A Socio-Legal Critique of Sports Regulation

A Socio-Legal Critique of Sports Regulation

Nothing to Do with Fair Play

Jonathan G. Merritt

BLOOMSBURY ACADEMIC
NEW YORK • LONDON • OXFORD • NEW DELHI • SYDNEY

BLOOMSBURY ACADEMIC
Bloomsbury Publishing Inc, 1359 Broadway, 12th Floor, New York, NY 10018, USA
Bloomsbury Publishing Plc, 50 Bedford Square, London, WC1B 3DP, UK
Bloomsbury Publishing Ireland, 29 Earlsfort Terrace, Dublin 2, D02 AY28, Ireland

BLOOMSBURY, BLOOMSBURY ACADEMIC and the Diana logo are trademarks of Bloomsbury Publishing Plc

First published in the United States of America 2026

Library of Congress Cataloging-in-Publication Data

Names: Merritt, J. G. (Jonathan G.) author
Title: A socio-legal critique of sports regulation : nothing to do with fair play / Jonathan G. Merritt.
Description: New York : Bloomsbury Publishing, 2026. | Includes bibliographical references and index.
Identifiers: LCCN 2025035686 (print) | LCCN 2025035687 (ebook) | ISBN 9781666916812 hardback | ISBN 9781666916836 paperback | ISBN 9781978760516 epub | ISBN 9798216267560 pdf | ISBN 9798881890858
Subjects: LCSH: Sports—Law and legislation | Sports—Sociological aspects
Classification: LCC K3702.M45 2026 (print) | LCC K3702 (ebook) | DDC 344/.099—dc23/eng/20250804
LC record available at https://lccn.loc.gov/2025035686
LC ebook record available at https://lccn.loc.gov/2025035687

ISBN: HB: 978-1-6669-1681-2
ePDF: 979-8-216-26756-0
eBook: 978-1-9787-6051-6

Typeset by Deanta Global Publishing Services, Chennai, India

Contents

Acknowledgements

I am grateful to a number of people for their contributions to this book. Firstly, my sports law and other students over the years who unknowingly helped me hone my skills in successfully conveying complex legal concepts in the context of sport. I am also lucky to work in a very supportive and cohesive school of law at De Montfort University. I would like to thank my colleagues for their suggestions, encouragement and good humour, which have helped me thrive in my academic career. They never fail to produce an atmosphere in which useful and interesting writing opportunities arise. My managers have also been instrumental in that they were patient and kind when I suffered an injury and could not work for over five months, including on this book. Without the support of, in particular, Alan East, David Hodgkinson, Tim Hillier and Martin Morgan-Taylor, this project would have sunk for sure. I continue to be grateful to John O'Leary for his work on sports law from a Gramscian perspective, which stimulated my research on that thread many years ago. My parents, Peter and Marjorie, both now no longer with us, imbued me with a curious mind and diligence, qualities which have helped me greatly as an author. I hope they would have been proud of what I have achieved. My brother Neville has done more than he knows with advice and encouragement, which boosted my confidence when it was flagging as well. My son Alex was influential in that his love for, and encyclopedic knowledge of, soccer provided insight that I would not have otherwise had. In addition, his focus and drive in his own life have been an inspiration. I am grateful to my editors at Lexington Books, now Bloomsbury, who gave this work a chance in the first place and who have been so very patient and flexible about deadlines during a tough couple of years for me. Finally, I would like to thank my old boss, Robert Bowes, who died recently. Without being aware at the time, he single-handedly created some of the best opportunities in my academic career. He was a gentleman and a scholar, and our chats over a beer will be sorely missed.

Any mistakes and omissions are of course mine alone.

Preface

This book has one purpose: to examine the contention that modern sport, because of the way it is regulated, has little or no connection with notions of fair play and sportsmanship. Other than isolated examples of 'gentlemanly' conduct on the field of play, sport has become a series of pastimes that seem regulated almost wholly in the interests of groups of people other than the participants themselves. This is not a sociological treatise, although such themes are part of the development of law. To consider the extent to which sports regulation serves the athlete or player rather than the ruling class of sport, the medium is an analysis of the way the law is applied to sport. This includes a discussion of how sports rules operate as law, why sports organisations are structured in the way that they are and whether national and international law is applied to sport in the same way that it is to citizens and corporate bodies outside sport.

Predominantly, English law is studied, not least because the self-regulation model dominant in that jurisdiction is so widespread around the world. Given that sport is now global, influences from other jurisdictions, such as the United States, Canada, Australia and the European Union, are considered as well. There are also legal and political themes which arise from Russia, China, South Africa, Saudi Arabia and Qatar, for instance. In order to achieve the aim of a deep analysis of sport, the law and fairness, it is imperative to fully consider the context in which the law is formed. Law develops from politics, which in itself is a product of the societies that are governed. Such sociological and religious factors, together with traditional notions and conventions, must be understood before the law can be usefully examined. Put another way, the law seeks to address the problems that sport has, but these are rarely unique to sport. There are issues with racism and sexism, for instance; however, those arise because the same contributory factors are being grappled with by society generally. Understanding the changes in social and economic attitudes across the populace and how they have impacted the development of the law helps to analyse the way the law operates in sport. Further, how the law is used, misused or ignored to the detriment of participants and fans.

The subtitle is drawn from a passage written by George Orwell, and his work is quoted elsewhere in the book. The words of Karl Marx and Antonio Gramsci also feature heavily. This is not, however, a Marxist critique of law, nor does it seek to raise Marxism as a solution to any of the problems of the world or sport. For one thing, communism has one fatal flaw; in order to survive, it must be overseen by an autocratic regime. Without the checks and balances that modern democracy, for all its faults, provides, despotism is nearly always the result in a Marxist regime. Having said that, free market capitalism should be put under close scrutiny as well. Sport is a business nowadays, but the sports business is unique in one key regard: it does not operate to eradicate competition. Tesco and Walmart would celebrate if competing supermarket chains went out of business. Nissan would be glad to see Honda go to the wall, as eradicating commercial competition means a greater market share for those left in the marketplace. However, Manchester United FC needs its competitors to survive. Other soccer premiership sides such as Arsenal and Liverpool must be credible adversaries for the tournament to have any meaning or to be good entertainment. The same is true of teams of the NFL in the United States and so on. Nevertheless, as a business, sport operates within the almost total dominance of global capitalism. Apart from the aberration around competition norms just described, sport is very much part of the free market and the patterns and values of the capitalist hegemony apply. Capitalism, which is largely unbridled, creates disturbing inequalities that plague almost all modern societies. These hierarchies are replicated in sport, which has its own versions of the 'ruled' and the 'rulers'. Understanding the power dynamics at play in society is necessary to fully understand whether sports' structures and processes aggravate or mitigate unfairness. Ultimately, though, Marxist ideas have corroded capitalism and produced some very good outcomes. These include employment rights, notions of social equality and mobility, and holding power to account. However, as Gramsci also said, the 'ruling class . . . reabsorbs the control that was slipping from its grasp. Perhaps it may make sacrifices . . . but it retains power', so it is with sport. Sport is not insulated from the structural changes society has undergone in the last century or so, nor is it immune from the attempts the ruling class have made to shore up their own position. In short, this book seeks to highlight what is going on in society, how the law is both succeeding and failing to protect people's health, well-being and happiness in an equitable way, and then applies that discussion to sport.

In many respects, this research builds on the author's other work in the area 'Regulating Sport for the Non-Human Athlete'. Some of the themes appear in both tracts. The first book had a much narrower focus, that is, sport involving equines. In carrying out that study, there were, however, many instances where it was evident that the issues covered had implications for human sport as well, hence the impetus for writing this monograph.

Introduction

Sport – 'War Minus the Shooting'

Orwell meant that the *playing* of sport when he penned those words, and they were a harsh indictment. There will be many instances of the 'Corinthian Ideals' still displayed on the field, but this book seeks to apply the point Orwell was making to include an examination of whether fair play extends to the management of sport in an increasingly commercialised and formalised sphere. The operation of law in sport is very much embedded in that discussion. Depending on the discipline, much of sport is actually controlled violence. Put another way, therefore, rather than violence on the pitch that Orwell referred to, this book concentrates on structural or institutional violence, which is categorised as unequal power and therefore unequal life chances from the 'violence' or violation built into the social structure,[1] in this case, the structure of sport. The first task is to define what is meant by 'fair' in this setting. Fair means being free of bias or injustice. Common synonyms include 'just', 'reasonable' or 'balanced', and to achieve fairness is to apply 'equity'. It is not the same thing as equality; after all, if you give both a starving person and a well-fed person a cookie each, you are treating them equally but not fairly, so context is everything. To be truly fair, allowance must be made for the other's needs and their journey to that point, regardless of the situation of their contemporaries. The debate then must be around the extent to which sport's hierarchies, structures, processes and organisation produce a fair result for competitors, support personnel, fans and other like stakeholders in that context.

A detailed discussion of the law in the key areas where it interfaces with sport is essential to discuss fairness away from the pitch because it underpins all of the structures, processes and rules of sport. This is primarily because sport has become a billion-dollar worldwide business, and where money and, linked with that, reputations are at stake, litigation is much more likely than in the days when sport was primarily an amateur pastime. Back in that time, the involvement of law in sport was much less likely, and even a rarity. Primarily, the law of contract provides the basis of most relationships in sport, whether between competitor and governing body, spectator and venue, board of directors and members, and so on. Statute is important in some areas, and torts such as negligence, together with some aspects of criminal law, all provide threads in the overall legal tapestry that covers sport.

National and international law does not operate in a silo; it is not divorced from the society from which it emanates. It is vitally important that the issues of race, gender, politics, religion, economics, disability, age demographics and culture that give rise to law are factored in to determine why the law still produces inequity. Law that is applied in a sporting context is no different. In 2023, there was a damning report into racism, elitism and misogyny in one important English sport. The England and Wales Cricket Board (ECB) commissioned the review, and it was carried out by the Independent Commission for Equity in Cricket (ICEC). It was seen as one of the most 'devastating' of its kind in UK Sport and branded the game as being 'racist, sexist and elitist'.[2] Of particular note, the report stated that the problems investigated are 'not, sadly, unique to cricket' and come from 'deeply rooted societal problems'.[3] The sports law books that exist tend to fall into two categories. They either consider the law as it applies to sport as if there were no sociological or other background, or they make little of it, or they are largely sociological works in themselves. These latter tend to take a few key themes, such as racism, sexism, transgender issues or human rights concerns, and delve deeply into the societal forces at work. However, they do not provide a complete guide as to how, as a result, the law has failed to address the power differential between sports participants, their supporters and the echelon which runs sport. There is a concentrated effort in this book to rectify this lacuna.

It has been said many times that sport and politics should not mix, or that sportspeople should not involve themselves in matters of wider state policy or perceived inequities in society. A sub-theme of the forthcoming discussion will be that this is a naïve view, both unworkable and undesirable. This is not to say that politicians should meddle in sport; almost always it is true that they should not, as they are too partisan, to put it kindly. The politics concerned is of a much simpler kind. As Chapter 1 considers, politics is not about the internecine squabbling that happens in the UK's Parliament, on Capitol Hill, or in the *Bundestag*. It is ultimately about what individuals feel should be done with problems in taxation, immigration, relations with foreign powers and the climate to name just a few areas. On a national level, politics is about what should be done because a doctor only has ten minutes to diagnose your condition or when class sizes in your local school reach a breaking point. It also encompasses when the roads are so poorly maintained that they damage cars and put cyclists and pedestrians at risk, and the list goes on. In other words, it is about the interaction of individual people and groups with the state and with institutions. Some of those people are sports competitors, from amateur to elite level, others work in the sports industry and still more watch sport for entertainment. The question to be asked is therefore: to what extent must sport necessarily involve consideration of these societal interactions? That, in turn, engages legal questions because of the intimate relationship between societal factors and the creation and implementation of law.

Orwell certainly thought sport was an extension of society, and he was not very kind about either of them, as he saw the same flaws in both. He was deeply cynical about the ability of humans to reshape their societies to be more egalitarian after his experiences in the Spanish Civil War.[4] It is perhaps unsurprising, then, that a physically and psychologically wounded Orwell wrote:

> Serious sport has nothing to do with fair play. It is bound up with hatred, jealousy, boastfulness, disregard of all rules and sadistic pleasure in witnessing violence: in other words, it is war minus the shooting.[5]

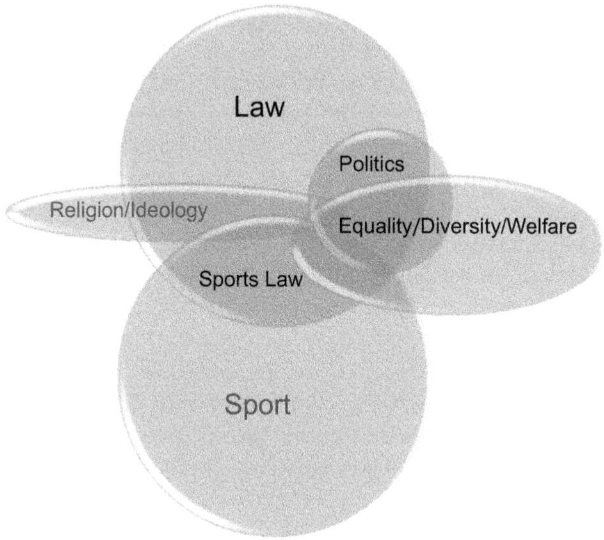

Figure 0.1 Intersections of sport and the law.

He obviously felt that whatever was wrong with society would be likely be wrong in sport as well. The extent to which he was right, in relation to the organisation of sport though, is the major focus of this book.

Perhaps the best way to continue the introduction to this book is to group the main areas of discussion into three: religion and ideology; equality, diversity and welfare; and finally, national and international politics (see Figure 0.1). This trifecta takes in the full gamut of influences that shape law and consequently explains why the law has not been as effective as it might be in creating an environment of egalitarianism in 'serious sport'.

Religion, ideology and sports law

Ideology is discussed as separate but overlapping with politics because it does not necessarily arise from there; it can have religious or cultural roots. Not all politicians are ideologues either. According to census figures, religion is declining in the UK;[6] this rather oversimplifies the picture, however. It is true that for the first time, less than half the population regard themselves as Christian; however, those who identify as Muslim or Hindu have increased in number. There can be a direct impact on the law from this demographic change. The crime of blasphemy, for instance, is based on Christian notions and is part of the common law. Consequently, what would qualify as such for a follower of Islam simply would not be covered by legislation arising from Christian beliefs. This crime was abolished in 2008[7] in England and Wales and in Scotland in 2021, but there have been no similar moves in Northern Ireland. Sport is influenced by religious ideology too; Anglo-American legal systems have grown up in the Judaeo-

Christian tradition. As such, many matters which were considered sins became law following those tenets. Welcome deviations from strict religious doctrine in the law, to account for the population's greater variations of faith and for those with none, have been relatively recent. They include the decriminalisation of male homosexual acts and liberalisation of marriage and abortion laws in the UK, for instance. It is consequently much more common now for a soccer or rugby player to come out as openly gay. In like vein, sports apparel that is allowed by sports governing bodies (SGB) has to now include the hijab or turban, according to the faith and culture of the competitor. To not do so would most likely fall foul of the Equality Act 2010, as discussed in Chapter 5. In other societies, change has been much slower, though, and the clash of cultures highlighted in Chapter 9 exemplifies this. The hosting of the soccer World Cup in Qatar brought criticism of its laws on LGBTQ+ issues, and Saudi Arabia's record on women's rights is part of the discussion on 'sportswashing'. This term identifies where investing heavily in sport worldwide is an attempt at distracting from a regime's poor human rights image, an example of how the ruling elite fights back against progressive ideas. Even Western society has not really reached an agreed position on transgender rights, however. In Chapter 5, there is a debate about how the lack of a broad consensus on gender identity matters has impacted unfairly on transgender athletes and relevant laws, to the detriment of athletes, irrespective of the science.

In turn, many of the themes of abstinence and moral purity found in religion feed into responses to the issue of doping in sport. These underpin a prohibitionist approach to street drugs found in many jurisdictions globally, and the UK is no exception. However, an increasing number of those territories are starting to go down the path of a 'public health' strategy such as Portugal, Scotland and Portland, Oregon have done. This is where drug takers are treated as in need of healthcare rather than as criminals. This is relevant to sport because no such drift away from a legalistic regime regarding illicit drugs in sport can be discerned, as Chapter 4 explores. The manifest failings of both the 'war on (street) drugs' and the incredibly resource-intensive anti-doping campaign in sport are easy to cite. Criminal justice policy is moving on, but anti-doping still relies on prohibition enforced by draconian legal measures like strict liability, spot checks out of competition and invasive health profiling. All this must be agreed to under contract if the athlete wants to compete professionally, and no alternatives are even countenanced, so deeply entrenched is the *status quo*. The advent of even the idea of a 'Steroid Olympics', with few restrictions on drugs, throws up an array of questions in that area too, however.

In terms of ideology, the struggles for dominance between the elites in both capitalism and communism have used and abused sport and its stakeholders from time to time as well. Chapter 9 looks at how China became re-integrated into global diplomacy with the unlikely help of table tennis. Russia has tried to revisit its former glory as a communist superpower by emulating the state-sponsored doping carried out by its former Soviet bloc partner, East Germany. In each case, the aim is to enhance the status of the country and its ideology on the world stage.

To establish who determines what is fair in sport management, it is essential to analyse the power dynamics in sports governance as a mirror of those that exist outside in the majority capitalist world. Chapter 2 explores the relationship of the athlete or player with the SGB, and Chapter 3 puts that in context to examine the legal basis for dispute resolution. Inequalities are embedded in capitalism, and it is therefore little surprise that diversity and inclusion are issues in SGBs, just as they are for wider society. Sport as a business is also a child of capitalism, as is the concept of intellectual property. It is not often discussed that there are alternative views to the prevailing moral status of copying, such as those in Confucianism, where it is effectively flattery. This and the 'commodification of ideas' are the basis for Chapters 6 and 7 on intellectual property (IP). Here, the law on the monetisation of images and brands, including how they impact on sports broadcasting, is analysed. Making a profit from sport also includes gambling in much of the world. This produces social policy conundrums for capitalist society, as considered in Chapter 8. Governments need the tax revenue gambling provides, and it can be a civil liberties issue to restrict citizens' pastimes unduly. Set against this, gambling is not considered morally acceptable by everyone, and further, can give rise to a dangerous and destructive addiction. The irony is that sport, with all its social utility, is largely funded in the UK from gambling in the form of the National Lottery. How effectively the law walks this particular tightrope is the foundation of this chapter.

Finally, sport also has an unfortunate but long history of being utilised by the ruling classes to distract the population from the excesses and failures of the ruling elites. Whether that be under neo-conservative ideology, communism or anywhere on the spectrum in between, this is a recurring theme in much of this book.

Equality and diversity legislation, athlete welfare and sport

Athlete welfare is a burgeoning area of sports law and policy, and it is therefore fitting that Chapter 5 on these topics is by far the largest in the book. The problem that sport has is that it is inherently discriminatory. It is designed to differentiate between those with higher or lower skills, abilities and stamina, both mental and physical. For fair competition, sport must sometimes also be segregated by age or by gender, although in key areas this is under challenge. However, into that mix comes the controversy about transgender athletes and women competitors with higher-than-usual testosterone levels. The degree to which the Equality Act 2010 meets the needs of sport and its stakeholders is considered in Chapter 5, but this legislation only goes so far in protecting athletes' and players' rights. It is also important to understand what other state apparatuses and the victims themselves can do to protect their welfare and seek redress. Consequently, the criminal law is applied in the context of violence on the playing surface, safeguarding, crowd control and health and safety. To continue the theme of setting the legal position in the context of wider societal problems, the issue of sexual offending and the poor statistics for convictions are considered. As there are barriers to reporting, recording and successfully prosecuting these crimes in general, so there are in terms of offending against vulnerable athletes. Just as in the world outside sport, some of the hurdles to tackle these crimes have come from indifference by elites or a desire to protect the reputation of an institution. In addition, the routes to compensation provided by the civil law, such as tort and contract, are explored. The next best thing to the prevention of wrongs in the first place is damages as redress. This helps the athlete or player rebuild their lives, but also, it acts as a deterrent, making those responsible for the injury or other loss take steps to address their failings for the future. In this way, the welfare of the whole sports community is potentially enhanced.

Chapter 5 may be where the debate on discrimination and other wrongs is concentrated, but these issues form threads in other discussions as well. For instance, in Chapter 2, the lack of diversity in sports governance is compared to the problems other institutions, from the judiciary to the UK Parliament itself, have in this area. This enables a clear understanding of the root causes in all these sectors to be had, which is preferable to looking at sport alone. Further, this chapter is where human rights feature to the greatest extent, but this thread runs through much of the book too. In Chapter 9, the struggles sport has had with how to deal with regimes the world over that have discrimination embedded in their structures and practices are considered as well.

Politics, geo-politics and the regulation of sport

In Chapter 1, the role of politics in sport is first encountered. Politics in a national, governmental sense is differentiated from politics with a small 'p', which is a feature of all human relations. In other words, and by way of example, politics at the government level influences funding for sport in schools, and unfortunately, politicians have attempted to run sport, with varying degrees of success in a number of jurisdictions, including the UK. Separately, politics and a limited form of democracy is a feature of many institutions, from company boardrooms to charitable trusts, and no less so in a sport governing body (SGB) or international sporting federation (ISF). There is potential for good work to come out of this governance, but, like in wider society, there is also the possibility of incompetence, poor representation of stakeholders, democratic failings, and even corruption. In a similar vein, bribery is a key part of match-fixing, which impacts on the gambling industry and on sports integrity. A detailed consideration of this in the context of UK social policy is to be found in Chapter 8. European Union (EU) law is the product of politics, and so too was the UK's decision to leave the bloc in 2016. It is difficult to know the full picture of which EU legal principles still apply in the UK going forward. This is because many of them were embedded in domestic legislation and case law, and not all of these have been repealed or overruled. Further, again due to local politics, Northern Ireland remains to an extent under EU jurisdiction, and not all the import and export controls consequent on Brexit have been implemented anywhere in the UK even now. In addition, the political relationship between the UK and the EU is not settled and may become closer again. This relationship impacts on sport in a number of ways, and how that manifests itself is another recurring theme throughout this book, but particularly in Chapter 3. Here, the methods of challenge to SGBs and ISFs under European law are examined. Despite the UK's exit from the bloc, sport straddles frontiers, as does the broadcasting of sport; therefore, consideration of those issues is a feature of Chapter 7 as well.

In terms of geo-politics, it is hard to divorce that from the climate emergency as this is a controversial political issue as well, so Chapter 9 deals with both subjects. The complicated relationship that the public and politicians have with the subject of climate change is at the root of a series of failures of leadership on the matter. This has led to climate activists feeling the need to target both sporting and non-sporting events and infrastructure. It is unsurprising then that the response of sports 'rulers' to climate change has been in words rather than actions in some instances. International politics and sport have had an uneasy relationship for a long time. The apartheid regime in South Africa posed particular challenges in terms of how sport should respond. That took thirty years to resolve, but it was merely one example of how tangled the relationship between sport and various regimes has become. Experiences with Russia, China and Saudi Arabia are also presented in Chapter 9 as examples of how sport can be misused on the world stage to the detriment of those actually involved in it. This is not to mention the oppression of minorities going effectively unchallenged.

A word about research, sources and acronyms

The traditional sources of peer-reviewed journals, cases and statutes are utilised in this book, but there are also a great many good-quality news outlets referenced as well. No apology is made for the quantity of these. Academic writing adds depth, but this is a socio-legal subject, and sometimes journalists from news organisations, particularly respected for their balance, are best at summarising key points and capturing the zeitgeist. It is important to be topical as well, and in some cases, the material is so new that, at the time this book was published, it had not yet been widely written about in academic journals. This is given the likely extensive timeline from events to writing, review and publication of a peer reviewed article.

There is also a deliberate policy of giving acronyms in full where they first appear in each chapter, rather than once for the entire book.

Notes

1 Claudio Colaguori, 'Violence, violent crime, and state violence', in *Crime, Deviance, and Social Control in the 21st Century: A Justice and Rights Perspective* (Toronto: Canadian Scholars, an Imprint of CSP Books Inc, 2023), 276.

2 Sean Ingle, 'English cricket is "racist, sexist and elitist," says landmark report', *The Guardian*, 27 June 2023, https://www.theguardian.com/sport/2023/jun/27/english-cricket-is-racist-sexist-and-elitist-says-landmark-report?CMP=oth_b-aplnews_d-5.

3 Ibid.

4 See generally, George Orwell, *Homage to Catalonia* (London: Penguin Press, 1938).

5 George Orwell, 'The sporting spirit', *Tribune*, 14 December 1945, 10.
6 'UK census – Religion, England and Wales, main points', accessed 29 November 2022, https://www.ons.gov.uk/peoplepopulationandcommunity/culturalidentity/religion/bulletins/religionenglandandwales/census2021#main-points.
7 Section 79 Criminal Justice and Immigration Act 2008.

1

What Is 'Sports Law'?

Sports law or sport and the law? '*Potato – potahto . . .*'

The central theme of this book is to analyse the reasons why the influence of law in sport does not, in practice, provide 'fairness'. Further, the book aims to show that this means modern sport as a whole has nothing to do with fair play, favouring, instead, existing power structures. To make that argument effectively at a deep enough level, it is essential to discuss in detail what the relationship between law and sport actually is. That is to say, the initial question in this journey is whether any body of law can be legitimately termed 'sports law' that operates *differently* from other law. Alternatively, is it more accurate to think of sports law as how existing and *generally applicable* legal processes and structures impact on sport? Without answering these questions, it is all the more difficult to analyse the role the law has in ensuring fairness in sport, or otherwise. To add form to this discussion, the debate will be conducted in relation to the nature and quality of sports governance rules, politics and sport, the contribution of academia, sport's 'judicial arm', sports law as soft law and the contribution of the European Union (EU) before concluding as far as is possible.

Firstly, the study of how the law and sport interact with one another is a distinct, worthwhile academic discipline. As the exponential growth of sporting commerce continues, so will the need for further specialist research to support expert practitioners in the field. Secondly, if there are proven to be systemic problems affecting fairness in sport, it will be an academic discussion that will expose these issues and suggest solutions. Additionally, there are practical consequences if sports law, as it is now, is not yet a fully coherent, consistent whole. Just by way of example, and as will be discussed later, in certain circumstances it is perfectly possible for a sports participant to simply switch sports after being given a disciplinary sanction such as a ban. This is not good for sport, nor does it imbue respect for sports law and its institutions. There are numerous other examples to come in this book of sports rules and structures that curry little favour with participants and fans but suit the ruling echelons of sport. Addressing these imbalances in one sport does not mean that they will be mitigated in another, because of the level of inconsistency. As a further instance, there are a number of sports that do not use the Court of Arbitration for Sport (CAS) for their disciplinary appeals, or do not do so as a matter of course. Some of these sports have considerable commercial and social impact, and not all sports are full signatories to the World

Anti-Doping Code (WADC) either. Soccer in the UK has its own disciplinary appeals mechanisms with recourse to CAS only if both parties agree, which happens rarely. In contrast, the Union of European Football Associations (UEFA) and the *Fédération Internationale de Football Association* (FIFA) fully utilise CAS. US sports such as the National Football League (NFL) (as distinct from various non-US American football leagues) and baseball also have their own appeal routes that do not routinely utilise CAS. International horse racing does not even have an International Sports Federation (ISF), merely a non-binding organisation that does not include all horse racing jurisdictions. There are no such jurisdictions that use CAS; instead, the British Horse Racing Authority (BHA) has an arms-length judicial function of its own. By contrast, most other horse sports, including the Olympic disciplines of show jumping, dressage, para-dressage and eventing, fully recognise the WADC and the jurisdiction of CAS. Elite sports horses in various disciplines can be owned by the same individual or organisation and so this is where the lack of consistency in sports law is most vividly displayed. It has been noted that at least one trainer has been banned in one sport but is free to train horses in a differently regulated discipline. This is because at the time there were no 'reciprocal arrangements between the [*Fédération Equestre Internationale* (FEI)] and international horseracing jurisdictions . . .' and so the individual remained free to 'train Thoroughbred racehorses while suspended'.[1] There are now some reciprocal arrangements between the BHA and FEI, which regulate most horse sport other than racing; even these, however, have not always stood up to the test in a tribunal.[2]

What this ultimately means, then, is that the current lack of a coherent, consistent and universally applicable body of sports law is not a purely academic discussion. This is especially true when reputation, livelihood, human and animal welfare, spectator enjoyment and potentially significant financial investment may depend on it.

Turning to how the law operates in sport, there are many domestic and international laws that apply to sport just as they do to any other individual or corporation. Players, referees and sports organisations can be sued for negligence, for instance. A wildly dangerous tackle can result in a criminal charge, and company law applies to sports associations that operate as limited companies and so on. Law is further embedded in sport, though, because, with very few exceptions, players and athletes are in a contractual *nexus* with national and international governing bodies. Agreeing to abide by the rules of a governing body places athletes in a contractual relationship with the rules as the terms of that contract, and transgressions, on the field of play or off it, mean the player has to accept the sanction as a matter of contract. The alternative is to challenge it, essentially as a matter of contract law, through the proper channels. The following discussion highlights the nuances in that understanding of sporting rules.

Commentators, lawyers and academics use the term 'sports law', but what does the phrase actually mean? There are a number of discrete bodies of law, 'family', 'employment' and 'consumer' being three examples. These categories are built around a collection of statutes and cases that are specific to them, however. Family law regulates families, using legal concepts found almost nowhere else in law, such as the emphasis on consensual settlements wherever possible and the avoidance, if feasible, of apportionment of blame. The body of matrimonial law is thus unique and esoteric. Employment and consumer law perform similar tasks in that they take the basic legal relationships that exist between contractual parties and alter the relative rights and duties to take account of a party in a weaker bargaining position. Thus, a corpus of law, based around statute, has grown up that protects employees and consumers from the harshness of pure contract law that would not apply if one party were not an employee or consumer. The question is, has sport created its own specialised set of legal principles applicable only to sport and its stakeholders? Sports lawyers claim it has; the term *lex sportiva* has been coined. This is rather like *Lex Mercatoria* or 'Mercantile Law', the term for a Europe-wide body of commercial law used in the Middle Ages. Traders operated under this system irrespective of which national jurisdiction they were conducting business in. This was a legal/judicial process but allowed for a certain amount of creativity. The rules were often to be ascertained and applied partly from custom as well as the law of the nation states themselves, as was 'appropriate and equitable'.[3] In law, though, what something is called is not necessarily what it is; the legal concepts need to be considered carefully.

There are undoubtedly statutes that apply only to sport, but these are few in number, because the 'self-regulation' European model of sport is paramount. The various sports prefer to keep government out of sports governance, and both the executive and judicial arms of the state have shown a marked reluctance to oppose that. In the UK, the Football Spectators Act 1989, as amended by the Violent Crime Reduction Act 2006, is an example of sport-specific legislation. This deals with banning orders and the like for unruly football spectators and is essentially public order law. The aim was to deal with crowd control issues at large sporting events, which straddle both the public and private spaces. Further, the world governing body for soccer, FIFA expressly forbids political interference with the running of football at the national level. FIFA has enforced that provision ruthlessly, such as with the threat of expulsion of Peru in 2008, as well as similar spats with Poland, Iran and Nigeria.[4] This makes former British Prime Minister Boris Johnson's threat to drop a 'legislative bomb' on the governance structures of English football rather puzzling. He did so in the wake of the decision of six Premier League teams to join the nascent European Super League (ESL) on 18 April 2021. In the end, it was all moot; however, because the clubs withdrew from the proposal less than three days later.[5] A future statute relating to certain aspects of soccer governance is currently being debated, but if eventually enacted, it will have to be somewhat 'light touch' to avoid the wrath of FIFA.

The courts have traditionally shied away from examining the decisions and inner workings of sports governing bodies (SGBs). As we shall see in more detail in Chapter 3, there are two main ways in which a decision or rule made by an SGB can be challenged under common law. These are through an 'indirect' judicial review or human rights action and separately, under the ruling in *Bradley v Jockey Club* [2004] EWHC Civ 2164 (QB) and other specific common law principles. Judicial review in its traditional, pure sense is something of a non-starter, as SGBs do not have a governmental function. The nearest an appeal of this nature has come to success was in *R v Disciplinary Committee of the Jockey Club, ex parte Massingberd-Mundy* [1993] 2 All ER 207. The court took the view that if there had been no authorities to the contrary, the 'near monopolistic' powers of the Jockey Club would have meant that judicial review of its decisions was possible. The same issues can be used indirectly, however, embedded in a private law claim, as can human rights, as shall be discussed in depth later. Despite its unwritten form, the UK does have a constitution, and this derives from statute, convention and common law. The 'right to work', for example, derives originally from case law. A capricious denial of this right to a racehorse trainer on the grounds that she was female was overturned in *Nagle v Fielden* [1966] 2 QB 633, reinforcing this right. Similarly, the common law 'right to a fair trial' (*audi alteram partem*) was upheld in *Ridge v Baldwin* [1964] AC 40. This was not a sports law case, but it would be applicable to SGBs.

R (Mullins) v Appeal Board of the Jockey Club [2005] EWHC 2197; establishes that the test for whether a body is sufficiently 'public' for judicial review is much the same as the equivalent test under S6 Human Rights Act 1998 (HuRA). This means that, without embedding in a private law claim, the domestic courts will not hear a claim against an SGB. The position has undoubtedly become a little more relaxed since *Bradley v Jockey Club*, which will be discussed further in Chapter 3. Suffice it to say, the judiciary needs a lot of convincing to unpick or even examine a decision by an SGB or ISF. As shall become apparent, the attitude of the judiciary and the consequent weaknesses in judicial oversight have limited the checks and balances that should protect the players and grassroots supporters from powerful sporting elites.

Sports governance, rules or law?

The question is, do the internal rules of SGBs and ISFs form a separate species of sports law? They certainly only apply to sports participants and other contractually linked stakeholders. This is similar to the way that consumer law only applies to consumers. That said, these internal rules are all underpinned by the general law of contract. Where there is disagreement, the interpretation of these contractual arrangements is determined in arbitration proceedings. This is carried out through CAS or another arbitral route within sports that do not utilise CAS. This process is 'the application of legal principles by the tribunals granted jurisdiction to hear disputes by the . . . governing bodies of sport'.[6] These powers are themselves created by contract, which highlights the wishes of these bodies to self-regulate disputes within their sports. Separately, it underlines 'their claims that they are developing through CAS a completely new branch of law that is often referred to as *lex sportiva*'.[7] This means that at least the rules relating to sports governance can be considered a distinct stream of law.

In terms of governance, there are, in fact, many parallels between corporations, nation states and SGBs. In each case, there is a regulatory framework with a hierarchy. There are also mechanisms for making new rules and for enforcing them. There are essentially two classes of people: a ruling 'committee' and the ruled mass population. In the case of limited companies, the directors act within the company's constitution (its articles of association) to manage and control the workforce. This is often heavily influenced by the agendas of the major shareholders. Sometimes, elements of the workforce have shares too, and they can participate in the decision-making process in a limited form of democracy. In most cases, though, the strategic direction is in the hands of a powerful elite within and behind the boardroom. In the same vein, a democratic nation state has a government, and periodically, the membership of that government is put to the people. In between times, however, the people are subject to that government, by and large without the ability to mount much of an effective challenge. SGBs have managing boards and committees as well, and people can be voted on or off those, usually at the end of their terms of office. Ultimately, though, athletes and players are subject to the rules and decisions that emanate from the governance framework of their SGB or ISF. It is little wonder, then, that similar academic 'tools' can be employed to analyse the power dynamics in all three sectors (see Figure 1.1). Corporate governance theories work both with companies and SGBs, for instance. Political theory can explain the relationships between the 'ruled' and 'rulers' at the national level. The same disciplines can also be employed to consider the equivalent dynamic between SGBs and players or athletes, and so on.

Democracy exists, to a greater or lesser degree in all of the above-mentioned human inventions, and these processes also seem prima facie to be able to produce similar controversies. For instance, there is a perceived lack of diversity in the boards and committees that govern English soccer. This was highlighted by an investigation by a UK Parliamentary Committee regarding racism and sexism in the game in late 2016.[8] This is an issue that has made the headlines with regard to other major sports too, and sanctions can be applied in the form of cuts to funding if the situation is not addressed.[9] The independent body, Sport England, has the remit to allocate National Lottery and government funding and would have the power to reduce financial support in this way. This assumes that the offending sport relies on lottery funding of course. Larger sports, from soccer to horse racing and even esports (for wholly different reasons), are not so reliant, so that lever to encourage change for the benefit of the stakeholders is virtually ineffective with them. The same concerns about diversity are frequently expressed about the dominance of white males of late middle age in government and corporate boardrooms as well. In UK politics,[10] the British judiciary[11] and at the executive level in industry,[12] specifically, there appears to be a problem, highlighting that sport reflects society-wide issues.

Research[13] has found that sport governance is a reality that evolves, a framework of rules and procedures that absolutely bind the parties but are wholly created by the individuals concerned.[14] An example may be illustrative; the only reason that the rules in the WADC matter to SGBs and athletes is because there is a broad consensus in place in both camps that these rules should exist and should be enforced. There is no national statute mandating this manner of regulation. The same could be said to be true of the 'whip rules' in horse racing, the constitution of the FA Council or indeed the very existence of World Rugby as an ISF. The stakeholders in each case made itso; there was no external coercion involved. This seems at first blush to be a positive model, but the corollary is that the lack of limits to the powers these organisations have can be quite staggering.

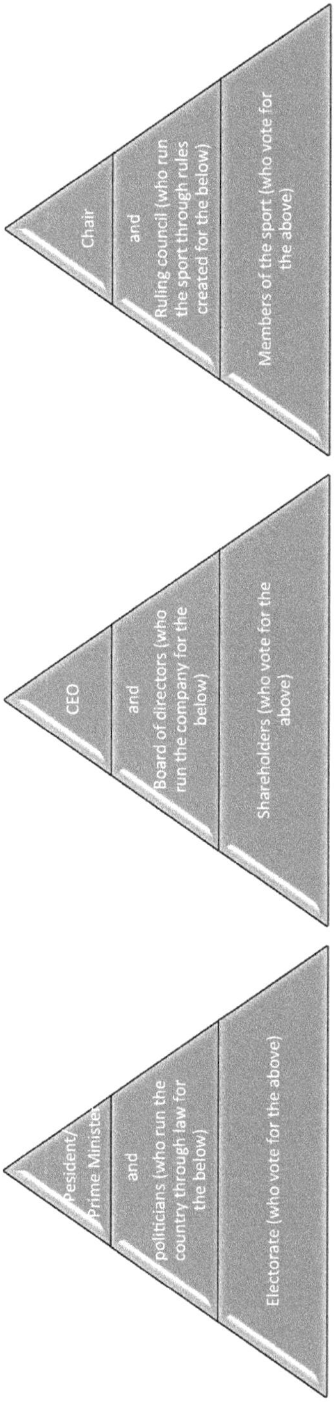

Figure 1.1 Similarity of structure between nation states, corporate bodies and sport.

The 'P' word and sport

There are proponents of the idea that politics should be kept out of sport. This is a naïve view; in the wider context, law derives from politics, and politicians enact laws according to their ideologies and perceived demand amongst the voters, many of whom consume sport or play it. The problem with the word 'politics' is that it is often understood to mean the convoluted manoeuvrings and sometimes impenetrable exchanges between members of political parties. These occur at national and international levels and thus can seem irrelevant to the majority of the population's daily lives. The reality is that politics is unfortunately inextricably linked to many facets of our existence. Whether to spend public money on fixing potholes in the street or on an LGBTQ+ helpline is a political decision, as is whether to increase or decrease funding to the National Health Service (NHS) or education. Both have a direct effect on the lives of ordinary citizens. The price of one's weekly shop is also affected by decisions on tax (or the knock-on effects of those), which are often ideologically driven, as was seen very clearly during Liz Truss' disastrous forty-nine days as British Prime Minister in 2022 and decisions made on tariffs by the Trump administration in 2025. In a different way, politics (with a small 'p') also invades every relationship we have. It may be 'politically' a good idea to include a senior colleague at work in a project because it is more likely to get approval. Befriending one's bank manager at the golf club was always politically astute before the advent of computerised credit decisions and so on. Politics like this also governs the relationships in human organisations and neither SGBs nor ISFs are immune.

In very broad terms, politics can be categorised as conservative versus progressive, with liberal (although not in the free market sense of the word) occupying the middle ground. These extremes are often termed 'right wing' (conservative, traditionalist, reluctant to accept change), 'left wing' (progressive, often with a restructuring of hierarchies towards a greater equality agenda) and 'centrist'. The latter has elements of the former two, often melded through pragmatism (see Figure 1.2). This characterisation of politics will be criticised as overly simplistic. It does, however, have the advantage of being broadly applicable to anything from parliamentary politics, company boardroom machinations, or what type of wedding a family is planning. All three of which require a degree of compromise, bluff, tact, trade-offs and coercion in some form or other.

Political gamesmanship is evident in the top echelons of sport, and thus, political analysis can also be helpful in analysing sports governance. From a left-wing perspective, it is possible to categorise the leaders of sport, such as the heads of ISFs and the ruling council of SGBs, as 'rulers' and the athletes or players as the 'ruled'. Marxists like Antonio Gramsci have had much to say about the relationship between the 'rulers' and the 'ruled' in a nation state. He was writing about the societal hierarchies that existed in the early twentieth century outside Russia, the country where Marxism first gained a foothold. Gramsci was talking about national human hierarchies that existed in prima facie democracies, so there are parallels with SGBs. It is therefore worth considering whether his and other politicos' theories might be useful in understanding why SGBs do as they do and whether athletes and players really have a say. This is after all the essence of sport governance.

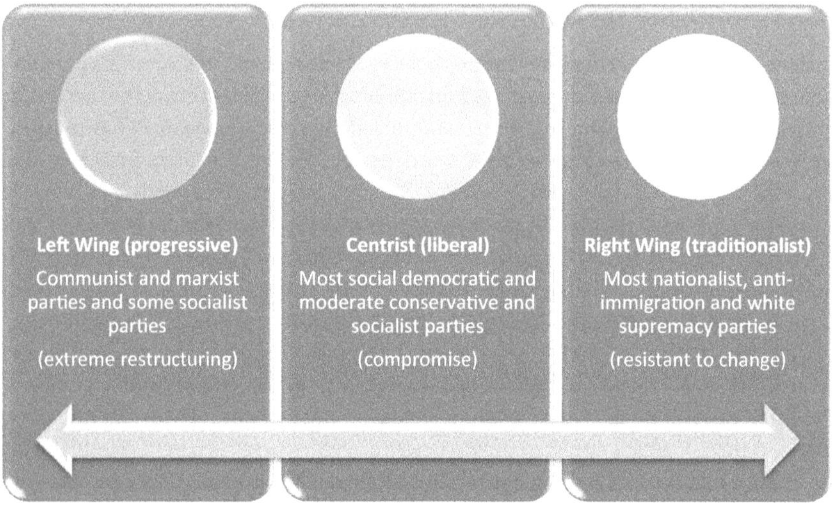

Figure 1.2 The political continuum, 'left' to 'right'.

Political ideas can be revolutionary, not necessarily in the violent sense of the word but in that they advocate radical change. Sport has had its fair share of 'revolutions'. Seismic examples range from the 1948 South American football league launched outside the auspices of FIFA[15] to the Kerry Packer League in cricket in the late 1970s and early 1980s. The advent of the Premier League in English football in 1992 and the stalled European Super League proposal in 2021 are worthy of note too. All of these have been driven by dissatisfaction with the status quo, sometimes because of a dispute within the sporting elite, more often because different elements of the 'rulers' are vying for control of the 'ruled' and the income they generate.

The structures of an SGB or ISF are created by the participants to enable those sportsmen and women to get on with competing. Those willing to serve sit on the various councils and boards, having been voted in by classes of persons involved with the sport and given the right to vote by its constitution. This is largely on the same basis as a democratic nation state, where the population selects representatives to attend a parliament so that the remainder can concern themselves with daily processes. These consist of working, founding a family, education and so on. This creates a ruling class that is granted special powers for the duration of the tenure of its individual members. Examples include the five years between national elections in the UK and the four-year term of a US president. These powers allow the passing of laws that regulate the whole population by society's ruling class. There are still other statutes that regulate how a parliament functions and the rights and privileges of that ruling class itself. The latter may be termed a constitution; sports bodies have those too.

In fact, from time to time, society's ruling class is perceived to be encouraging the mass of the population to be concerned with their day-to-day lives rather than the activities of the rulers. This is despite what politicians may say they are doing to combat voter apathy. After all, a challenge to the social status quo by the population is less likely[16] if they play no part in the democratic process. Sport plays its part in this subterfuge; the word 'sport' comes from the Latin word 'dēportō', which means to 'carry away'. In other words, whilst sports fans are passionately discussing the successes of their teams or the relative merits of sports personalities, they get carried away, or distracted, from their humdrum lives. Of more concern, the populace is thus less aware of the activities of the nation's ruling class, which may not always have the population's best interests at heart.[17]

Notwithstanding the foregoing, sometimes the public's attention *is* focused on those governing them, perhaps because of a scandal such as the 1998 Monica Lewinsky presidential perjury allegations in the United States[18] or the UK Members of Parliament expenses debacle in 2009.[19] When this happens, reform is promised, but this never really alters the basic power dynamics between the people and the rulers.[20] This fundamental power imbalance[21] also exists within SGBs and ISFs as well, and there is little encouragement from the top echelons of sport for the athletes or players to try to change or, less still, challenge the rules in a legal process. To allow such dissent, or even debate, is dangerous for those seeking to rely on the rules. This is irrespective of any stated intention by the elites of merely furthering the interests of the sport in question.[22] Thus, the politics of sport influences the rules in sport, and these, underpinned by contract, are sport-specific law. Put another way, the legal force comes not from the rules themselves but the law that gives them effect.

To avoid heated debates, 'never discuss religion or politics', or so the saying goes. The fact is, though, that there is a deep connection between the two. Thus, if politics is embedded in sport, so is religion. For instance, much law in Western democracies is still derived from interpretations of the Bible. In the UK, the ban on homosexual acts and the criminalisation of suicide, both only relatively recently repealed, owe their roots to rigid interpretations of the Old Testament. Many rigorously enforced dietary restrictions and even controls on marriage and citizenship in Israel derive from a similar construal of the Torah. *Sharia* Law is a legal system that applies the religious rules in the Quran, strictly and literally, in countries and provinces where Islamic Law is dominant. In the United States, the debate about whether abortion should be illegal is closely tied to fundamentalist Christian beliefs. This is also true of the legal debate around teaching creationism, intelligent design and evolution in schools in some states.[23] Turning to sport, it would be impossible, for instance, to discuss the position of transgender athletes without considering the position of people with gender dysphoria in society generally. The development of the legal rights of transgender people is a political process, one not assisted by entrenched religious beliefs about the primacy of biological gender. In turn, there has been debate in various countries about the legality of the hijab, niqab and burka in some public spaces. Accordingly, sport has to develop its rules on sportswear to accommodate religious garments in a highly charged atmosphere.[24] Unsurprisingly, therefore, the connection between sports regulation, law and religion must be addressed for a full treatment of sports law and to analyse where the law has failed to underpin basic notions of fairness there.

The academic discussion

Turning to the commentary in published works on what *lex sportiva* really means, very few sports are limited to being played in one jurisdiction only; most are international at the top level. A distinction can be made between international sports law and global sports law. This might seem like semantics, but words and their meanings are central to any study of law. International sports law has been argued to be 'an authoritative process of decision-making and legal discipline'[25] and in practice, international law norms and values are central to that. In other words, we may refer to it as international sports law, but what is really being discussed is how legal force can be applied to enforce sports rules in an international setting. International trade operates in a similar arena. International treaties and trade deals apply legal rules across multiple jurisdictions because there is no overarching global legislature or judiciary in the true sense. Adhering to these treaties and agreements is often as much a matter of pragmatism as anything. No country wants to be excluded or disadvantaged in an international marketplace because it is not performing its treaty obligations. In the same way, international sports law is about using treaties and treaty-like arrangements, such as the WADC, to ensure parity of rules and enforcement across sport globally.

Global sports law, on the other hand, can be seen as 'a transnational autonomous legal order created by the private global institutions that govern international sport'.[26] This means that at times it can be at odds with, or even mandate change in, national law. The International Olympic Committee (IOC) has the power to insist on national legislation specific to the Games before they are awarded to a host nation, for instance.[27] It may be concluded from this, then, that global sports law only really applies to sports governance. This is because the rest of sports law contains aspects of existing statute and case law on contract, criminal, tort and intellectual property, for example, but these can only be applied to sport in a specific jurisdiction. As an example, image rights pertaining to sport in the United States are markedly different from those that exist in the UK. Sports 'autonomous legal orders', however, are not created by national statute but by private global institutions like the IOC, FIFA, World Rugby and so on. Thus, the two concepts of sports law are separate.

According to the academic commentary, there are three main positions that can be taken with regard to whether sports law exists as a distinct discipline. In the first place, traditionally, sports law as a distinct discipline did not exist. It was an amalgam of laws that already applied generally and thus could be applied to sport.[28] There are those who argue nothing has changed and that a 'moment's thought reveals that no discrete area of law exists to which can aptly be attached the label "sportslaw" [and human] activity is subject to the law in all its aspects and sport can plead no special exemption'.[29] The alternative view is that sports law has a separate and identifiable body of law, both common law and statute, which is unique to the sports industry.[30] There is a 'third way'; however, this is the view that sports law is in transition between the two extremes and may yet develop into a distinct and discrete body of law.[31] As evidence of this, one can point to the standard of care applied in sporting personal injury cases. This is dealt with in more detail in Chapter 5. Suffice it to say here, though, there is an unresolved argument as to whether there is indeed a new and different standard of care there. Specifically, a test that is more lenient towards the defendant and allows for sporting endeavour and the 'agony of the game'. Alternatively, it is argued that the test is the same as in ordinary negligence actions but merely requires a higher evidential standard to be met. If there is, in fact, such a distinct and separate test, this militates towards the conclusion that a distinct body of sports law is emerging. If, however, case law determines that the test in sports personal injury does not differ substantively, then this indicates that the law is simply being *applied* to sport.

The Court of Arbitration for Sport

CAS has a body of case law emanating from it; this and its relationship with the domestic law of various nations provide the best evidence of a real *lex sportiva* rather than a putative one. The jurisprudence of this arbitral body is derived from a unique set of legal processes. It is referred to as a 'court' but is in fact a highly developed form of Alternative Dispute Resolution (ADR) in that it settles legal disputes primarily by arbitration. There is what seems at first glance to be an odd mix of common law principles juxtaposed with civil code concepts, though. Thus, strict liability and the concept of some form of precedent, both very much Anglo-American legal traditions, are overlaid by, for instance, a 'comfortable satisfaction' standard of proof. This standard is much more commonly found in Romano-Germanic legal systems like the French, German and Italian Civil Codes. This jurisprudence is of little interest or assistance to anyone outside the sports industry and associated academia, however. One of the features of CAS case law is that it has produced a 'degree of harmonisation on the decision-making procedures' of different ISFs.[32] This suggests a coherent body of *lex sportiva*, but this is law which cannot apply to all sportspeople, regardless of their discipline. This is because there are sports, including major actors like Formula One, horse racing and even English soccer,[33] with its global influence unmatched by almost any other country, that have in-house disciplinary procedures. These do not have an ordinary appeal route to CAS. This must be a significant obstacle for arguments that CAS is a 'supreme court' for sport. After all, to take the Supreme Court of the UK, the US Supreme Court and the French *Cour de Cassation* as just three examples, all pass judgements that every citizen of those countries is potentially subject to. The equivalent population for CAS should be every sports participant, but in fact, it is much more limited than that. No CAS decision will have any direct effect on the way a horse racing jockey operates, for instance. Thus, if 'coherent' implies 'complete', then there is in fact no coherent body of sports law that emanates from CAS.

The counterpoint is that although some sports, even those with as large an impact as football, horse racing and Formula One, do not routinely contribute to CAS jurisprudence, they have their own arbitration systems. These arbitral mechanisms do generate case law of a sort as well. There is therefore a stronger argument that *lex sportiva* could usefully refer to the totality of arbitration awards in sport, rather than just those issued by CAS. Interpreting *lex sportiva* this way, however, means that such a body of law must derive from different, sometimes conflicting, legal rules.[34] This is rather than a single codified set like the WADC. There is significant common ground, though, the overwhelming reliance on strict liability in sport arbitration rules being a key example. Domestic legal systems with sufficient congruence often refer and even defer to one another, however. This produces a body of precedents that straddles many jurisdictions. The presence of Australian, Canadian and (pre-1997) Hong Kong appeal decisions in English law is clear evidence of that. In like vein, CAS awards do inform those made by the British Horse Racing Authority (BHA) judicial process from time to time, for example, even though it is not bound so to act.[35]

Sporting rules as 'Soft Law'

It may well be useful to now discuss what elements of sports law, if any, are 'soft' law in determining the true nature and quality of this legal category. Firstly, though, it is important to be clear about the term. In the wider legal context, sports law aside for now, 'hard' law is what 'law' is usually constructed as. Whether by laypeople or students on first encountering legal study or indeed by many High Street legal practitioners and their clients, that is, law is what statute and cases say it is. For example, in the UK, the Fraud Act 2006 is hard law and so is case law that clarifies rights and duties in negligence cases like *Donoghue v Stevenson* [1932] AC 562 on negligence. In the United States, the Patriot Act on anti-terror measures is an example of hard law, and so is the case of *Roe v Wade* 410 US 113, now of course, overruled. In countries with a Romano-Germanic legal tradition, the equivalent hard law can largely be found in a 'Civil Code', an extensive single body of written law such as the French *Code Civil* or '*Code Napoléon*'. 'Soft' law, on the other hand, is best described as collection of norms and values that are not breached because to do so would potentially deprive the transgressor of access to a given market, organisation, community or other beneficial environment or arrangement.

Examples of soft law can be found in international trade. This is governed by a number of treaties signed by nation states. There are treaties that are capable of being enforced by a judicial body, such as the European Court of Justice (ECJ) in relation to the Treaty on the Functioning of the European Union (TFEU). Still others, however, lacking any real judicial body to enforce provisions, rely on practical consequences that flow from non-adherence to treaty provisions. For instance, if a business or even a state does not comply with, say, trade tariff rules, the consequence might be that it is excluded from international trade or heavily restricted, based on the decision of other signatories. This is where the coercion and standardisation come from, not hard law legal consequences such as judicial pronouncements on statute law.

Another, more specific example of soft law can be found by studying the Kyoto Protocol and the UN Framework Convention on Climate Change.[36] The former will be revisited in Chapter 9, but in these cases, signatories' compliance with commitments to reduce harm to the environment is reliant on a range of coercive factors. None of these is the result of a binding legal obligation. It is best to think of hard and soft law as existing on a continuum rather than being absolutes, however. It would further be useful to have a framework to analyse where any given set of rules fits on this sliding scale, the polar extremes being traditional hard law enshrined in statute versus true soft law with goals that are at best vague and aspirational.[37] In international legal orders, there are three key factors at play; these might be summarised as binding obligation, precise wording, and a provision for some form of delegation in the implementation of the law[38] (see Figure 1.3). If any one or more of these factors are weak in an international legal framework, that regime is better characterised as soft law, or at least with significant soft law elements.

Other international legal frameworks exist that are at the sub-national state level. That is to say, they are not the product of arrangements between national governments but are essentially extensive, but private 'normative co-ordinations'.[39] This is again a topic relevant to Chapter 9 and a discussion of climate change and sport. Sports law, or key strands of it, can be considered an example of such legal co-ordinations. To be specific, the WADC and rules made by the IOC fit very well in this category. The WADC has a highly developed judicial apparatus to enforce it in CAS, as already discussed. The soft aspects of this international legal order are that submission to it is entirely voluntary, however. Put another way, signing up to the WADC is the gateway to competing at the elite level in a number of key sports, but there are alternative choices. These choices may be unattractive, such as competing only at the amateur level or pursuing another career altogether. The real or otherwise nature of such alternatives for the competitor has been discussed in the European Court of Human Rights (ECtHR),[40] for instance, in relation to the alleged 'forced' nature of the arbitration clause in the rules. Alternatively, the choice may be between sports with differing sets of rules

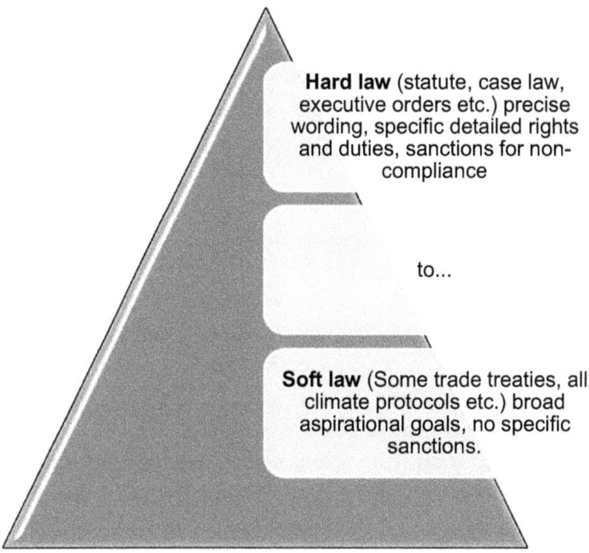

Figure 1.3 The hard law – soft law continuum.

but essentially a similar activity, Olympic equestrianism (WADC) and horse racing (Orders and Rules of Racing), for example. This choice is sometimes forced upon participants in some instances by a ban in one or other discipline.[41] Once signed up, however, the elite athlete has entered into binding obligations under precise wording, with enforcement delegated to a specialist judicial arm, and is very much encountering hard law in the form of contract.

In terms of statute law, though, in the UK, the state has long resisted being overtly and directly involved in governing sport. The closest any administration has come to this is in respect of the national game, football. There have been threats to reform the English FA[42] in relation to diversity issues raised in 2016 and football governance generally in 2021. A football governance bill is currently making its way through Parliament as a result. These developments were in large part in response to the abortive moves to create an ESL already discussed. Legislation aside, several judicial decisions have established that SGBs are not susceptible to either Judicial Review or a Human Rights Act action as they are not sufficiently 'governmental' in function. The courts have accepted a supervisory jurisdiction over SGBs, however,[43] in *Bradley v Jockey Club*, which will be examined further in Chapter 3. In sum, the UK has a largely non-interventionist approach to sports governance compared to a significant number of other countries.[44]

Nevertheless, the decisions of SGB tribunals and CAS have binding force as they are underpinned by the laws of contract and arbitration and so far, sports law may seem to have more hard law in it than soft. It is a complex area, however, because as a whole, sports law includes in it the overarching notion of needing to adhere to norms and values in order to compete at the highest level. This is in addition to domestic and supranational case law, statute and treaty. In turn, there are arbitral awards which are contractually binding, but submission to those contracts is effectively coerced by a very persuasive moral imperative, constantly championed by sports 'rulers'. This is often badged as the need to maintain 'Clean Sport', or sport free from drugs. This all may seem a philosophical discussion, but the contested nature of 'sports law' and *lex sportiva* can have real and practical consequences, as discussed at the beginning of this chapter.

A discussion has already been opened about how to study sports law by using tools more commonly found in examining corporate bodies and how they function. The creation of sporting rules was described there as a set of 'emergent social processes'. This is a term used to analyse the power dynamics and human relations within a juristic person, a limited company[45] and is entirely an internal organisational matter. Comparisons can also be made with the way that corporate life is governed by the UK Corporate Governance Code (UKCGC), which has strong soft law elements. Albeit that its soft elements are said to be to its detriment.[46]

At the other extreme, countries such as Greece and Belgium have criminalised doping in sport[47] but, for most jurisdictions, sporting rules are a structural matter for autonomous SGBs and ISFs. In common law jurisdictions, though, the national law can also be derived from case law. Therefore, when it falls to the courts to adjudicate on sporting rules, the resulting judicial determination does become part of the law of the land. *Bradley v Jockey Club*, involving a racing jockey, is a good example of this process. In this case, it was confirmed that SGBs are under a supervisory jurisdiction provided by the national courts, at least where the fundamental rights of the athlete or player are threatened. Outside the UK, the case brought by the footballer *Matuzalem*[48] established that the types of appeal possible against CAS awards through the Swiss Federal Tribunal (SFT)[49] are much wider than previously thought. It had long been possible to take such an award to the SFT on procedural grounds, rather like the common law Judicial Review process in the UK. *Matuzalem* effectively expanded the appeal route to include matters of substantive law, not just, for example, issues of bias in the panel. In this case, the award itself was found to breach Swiss public law and the rights of the individual enshrined therein.

Claudia Pechstein, an international skater, also brought forward claims initially in Germany. The *Pechstein*[50] cases originally involved just her, but later were in conjunction with the soccer player Adrian Mutu. The judgements ultimately provided guidance as to what constitutes a fair trial in sports arbitration[51] amongst other procedural matters. The ECtHR applied Article 6 of the European Convention on Human Rights (ECHR) to determine this. It is true that these cases mostly address conflicts of laws. That is to say, they provide adjudication where sporting rules and domestic law, or that of a supranational body such as the EU[52] are at odds. Nevertheless, in this sense at least, sports law can become part of the general law through the courts. As shall be discussed, in a subtle way, therefore, the power dynamics which serve the interests of society's elite also serve those of sports 'rulers' and not necessarily the needs of participants and fans.

European Union (EU) law

Having journeyed through various ways to analyse the nature and quality of sports law, it has been established that, taken as a whole, it is difficult to easily deem it a distinct category. The position is a little clearer with regard to the law of the European Union (EU); however, the UK has now left the EU, but the remaining twenty-seven member states are still subject to the EU treaties and ECJ judgements. Sport is an international phenomenon, so studying how it is legally regulated solely in the UK is unproductive. For example, soccer and rugby players are still recruited from the EU, and both equestrians and cyclists are governed by ISFs based in Switzerland.[53] Thus, EU law remains an important factor in UK sport regulation. Furthermore, it will take time to determine which laws that came into being during the UK's forty-seven-year membership of the EU will not be repealed. It is therefore not possible to study sports law in the UK as if in a vacuum. There is strong evidence that there is a level of distortion in EU law when it is applied to sport, which operates to create a more or less distinct 'EU Sports Law'. The treaties and subsequent ECJ judgements operate together to create what has come to be termed the 'specificity of sport'.[54] This derives from sport's unique influence on society for the good; it promotes social integration, provides employment, addresses many health concerns and so on. This is still true when sport is operated as a business, and this discussion will be explored in more detail in various later chapters. The net result, though, is that sport business is treated differently from enterprises unrelated to sport in treaty provisions, policy documents emanating from the treaties, and in case law from the ECJ.[55] This body of law, solely created to cater for the special nature of sport and sport business, is a separate *lex sportiva* or at least a *lex sportiva Europa universalis*. This then is the law that all citizens of all member states are potentially subject to, without having to opt in via participation in sport.

It could be argued that sport has always been special, but the specific legal concept of the 'specificity' of sport can be traced back to Article 165 of the TFEU of 2007 and the 'White Paper' of the same year. The ECJ also 'admitted that . . . sport in general, possesses unusual characteristics that distinguishes it from "normal" commercial sectors'.[56] This specificity has produced judgements such as Case C-176/96 *Jyri Lehtonen and Castors Canada Dry Namm-Braine ASBL v Fédération royale belge des sociétés de basket-ball ASBL (FRBSB)* (the *Lehtonen* case) and Case 415/93 *Union Royale Belge des Societes de Football Association ASBL v Jean-Marc Bosman* [1995] ECR I-4921 or '*Bosman*' case. In these, the extent to which EU law applies to the activities of sport businesses was delimited. These are activities emanating from the playing of the sport itself, rather than the sport's operation as a business. In sum, only sporting rules that have no commercial element to them, mostly rules that solely operate on the field of play, are outside EU jurisdiction. There is of course a complication in that some rules may have, for example, the maintenance of competitive balance as their motivation, but they may have commercial implications too. The Financial Fair Play Rules (FFP) and transfer arrangements in soccer being prime examples. There is undoubtedly a commercial element to these rules as well as trying to ensure a 'level playing field', and thus they may be termed 'hybrid' rules. These categories are discussed further in Chapter 2. In *Deliège*,[57] a competitor claimed that regulations for international selection written by her ISF, based in the EU member state of Belgium, had frustrated her career unfairly. Specifically, there were limits in these rules on the number of participants that could be put forward by each national federation in her sport. The ECJ ruled that there was an economic aspect to these rules, irrespective of any co-existing motivation to maintain sporting fairness. It seems equitable that businesses and corporations should not escape the operation of law entirely simply because their enterprise is the playing of a sport. It is good that the EU has social and cultural aspirations as well as commercial ones, and 'sport has been identified by the EU institutions as one of the tools through which these goals can be achieved'.[58] On the other hand, as will be discussed later, firstly, the primary goal of EU law is to ensure harmony in trading practices across member states' borders, not sporting fairness; politicians and judges are not experts in that. Further, it is very difficult to discern clear water between rules that affect play and those that affect the business. Consequently, the judgements are hardly a model of clarity and consistency. With that in mind, it may prove difficult for SGBs and ISFs to devise rules in the future that are certain not to be subject to EU law. This is because of the inexorable direction of travel towards increasing commercialisation in the sector.[59] *Deliège* makes the point that the rules on selection were no doubt part of how the sport is organised. The reality is, though, paying spectators and broadcasters wanting to negotiate exclusive rights with the ISF inevitably introduced an economic facet to those same rules. It is unlikely that this commercial strand in the interpretation of those rules was in the minds of those drafting them, much less their intention. The fact that EU sports law will increasingly need to be taken into account when drafting sports rules militates towards viewing EU sports law as a distinct entity, one that is strongly influential on international sport.

Where are we? Well, 'Potahto' . . . almost.

So, what is law to sport? Whilst there may be soft law elements in sports law, it is much more than that; for instance, it addresses 'a unique set of relations among persons and undertakings involved in the playing and organisation of sport'.[60] It has elements of coherence that are like those found in health law and family law. There are rules such as contract and tort, which are often varied to take account of the special nature of the relationships involved.[61] The difficulty is of course, that the comparison is a limited one; everyone is a member of a family. This may be distant and fragmented or close and traditional, but biology dictates belonging. It is not possible to opt out of the jurisdiction of the family courts. Sports law, on the other hand, contains aspects like governance regulations that have no relevance to those who have no connection with the sport regulated, or indeed any organised sport.

That said, some components of sports law are merely domestic legislation and case law that are applied to a dispute arising in a sporting context. However, there is an argument that where tort and contract law are so applied, the legal principles are sometimes adjusted by the judiciary to such a degree that these variations constitute a new species of law. In negligence, for instance, with an injury caused to a player, official or spectator during a recognised, regulated sporting event, a claim for damages can be made. Proponents of the argument that sports negligence is so distinct that it is a part of sports law and different from 'ordinary' negligence point to the standard of care that is applied when the injury is a sporting one. Some cases indicate that, so as not to interfere with 'sporting endeavour', sports participants and so on are held to a lower standard.[62] Specifically, instead of the familiar tests applied for breach of a standard of care, the sportsperson will not be liable unless they have shown 'reckless disregard'.

The alternative view is, however, that reckless disregard is merely a rule of evidence to be applied in judging whether the traditional tests have been met and not a new test at all.[63] This argument draws on the fact that the standard of care test in 'ordinary' negligence remains the same in an emergency[64] and when the injured party is in a category of people particularly vulnerable to the negligence alleged.[65] However, the evidential considerations applied as to whether a breach has occurred in those circumstances take account of their special nature, without a completely new test being created. This suggests the ordinary negligence test is still in play in sport, and the full ramifications of this debate will be considered in Chapter 5.

In the final analysis, there are *aspects* of sports law that are sport-specific and applicable nowhere else in the legal landscape. Governance rules, even underpinned by contract, only matter to stakeholders in that particular sport. Further, a sports participant who is banned from a sport by its disciplinary process feels no effect of that ban if they voluntarily leave the sport and take up other employment. There are even documented examples of persons subject to a ban switching to a sport with a different disciplinary process and no effective reciprocal banning provisions.[66] In addition, EU sports law is indeed different when applied to sport. Any business that provides both sporting and non-sporting entertainment would find essentially different law applied by the ECJ, even if more or less the same dispute arose regarding both arms of its operation. Here, at least then, sports law is different law. A significant amount of law applied in a sporting context, tort being an example, does not differ because of sporting considerations, or such difference as there may be, is contested. Furthermore, the tortfeasor cannot escape the effect of the outcome of the case simply by no longer playing the sport.

The summary position must be that sports law is not 'there' yet as a distinct, consistent, coherent legal category, but it may evolve to be so in due course.

Notes

1 Pippa Cuckson, 'Maktoum family endurance horse trainer banned for steroids offence', *Horse Sport Website*, 2023, accessed 25 March 2025, https://horsesport.com/horse-news/maktoum-endurance-trainer-banned-steroids-offence/.

2 See generally, Jonathan Merritt, '"Don't look a gift horse in the mouth" – Regulating for integrity, what equestrianism can learn from Thoroughbred racing', *International Sports Law Journal*, 16, no. 3 (2017): 198–216.

3 Ole Lando, 'The lex mercatoria in international commercial arbitration', *International and Comparative Law Quarterly*, 34, no. 4 (October 1985): 747.

4 'World Cup 2010: Fifa issues ban deadline to Nigeria', *BBC Sport*, 2 July 2010, http://news.bbc.co.uk/sport1/hi/football/world_cup_2010/8780028.stm.

5 Jonathan Merritt and Genevieve Gordon-Thomson, 'European Super League: What can its opponents legally do?', *The Conversation*, 20 April 2021, https://theconversation.com/european-super-league-what-can-its-opponents-legally-do-159393.

6 Mark James, *Sports Law* (Basingstoke: Palgrave Macmillan, 2013), 5.

7 Ibid.

8 Dan Roan, 'FA reform: Former chiefs say, "elderly white men" block change', *BBC Sport*, 12 December 2016, http://www.bbc.co.uk/sport/football/38274152.

9 Andrew Bull, 'Sports bodies face cuts over lack of women in boardrooms', *The Guardian*, 8 March 2017, 7.

10 See generally, Pippa Norris and Jonni Lovenduski, *Political Recruitment: Gender, Race and Class in the British Parliament* (Cambridge: Cambridge University Press, 1995).

11 Francis Gibb and David Brown, 'Verdict on the judges: Too male, too white, too elitist', *The Times*, 6 July 2011, 1.

12 Sarah Gordon, 'Women hold just a sixth of senior roles at top UK companies', *The Financial Times*, 15 March 2017, https://www.ft.com/content/0713fe70-18f8-11e6-bb7d-ee563a5a1cc1.

13 Gibson Burrell and Gareth Morgan, *Sociological Paradigms and Organisational Analysis* (Aldershot: Ashgate, 2005), 32.
14 Ibid., 28.
15 Jonathan Wilson, 'A lesson from history: The European Super League battle is not over', *The Guardian*, 22 April 2021, https://www.theguardian.com/football/2021/apr/22/a-colombian-lesson-from-history-the-super-league-battle-is-not-over.
16 David Karen and Richard Washington, eds, *Sociological Perspectives on Sport – The Games Outside the Games* (London: Routledge 2015), 21.
17 Ibid.
18 Richard Posner, *An Affair of State: The Investigation, Impeachment and Trial of President Clinton* (Cambridge, MA and London: Harvard University Press 2012), 1–15.
19 Matthew Flinders, 'MP's expenses: The legacy of a scandal', *BBC*, 7 May 2019, https://www.bbc.co.uk/news/uk-politics-48187096.
20 Antonio Gramsci and David Forgacs, *The Gramsci Reader: Selected Writings, 1916–1935* (New York: Schocken Books, 1988), 218.
21 See Mark Pieth, *Reforming FIFA* (Baden-Baden: Nomos Verlagsgesellschaft, 2014), especially – Introduction, 'Governing FIFA'.
22 Sebastian Coe, 'We cannot move from strict liability rule', *Daily Telegraph*, 25 February 2004, http://www.telegraph.co.uk/sport/othersports/drugsinsport/2373729/We-cannot-move-from-strict-liability-rule.html. There is also a discussion of Juan Antonio Samaranch's 'moral death' speech in Anne Amos, 'Inadvertent doping and the WADA code', *Bond Law Review*, 9, no. 1 (2007): 1.
23 See *Kitzmiller v Dover Area School District* 400 F Supp. 2D 707 (M.D. Pa. 2005).
24 Emily Dawling, 'The sports hijab dividing opinions', *BBC*, 10 January 2018, https://www.bbc.com/culture/article/20180110-the-sports-hijab-dividing-opinions.
25 Ken Foster, 'Is there a global sports law', in *Lex Sportiva: What is Sports Law?*, ed. Robert Siekmann and Janwillem Soek (The Hague: T.M.C. Asser Press, 2012), 37.
26 Ibid., 35–7.
27 Mark James and Guy Osborn, 'The Olympics, transnational law and legal transplants: The International Olympic Committee, ambush marketing and ticket touting', *Legal Studies*, 36, no. 1 (March 2016): 93–110.
28 Timothy Davis, 'What is sports law', in *Lex Sportiva: What is Sports Law?*, ed. Robert Siekmann and Janwillem Soek (The Hague: T.M.C. Asser Press, 2012), 3–7.
29 David Griffith-Jones, *Law and the Business of Sport* (Haywards Heath: Tottel, 2007), Preface.
30 Simon Gardiner et al., *Sports Law* (London: Cavendish, 2011), 83–5.
31 Davis, 'What is sports law', 3–7.
32 James, *Sports Law*, 52.
33 *Stretford v The Football Association Ltd & Another* [2007] EWCA Civ 238, regarding the FA's 'Rule K'.
34 Jonathan Merritt, *Regulating Sport for the Non-Human Athlete* (Lanham: Rowman and Littlefield, 2019), 37–74.
35 Ibid., 52–7.
36 Kenneth Abbott and Duncan Snidal, 'Hard and soft law in international governance', *International Organisation*, 54, no. 3 (2000): 421–56.
37 Sylvia Karlsson-Vinkhuyzen and A. Vihma, 'Comparing the legitimacy and effectiveness of global hard and soft law: An analytical framework', *Regulation & Governance*, 3, no. 4 (2009): 400.

38 Ibid., 402.
39 Neil Walker, 'Beyond boundary disputes and basic grids: Mapping the global disorder of normative orders', *International Journal of Constitutional Law*, 6, nos. 3 and 4 (2008): 377.
40 *Mutu and Pechstein v Switzerland* (2018) App. Nos. 40575/10 and 67474/10.
41 Cuckson, 'Maktoum family endurance horse trainer banned for steroids offence'.
42 Richard Coway, 'FA reform: As MPs debate the issue, is real change a stretch too far?', *BBC Sport*, 8 February 2017, http://www.bbc.co.uk/sport/football/38907978.
43 See also generally Merritt, *Regulating Sport for the Non-Human Athlete*.
44 James, *Sports Law*, 7.
45 Burrell and Morgan, *Sociological Paradigms and Organisational Analysis*, 32.
46 See Andrew Keay, 'Comply or explain: In need of greater regulatory oversight?', *Legal Studies*, 34, no. 2 (June 2014): 279–304.
47 John O'Leary, *Drugs & Doping in Sports: Socio-legal Perspectives* (London: Cavendish, 2001), 259.
48 See Roy Levy, 'Swiss Federal Tribunal overrules CAS award in a landmark decision: FIFA vs Matuzalem', *International Sports Law Journal*, 12, nos. 3–4 (2012): 35–9.
49 CAS is based in Switzerland. The SFT is the Swiss Supreme Court.
50 Landgericht München, judgement dated 26 February 2014, file no. 37 O 28331/12.
51 *Mutu and Pechstein v Switzerland* (2018) App. Nos. 40575/10 and 67474/10.
52 For instance, Case T-313/02 *David Meca-Medina and Igor Majcen v Commission of the European Communities*.
53 Switzerland is not a member of the EU, but the parties have a free trade agreement dating back to 1972, effectively incorporating many EU policies, such as freedom of movement, into Swiss law.
54 Art. 165 Treaty on the Functioning of the European Union (TFEU).
55 Karen Davies, *Understanding European Law* (Oxford: Routledge, 2013), 53–62.
56 Steven Weatherill, '"Fair play please!" – Recent developments in the application of EC Law to sport', *Common Market Law Review*, 40 (2003): 53–4.
57 Case C-51/96 and C-191/97, *Christelle Deliège v Ligue Francophone de Judo et Disciplines ASBL*.
58 Richard Parrish, 'The birth of European Union Sports Law', *The Entertainment and Sports Law Journal*, 2, no. 2 (2003): 22.
59 Ibid.
60 Jack Anderson, *Modern Sports Law* (Oxford: Hart, 2010), 25.
61 Einer Elhauge, 'Can health law become a coherent field of law?' *Wake Forest Law Review*, 41 (2006): 365.
62 *Wooldridge v Sumner* [1963] 2 QB 43.
63 *Caldwell v. Maguire and Fitzgerald* [2001] EWCA 1054.
64 *Watt v Hertfordshire County Council* [1954] 1 WLR 835.
65 *Paris v Stepney Borough Council* [1950] UKHL 3.
66 Cuckson, 'Maktoum family endurance horse trainer banned for steroids offence'.

2

Sport, Sporting Organisations and Their Rules

Running sport – 'Every State Is a Dictatorship'[1]

It has been established in Chapter 1 that even democracies are effective dictatorships, for the duration of the electorate's mandate. Furthermore, this is also true of sports organisations at the elite level; this is because sports governing bodies (SGBs), national governing bodies (NGBs) and their international sports federations (ISFs) bear considerable similarity in form and function to miniature nation states. They have members as a populace, they have a governing committee capable of passing statutes that regulate their constituents, and usually there is a constitution and a judicial arm. As such, they are creatures of capitalism because, in modern times, with very few exceptions, nations are run according to a capitalist hegemony. Gramsci opined that a vital function of power in these states was to 'preserve the ideological unity of a whole bloc'[2] and so likewise, dissent as to the basic notions of how sport is run gets short shrift. It is thus unsurprising that SGBs suffer from some of the ills of governance that nation states also do. SGBs are not co-operatives; they have hierarchies and a limited form of democracy to install officials. They are also, in the modern world, commercial entities striving to maximise income for their sport. The following will evaluate the precise functioning of these bodies as well as the extent to which Gramsci's analysis is applicable to sport.

Sport and its regulation

Sport has not always been heavily regulated and professionalised. The transition from amateur pastime to professional activity is more advanced in some sports than in others. Sports governance has been seen as too often 'fragmented' and 'unprofessional'[3] although much has improved since the introduction of a Sports Governance Code. From a legal perspective, the coherence of sport structures and rules is of considerable importance. It becomes difficult to apply a framework to make sense of how sport operates under the law if the systems and processes in different sports are too disparate in terms of the principles at heart. As will be discussed, these disparities can lead to outright inequity as well. Differences in detail, such as being a signatory to the World Anti-Doping Code (WADC) or not, and specific differences in rules, such as between Soccer and American Football, are inevitable, but basic notions of governance, integrity, constitutionality, equity and justice need to be common. The term *lex sportiva* has been coined for the study of sports law, but the term needs to be properly examined.

Sports governance and lex sportiva

In Chapter 1, the question of a distinct legal discipline of sports law was examined in detail. It was concluded that whilst there may be an emerging discipline of sports law, it is incomplete. It may be that a discrete body of sports law will emerge, but it is not there yet, and at that future stage, it may be in a better position to reduce unfairness in sport rather than enhance it or ignore it. Nevertheless, it is worth revisiting in summary some of the issues raised in that chapter and applying them directly to sports governance. Unequal power dynamics exist in sport between those who organise or regulate and the members. These lower orders are mostly, but not exclusively, made up of competitors. This dynamic is not unlike that in a state, in that there is a similar dominance of 'rulers' over 'ruled'.[4] The degree to which the ruled can influence or even replace individual 'rulers' varies across nations of course but even in a modern democracy, the best that can be achieved is an 'elective dictatorship'.[5] In the United States, this temporary autocracy lasts for four years and in the UK, five years, after which in each case a general election must be held. During these periods, it is very difficult for the ruled to influence the government policies that are implemented. This is also true of members vis-à-vis the ruling council of their SGB. Furthermore, as already argued, just as the modern SGB mirrors the nation state, there are certain comparisons to be made with limited liability corporations, another feature of capitalism. Both operate under a constitution and have members with the ability to vote for or against directors sitting on a ruling council in the form of the management board. In fact, many SGBs and ISFs have turned themselves into these juristic persons under various jurisdictions to formalise their business activities. It is useful therefore to study sports governance with similar tools to those that are used in analysing corporate governance. The similarity with states and corporations does not end with the voting process, however. Like the other two, sport seems to be beset from time to time by the same sort of controversy over inequities. For instance, in 2016, in English soccer, a lack of diversity at the governance level was very much the subject of debate.[6] Parliament even threatened sanctions[7] if the national game did not review the gender balance in its top echelons. These concerns replicate those made about the prevalence of late middle-aged white males in UK politics,[8] the judiciary[9] and in British corporate boardrooms.[10]

In Chapter 1, whether sports governance, like corporate governance[11] is also 'an emergent social process which is created by the individuals concerned'[12] was considered. Members of a given SGB will be the sole source of the social processes within the organisation. Some of these will become officials through election; the rest are responsible for placing those people in positions of power through the electoral process. Governance rules and processes will be influenced by the need to adopt the Sports Governance Code in order to obtain Lottery funding, but the ultimate decisions that govern the sport are those of the SGB ruling council alone. It is therefore not surprising that similar complaints emerge about the way SGBs and ISFs are governed as are voiced about the way society is run. The leadership structures in a sport are created, and people are elevated to them, so that competitors can get on with training and competing. In like vein, the proletariat elects a parliament or local government so that the electorate can concentrate on the day-to-day mundanities of living. Such parliaments exist within a larger pool of power brokers connected with it, however. Judges, industrialists, aristocrats, senior law enforcement and military figures all contribute to what has been termed the 'ruling class'. Indeed, individuals often move between the government and these satellite roles. A senior executive being elected to parliament would not be unusual, for instance. The rulers in both society and SGBs and ISFs tend to encourage the lower echelons to leave them to get on with governing, whilst the ruled get on with life. This is advantageous to the rulers because there is less likelihood of the status quo being questioned.[13] In sport, as in society or corporate life, promised major reform almost never affects the imbalance of power between the two groups.[14] For example, as discussed with regard to doping rules in Chapter 4, competitors are encouraged to not question the rules, merely to abide by them.[15] In all of this power framework, the contractual *nexus* between member, SGB, ISF and such as the IOC and the World Anti-Doping Agency (WADA) is the source of most of the coercion, not government control. In fact, ISFs can have the de facto power to mandate that governments do not interfere here, on pain of expulsion from the international body, and *Fédération Internationale de Football Association* (FIFA) statutes are a case in point.[16]

SGBs and their ISFs

The overwhelming majority of international professional sports have both a national and international governance structure. Soccer, for instance, has FIFA as its world governing body. This ISF has a similar number of member states to the United Nations and has been in existence since 1904, making it one of the most well-established ISFs. Each of the nations of the UK has its own NGB. The English Football Association (FA) owns and operates the prestigious FA Cup competition, for instance. Germany has the *Deutscher Fußball-Bund*, the United States has US Soccer and so on. There is a Europe-wide ISF as well, the Union of European Football Associations (UEFA), with fifty-five members. It is one of FIFA's subordinate continental confederations, similar in form and function to equivalents governing North America, South America, Asia, Australasia-with-the-Pacific and Africa. FIFA has known its fair share of governance scandal,[17] but now seeks to present itself as 'fast evolving into a body that can more effectively serve our game for the benefit of the entire world',[18] it enthusiastically promotes both the men's and women's games and has several important functions in standardising and maintaining the integrity of international soccer. These include harmonising the technical rules of the game, such as the size and weight of the ball, the dimensions of the pitch and goals and so on. Establishing and reviewing the rules relating to the game's integrity, whether the threat be from doping, match-fixing, or any other source, also falls within its remit. Further, FIFA organises and facilitates national and international tournaments; it owns and manages the 'World Cup' tournament, for instance. Each level of the game is 'affiliated' to the one above it in the hierarchy; Manchester United FC is affiliated to the English FA, who are in turn affiliated to UEFA and ultimately FIFA. US soccer teams like LA Galaxy are affiliated with US Soccer, which is part of the Confederation of North, Central American and Caribbean Association Football (CONCACAF) and, through that membership, FIFA.

This process of affiliation is based on contract and is replicated through almost all major sports. Cycling has *Union Cycliste Internationale* (UCI) as its world governing body, with such as British Cycling and US Cycling as subordinate NGBs. World Athletics is the new name for the International Association of Athletics Federations (IAAF), headquartered in Monaco. This is the global body, with such as UK Athletics and the *Federazione Italiana di Atletica Leggera* (FIDAL) from Italy as its members. In the early days of professionalisation and commercialisation of international sport, there were doubts about the true contractual nature of the relationship between competitor/club/NGB and ultimately ISF. There were instances where the common law traditions of offer, acceptance, consideration, capacity or intention to create legal relations were held to be too difficult to establish. This was because of the less formal ways that athletes used to agree to compete. In *Modahl v British Athletics Federation* (No 2) [2002] 1 WLR 1192, for instance, runner Diane Modahl sued for breach of contract between herself and her NGB. This was the result of a previous case between the two parties where poor laboratory procedures led to her exoneration regarding a positive doping finding. Modahl sought damages because she suffered a loss of chance to compete and consequently potentially lost revenue. On the basis of the specific facts of the case, however, the court was unwilling to find that a formal contract existed between the athlete and the BAF. These issues are unlikely to reoccur, though, as increasing commercialisation means resorting to litigation is more likely. Consequently, teams of lawyers in most organisations will have ensured that in the majority of cases a contractual relationship can be clearly evidenced. One of the Olympic equestrian sports can be taken as an example. On applying to join British Dressage (BD) using an online form (offer/acceptance) and on payment of a registration fee (consideration), a 'handbook' of rules is supplied. These are the terms and conditions of membership. If the applicant is under eighteen, an adult will have to sign for them online, which caters for the requirement of capacity. BD is a commercial organisation so the presumption is for this being a legal relationship, not a domestic one. The requirements for a valid contract are met. Further, the 2023 Handbook makes it clear that the document represents an 'Agreement to be bound by the rules' and that:

> 'All members of British Dressage (BD) are bound by the Memorandum and Articles of BD, together with the rules, Code of Conduct, regulations, terms and conditions and bye-laws made under them'. [Further,] 'in becoming a member of British Dressage, members have also agreed to be bound by: The FEI rules when competing in international classes, the BEF Equine Anti-Doping Rules (BEFAR), the BEF Anti-Doping Rules for International Athletes.'[19]

The member agrees to be bound by the BEF or British Equestrian Federation (now 'British Equestrian') Rules and those of the *Fédération Equestre Internationale* (FEI). This indicates that the contractual nexus extends from the member to the SGB, then to the NGB and finally to the ISF as well. Similar documents and processes are evident in the vast majority of international sports, even, like BD here, at the grassroots level.

What is an 'official' sport?

Not every pastime has recognition as a sport in the UK. This does not affect the enjoyment of those engaged in these activities nor their validity, but it does affect the way they are funded. The UK Sports Councils, one for each of the four nations of the UK, are Sport England, Sport Scotland, Sport Wales and Sport Northern Ireland. The umbrella organisation responsible for distributing government and lottery funding is UK Sport. Each is an executive non-departmental public body sponsored by the Department for Culture, Media & Sport (DCMS). The Sports Councils were created by Royal Charter in 1996 and share a common vision: 'to invest in sport and physical activity to make it a normal part of life for everyone . . . regardless of who you are'.[20] It is an important part of government policy to encourage sporting activity. In addition to the tax income that encouraging professional sport provides, facilitating grassroots sport is thought to lead to a fitter, healthier population. Such a society is happier, more productive and less of a drain on healthcare and other social resources. George Orwell was rather more scathing. He had the view that encouraging emotional investment in sport made it less likely that the people would pay attention to what the government was doing to further its own interests:

> the care of home and children, petty quarrels with neighbors, films, football, beer and above all, gambling filled up the horizon of their minds. To keep them in control was not difficult.[21]

Put another way, being preoccupied with sport eats away at the motivation to question the way that capitalist society operates:

> the collective passion towards sports distracts people from the vagaries and exploitations of everyday life: When the workday is over, I can root for my beloved Rangers/Giants/Titans and not think about my nasty boss.[22]

This is a very effective way for governments to create and maintain the 'consent of the governed'[23] after all. If institutional violence is when unequal life chances are woven into structures,[24] then the distraction of sport is a useful way to embed that and minimise pushback from the ruled. The National Lottery was created by the National Lottery Act 1993, and it is funds from this source, together with a limited amount of income drawn from tax, that the sports councils are charged with distributing. This in itself creates another paradox, and the uneasy relationship this state-sponsored gambling has with government efforts to deal with gambling addiction is dealt with further in Chapter 8. Inevitably, though, demand for funding is greater than supply, so the Sports Councils will only entertain bids from 'official sports'.

Sports council recognition criteria

The argument in this book is focused on 'official' sports, so it is important that the criteria for recognition are examined. For funding purposes, both the sport and the NGB must be recognised by the relevant sports council. The application process is the same throughout the four nations, and the various Councils are at pains to point out that they do not decide what is and what is not a sport. They acknowledge that this can be a matter of opinion and is, to a degree, subjective. The process is designed to determine which sports the Councils are prepared to work with or 'recognise'. The essential criteria are whether the sport, 'meets the Council of Europe's European Sports Charter 1993 definition of sport, and whether it's well established and organised within our jurisdiction'.[25] The Charter definition is:

> 'Sport' means all forms of physical activity which, through casual or organised participation, aim at expressing or improving physical fitness and mental well-being, forming social relationships or obtaining results in competition at all levels.[26]

Being 'well organised', will require the NGB concerned to have adopted the Sports Governance Code, which will be discussed further later in this chapter. The UK government does not officially interfere with the running of sport, as discussed earlier, but has, by this indirect means, forced a standardised form of governance on sport. To refuse to abide by this code would effectively bar any access to government and Lottery funding. This will be less meaningful to sports that have a strong relationship with betting and/or have significant gate and broadcasting revenue streams, like soccer and golf. However, for the majority of 'lesser' sports, such a loss of funding opportunities would be catastrophic.

It may be difficult to picture a 'sport' that does not qualify as 'official'. To illustrate this, consider the differing fates of two pastimes, pub darts and the card game, bridge. Neither requires players to be in the peak of physical fitness by any means. Nevertheless, darts has won official recognition, whereas bridge, even after litigation, has not. Professional darts players have been around at least since the 1980s, when the sport first started to attract lucrative television deals and could offer significant prize money. These potential winnings dwindled somewhat as the game became associated with an unhealthy lifestyle. This was just when keeping fit and dietary concerns were starting to feature in the national conversation in a big way. Unfavourable media attention beginning in the early 1990s on the smoking, drinking and eating habits of the stars of the sport made sponsors wary. The British Darts Organisation (BDO), one of two NGBs for the sport, the other being the Professional Darts Corporation (PDC), engaged lawyers and started preparing evidence. By March 2005, amongst other things, they could prove that a player could walk up to 16 miles during a competition, and Sport England agreed to recognise the sport.[27] Bridge had a less happy experience by comparison. The English Bridge Union (EBU) had its application to Sport England rejected on the basis that no appreciable physical activity was involved in the game. In October 2015, the EBU's application for judicial review was rejected in the High Court, so the EBU took the matter to the European Court of Justice (ECJ). The claim was that this decision would disadvantage bridge with regard to VAT,[28] with sport being exempt from this tax under EU law.[29] Framing the claim like this brought the matter within the purview of the ECJ as it became an economic matter. In its 2017 decision[30] the court was not persuaded that there was sufficient physical activity to bring Bridge within the definition of 'sport' in the Directive. This indirectly vindicated Sport England's decision and was despite an earlier ECJ Attorney General's opinion to the contrary.

An obvious outlier in this discussion is Esports. The closest thing to an NGB in the UK is the British Esports Association, and there is a world body, the International Esports Federation (IEF), based in South Korea. The IEF does have ambitions for the sport to be officially recognised but can be relatively ambivalent as to whether any UK government or Lottery funding is forthcoming or not. It is similarly less important for them to gain Olympic recognition. This is because Esports has had an entirely different journey to its current status as a multi-billion-dollar enterprise compared to traditional sports. Sports like soccer and rugby have comparable earning power, but they began as pastimes. Eventually, these became official sports, and as a result of that, started to attract revenue through selling their intellectual property as well as ticket sales. Conversely, the various esports themselves were the intellectual property of the publishers of the games from the outset. That is where the generous funding comes from for the organisation of the sport, huge prize money[31] and competitions.

Self-regulation – virtue or sin?

The fact that sports in the UK follow the 'self-regulation' model can be a limiting factor and also an expansive one. It will be useful to consider in what ways this mode of operation is both a positive and a negative factor in sports governance. In turn, this will assist in understanding how powerful the ruling bodies of sport are and how difficult they are to challenge by spectators and participants.

Where self-regulation helps

Proponents will point to the degree to which sport is freed from national politics by not being regulated to any appreciable degree by the state. There may well be a benefit from the legislature keeping itself at arm's length from sport regulation, but it will be argued later that the same may not be true of the courts' reluctance to intervene when inequities are highlighted in sporting rules and decisions. As discussed earlier, there is some control from the government indirectly imposed through the strictures applied to funding. In large part, however, sport is left to its own devices. Further, advocates would say there is democracy at the heart of sport. The members can vote officials on or off boards of control in free and fair elections. However, these elections are not immune to the degree of disillusionment with democracy seen in voter apathy generally in society. Both regarding local and general elections in the UK, there has been a steady decline in turnout since 1950.[32] If there is a lack of interest in voting even when the nature and extent of national government is at stake, this does not bode well for engagement with sports organisations' internal democracy.

It has been established that, in the absence of statutory control, the relationship between the sports and their members is a contractual one. The legal rights and obligations of each party are determined by the terms and conditions of membership. This means that each sport can tailor its relationship with its athletes or players and other stakeholders. The expertise and experience required certainly reside within sport itself. In addition, this web of contractual relationships or *nexus* can be very useful in dealing in a proactive and responsive way with persons who are not members. That is to say, those who exhibit problem behaviours but are not in a direct contractual relationship with the SGB concerned. This can be achieved without the weighty process and delays that statutory intervention means. For example, as discussed in Chapter 5, soccer hooliganism was a problem in the UK and Europe long before the Football Spectators Act 1989 was finally enacted. By contrast, the British Horse Racing Authority (BHA) is in a good position to promptly deal with undesirable spectators without the efforts of lawmakers. This ability derives in part from the BHA's ownership of, or close contractual links with, racing venues insofar as it can dictate to those tracks who may or may not be allowed entry. The nefarious activities of these spectators might vary from involvement in race fixing to drunken disorderly behaviour, but the Rules of Racing entitle the BHA to prevent entry to anyone. Rule L13 states that, 'the BHA may issue an Exclusion Order against any person, whether or not they are subject to the Rules, where it is in the interests of racing to do so'. Rule L53.2 further states that such a person may not enter Licensed Premises.[33] The breadth of this contractual reach is very wide indeed when *Davis v Carew-Pole* [1956] 1 WLR 833 is also taken into account. It was determined in that case that the racing governing body can have jurisdiction over a person even if they are not licensed by them. This is in the circumstances where such a person attends a disciplinary hearing, thereby entering into the contract by conduct, irrespective of having no live membership. The reach of the rule makers in this sport is quite unprecedented.

The contractual *nexus* (see Figure 2.1) is also useful in grassroots sport. Problems have arisen with regard to the welfare of very young participants, where the SGB concerned does not necessarily have the luxury of a close-knit relationship with the venues that host its youth competitions. These problems range from overbearing, even abusive or violent parents to those whose interest in viewing the young people playing is sexual. In the case of the abusive parent on the touchline, this may be in a public park where there is no controlled access. Further, whilst the child player can be considered a member of the FA, Rugby Football Union (RFU) and so on, the parent may well not be. The only recourse for the SGB is effective but clumsy and undesirable, so it would be a

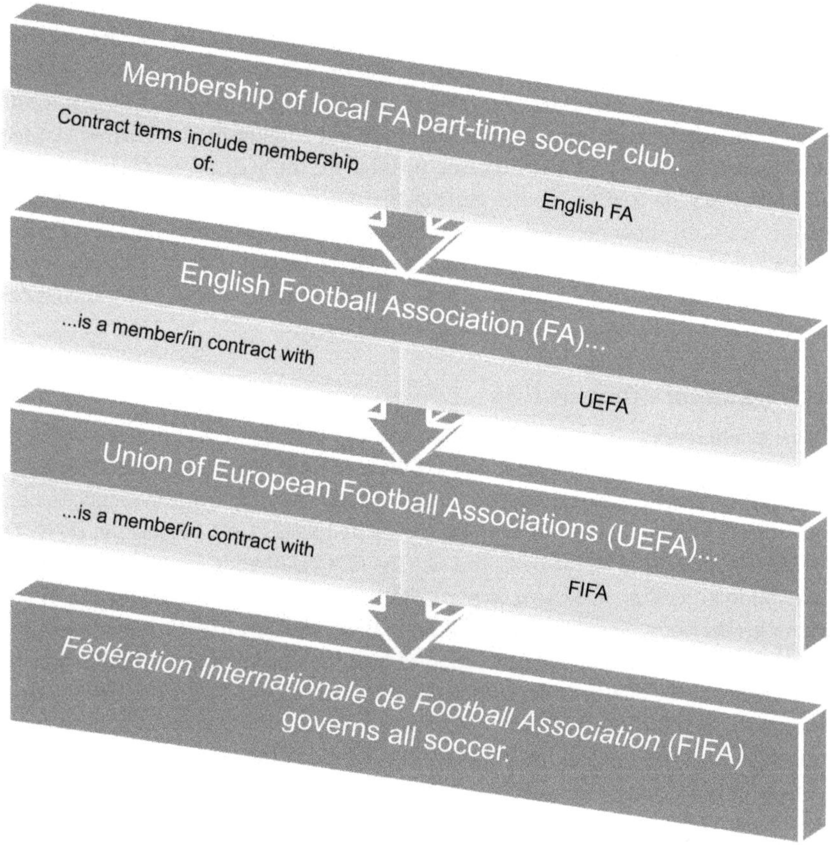

Figure 2.1 Contractual nexus – an individual amateur player becomes subject to FIFA rules.

last resort. The young player or athlete would have to be banned from competition in order to attempt to prevent the parent from attending the matches. This is achievable because of the contractual relationship of the grassroots club and the SGB, for example, the FA in the case of an under-11s local soccer team. This would impact very unfairly on the child, so the SGB would have to carefully weigh the competing interests before acting. Specifically, the factors to be considered would be the impact on the young person of such a ban and the likely attendant unfavourable media coverage. Against this, there is a benefit for the team members, voluntary staff and other properly behaved spectators.

As well as their friends, families and supporters, young people engaged in activities such as swimming and athletics sometimes attract thoroughly unwelcome spectators. Persons unrelated to the participants may be filming the children on their mobile phones or cameras for their own sexual gratification. The amateur competition may be held by a club affiliated to an SGB such as Swim England, but the venue, the local swimming baths operated by the local authority in most cases, is not under the SGB's control. It may take years to have legislation enacted to bar such individuals from these events. Sexual Harm Prevention Orders (SHPO) already exist and would restrict undesirables' ability to attend. However, they might be too narrow in their provisions to be effective.[34] It is, however, possible for the SGB to require these events to be effectively 'policed' by leisure centre staff. Failure to prevent the entry of, or eject, persons who can show no good reason for recording an event would mean that such venues could be 'blacklisted' from being a suitable venue by the SGB. This would present a very serious public image problem for the private owners or local councils that operate these facilities, so compliance is very likely.

Self-regulation – the negatives

The neat coherence and professionalisation that self-regulation in accordance with the Sports Governance Code presents may be illusory to an extent, however. Not every sport has the benefit of one governing body. Golf has the 'R & A' or Royal and Ancient based in St. Andrews, Scotland, but also the United States Golf Association (USGA). UK Darts had, until 2020, the BDO and also the PDC, as already noted earlier. Boxing, Taekwondo and others have two or more SGBs or ISFs as well. Horse Racing in fact has no global body. There are NGBs like the BHA and Royal West India Turf Club (RWITC), but no International Federation as such. This means that a sport bearing the same name may be played under completely different rules and with a wholly different governance structure. One NGB or ISF may respond to public or political pressure to reform its rules and procedures, but that does not mean the same sport played under another body will follow suit. Each body has to democratically vote to follow the other down a particular path of reform or diverge from it. Ultimately, the board or council running each variant of the sport makes the final decision.

When Churchill said 'Democracy is the worst form of government, except for all the others',[35] he was thinking of his own woes at the hands of the British electorate, but democracy wherever it is found, is not a perfect system. SGBs and ISFs are democratic; many always have been, but all must now be so to comply with the Sports Governance Code. It is true that the constitutional mechanisms in a sports body are more flexible and responsive than those at the government level, but they can still be more unwieldy and cumbersome than is ideal. The sporting rules developed in this way can be disjointed and lack a holistic framework as well:

> rules of domestic or international federations tend to resemble the architecture of an ancient building: a wing added here; a loft there; a buttress elsewhere, without adequate consideration of whether the additional parts affect adversely the symmetry of the whole.[36]

Sometimes, reform of the rules can appear to be merely a reaction instigated by one scandal or another rather than a process of continuous review. For instance, UK horse racing has had a series of integrity reports this century already, including the Neville[37] and Quinlan[38] Reviews. The former suggested some major changes to the Rules of Racing because it was an arcane and complex document, encompassing far more than sporting rules normally would. These even included what were effectively employment provisions. The implementation of these findings was a slow process and was only accelerated when an appeal was threatened by trainer Jim Best in 2016. This regarded procedural defects in the way his case was handled by the BHA disciplinary mechanism as it was then constituted.[39] As will be discussed in Chapter 3, no doubt the ruling in *Bradley v Jockey Club* assisted his case.[40] Christopher Quinlan QC was instructed, and after he reported, large sections of the Rules of Racing and attendant venues and processes were thoroughly revamped to ensure they complied with fundamental human rights principles. This move was welcomed, but given that the European Convention had existed since 1948 and the Human Rights Act 1998 had been in force since 2000, the changes can hardly have been heralded as proactive. After all, giving way to progressive change is best termed 'reformist corrosion',[41] in that inequities are often chipped away at over a long time rather than sweeping reform being the norm.

The sports governance code

Even at the turn of this century, the then Labour administration identified that governance in sport could be 'fragmented and too often unprofessional'.[42] However, it was not until the Conservatives next won an election outright, and after various sporting scandals had been discovered by the press, that there was concrete action. A policy document was published introducing the notion of a 'voluntary' code for sports governance. David Cameron, the then prime minister, wrote in the Foreword that he welcomed the role the media had played in revealing corruption and governance issues at the highest levels and the establishment of 'a new governance code that will be rigorously enforced at home and set a new standard internationally. The code will be mandatory for all sports bodies that want to receive public funding from 2017'.[43] This comment emphasises the fact that the Code is not a statute with penalties for non-compliance and sports are free to ignore it, unless that is, government or lottery funding is needed. This policy development mirrored moves in other European countries. The Council of Europe, having made a resolution on sports governance in EU member states in 2016, the principles of which were later adopted by the EU Parliamentary Assembly in 2018. The resolution encourages those states to 'foster good governance of sports organisations . . . and adopt binding national codes on sports governance'. The resolution goes on to recommend that the award of public grants be made conditional on compliance with these codes.[44]

There are five principles of good governance at the core of the Code; they are 'Structure', 'People', 'Communication', 'Standards and Conduct' and 'Policies and Processes'[45] (see Figure 2.2). A full analysis of the Code provisions and their effectiveness compared to other forms of governance around the world is beyond the scope of this book.[46] It will, however, be of benefit to look at some examples of the

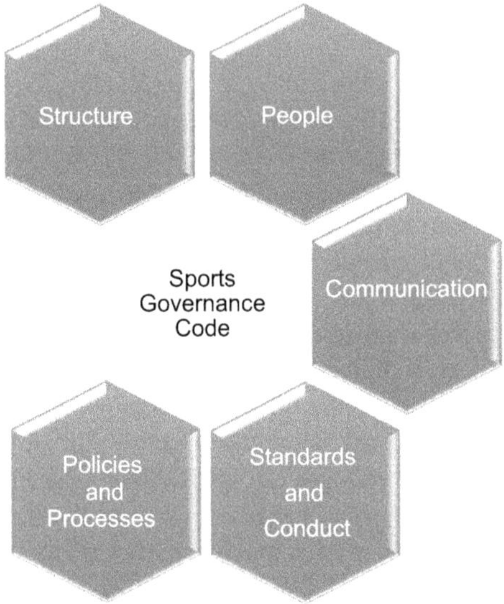

Figure 2.2 The principles in the sports governance code.

principles to serve as an illustration. For example, Principle 1 – Structure requires Code signatories to have:

> a clear and appropriate governance structure, led by a Board which is collectively responsible for the long-term success of the organisation and exclusively vested with the power to lead it. The Board shall be properly constituted and shall operate effectively.[47]

In turn, Principle 3, Communication, emphasises 'nurturing internal democracy',[48] which requires such a board to be democratically elected by those who are ordinary members of the SGB. This might seem the obvious way to run a sporting body, but prior to the Code, experiences varied. For instance, English soccer and rugby have long had elected boards such as the FA Council and RFU Council respectively. This did not prevent controversies regarding the former from leading to reform post-2016, as shall be further discussed shortly. However, there has been, for a considerable part of the game's history, an elected 'legislative'. By contrast and as an example, throughout the 1980s and 1990s, the game of professional darts had one SGB, the BDO, encountered earlier in the context of sport recognition. The BDO was, for most of that period, effectively the fiefdom of one man. Mr Olly Croft ran the organisation from its inception, out of an office in his home borough of Muswell Hill, London. Mr Croft was the driving force in taking the game from its base as a pastime in public houses across the land to prominence as a professional sport. Contracts for considerable TV airtime were signed within only a few years of the start of this development, and forming the BDO was part of that strategy. The BDO went into liquidation in 2020, but such an autocratic governance structure would be unlikely to meet the requirements of the Code nowadays.

Can government get away with intervention?

It has been established that in the UK, in common with some other European countries, the government and the judicial branch generally prefer there to be a distance between them and the administration of sport. It has also been noted that major ISFs like FIFA would not tolerate direct government intervention, but indirect control has been instituted through the Sports Governance Code. There have been some statutory interventions in soccer, but these are on the periphery of the governance of sport. Some should be considered public order measures relating to spectators rather than providing for the running of the sport itself. That said, they do cover the licensing of soccer venues and seating arrangements, which is bordering on the usual remit of an SGB. More detailed consideration of laws such as the Sporting Events (Control of Alcohol etc.) Act 1985 and the Football Spectators Act 1989 fall under Chapter 5 on athlete welfare, but these laws are the only major example of any UK administration legislating on a specific sport so far.

There is also the Games legislation that the IOC mandates is passed by the parliament of the successful bidder to host the Olympics. For the London 2012 Games, that was the London Olympic Games and Paralympic Games Act 2006. This statute covered many aspects of the Games, from protecting the intellectual property of the Olympic movement to traffic control and street trading in merchandise. Similar laws were passed by Brazil in preparation for the 2016 Games and in Japan ahead of the delayed 2020 Olympics. This kind of legislation creates no tension between the state and sport; however, as the IOC requires statutory intervention as a condition of awarding the Games. It must be said, though, that a private international sporting body having the power to insist that state governments pass laws is quite unparalleled in any other sphere.[49]

With regard to the judiciary, there have been some 'near misses' in terms of the courts being prepared to intervene in the administration of sport. In *R v Disciplinary Committee of the Jockey Club, ex parte Massingberd-Mundy* [1993] 2 All ER 207, the 'near monopolistic' position of the Jockey Club[50] was considered a powerful argument for allowing judicial review. In the end, though, the court was bound by authority to consider the claim to be not a matter of public law. Nevertheless, the position of that particular NGB in public life would mean that if it failed, the government would have to run the sport, at least temporarily. That has never happened with any sport, but it has been threatened in relation to soccer twice. In 2016, the FA was so mired in allegations of sexism and racism,[51] despite it being run as a democratic body, that it was brought before a Parliamentary Committee. There, it was warned that if it failed to address these concerns, Parliament would legislate on the running of the organisation.[52] Further, in 2021, a breakaway European Super League was launched by twelve clubs who initially signed up. The move was bitterly opposed by the FA, UEFA, politicians and supporters' groups alike. The then Prime Minister, Boris Johnson, threatened to drop a 'legislative bomb' on UK soccer with enforced reforms to football governance and structures.[53] At the time, it was unclear how practical those moves would be and what FIFA's reaction might look like, especially, given its statutes specifically prohibit political intervention in the game, and FIFA has previously expelled NGBs to enforce this. Considering Mr Johnson's spectacular fall from grace in 2023 following a Parliamentary Report on his dishonesty and poor judgement whilst in office,[54] perhaps now these comments should be dismissed as political posturing and hubris.

Categories of sporting rules

The ruling councils of each sport coerce and control the participants with a host of rules that regulate the playing of the sport and matters of the playing surface. To aid in understanding the mechanisms of coercion, these rules can be grouped by purpose. It is worth reiterating here that these rules engage domestic and international law because they are the 'small print' of the contract between the participant and the SGB (see Figure 2.3). It is in this way that sanctions for breaches of these rules can be enforced, as they are a breach of contract. These rules are for consistency in how the game is played, preserving integrity, financial fairness, welfare, safeguarding and so on. They fall into a number of broad categories; however, depending on their primary motivation. There is no definitive set of categories throughout the sporting world; however, generally, rules fall into one of the following sub-types: technical, sporting conduct, sport as a business and 'hybrid'. To this can be added what remains of the unwritten code that is not technically rules. These are notions by which competitors abide voluntarily, in line with the 'Corinthian Ideals' or the spirit of fair play.

Technical rules

These rules are primarily to ensure the game or event is a consistent experience for the competitors wherever it is played, even internationally. In soccer, cricket, baseball, basketball and rugby, for instance, there are standards for the dimensions and weight of the respective balls used. The Marylebone Cricket Club or MCC is the pre-eminent organisation in the UK and is the custodian of the 'Laws' of the game. Under the 'Ball Law', the weight and size of the ball are prescribed in para. 4.1:

Figure 2.3 Breach of sporting rules as breach of contract.

> The ball, when new, shall weigh not less than 5.5 ounces/155.9 g, nor more than 5.75 ounces/163 g, and shall measure not less than 8.81 in/22.4 cm, nor more than 9 in/22.9 cm in circumference.[55]

If such standardisation did not take place, then playing cricket in different counties could be a very unsettling experience, and international competition would be fraught with difficulty. These are relatively simple requirements, but some sports need much more complexity. Motorsport, for example, must have rigorous technical specifications in place for the vehicles and racetracks to be safe and for the races to be of consistent difficulty at the required level wherever in the world they may be held. It would require specialist engineering qualifications and experience just to fully understand them, much less apply them to the cars and venues. The following extract on the relatively simple matter of Formula 1 car permitted engine cover shapes makes the point perfectly:

> On each side of the car, the combined external Coke Panel and Engine Cover surfaces must: a. On any X section, form one tangent continuous curve. Furthermore:
>
> i) Outboard of Y=25 the radius of curvature of any such section must not be less than 75mm if convex, or 50mm if concave, with the exception of a rectangular region bounded in plan view by (XC=20, 125) and (XC=150, 375) where the radius of curvature must not be less than 25mm and within a 20mm offset from the lower side impact structure defined in article 13.5.1 where the radius of curvature must not be less than 10mm.
>
> ii) Between Y=5 and Y=25 the radius of curvature of any such section must not be less than 25mm.[56]

There are still variances that either cannot be avoided or are features of the competitions that make them interesting to follow. Playing tennis on a clay court is not quite the same as playing on grass, for instance. No two cricket grounds are exactly alike, and neither are the ground conditions, due to local climates. Formula One races are not conducted on identically shaped tracks either. In such cases, general parameters are produced to ensure the sporting experience is similar enough to be comparable, wherever it is to be had.

Rules of sporting conduct – competitive balance and integrity

The two concepts of competitive balance and integrity are linked in the sense that if there is cheating, that balance is upset. Malpractice aside, it is important that the rules allow a fair game to be played or a race to be run. Changing ends after half-time in a soccer match allows for any advantage provided by the ground conditions or view to be evened out, for instance. Adding weights to a jockey's saddle to ensure the burdens for all the horses in a race are roughly equal is another example.

Competitive balance is also important because it is vital for a competition to have an unknown or largely unpredictable outcome. Viewing figures and gate receipts would be negatively affected if there were little doubt about the outcome of a fixture based on an obvious advantage to one or the other opponent. Examples of these types of rules can be found in the sport of Ski Jumping. Like many sports, the interests of competitive balance are served by having age categories for competitors. This prevents the obvious, if unlikely, presence of a 15-year-old competing against a jumper in their thirties. The difference in experience alone would not make this a fair match. One of the International Ski and Snowboard Federation (FIS) rules on age classification reads as follows at paragraph 406.1:

> The following age classifications have been established for FIS Ski Jumping competitions:
>
> Youth I and II [determined by year of birth at date of competition]
> Juniors up to 20 years of age on 1st January of the current calendar year.
> Seniors: all competitors over the age limit for juniors.[57]

Competitive balance is also the main reason cited for banning most transgender athletes from entering women's competitions, such as those in cycling and athletics. The extent to which these rule changes have affected the life chances of such athletes is discussed further in Chapter 5.

The foremost rule frameworks designed to protect the integrity of sports are those concerned with doping. There is some limited consistency here since the advent of the World Anti-Doping Agency (WADA) and its published Code. Sports that are adherents of the Code need only state in their rules that athletes must abide by those provisions or alternatively the SGB must provide their own code which is compatible with WADA's satisfaction. This does not mean that all sportsmen and women across the globe have to operate to identical standards in this regard, however. Significant sections of the sporting world are not members of WADA. Therefore, the drugs that are permitted to be administered to racehorses may not be permissible in Olympic show jumping, for instance. The anti-doping regulations in baseball mean that a player would not necessarily be barred from taking all the drugs that are prohibited in, say, athletics and so on. These inconsistencies are dealt with at greater depth in Chapter 4 on doping and other prohibited measures.

Another key area where integrity is under threat is in terms of match and race fixing. The relationship between sport and gambling is almost as old as modern sport itself.[58] It is not just the seemingly obvious sports like horse racing and soccer that have suffered integrity crises of this nature. Even in the nineteenth century, cricket and baseball had already been mired in controversy over match-fixing.[59] Concern about the prevalence of fixing is mounting, though. A previous Director General of WADA even talked of the need for an agency with a wider remit than his own to deal with betting, bribery and corruption as well as doping.[60] At present, most of the major sports have rules about players not being allowed to gamble on games in which they have an involvement. For instance, English soccer's FA rules state:

> No Participant can bet on a match or competition in which they are involved that season, or which they can influence, or any other football-related matter concerning the league that they play in. Participants are also prohibited from using or passing inside information for betting.[61]

The advent of spot, in-play and lay betting, where the bet is placed on a competitor to lose, has exacerbated concerns about corruption.[62] Some sports, such as horse racing, have long had rules sanctioning a jockey who deliberately does not ride his or her horse to its full potential. However, as will be argued later, the most important paradox that neither law nor public policy has addressed is that gambling is potentially very harmful, yet it is the lifeblood of some major sports and the source of considerable tax revenue. Furthermore, the funding of much of sport in the UK comes from state-sponsored gambling, the National Lottery.

Rules concerning the business of sport

In large part, this category of rules is brought about by the existence of European Union law. This is because EU law has within it a limited sporting exception. Article 165 of the Treaty on the Functioning of the European Union (TFEU) enshrines sport as having special significance in society, with its health and welfare benefits and propensity to promote social cohesion, amongst other things. This has the effect of allowing EU law to be applied with a little more flexibility when the business concerned is a sporting one, albeit this is predicated on being able to clearly delineate the boundary between rules concerning the sport and those pertaining to the business of sport—something the law is yet to achieve. The UK has completed 'Brexit' and left the European Union on 31 January 2020. Nevertheless, Northern Ireland still remains under some EU jurisdiction and is a country within the UK. This is because of the practical difficulties of policing the UK's only land border with the EU in terms of customs and immigration. Uniformed guards and checkpoints could be inflammatory with regard to what is still a relatively recent peace accord after over thirty years of armed conflict to suppress an independence movement. Further, since sport is an international phenomenon with the possibility of rules being made at continental level, say by UEFA (in respect of soccer), it will be worth a brief summary here. Furthermore, the prospect of the UK rejoining the bloc, whilst not a real possibility yet, is not the fantasy it once was.[63]

Essentially, rules that are purely about the way the sport is conducted do not engage with EU law[64] (see Figure 2.4). This is because they have nothing to do with what the EU is there for, which, put very simply, is harmonising trade laws between member states. That said, the ECJ case of *Meca-Medina and Majcen v Commission* (2006) C-519/04 P tested the boundaries of the distinction. Swimmers David Meca-Medina and Igor Majcen failed doping tests. They alleged that the fixing of the limit for nandrolone permissible in the blood was a deliberate commercial arrangement between the IOC and the then twenty-seven accredited laboratories and was in breach of EU law. The ECJ ultimately ruled that doping could come under EU jurisdiction in

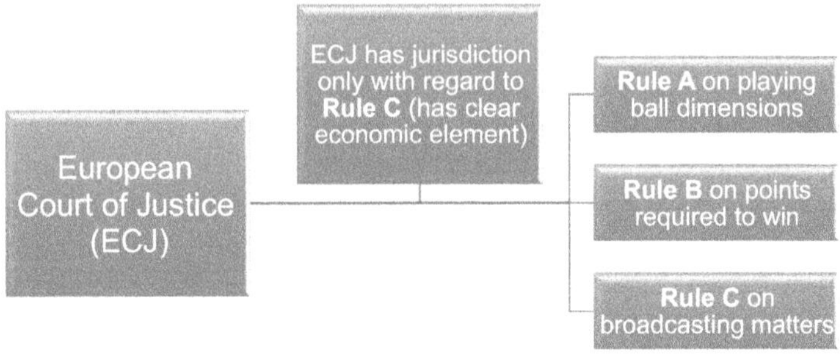

Figure 2.4 The jurisdiction of the European Court of Justice to hear disputes about rules.

such circumstances. Consequently, examples of rules on integrity that might be liable to scrutiny under EU law can be found throughout Chapter 4 on doping.

In addition, some rules that SGBs enact are not about how the game is played but are to do with how the sport operates as a business. These rules would be subject to EU law without much argument. An example would be UEFA's Financial Fair Play (FFP) rules for soccer. These requirements seek to limit the ability of clubs to spend more than they earn and risk insolvency. They also place limits on the ability of wealthy benefactors to unfairly enhance the ability of a club to purchase the best players. This is especially true when compared to clubs that are operating within their balance sheet or without a billionaire owner. These rules are obviously aimed at maintaining competitive balance, but they primarily affect the profit and loss of soccer clubs as trading enterprises. To ensure that these rules were compatible with EU law, UEFA and the European Commission released a joint statement in 2012.[65] This essentially said that FFP rules were broadly in line with the EU's stance on competition law. Thus, any challenge to FFP would seem to be capable of being brought to the ECJ (see Figure 2.4).

Followers of UK soccer will have heard of the 'Bosman Rule'. This change in the way players are recruited came about because of the landmark judgement in Case 415/93 *Union Royale Belge des Societes de Football Association ASBL v Jean-Marc Bosman* [1995] ECR I-4921. Bosman was a Belgian footballer who was denied a transfer to another club despite being out of contract with them. The stumbling block was that UEFA rules allowed the selling club to demand a transfer fee even though the player's contract had expired. In this instance, the new club refused to pay. Bosman languished at his home club and, to add insult to injury, was paid wages that were reduced by 75 per cent. This dispute triggered EU law because one of its central pillars is the free movement of persons, especially between member states. Bosman won his case, although his personal life led him down a path to alcoholism and decline in any event. The result of the ruling was that players can move from one club to another after the expiration of their contract without a fee being payable. It was also ruled under a separate limb of the case that there can be no cap on the number of foreign players recruited to a club from other member states, save in the national team. This again overturned UEFA rules on the subject and was followed by the ruling in Case C-438/00

Deutscher Handballbund eV v Maros Kolpak, the 'Kolpak' case of 2003. This extended the key findings of *Bosman* to countries that are not member states but have signed European Association Agreements with the EU. These have the aim of developing trade, cultural and other links, and countries like Switzerland and Norway would fall into this category. For the argument in this book, what is interesting here is that, despite being democratic bodies, soccer's ruling elite were perfectly happy to tolerate clearly unfair rules until a court ruled against them. When courts are persuaded to intervene in sporting matters, it is more often than not to the benefit of athletes, players, fans and support personnel. 'Brexit' has not directly removed the Bosman rule; it is still part of UEFA's transfer system. That said, there is no free movement between the UK and the remaining twenty-seven EU member states. Football clubs wishing to recruit players from those countries must ensure the footballer has the required visa, just as they always have if they recruited a player from South America or West Africa, for instance. Those visas are subject to Home Office immigration rules.

In this book, whilst examining the law's ineffectual impact on fairness in sport, it has been established that this is intertwined with how embedded politics and society are in law. These 'economic' rules that SGBs make are a good example. The initial position was that the rules on the playing of sport were not subject to EU law because of the 'specificity' of sport. That position has been consistently eroded by a political law-making body, the EU. *Meca-Medina* was itself a continuation of emerging jurisprudence that was seen in Case 36/74 *Walrave and Koch* [1974] ECR-01405. It was decided here that discrimination based on nationality in sporting rules did engage EU law. In this case, it was about rules specifying the nationality of cycling pacemakers in a race. In 2000, Case C-51/96 *Christelle Deliège v Ligue francophone de judo et disciplines associées ASBL, Ligue belge de judo ASBL, Union européenne de judo* further entrenched this mode of thinking post-*Bosman*. The *Deliège* case was about national quotas in judo for selection for international competitions. These rules too were deemed subject to EU law as they infringed on EU freedoms of movement and to provide services. Further, the UK's vote to leave the bloc, taken by referendum in June 2016, was in large part driven by public perceptions about immigration. There are indeed fewer immigrants from the EU since Brexit, but the overall immigration figure is far higher now than in 2016. Workers from other parts of the world have had to be recruited,[66] and it has become harder to repatriate refugees to another safe member state that they have passed through before arriving in the UK. This exposes that particular line of argument by 'Leave' campaigners as having been vastly overrelied on. In any event, it is these public sentiments, based on little evidence, about the perceived erosion of national identity and pressure on public services from immigration that largely triggered Brexit. The effect is that whilst ECJ case law on sporting rules may mostly still be followed in principle in the UK, there is nothing now to stop those rulings being overturned in a UK court. Further, they may be eradicated by means of statutory action aimed at post – Brexit relations with the EU. In short, xenophobic attitudes, prevalent in many societies,[67] in this case influenced politics, which has in turn changed the relationship between settled jurisprudence and UK sporting rules. Here, politics was very definitely not kept out of sport.

Hybrid rules

The term here does not refer to hybrid sports where one or more sports are combined to make a new pastime. Polocrosse (lacrosse and polo), baseketball (baseball and basketball) and equestrian vaulting (gymnastics and horse riding) are examples of these. This is about a category of rule that can be found in any sport. The categories are presented in this chapter based on the motivation behind the rules. Doping regulations are prima facie clearly made with the preservation of sporting integrity and keeping the playing field level in mind. It is apparent from the foregoing section, though, that these sometimes might be considered to have an economic element even if that was not the primary driver (see Figure 2.5). Put another way, some rules may have twin motivations. They may be made as, say, technical rules but have a strong economic element; these are best described as 'hybrid'. Mandatory rules on safety equipment are a suitable example. SGBs often require safety protection to be worn for the health and welfare of competitors. Helmets and padding are required in American football, riding hats and body armour in certain equestrian disciplines, head protection in skiing and so on. These pieces of equipment usually have to meet certain industry standards and sometimes, although rarely, must be from a particular manufacturer. The following is an example from British Dressage:

'Protective hats must meet one of the following standards:
British – All PAS 015 (1998 and subsequent dates)
European – VG1
European – EN1384 – 2017(Only in conjunction another accepted standard from this list)
American – SNELL E2001, E2006 . . .'[68]

Riding helmets that pass these exacting safety tests are only available from certain manufacturers, although there are a number of those companies. The remainder concentrate on protective hats for leisure riding. There are currently no domestic laws in the UK that mandate a certain safety standard or even that protective equipment

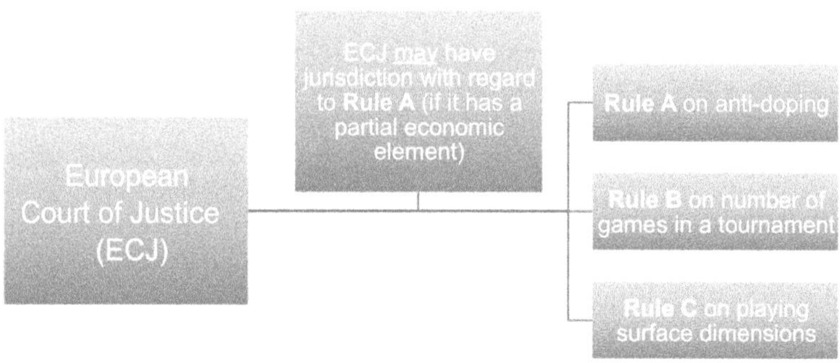

Figure 2.5 Hybrid rules and the European Court of Justice.

must be worn at all for leisure horse riding, on or off the road. Therefore, no legislated minimum safety standard is required in the way that applies to, say, motorcycling.

These BD rules are technical, but if this SGB were to acquire a large financial stake in one or more of the companies that manufacture to the above standards, or if major sponsorship deals were struck[69] that would change. In such circumstances, there would be such a significant economic element that these rules would become hybrid.

Corinthian ideals

The final section of this chapter deals with behaviour that is coerced by peer pressure and a general desire to behave morally and ethically rather than by specific regulation. These rules are not enforceable under any contract between the competitor and his or her SGB. This is apart from the fact that a breach of them might fall under a general 'bringing the sport into disrepute' type of charge. This would not be automatic but would depend on the wording of such a rule and the discretion within any disciplinary process.

The origins

These moral codes are based on what are termed the 'Corinthian Ideals'. Far from harking back to any sporting ethics from Ancient Greece, these notions stem from the actions of an English soccer team founded in the nineteenth century, Corinthian FC. This club was based in London between 1882 and 1939 and is often credited with embodying the golden age of amateurism, playing solely for the love of the game and gentlemanly fair play.[70] For example, it was said that as no 'gentleman' would conduct a foul, the Corinthian goalkeeper would not even attempt to save the resulting penalty.

Nowadays, sport is so competitive and commercialised that winning is paramount. Therefore, there are few competitors who would risk losing based purely on ideas of unsporting behaviour. Examples of abusing the spirit of a game, even if no rules are broken, might nevertheless be detrimental to a professional career. Social media can nowadays heap pressure on a competitor to the point where they are forced to publicly address their behaviour, even if it is out of character. This was the case for a Swiss international hurdler at a leading 2023 athletics event, where he celebrated his win ostentatiously, apparently unconcerned that a fellow competitor was gravely injured.[71] There was no doubt a 'one-off' lapse of judgement there, but in more extreme cases, especially where a competitor becomes 'known' for repeated wrongdoing, there can be tangible negative consequences. Sponsors and the like might be loath to be associated with such a public image, so these moral codes may therefore have more 'teeth' in the modern media-soaked world than they once did.

There can be other ramifications in the mainstream press and even diplomatic circles as well. In cricket during the 2023 Ashes series, there was a visceral reaction to a controversial 'stumping'. English batsman Jonny Bairstow wandered away from the crease thinking that the ball was 'dead'. When the wicketkeeper stumped him, the umpire decided this was within the rules. The crowd obviously felt this was unsportsmanlike, and there was even an unprecedented oral altercation in the MCC rooms afterwards.[72] This resulted in the Australian media saying that it was the MCC members who were not acting with the values of the game at heart. Ultimately, this led to the sitting UK prime minister, Rishi Sunak, commenting that 'he simply wouldn't want to win a game in the manner Australia did'. The Australian Premier hit back almost immediately, defending his team.[73] Claims that this is a full diplomatic incident may be overblown, but it would be a written rule breach case of some magnitude that would have two Prime Ministers talking about it in such a manner. This emphasises the soft power of Corinthian sporting ethics.

Modern conundrums – 'Taking The Knee'

One way in which considerations of acting within the spirit of sport really came to the fore was with the actions of the US football player, Colin Kaepernick. There are a number of topics within this book where this controversy might be discussed, but it left sports officials, politicians and the wider public divided. Kaepernick first sat, then got down on one knee when the US National Anthem was played ahead of games.[74] The sportsman was protesting against the oppression of black people in America and in support of the 'Black Lives Matter' campaign. Public reaction fell largely into two camps: those who supported his actions and those who felt it was either unpatriotic, unsporting or both. There seemed to be an unwritten rule that participants should not have their politics and social activism on view at or near the field of play.[75] The difficulties that some people have with acknowledging that politics cannot be divorced from sport are dealt with further in Chapter 9, but this was a domestic social issue. The campaign did spread beyond the borders of the United States, though, with even the UK's Premier League soccer teams taking the knee in support for a time, however.[76] This was despite the fact that the numbers of UK deaths of ethnic minorities at the hands of the police are tiny compared to the figures from the United States. It became part of English Soccer's general anti-racism campaign, so it was not controversial.

In the United States, though, a majority of news outlets framed the protest as 'antimilitary, antipolice, and fundamentally anti-American' and those who spoke in support were largely undermined in the reporting.[77] Other American sports personalities showed their support, from Megan Rapinoe of Women's Soccer[78] to Denver Broncos linebacker Brandon Marshall.[79] Some even lost sponsorships over it. Ironically though, Nike actually increased their sales, despite their sportswear being burned in the street during the public backlash, by electing to use Kaepernick as the frontman for their advertising.[80]

Given the polarisation driven by Kaepernick's actions and the ripple effect extending well outside the world of sport, the SGB concerned was uncertain as to how to respond. In 2018, the National Football League (NFL) introduced a rule requiring players to stand during the national anthem, backed by the sanction of a fine. However, after the death of George Floyd at the hands of the police and prominent players speaking out, this move was put on hold in 2020. The NFL ultimately admitted they had been 'wrong for not listening to NFL players' and said, 'this is a time of self-reflection for all – the

NFL is no exception. We stand with the black community because Black Lives Matter' and protests during the playing of the national anthem were no longer banned.[81] Kaepernick himself gave up his NFL team place voluntarily, but his lucrative career with Nike continued.

The unwritten moral codes that athletes play by do not receive much attention in many sports law books, many preferring to concentrate on the rules and laws of the game, which are less nebulous. However, the story of Colin Kaepernick further shows that determining these moral and ethical norms, together with whether they have been breached, can be as important as analysing the rulebook, if not more so.

Notes

1 Thomas Bates, 'Gramsci and the theory of hegemony', *Journal of the History of Ideas*, 36, no. 2 (April–June 1975): 351.
2 Ibid.
3 Department of Digital, Culture, Media and Sport, *A Sporting Future for All* (London: DCMS, 2000), 6.
4 Berch Berberoglu, *An Introduction to Classical and Contemporary Social Theory: A Critical Perspective* (Lanham: Rowman and Littlefield, 2005), 57.
5 'Lord Hailsham's Dimbleby lecture', *BBC*, 14 October 1976, audio, 21:25. https://www.bbc.co.uk/programmes/p00fr9gh.
6 Dan Roan, 'FA reform: Former chiefs say, "elderly white men" block change', *BBC Sport*, 12 December 2016, http://www.bbc.co.uk/sport/football/38274152.
7 Andrew Bull, 'Sports bodies face cuts over lack of women in boardrooms', *The Guardian*, 8 March 2017, 7.
8 See Pippa Norris and Jonni Lovenduski, *Political Recruitment: Gender, Race and Class in the British Parliament* (Cambridge: Cambridge University Press, 1995).
9 Francis Gibb and David Brown, 'Verdict on the judges: Too male, too white, too elitist', *The Times*, 6 July 2011, 1.
10 Sarah Gordon, 'Women hold just a sixth of senior roles at top UK companies', *The Financial Times*, 15 March 2017, https://www.ft.com/content/0713fe70-18f8-11e6-bb7d-ee563a5a1ccl.
11 Gibson Burrell and Gareth Morgan, *Sociological Paradigms and Organisational Analysis* (Aldershot: Ashgate, 2005), 32.
12 Ibid., 28.
13 David Karen and Richard Washington, *Sociological Perspectives on Sport – The Games Outside the Games* (London: Routledge, 2015), 21.
14 See Mark Pieth, *Reforming FIFA* (Baden-Baden: Nomos Verlagsgesellschaft, 2014), especially – Introduction, 'Governing FIFA'.
15 Sebastien Coe, 'We cannot move from strict liability rule', *Daily Telegraph*, 25 February 2004, http://www.telegraph.co.uk/sport/othersports/drugsinsport/2373729/We-cannot-move-from-strict-liability-rule.html. See also Anne Amos, 'Inadvertent doping and the WADA code', *Bond Law Review*, 9, no. 1 (2007): 1.
16 'FIFA regulations – Article 17', FIFA, accessed 4 October 2023, https://digitalhub.fifa.com/m/41c272bcbc3b19df/original/c83ynehmkp62h5vgwg9g-pdf.pdf.

17 See for instance, Roger Pielke, 'How can FIFA be held accountable?' *Sport Management Review*, 16, no. 3 (2013): 255–67 and John Verver, 'Lessons from the FIFA corruption scandal', *Risk Management*, 62, no. 7 (2015): 16.
18 'FIFA - About FIFA', accessed 4 October 2023, https://www.fifa.com/about-fifa.
19 'British Dressage – British Dressage members handbook 2023', 51, accessed 4 October 2023, https://www.britishdressage.co.uk/news/2023-bd-members-handbook-now-live/.
20 'Sport England – About us', accessed 4 October 2023, https://www.sportengland.org/about-us.
21 George Orwell, *Nineteen Eighty Four* (Glasgow: Collins, 1949), 48.
22 Karen and Washington, *Sociological Perspectives on Sport – The Games Outside the Games*.
23 Ibid.
24 Claudio Colaguori, 'Violence, violent crime, and state violence', *Crime, Deviance, and Social Control in the 21st Century: A Justice and Rights Perspective* (Toronto: Canadian Scholars, an imprint of CSP Books Inc, 2023), 277.
25 'Sport England – The recognition process', accessed 4 October 2023, https://www.sportengland.org/our-work/national-governing-bodies/sports-that-we-recognise/.
26 Council of Europe's European Sports Charter 1993, Article 2(1)(a).
27 Paul Kelso, 'Bull's-eye! Darts achieves sporting recognition', *The Guardian*, 3 March 2005, https://www.theguardian.com/uk/2005/mar/25/sport.paulkelso.
28 VAT or 'Value Added Tax' is the term for sales tax in the UK and Europe.
29 Article 132(1)(m) of Council Directive 2006/112/EC of 28 November 2006.
30 Case No. C-90/16 (The English Bridge Union).
31 Jay Castello, 'Why do female pro gamers earn millions less than men?' *The Guardian*, 10 October 2021, https://www.theguardian.com/games/2021/dec/02/why-do-female-pro-gamers-earn-less-than-men-esports.
32 Elise Uberoi and Neil Johnston, 'Political disengagement in the UK: Who is disengaged? – Research Briefing, House of Commons Library', 7, accessed 21 November 2022, https://researchbriefings.files.parliament.uk/documents/CBP-7501/CBP-7501.pdf.
33 'BHA rules of racing, chapter L – BHA investigations and disciplinary action, rules 13 and 53.2', accessed 4 October 2023, https://rules.britishhorseracing.com/#!/book/34/chapter/s3489-bha-investigations-and-disciplinary-action.
34 See *R v Aldridge, R v Eaton* [2012] ECWA Crim 1456, a case on the previous Sexual Offence Prevention Orders (SOPO), which remains relevant in that orders will not be granted with too wide a remit.
35 Attr. Winston Churchill.
36 Michael Beloff, 'Drugs laws and Versapaks', in *Drugs & Doping in Sports: Socio-legal Perspectives*, by John O'Leary (Abingdon: Cavendish, 2001), 40.
37 Dame Elizabeth Neville, 'The British Horseracing Authority and integrity in horseracing: An independent review 2008', accessed 4 October 2023, https://www.britishhorseracing.com/wp-content/uploads/2008/05/Neville-Review-Pr-Rel-Exec-Summ-Recomm-City-of-Lon-May-08.pdf.
38 Christopher Quinlan QC, 'The British Horseracing Authority and integrity in horseracing: An independent review 2016', accessed 4 October, https://www

.britishhorseracing.com/wp-content/uploads/2017/03/Christopher-Quinlan-QC-Report-29-09-16.pdf.

39 'Jim Best may seek High Court ruling over rehearing dispute with BHA', *The Guardian*, 8 August 2016, https://www.theguardian.com/sport/2016/aug/28/jim-best-high-court-ruling-rehearing-bha.

40 *Bradley v Jockey Club* is a key case enabling the courts to seize jurisdiction over SGB decision-making if fundamental rights are at stake, discussed further in Chapter 3.

41 Antonio Gramsci, *Selections from the Prison Notebooks*, trans. Quintin Hoare and Geoffrey Nowell-Smith (New York: International Publishers, 1971), 44.

42 Department of Digital, Culture, Media and Sport, *A Sporting Future for All.*

43 'Sporting future: A new strategy for an active nation – Foreword', Department of Digital, Culture, Media and Sport, accessed 4 October, https://assets.publishing.service.gov.uk/government/uploads/system/uploads/attachment_data/file/486622/Sporting_Future_ACCESSIBLE.pdf.

44 Stéphanie De Dycker, 'Good governance in Sport: Comparative law aspects', *The International Sports Law Journal*, 19 (2019): 118.

45 'UK Sport – A code for sports governance', accessed 4 October 2023, https://www.uksport.gov.uk/resources/a-code-for-sports-governance.

46 See generally, De Dycker, 'Good governance in sport: Comparative law aspects', for a useful comparative study of sports governance in the UK and other countries.

47 'UK Sport – A code for sports governance: The principles', accessed 4 October 2023, https://www.uksport.gov.uk/resources/a-code-for-sports-governance/the-principles.

48 Ibid.

49 Mark James and Guy Osborn, 'The Olympics, transnational law and legal transplants: The International Olympic Committee, ambush marketing and ticket touting', *Legal Studies*, 36, no. 1 (March 2016): 93–110.

50 The predecessor of the British Horseracing Authority.

51 Richard Coway, 'FA reform: As MPs debate the issue, is real change a stretch too far?', *BBC*, 8 February 2017, http://www.bbc.co.uk/sport/football/38907978.

52 Roan, 'FA reform: Former chiefs say, "elderly white men" block change'.

53 Jonathan Merritt and Genevieve Gordon-Thomson, 'European Super League: What can its opponents legally do?' *The Conversation*, 20 April 2021, https://theconversation.com/european-super-league-what-can-its-opponents-legally-do-159393.

54 'House of Commons Committee of Privileges matter referred on 21 April 2022 (conduct of Rt Hon Boris Johnson): Final report, fifth report of session 2022–23', accessed 15 June 2023, https://committees.parliament.uk/publications/40412/documents/197199/default/.

55 'MCC Laws of Cricket – The Ball Law, para. 4.1', accessed 4 October 2023, https://www.lords.org/mcc/the-laws-of-cricket/the-ball.

56 'Fédération Internationale de l'Automobile (FIA) 2023 – Formula 1 Technical Regulations, para. 3.7.4, "Coke Panel and Engine Cover Shape"', accessed 4 October 2023, https://www.fia.com/sites/default/files/fia_2023_formula_1_technical_regulations_-_issue_4_-_2022-12-07.pdf.

57 'Fédération Internationale de Ski et de Snowboard (FIS) – The International Ski Competition Rules (ICR) Book III, Ski Jumping 2022/23, 46', accessed 4 October,

https://assets.fis-ski.com/image/upload/v1671441414/fis-prod/assets/ICR_Ski_Jumping_2023_clean.pdf.

58 David Forrest, 'Betting and the integrity of sport', in *Sport Betting: Law and Policy*, by Paul Anderson et al. (The Hague: T.M.C. ASSER Press, 2011), 14.

59 Ibid., 15.

60 David Howman, 'Supporting the integrity of sport and combatting corruption', *Marquette Sports Law Review*, 23 (2012): 247.

61 'FA – Know the rules: Betting, match fixing and inside information', accessed 4 October 2023, https://www.thefa.com/football-rules-governance/policies/betting-rules.

62 Forrest, 'Betting and the integrity of sport', 23.

63 Jon Henley and Michael Goodier, 'Britons who want to rejoin EU at highest levels since 2016, survey finds', *The Guardian*, 23 June 2023, https://www.theguardian.com/politics/2023/jun/23/britons-who-want-to-rejoin-eu-at-highest-since-2016-survey-finds.

64 *Edwards v BAF and IAAF* [1998] 2 CMLR 363.

65 'EC/UEFA Joint Statement on Financial Fair Play (FFP) rules and state aid control in professional football', 21 March 2012, accessed 4 October 2023, https://ec.europa.eu/competition/sectors/sports/joint_statement_en.pdf.

66 Sachin Ravikumar and M. Muvija, 'Record net arrivals highlight UK's post-Brexit migration dilemma', *Reuters*, 25 May 2023, https://www.reuters.com/world/uk/net-migration-uk-hits-record-606000-2022-2023-05-25.

67 Katya Adler, 'Far-right parties on the rise across Europe', *BBC*, 30 June 2023, https://www.bbc.com/news/world-europe-66056375.

68 'British Dressage – British Dressage handbook 2023', 118, accessed 4 October 2023, https://www.britishdressage.co.uk/competitions/competition-rules/.

69 This is an illustrative and hypothetical example; no such financial arrangements are alleged here.

70 See generally, D. J. Taylor, *On The Corinthian Spirit: The Decline of Amateurism in Sport* (London: Yellow Jersey Press, 2006).

71 Ben Parsons, 'Hurdler issues apology for unsportsmanlike behaviour as rival placed in neck brace', *Daily Mirror*, 7 March 2023, https://www.mirror.co.uk/sport/other-sports/athletics/jason-joseph-european-athletics-news-29392603.

72 'Ashes: "Wholly unacceptable" – Lord's bosses suspend cricket fans after clashes with Australia players following controversial Bairstow stumping', *Sky News*, 3 July 2023, https://news.sky.com/story/ashes-emotions-were-running-high-lords-bosses-apologise-after-fans-clash-with-australia-players-12913481. See also, Geoffrey Boycott, 'Australia should issue public apology over Jonny Bairstow stumping – If they are man enough', *The Telegraph*, 3 July 2023, https://www.telegraph.co.uk/cricket/2023/07/03/boycott-australia-should-apologise-bairstow-stumping/.

73 'Albanese "proud" of Australian cricketers after British PM weighs in on Lord's stumping', *Sydney Morning Herald*, 3 July 2023, https://www.smh.com.au/world/europe/rishi-sunak-weighs-in-on-jonny-bairstow-dismissal-at-lord-s-20230703-p5dlhe.html.

74 Joon Kyoung Kima, Holly Overton, Nandini Bhallac and Jo-Yun Lid, 'Nike, Colin Kaepernick, and the politicization of sports: Examining perceived organizational motives and public responses', *Public Relations Review*, 46, no. 2 (2020): 1–2.

75 Danielle Sarver Coombs, Cheryl Ann Lambert, David Cassilo and Zachary Humphries, 'Flag on the play: Colin Kaepernick and the protest paradigm', *Howard Journal of Communications*, 31, no. 4 (2020): 319.
76 'Premier League captains confirm players to continue taking a knee', *BBC*, 3 August 2023, https://www.bbc.co.uk/sport/football/66443693.
77 Coombs, Lambert, Cassilo and Humphries, 'Flag on the play: Colin Kaepernick and the protest paradigm', 324.
78 Ibid., 326.
79 Ibid., 330.
80 Kima, Overton, Bhallac and Lid, 'Nike, Colin Kaepernick, and the politicization of sports: Examining perceived organizational motives and public responses', 1.
81 'Colin Kaepernick: How the NFL made its U-turn', *BBC*, 6 June 2020, https://www.bbc.co.uk/sport/american-football/52948942.

3

Challenging Sports Governing Bodies

Redressing the balance, 'Power corrupts . . .'

The first point to make is that the 'activist athlete' is a very rare beast indeed. That is to say activism against their own governing body rather than in a wider social context. The focus of a newcomer, even a seasoned sports person, is winning. Practice, funding, competing and earning are all quite rightly paramount. Much of the foregoing is reliant upon the grace and favour of sports governing bodies (SGBs) and international sports federations (ISFs), so challenging their decisions is not attractive. At least not for the sole purpose of simply promoting justice for its own sake. An athlete or player relies on membership of the appropriate body for selection and competition at the highest levels. These factors militate against raising one's profile as a person likely to challenge the status quo, a perceived 'troublemaker' perhaps. As Richard Pound said of the increasingly authoritarian IOC, 'I paid the price for publicly expressed opposition to the IOC's decisions, through my removal . . . If the senior member of the IOC was punished for showing the temerity to question the IOC's decisions, how can we expect junior members not to stay in line?'.[1]

Fundamental challenges to the decisions, structures and the like of sports governance are mostly limited to two broad areas. Firstly, the athlete or player who deems themselves unfairly disadvantaged by an inequality embedded in the processes of the organisation. This may involve a specific decision, often a disciplinary one. Secondly, these sports bodies operate with a limited form of democracy. There are therefore opportunities for individuals to be voted in or out of a governing council or for specific issues to be raised as a campaign for change. Transformation can be achieved, or at least pressure applied for a rethink, in much the same way as can be seen with national government. Grudgingly, there is a response to such demonstrations, social media backlashes and petitions. It has to be said though, in neither context is this process easy or success guaranteed.

'All Hail The SGB'

Voting for or against a candidate or proposition is of course only part of the democratic process. In national politics, an idea or objection might be raised by, say, a petition. However, the issue concerned may very well not be one that an elected administration thinks is pressing enough to act on, that is, until such as opinion polls make confronting the concern unavoidable. Examples of such responses to societal attitude change include the successful early twentieth-century Suffragette votes for women campaign in the UK and the civil rights movement in the United States. The latter led to the removal of de facto barriers to black people exercising their right to vote by 1965.[2] More recent, albeit less seismic, instances have been the UK government's abrupt U-turn on animal rights after an intense social media storm.[3] The plan had been to remove the European Union (EU) definition of animal sentience from law as part of 'Brexit', but without a clear plan as to what would replace it. There are also examples from sport of issues being brought to the attention of those charged with governance by popular 'internal' protest in recent times. These include the narrowly avoided jockey's strike in response to the British Horse Racing Authority's (BHA) changes in the rules around the use of the whip in 2011.[4] In 2021, an intense public outcry put paid to the creation of a multi-billion-pound European Super League (ESL) for soccer also, basically within seventy-two hours of its launch.[5] Certain Premier League clubs and their equivalents in other European countries had a plan to create a super league with just the elite teams in it. This was not to the liking of the fans, the Premier League or the relevant SGBs and led to mass protests online, the weight of which forced an abrupt rethink. There is no indication from these isolated examples that SGBs are getting into the business of broader power sharing with their stakeholders, however.

In sum, and as encountered in Chapter 2, in between elections to the national executive and legislative there can exist an 'elective dictatorship'.[6] This term acknowledges that it is extremely difficult for the electorate to influence the decisions made by a government during its term of office. To coin a phrase, it can do what it wants until it is election time again. SGBs enjoy a similar freedom from interference from the players, athletes and other stakeholders that they 'govern' during their terms of office. This is worthy of note because, as further discussed in the last chapter, the extent and depth of the power that SGBs and ISFs wield is considerable and comparable to state-level international orders. For instance, before a country can win a bid to host the Olympic Games, it must agree to enact Olympic-specific legislation; a private organisation, the International Olympic Committee (IOC), can mandate that legislation is passed by a nation.[7] This is akin to the power the European Union (EU) has over its member nations as a condition of membership. As discussed in Chapter 9, these bodies can enter into the geo-political sphere with some influence as well. This usually involves barring players and athletes with certain nationalities from international competition when the regimes concerned are deemed to have acted inhumanely.

Further, at the level of the individual, the maintenance of 'Clean Sport' is a worthwhile cause. However, most SGBs, whether they have adopted the World Anti-Doping Code (WADC) or not, seize for themselves the power to police and act against recreational drug *ingestion*, something which most nation states do not. Most drug enforcement legislation, taking the UK's Misuse of Drugs Act 1971[8] as an example, criminalise dealing, trafficking and possession of drugs. A person will not normally be prosecuted for having drugs in his or her bodily system, albeit there is other legislation which prohibits ingestion in specified circumstances such as flying or driving. The

Road Traffic Act 1988 is one example, but there are no statutes to prohibit ingestion in everyday life. There are also laws about public inebriation, but these are about exhibited behaviours resulting from ingestion and are not applicable to private spaces. By comparison, SGBs can sanction athletes who use recreational drugs even when they are not actually competing on the track, racecourse, or field of play.[9] That said, there are time limits on either side of a competition when this can happen. This would still be akin to the police randomly drug testing car drivers in their homes even if they had no plans to drive for some days or even weeks. In sum, the power in the hands of the managing board of a sport, between elections, can be enormous.

Voting for change

From the above discussion, in respect of their 'populace', the athletes and players, ISFs and SGBs exercise effectively autocratic control in almost all matters related to competing in their sport. Some SGBs, such as the BHA, go further and have contrived control of even spectators through their close relationship with most racing venues in the UK. Many horse racing bodies around the world also do this by modelling their rules on the BHA's Orders and Rules of Racing.[10] Drawing again on the discussion in Chapter 2, SGBs operate with a limited democratic process within a constitutional framework. They are in many ways 'quasi-state entities'[11] or corporations, and research on how these are governed is applicable to sport.[12] In all three contexts, there is a group of 'ruled' controlled by a much smaller group of 'rulers', often ruthlessly guarding their power:

> The traditional ruling class . . . changes men and programmes and, with greater speed than is achieved by the subordinate classes, reabsorbs the control that was slipping from its grasp. Perhaps it may make sacrifices, and expose itself to an uncertain future . . . but it retains power.[13]

Gramsci was referring to governments in the 1920s, but there is a strong analogy with the way that the ruling councils or boards of SGBs and ISFs operate. Studying power through the lens of sport helps explain how cultural politics weave across and between the sporting and non-sporting world. This in turn assists in making sense of how inequalities in wider society are replicated in sport. This, in turn, helps to promote tolerance of unfairness in both arenas. Put another way, '[t]he cultural politics of sport engages with battles over identity, meaning, inclusionary and exclusionary processes, and explores how all this relates to the distribution of social and economic capital inside and outside the sporting arena'.[14] Like governments, SGBs and ISFs do tend to give way on certain issues when persuaded, such as technical rule changes and tweaks. However, they will almost never relinquish the main levers of control to the athletes whom they regulate. Examples of this can be seen with respect to the WADC. All Olympic sports have adopted this as their anti-doping rules, and many other disciplines as well. These SGBs have the ability to influence its content. As to be considered in Chapter 4, after pressure, the WADC now has more relaxed rules around burdens of proof and levels of sanctions. At no point, though, has the World

Anti-Doping Authority (WADA) been prepared to consider a move away from the cornerstone of those rules, strict liability. Ostensibly, this is argued to be because of a lack of a viable alternative despite its potential for injustices, but competitors' fear of this unforgiving regime is also a strong weapon of control.[15]

The 'monopolistic' control that many SGBs exert has been mentioned in case law, and it has not escaped the attention of competition regulators either, at least in terms of broadcasting. The detail on those points will appear in Chapter 7, however. There are of course exceptions and sometimes there is a 'duopoly' or more. For example, the sport of golf has the United States Golf Association (USGA) and the Royal and Ancient Golf Club (R&A); these jointly publish rules and updates that affect golf globally. However, the USGA primarily has jurisdiction over the United States and Mexico, whilst the rest of the world is mostly governed by the R&A. Furthermore, in boxing, there are two ISFs that would claim to be the world governing bodies: the World Boxing Council (WBC) and the World Boxing Organisation (WBO). These are first and foremost commercial organisations though, which promote world boxing events and award the relevant titles. These bodies do not operate across grassroots to elite level in the way that many ISFs do.

The mechanics of sporting democracy

In the UK, sports governing councils or boards have to be democratically elected to receive funding from the UK Sports Councils. This is because these bodies, such as Sport England, require that the Code for Sports Governance is adopted.[16] That Code mandates that, 'Committee members are subject to regular election and ideally should serve no more than nine years'.[17] There are also stipulations around transparency of decision-making, personal relationships between board members and more detail on term limits, for example. Whether an acceptably high enough number of athletes and other stakeholders entitled to vote actually do so is a matter for debate. As with national politics, there may be a lack of information about entitlement to vote and also a degree of apathy. Nevertheless, there is a democratic process such that particular rules and decisions can be challenged by voting for candidates for the board who favour change. There are also 'checks and balances' in place in this model of democracy. For instance, like in a nation state, or for that matter, a corporate entity, a sport's constitution requires a process and certain majorities to effect change. Therefore, the executive in each context should not be able to make decisions that are not in accordance with that overarching body of rules. Sometimes, however, agreement cannot be reached over fundamental issues. This can lead to the winding up of a company,[18] the break-up of a nation sate[19] or 'civil war' in an SGB. This outcome will be discussed in the next section. As in states that are nominally democratic, though, a particularly autocratic style of SGB leadership can frustrate the spirit, if not the letter of a constitution.[20]

Challenges from other SGBs

Challenges from within the organisation under a democratic process are not the only way that an SGB or ISF can evolve. In some circumstances, 'breakaway' governing bodies can form. This is usually the result of irreconcilable differences between groups inside an SGB that cannot be resolved within the constitution and a democratic vote. It is also important to recognise that not all SGBs are well constituted or run as professionally as would be ideal.[21] This situation is improving with the widespread adoption of the Code for Sports Governance, however. There have been a number of examples of a sort of sporting 'mitosis', or breeding by division rather than progeny. Cricket had to contend with the breakaway 'World Series Cricket' organised on a commercial basis by the Australian media tycoon, Kerry Packer. Whilst this was short-lived, it definitely changed the governance landscape for English cricket[22] as well as opening up commercial possibilities, such as in Southeast Asia. Whilst cricket has become commercially more successful, this is undoubtedly an example of 'piratical capitalism', which is a 'a volatile, extractive brand of rapacity that exacerbates inequality . . . Today's hyper-capitalism transforms all human existence into a network of commercial relations'.[23] That does not militate towards fairness (in the broadest sense) in sport regulation.

Another example of a single, dominant SGB suffering a schism on the basis of commercial pressures is the British Darts Organisation (BDO). Ultimately, the challengers, the Professional Darts Corporation (PDC), became as important in the world of darts as the BDO. A form of darts was played from about 700 years ago, but the status of the game increased during the early half of the twentieth century. This was helped by the popularity of the game amongst servicemen during the Second World War, including American soldiers and airmen stationed in the UK. By the 1960s, however, darts was still simply a well-liked game played in public houses, community centres and even homes; it was not a sport. Movement towards 'official' recognition really began with the foresight and enthusiasm of one man, Mr Olly Croft and his wife Lorna, together with eleven other people, who formed the BDO in 1973.[24] It was based for many years in a shop premises in Muswell Hill, London. Through better organisation of tournaments and capitalising on television deals, under the BDO, the game grew to the point where major players achieved fame and played for prize money proportionate to that. Such as Jockey Wilson and Eric Bristow became household names and could command viewing figures in the tens of millions. This in turn attracted sponsors like Imperial Tobacco and a number of breweries, increasing the personal wealth that successful darts players could expect to enjoy.

Cracks began to appear in the governance of darts once public opinion began to shift against the playing culture. By the mid-eighties, the push for healthier lifestyles was in full swing and the predominance of drinking and smoking during darts matches, together with the perceived unhealthy diets of the competitors, did not chime well with that new age. By 1989, audiences were declining and sponsors were moving away from a pastime they felt might now hurt their brand image. Darts celebrities like Eric Bristow started to complain about the resultant drain of prize money away from the game and the BDO's inability to address these issues. This was in large part because the BDO was not democratically run and was really the fiefdom of Mr and Mrs Croft, and the wider consequences of this were addressed in Chapter 2. Olly Croft resisted calls to engage a public relations guru and ultimately darts' sixteen top-ranked players

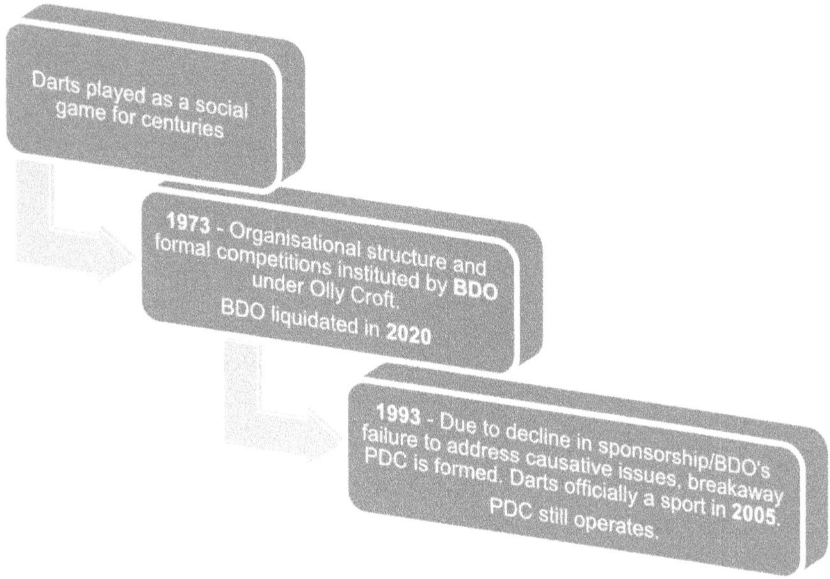

Figure 3.1 The process of breaking away from the British Darts Organisation (BDO) by the Professional Darts Corporation (PDC).

lost patience. This included a good number of previous world champions.[25] In 1993, these players formed the World Darts Council (WDC), which ultimately became the PDC (see Figure 3.1). As argued previously, an SGB with one man in an unassailable leadership position was hardly a model of good governance.

There followed a legal battle as the BDO banned those who had signed with the PDC from its competitions. This was resolved with a *Tomlin* Order, a form of confidential consent order staying proceedings. This meant that players could compete in tournaments under either governing body.[26] Both ultimately came to recognise the World Darts Federation (WDF) as the single ISF for the game. Both ran tournaments and world championships until 2020 when the BDO folded. The PDC had proved itself rather better at promoting its image, retaining viewers, obtaining lucrative sponsorship and broadcasting contracts with such as Sky TV. It was therefore able to maintain prize money levels. The game of darts first became officially recognised by Sport England in 2005 and can now be truly referred to as a sport.

The process just described was expensive, acrimonious and ultimately fatal for the BDO. However, the tale ably illustrates how, when internal sporting democracy fails, the 'war' that follows can bring about fundamental change. The story also serves to highlight the enormous influence that sports broadcasters can have on SGBs' strategic thinking, far more so than participants and fans. Without the financial muscle that Sky TV could muster, it would have been much more difficult to encourage so many star players to defect to the PDC.

Challenging disciplinary outcomes

There is a wholly erroneous impression, mostly generated by sports journalism, that breaking a rule in sport can be categorised as an 'offence' and words from the criminal lexicon soon follow. Terms like 'charged', 'prosecuted' and 'guilty' are commonly used. In fact, these phrases are not appropriate at all because a sports disciplinary is essentially a breach of contract civil case, carried out through an Alternative Dispute Resolution (ADR) process, namely arbitration. In fact, would that it did follow criminal processes because at least then there would be some involvement of genuine lay people for a common-sense view. There would also be the proper checks and balances on standards and burdens of proof, evidence, procedure and the like that, for all its faults, the criminal law has developed over centuries. This is especially pertinent because it should be borne in mind that the sanctions available to a sports disciplinary panel can be as equally shattering to a sports person's life as those that might be applied by a criminal court. For instance, possession of cannabis for personal use might not even be treated as warranting a trial in many jurisdictions. Such matters are often dealt with through a police reprimand and so the impact on the offender's life is limited. If possession of the same amount was the subject of a disciplinary brought by the relevant SGB, however, the outcome could be a ban on competing and thus severely damage the income for that person. As well as the lost chance of winnings, revenue from sponsors may significantly diminish. To reinforce the point, sports personalities have continued their sporting careers even after a spell in prison. Not many, if any, fully recover from a lengthy ban, however.

The exact nature of the contract between the SGB or ISF bringing the case and the wrongdoer is itself not always clear-cut. It is a basic tenet of contract law that, with very few exceptions, only the parties to a contract can seek redress under it.[27] Therefore, an important preliminary step is to consider whether the contractual relationship is with the sports participant or whether it could apply to their support personnel, such as a coach. Further, whether the contract can extend to spectators and supporters. It was established earlier that unruly spectators attending a horse racing fixture can be the subject of a sanction; so also can badly behaved soccer fans. The exact contractual relationship utilised is different in these two examples, however, and needs to be clearly set out. A lack of clarity could lead to the wrongdoer successfully arguing that the tribunal does not have jurisdiction over them.

The different categories of rules were discussed in Chapter 2, and challenging SGBs in an adversarial legal setting most often involves integrity matters. The accusation is framed not in moral terms but rather that one or more of the rules have been breached. The rule broken could be anything from a very broad, 'bringing the sport into disrepute', not even necessarily in competition,[28] to a specific cheating allegation at a named venue. It is extremely rare for an athlete or player to challenge a perceived inequity in a rule simply in the interests of justice. Nearly always, the motive is to defend a career hanging in the balance. The challenge might be based on the facts, the nature of the contractual relationship with the accusing SGB, or whether the rules themselves accord with human rights principles.

A challenge based on the facts would be a challenge to the SGB's factual account of the incident. In a doping or fixing case, that might involve questioning the scientific or technological evidence, together with possibly queries over the 'chain of custody' of any urine sample, for instance. A discussion on challenging whether the rules and processes themselves are 'just' will take up a significant part of this chapter, but first, questioning whether the SGB has jurisdiction based on its contractual position should be considered. If such jurisdiction does exist, this provides the framework for the SGB to exercise its enormous power.

Challenging the contractual relationship itself

The argument that the basis of the relationship between a sports participant or other stakeholder is founded on the law of contract arises because the athlete is offered the chance to compete at a certain level in organised competitions. In return for that, there are rules and restrictions, structures and policies that must be followed. There have been instances where this conception of the relationship has been questioned. However, arguments that something less formal than a binding contract exists are becoming less tenable as SGBs and ISFs become better organised. *Modahl v British Athletic Federation* (No 2) [2002] 1 WLR 1192 is nevertheless, one such example. At the time, the UK SGB for athletics was the British Athletic Federation (BAF), the forerunner to UK Athletics. In 1994, Dianne Modahl, an English middle-distance runner, was suspended following a positive doping finding at a competition in Lisbon, Portugal. Modahl appealed successfully within the BAF's systems and rules because of serious questions about the reliability of the testing process. The ban was lifted, and she returned to competition in 1996.

Modahl felt that there was a contract between her and the BAF and, *inter alia,* that contract impliedly guaranteed fair and due process in disciplinaries. Modahl had shown that the testing facilities and processes were inadequate, and she further argued this constituted a breach of this guarantee. Modahl sued in the domestic courts for lost income she would have received from the sport and other consequential losses stemming from the false positive finding. The court of first instance held there was no contractual relationship however, and separately that the disciplinary committee had acted fairly and without bias. Modahl appealed to the Court of Appeal alleging the existence of a contract between herself and the BAF, and her argument rested on three main planks. Firstly, her membership of her local running club, which operated under the auspices of the BAF, meant she was bound by the BAF rules. Secondly, Modahl's participation in overseas competitions, such as the one at which the erroneous drug result occurred, required BAF permission under those rules. Thirdly, the BAF's affiliation to the International Association of Athletics Federations (IAAF) meant she submitted to the latter's disciplinary processes which must, as arbitration, be a contractual process. That is to say, her rights to be heard and to take advantage of the appeal process were contractual ones, especially as in doing so, she agreed to be bound by the outcome.

The BAF's counterargument was shrewd, if somewhat potentially self-defeating in the long term. In most common law legal systems, including that of the UK, a contract does not need to be written down except in certain circumstances, normally specified by statute. An example of these would be the sale of land or shares. The components required for a simple contract, though, are; an offer, an unequivocal acceptance, consideration,[29] that the parties have the legal capacity to make the contract, and finally that the parties *have the intention to be legally bound*. It was this latter point that the BAF contested, saying there was no such intention. Indeed, contracts are perfectly valid with an express clause stating that there is no intent to create a legal relationship.[30] This just makes the contract unenforceable in court. Unfortunately for Modahl, the judges agreed with the BAF on this point, albeit after considering the existence or otherwise of a contract at some length, and the claim was dismissed. The cost of the case contributed to the BAF being declared insolvent in 1997 and soon after being replaced by what is now UK Athletics. Modahl herself was financially ruined by legal costs as well, although she now enjoys a successful career post-competitive athletics. Generally, SGBs and ISFs now proceed on a much more organised, formalised basis than they did in the 1990s. In the relationships that they have with their participants, there has to be a clear contractual relationship. A lack of clarity in this regard would make it difficult for SGBs to argue that internal disciplinary tribunals have jurisdiction over members. Therefore, nowadays, it is very unlikely that any SGB, NGB or ISF could realistically argue that there is no legally binding contract in place.

The finding in *Modahl* is all the more surprising given earlier instances where the courts were more relaxed in finding that such a contract did exist. In *Davis v Carew-Pole* [1956] 1 WLR 833, the facts were that Davis, a stable keeper, was disciplined by the National Hunt Committee (NHC). This body regulated certain types of horse racing not at the time catered for by the Jockey Club. The allegation was that the claimant did not have the required NHC licence but had nevertheless trained a horse for a 'steeplechase'.[31] The outcome of the disciplinary hearing was that Davis was found to have breached NHC rules and was declared a 'disqualified person' in that sport permanently. Davis responded by taking the NHC to the High Court on the basis that it had acted *ultra vires* in that the tribunal had no power to disqualify him. Davis argued that due to the very fact that he lacked an NHC licence, there was no contractual relationship between him and that SGB. The High Court held, however, that Davis' attendance at the disciplinary hearing meant he submitted to the NHC's jurisdiction and thus created a contract via the conduct of the parties, rather than under any written document.

It is worth mentioning here that even if no contractual link between the parties can be shown, that will not always be fatal to a challenge in the courts. Later in this chapter, the case of *Bradley v Jockey Club* [2005] EWCA Civ 1056 will be discussed and deserves its own section, such is its importance. Even long before that ground-breaking case, however, in *Nagle v Feilden* [1966] 2 QB 633, a woman had been refused a licence to train racehorses, purely due to her gender. The BHA's forerunner, the Jockey Club, had a practice of refusing licences to women at the time. The court held that the long-established English common law 'right to work' was paramount and that the Jockey Club had ignored that in an arbitrary fashion. This was found to be egregious enough to allow intervention by the courts without it being necessary to establish the existence of a contract.

The devil is in the detail

If the relationship between athlete, player, support personnel etc. and their SGB is one of a formal legally binding contract, the question then arises as to what terms that contract actually contains. It has been established that the contract is created when an athlete accepts, usually either by conduct or in writing, the SGB or ISF's rules. What these rules are is dictated by the managing portion of the organisation. Sometimes these will contain adopted rules or codes from other organisations, such as the WADC, but the adoption itself is a management decision. In addition, there will be self-drafted rules on anything from employment conditions to financial governance and internal democratic processes to rules of the game on the field of play. A key point is that these bodies are enormously powerful and can make or unmake any rule they want unless successfully challenged by the internal democratic means already discussed. The other methods of challenge being primarily through sports tribunals such as the Court of Arbitration for Sport (CAS), the courts[32] or by being limited by the few statutory provisions that exist pertaining to sport.[33]

The fact that SGBs are not part of the state apparatus can potentially add to the lack of accountability and transparency as well. This point may be blurred under some regimes, such as authoritarian ones, but ISFs usually take great pains to ensure NGBs and SGBs within their jurisdiction do not suffer too much state interference.[34] They are therefore very unlikely to tolerate an SGB that is an arm of the state. As discussed in Chapter 2, SGBs are private self-regulating bodies that have developed and formalised over time, not necessarily in a logical, evolutionary way, however. Consequently, the rules of SGBs and ISFs may lack a sufficiently logical structure and 'symmetry'.[35] Where rulemaking and adjudication do result in injustice, state mechanisms to deal with this are not always able to properly engage in the way they would if SGBs were state actors. More recent official recognition based on observance of the Code for Sports Governance has, however, led to some improvements in rulemaking and organisation. This goes hand in hand with more effective, if not ruthless, capitalisation on lucrative sponsorship, merchandising and broadcasting deals. Nevertheless, the inconsistencies that remain, where they lead to potential and actual miscarriages of justice in sports tribunals, can lead to expensive and protracted cases. Both SGBs and ISFs are finding themselves subject to the law to an increasing degree in a more litigious society.

As an interesting aside, not all SGBs have developed in this piecemeal fashion. 'Esports', whilst not yet enjoying the status of a fully-fledged sport, have a relatively short history. Despite being the 'new kid on the block', there is a formal organisational structure, well-funded competitions[36] and a developing disciplinary function (see Figure 3.2). This is because these pursuits, which may become a recognised sport in some form in the future, are really the child of the video gaming industry. As such, it benefits from all the clear intellectual property ownership and optimised commercialisation that goes with that from the outset.

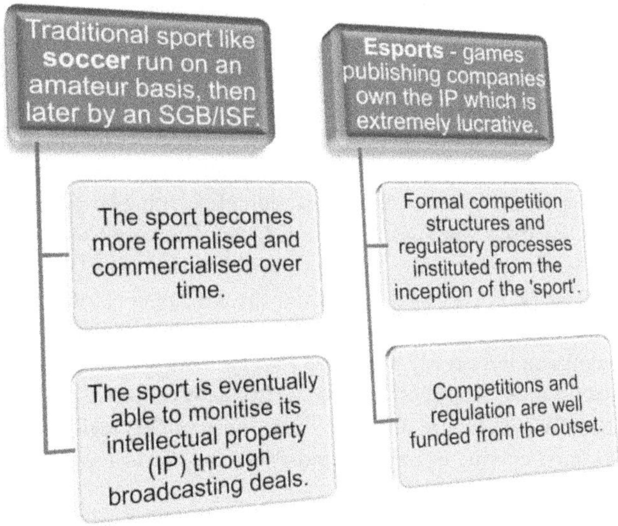

Figure 3.2 Comparison of the commercial and organisational development of Esports compared to 'traditional' sports.

The legal frameworks within SGBs and ISFs are becoming more formalised with more checks and balances in place. Nevertheless, there will always be the potential for arbitrary or unjust decision-making where human beings are concerned, however well-intentioned they may be. There have been mechanisms in the court system for reviewing decisions for a very long time, such as judicial review, human rights processes and even from the common law itself. In the context of this book, one aspect of the lack of fairness in sport is rooted in the fact that applying these review processes to sporting disputes is by no means straightforward, and this requires a detailed analysis, which follows.

Judicial review

The Judicial Review and Courts Act 2022 has introduced changes to avenues of challenge under this heading. However, the major modifications will apply only to specific routes of appeal in immigration cases, so need not be a focus here. Aside from this statutory intervention, judicial review is a doctrine developed by the courts over centuries. This process allows decisions, originally from more or less any tribunal, whether public or private, to be reviewed by the courts if due process was not followed. This is quite distinct from retrying the facts that led to the decision. The courts can only rule that due process has not been followed and, *inter alia*, order the matter to be considered again. Furthermore, provided the body acted fairly the second time, they could arrive at the same decision without further review being possible. The decision-making bodies concerned can be the lower courts.[37] However, more commonly, they have been tribunals, committees and even government ministers[38] who are not courts per se but are passing judgement on a matter that affects individuals in a similar way.

It is the High Court that exercises the supervisory function of judicial review. The High Court's jurisdiction here is over inferior courts, tribunals, bodies or persons who make quasi-judicial decisions. There is also the ability to review the performance of public acts or duties; for instance, the application of planning laws by a local council. The matter can go from the High Court up to the Supreme Court on appeal. For example, in *R v Bow Street Magistrates ex parte Pinochet No (2)* [2000] 1 AC 119 (HL), the *Pinochet* case. This matter involved the attempted extradition of a foreign ex-head of state residing in the UK. The focus is not on the merits of either side's substantive argument but on whether there was, for instance, actual or even potential bias. Alternatively, if the subject of the decision was allowed to exercise their right to be heard fully. The Civil Procedure Rules are a piece of secondary legislation that governs how the civil courts operate in England and Wales, and Part 54 specifies how judicial review cases are to be brought.

Up until *O'Reilly v Mackman* [1983] 2 AC 237, there was no real divide between public and private decision-making bodies as far as judicial review is concerned. Before that, a case for judicial review could be brought in relation to a decision made by an organ of the state, such as a local authority landlord or, alternatively, a private body such as the membership committee of a sports or social club. *O'Reilly* marked the point at which the judicial system would henceforth only review the decisions of public bodies (see Figure 3.3). Much of the case law after that was concerned with what was meant by a public body. After all, many private contractors carry out public functions, such as private prisons and household waste collection and treatment companies. Within that history, there have been consistent attempts to determine whether SGBs, NGBs and ISFs carry out public or private duties. One particular stumbling block is that if the parties' relationship derives from contract, which in sport it mostly does, that precludes judicial review by the courts. As shall be discussed later in the chapter,

Figure 3.3 The effect of *O'Reilly v Mackman* on judicial review.

this may not prevent the inclusion of judicial review principles in a decision framed in a different way, however.

An important sporting case is *Law v National Greyhound Racing Club Ltd* [1983] 1 WLR 1302. Here, Mr Law was challenging a decision to suspend his licence to race greyhounds because of a breach of the National Greyhound Racing Club (NGRC)'s rules. Law argued that the ability to issue, suspend and withdraw licences had a public element as it would affect at least a section of the populace concerned with greyhound racing. The judgement dismissed this contention, however:

> A stewards' inquiry under the defendants' Rules of Racing concerned only those who voluntarily submitted themselves to the stewards' jurisdiction. There was no public element in the jurisdiction itself. . . . such powers as the stewards had to suspend the plaintiff's licence were derived from a contract between him and the defendants.[39]

The judgement did acknowledge that the decisions made by such 'domestic' (private) tribunals could benefit the public. That is to say, as it was in this case, adverse effects on enjoyment of the sport and on betting markets would be prevented. The court was not persuaded, however, that this in any way eroded the courts' general reluctance to exercise judicial review other than in the public sphere.

Since *Law*, the same issues have been further addressed in other cases, not all of them sporting. Nevertheless, these still create applicable precedents, and one such is *R v Panel on Take-overs and Mergers, ex p Datafin plc* [1987] QB 815, the *Datafin* case. The City Panel on Take-overs and Mergers wrote and applied the Code on Take-overs and Mergers. This aimed to safeguard the treatment of shareholders when one company took over another. At the time, it had no statutory or prerogative power, although it has a statutory footing now by virtue of the Companies Act 2006. As a private self-regulating body, it has certain analogies to an SGB, and so the case is relevant. Datafin was a company that had made a takeover bid for another corporation and was adversely affected by a decision made by the Panel. The claimant, therefore, brought a case for judicial review. Despite its non-statutory basis or formal legal powers, it was adjudged that the panel did perform public law functions.[40] This meant that judicial review of Panel decisions was possible. Key to this finding was that the court held if there was no such panel, the government would have to set up a public body to perform the same function. A further nuance was added by the judges in this case. They differentiated between the public or private nature of the power itself and functions that have public law *consequences*, despite those functions being technically private ones.[41] This is a much more holistic and realistic approach in that a power or function may not be 'public' if viewed narrowly. Conversely, if the exercise of that power affects the public sphere sufficiently anyway, judicial review could be available. Thus, if it is successfully argued that a body, like an SGB, is making decisions that affect a large enough portion of public life, then judicial review might be available. It may be, of course, that such an organisation would have to be in charge of a very large and popular sport to do this.

The governmental test

In *R v Jockey Club ex parte Aga Khan* [1993] 1 WLR 909, the Court of Appeal clarified and simplified the question to be asked to determine susceptibility to judicial review. Namely, whether the domestic tribunal in question is sufficiently governmental in its operation and nature. This has been entitled the 'governmental test'. In applying this test, the court had to consider the nature of the Jockey Club, one of the predecessors of the British Horse Racing Authority (BHA). It was recognised that the Jockey Club had monopolistic control of an activity that was of national interest. In common with the soccer Cup Final and World Cup tournaments, certain horse racing events such as the Grand National are enjoyed by many people who would not normally follow the sport. This is because of their traditional place in society and national or international scale. This is a key reason for all of these sporting fixtures being included in the list of 'Crown Jewel' events which must be offered first to 'free-to-air' broadcasters, as discussed in Chapter 7. With the Club's exclusive purview in mind, the court recognised its decisions affected a large section of the public. That said, the judges were not prepared to say that this took the Club as far as having a governmental role, and judicial review was denied. This view was later confirmed in 2005 in *R (Mullins) v Appeal Board of the Jockey Club* [2005] EWHC Admin 2197.

The governmental test was most nearly passed in *R v Disciplinary Committee of the Jockey Club, ex parte Massingberd-Mundy* [1993] 2 All ER 207. This would have allowed judicial review against an SGB. The case again concerned the regulation of the sport of horse racing, and it was further acknowledged that the Jockey Club had 'near monopolistic' powers in relation to that activity. The Court was of the opinion that, left to its own devices, it could have ruled that the nature and quality of the Jockey Club made it a public body. The problem was that there were authorities the Court could not ignore that ruled the opposite. It seems therefore that the only bar to such a paradigm shift in judicial thinking was the Doctrine of Precedent itself. The Court was clearly of the view that it would be in the interests of fairness and justice to intervene if it could.

As the development of case law stands now, it may seem that an action for judicial review cannot succeed against an SGB or ISF, as the courts view them as private bodies with no 'governmental' function. Nevertheless, just because a body is seen as private or public now does not mean that it always will be. The functions of such a body may change, as can the potential effect of its decisions upon the public. Further, indications may increase that the government might step in to regulate the members and stakeholders concerned in some important way, specifically if the body could not function satisfactorily. In such circumstances, the claim that the SGB concerned should be subject to judicial review would be stronger. Attitudes to governmental intervention can change. For example, in April 2021, a European Super League (ESL) was proposed for soccer, which would have eventually had around twenty teams from the English Premier League and equivalent major European leagues. This was an open attempt to challenge the dominance of the European Champions League and to open up better broadcasting income streams. There was widespread antipathy to the idea, not least from soccer fans. The genesis of this idea had not come via supporters but from a desire by the clubs to maximise their revenue. Within around seventy-two hours of launch, the scheme was in disarray, with most of the initial signatory clubs having withdrawn owing to the public backlash. Without a significant shift in the corporate governance of soccer, the concept could resurface however.[42] There were threats at the time from politicians to legislate on soccer governance given the furore, and a Football Governance Bill is making its way through Parliament at the time of writing. The history behind these warnings is worth exploring.

Such breakaways have had more successful precursors, and whilst history does not repeat itself, it does rhyme. In the early 1990s, the Premier League emerged in English soccer to challenge the existing Football League and its then elite status within the English game. There were four divisions in the Football League, Division One containing the most successful clubs of the time, like Manchester United FC and Arsenal FC. It was these clubs and others like them that resigned from Division One to join the new league. The Premier League was affiliated with the Football Association (FA) from the outset and as such is known as the FA Premier League. Sky Broadcasting entered into a very lucrative deal with the FA, with then unheard-of sums of money involved for broadcasting rights. However, the Football League sued, considering that the FA's actions should be judicially reviewed. This was on the basis that, given it had governance monopoly over the National Game, the FA should not also be the pre-eminent commercial promoter of it. The Football League was unsuccessful in *R v Football Association Ltd ex parte Football League* [1993] 2 All ER 833. This was on the basis that the High Court could not so review a body that was not a 'public' one. The court first pointed out the contractual link between the Football League and the FA, which, as discussed above, was already considered fatal to a judicial review action. That said, the most interesting reasoning in the judgement was that there was no 'governmental interest . . . nor is there any evidence to suggest that if the FA did not exist the State would intervene to create a public body to perform its functions'. This is pertinent because since then, there have been significant threats by the state to intervene significantly in the running of English football, admittedly not all of them that well thought through. In 2016 through into 2017, the FA was under scrutiny for its handling of historic allegations of sexual abuse and issues of racism and sexism. Five former FA executives made public their concerns that the FA structures were complicated and arcane, together with the fact that the game was run by 'elderly white men' unqualified to carry through the change needed. They further cited that 'the FA Board is neither an independent board nor an independent regulator' in their criticisms.[43] By early April 2017, a Commons debate was being held as to whether the 'FA has the ability to reform itself, or whether legislation is needed to force it to change'.[44] This prompted reform in the FA from within, but legislation to regulate the governance of soccer is currently being debated in Parliament. Proposed legislative interference is not necessarily the same thing as the Government taking over the running of English Soccer, something FIFA would have plenty to say about. Nevertheless, this sequence of events does start to show an emerging mindset that failed governance at the heart of the game *could* be a 'public' enough issue for an organ of the state to get involved.

Further circumstantial evidence to support this argument comes from the ESL fiasco in 2021. The public outcry and that from most of the domestic game were so loud that even the Prime Minister felt moved to comment. At the height of the crisis, Boris Johnson threatened to drop a 'legislative bomb' to make sure the ESL did not become a reality.[45] Exactly what statutory intervention the Prime Minister had in mind was unclear, and his words were never tested. This was because the plan for the ESL fell apart within three days, but it is clear that the state was willing in principle to curtail or direct the powers of the FA. To what extent will only become clear when the Football Governance Bill becomes law. Admittedly, the possibility of the state functioning to control sport probably only realistically extends to the major sports such as horse racing and football. However, if the BHA or FA were to face an application for judicial review, the court might now be persuaded to distinguish *R v Football Association Ltd ex parte Football League*. There is evidence of 'governmental interest' in the largest sports, and any move towards court intervention becoming more likely is welcome. This is because the ruling elite in SGBs would need to pay greater attention to whether their rules, decisions and processes met with wider notions of fairness than just their own. There has after all been movement in the way that courts have viewed the public/private nature of decision-making bodies in other sectors, most notably in housing. Admittedly, the following discussion of judicial consideration of the public/private nature of bodies is in the context of a mixture of judicial review and human rights law. That said, the divide is treated in a very similar way under the Human Rights Act 1998, and this legislation will be discussed specifically later in this chapter.

Alongside local government, housing associations are not-for-profit organisations that provide social housing in the UK. At times, these associations have been challenged on their decisions, such as evictions or allocations of housing. For the first few years after the Act came into force, these associations were viewed by the courts as private, for instance, in *R v Servite Houses ex parte Goldsmith* [2000] 5 WLUK 415. By the time *Donoghue v Poplar Housing & Regeneration Community Association Ltd* [2001] 3 WLR 183 was decided, though, this view had changed. Housing associations could be seen as sometimes public when they had been created by a local council to manage that council's housing stock. Finally, it was acknowledged in *R (on the application of Weaver) v London and Quadrant Housing Association* [2009] EWCA Civ 587 that they are generally public bodies.

In summary, there are several reasons to consider whether the outcome of *R v Football Association Ltd ex parte Football League* would be the same if decided today. There is now persuasive evidence that some of the most prominent SGBs in the UK would be able to pass the 'governmental' test. Judicial review may therefore still come to be a relevant threat for some SGBs, NGBs and ISFs. However, there are still strong forces that militate against these developments. The courts' policy position that sporting bodies, particularly their disciplinary proceedings, should be free from the interference of the courts is long-standing. This is so long as fundamental notions of fairness are met.[46] This is especially so when there is potentially a contractual remedy. Paradoxically though, the judicial review process could be more attractive to SGBs because, in contrast to contract actions, there is a shorter limitation period. Further, cross-examination does not happen and damages are not available, nor is interim relief. The result is a temporary order protecting the parties' interests until the conclusion of the matter.[47]

The English courts' reluctance to allow judicial review of SGBs is not shared by those in other common law jurisdictions. For instance, in Australia, in *Forbes v NSW Trotting Club Ltd* (1979) 143 CLR 242, the High Court there held that the club's decision to bar Forbes from its tracks could be judicially reviewed. This was because that body controlled a form of harness racing which a large section of the public follows and gamble on in Australia. The sport is also much more popular in the United States and France than in the UK.[48] The club was held to be controlling a public activity. Later, in New Zealand, in *Finnegan v New Zealand Rugby Football Union* [1985] 2 NZLR 190, it was also held that judicial review could be used against SGBs. A view also taken by the Scottish courts in *Lennox v British Show Jumping Association (Scottish Branch)* 1996 SLT 353.

The discussion has arrived at a point where it can be concluded that judicial review against an SGB, NGB or ISF has not succeeded thus far in the English courts. However, there is evidence that the position might change regarding the most prominent SGBs, such as soccer and horse racing. For this reason, it is important to consider what causes of action are relevant to sports governance under this doctrine. Further, as dealt with later in this chapter, these causes of action could be effectively inserted into a private law claim, such as breach of contract by an SGB. The criteria are 'fairness' or, put another way, 'natural justice', the essential components of which are the 'rule against bias' and the 'right to a fair hearing' (see Figure 3.4). It has already been noted that SGBs are quite capable of acting capriciously and flying in the face of these fundamental concepts of equitable behaviour, and further instances will emerge throughout this book.

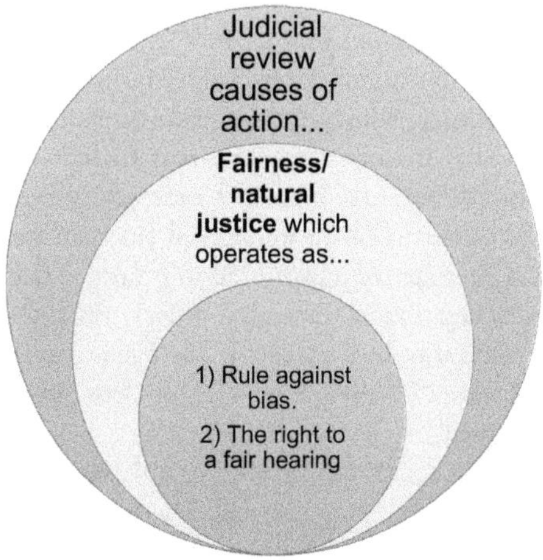

Figure 3.4 Judicial review cause of action.

Fairness or natural justice

The domestic tribunals of sports regulatory bodies are not courts but arbitration procedures, although they are rarely referred to as such. The jurisdiction and power of these panels derive from contract, *Modahl* notwithstanding. Implicitly or explicitly, the athlete or player agrees to be subject to arbitration and bound by the outcome. If the SGB concerned were to be ruled to be exercising public functions, the principles of natural justice could be examined through judicial review, as discussed above. Although the full gamut of court procedures is not followed in arbitrations, certain basic tenets of fairness are inalienable. Consequently, the disciplinary procedure, including evidence harvesting, processing and storage must have been carried out fairly and with due process. Essentially, the decision mechanism must not be affected by real or even potential bias, and there exists a right to a fair hearing.[49]

The concept of natural justice is not limited to hearings but extends to decision-making. In *Council of Civil Service Unions v Minister for the Civil Service* [1985] AC 374, the protagonists were the Conservative administration under Margaret Thatcher and civil servants working for the government electronic surveillance operation known as 'GCHQ'. These workers were civilians, but the government sought to ban them from being members of trade unions to align them with their military colleagues. This became known generally as the 'GCHQ Case'. This organisation also works closely with MI5, MI6, and the police, and mostly tracked Soviet communications for espionage purposes at the time. Since 1991, the focus has been much more on domestic and international terrorist activity, but with the war in Ukraine, the likelihood is its attention has been largely drawn back to Russia again. The reasoning in the 1980s was that those civilians working in such a security-sensitive environment should not be able to strike. Also, there were concerns that trade unions, being overwhelmingly left-wing organisations with socialist agendas, might contain members with sympathies towards the Union of Soviet Socialist Republics (USSR). Finally, this was also part of a general push to curtail the power of unions and curb strikes during a particularly turbulent time for industrial relations in the UK.

The decision to ban union membership at GCHQ was judicially reviewed, and the principle of natural justice, which derives from the notion that there should be no 'procedural impropriety' in such decisions, was further developed in the case. Ultimately, it was ruled for the first time that prerogative powers, like the Orders in Council used by the Government to implement the ban, were subject to judicial review. More recently, a prerogative power used to prorogue (suspend) Parliament as a tactic to get the Brexit legislation through a bitterly divided House of Commons was challenged in the same way. In *R (Miller) v The Prime Minister; Cherry and Ors v Advocate General for Scotland* [2019] UKSC 41, that Order in Council was judicially reviewed and held to be void.

The preceding reasoning could also be used to adjudge the fairness of SGBs' acts and omissions in judicial review, were allowed. There are two types of decisions an SGB might make; the first is a 'judicial' decision and the second an 'executive' one. An example of the former might be a disciplinary outcome; the latter, a decision on eligibility for international competitions. During the development of the Doctrine of Judicial Review, it was thought that procedural impropriety could only be alleged against a panel or individual acting in a judicial capacity. In *Ridge v Baldwin* [1964] AC 40, however, a case where senior police officers were not afforded the right to defend their actions before dismissal, the right was extended to executive decisions. This case concerned the actions of local authority functionaries who had the power to terminate Ridge's employment with his force. Since then, the test is whether the effect of the decision is a 'judicial' one. In *Ridge*, arbitrarily imposing a severe sanction on someone following alleged misconduct was an executive outcome but had a judicial effect. Thus, non-disciplinary decisions of an SGB that are nominally executive and related to the running of the organisation could also fall into this category if they have the consequence of sanctioning someone.

The rule against bias

Every right-thinking person would feel unfairly treated if the panel before which they appear is not free of potential or actual bias. This applies whether it be a court of the land or a sports disciplinary, unfortunately, examples of bias can be found in both, yet as things stand, only the courts can be judicially reviewed on this ground. *R v Bingham Justices ex p Jowitt* (1974) QBD involved a charge of speeding heard before the magistrates' court. This was before the widespread use of speed cameras, and then as now, it is possible to convict on the basis of opinion, although that option is almost never used today. The police officer said Jowitt was speeding, and the defendant said he was not. In convicting Jowitt, acknowledging that it was his word against the officer's, the magistrate said, 'my principle in such cases has always been to believe the evidence of the police officer'. That decision was found by the High Court to be tainted by obvious bias. Potential bias is also iniquitous, such as a financial interest in either party or the outcome, however unlikely that actual bias was present. In the *Pinochet* case mentioned earlier, the original decision to be reviewed was that of a District Judge at Bow Street Magistrates' Court. The case was very high profile and involved General Augustus Pinochet, ex-dictator of Chile, in the UK for medical treatment. During Pinochet's brutal rule, some of the people he allegedly ordered to be tortured were Spanish citizens living in Chile. Once he arrived in the UK, the Spanish authorities took advantage of extradition arrangements that they did not have with Chile and asked for his arrest. This was with a view to investigating the General and possibly trying him in Spain. The initial hearing before the magistrate would have resulted in extradition, but judicial review was undertaken three times in total in an attempt to prevent this. The first case was presided over by a House of Lords (now Supreme Court) panel which included Lord Hoffman. This senior judge had not disclosed his personal links with Amnesty International, a charity that campaigns *inter alia* for torture victims. He and his fellow judges made a ruling that Pinochet did not have immunity from prosecution by virtue of being an ex-head of state. This was overturned by a differently constituted House of Lords panel, reasoning that apparent or potential bias was enough to render the previous decision unsafe.

The disciplinary case the BHA brought against a racehorse trainer, renowned in racing circles as the *Jim Best* case, suffered a similar fate. Best was alleged on multiple occasions to have instructed his jockeys to 'stop' horses. This is usually done because of illicit betting practices taking advantage of the fact that it is now legal to bet on a horse to lose, so-called 'lay' betting. The practice of stopping was also in breach of Rule (D) 45 of the Orders and Rules of Racing. The disciplinary panel contained a solicitor, one Matthew Lohn, and it emerged that he had previously worked for the BHA. He had been a consultant, which evidenced an obvious financial interest in one of the parties.[50] The BHA's Appeal Board agreed that there was a potential for bias; the case was adjourned, and all of the cases that Mr Lohn had previously sat on were re-examined. Further, Christopher Quinlan QC was asked to carry out a general review of the BHA's disciplinary, licensing, and appeal functions to ensure they:

> remained legally robust and would withstand legal challenge . . . [further] . . . that proceedings before such bodies comply with the highest standards of procedural fairness.[51]

After Quinlan's report, the case against Best continued. He was found to have breached the Rules of Racing, but his sanction was set at a much lower point in the range available to the panel than might have been expected. This exemplifies the earlier note about appeals where the process is examined rather than the substantive law. A successful outcome for the complainant always means simply having the matter referred back to the original venue for the process to be applied correctly. It is never to have the matter quashed entirely. In many cases, the outcome of the retrial will be a reversal or, at least, as in this case, a mitigation of the original finding, but by no means does this happen all the time. There is every possibility that a differently constituted panel or properly applied due process might achieve the same outcome as the flawed proceedings. It may be argued that if this outcome is possible in private disciplinary proceedings, then there is no necessity for judicial review to be available in a challenge to unfairness. However, these proceedings were extensively and exhaustively covered by the mainstream press and were thus very much in the public eye. It is not automatically so that cases within smaller SGBs would garner so much attention and create such a public relations nightmare for them. Undoubtedly, there was pressure on the BHA to 'do the right thing' in the court of public opinion rather than any court of the land.

The right to a fair hearing

Irrespective of the non-availability of judicial review, the common law can thankfully step in here. This right is not just a cause of action in judicial review; it is additionally founded in English case law. A version is also found in human rights frameworks around the world, so integral is it to basic tenets of fairness. Again, though, that right has not always been acknowledged in internal sports matters. The principle of *audi alteram partem* is central to the right to a fair hearing. This is a long-standing legal maxim which means 'let the other side be heard'. In practice, this also means a right to adequate legal representation. *Russell v Duke of Norfolk* (1949) 1 All ER 109 was a case involving the grant of licences to train racehorses and was cited in *Ridge v Baldwin*. It was held that:

> Common justice . . . requires that before any man can be found guilty of an offence carrying such consequences, there should be an inquiry at which he has the opportunity to be heard.

This case also referenced the monopoly that the Jockey Club had over such a large and important sport. Coupled with that, the decisions reached by the Club had great potential to be destructive to the lives and livelihoods of such individuals as jockeys, trainers and owners. Consequently, the need for the principles of natural justice to be respected was highly apparent.[52] The Irish High Court adopted similar reasoning in *Quirke v Bord Luthchleas na hÉireann (BLÉ)* [1988] IR 83. An athlete left a venue without providing a requested doping sample. His case was that he had not been told of the consequences of this kind of non-compliance and that he would have returned if he had known. The penalty for Quirke's actions was an 18-month ban, potentially ruling him out of the 1988 Olympic Games in Seoul. Understandably, this was his life's ambition, and the *An Ard-Chúirt* sitting in Dublin took the view that the significance of the penalty alone was enough to require the very highest standards of due process to be met.[53] Further, in *Enderby Town Football Club Ltd v The Football Association Ltd* [1971] Ch 591, a particularly dim view was taken of any steps an SGB might take which, 'lay down procedure contrary to natural justice.' Finally, in *McInnes v Onslow-Fane* [1978] 1 WLR 1520, criteria were considered that might merit intervention by the courts. These were the revocation of membership or licence or a refusal of an application for the same. This would be especially true where there is a reasonable expectation from previous conduct that such a licence or membership will be granted.

To sum up, a previous section established that judicial review per se is not currently possible against an SGB because of the precedents which have ruled them to have no governmental function. That approach takes away a potential and much-needed safeguard against unfairness but may not last indefinitely, however. Indeed, *R v Football Association Ltd ex parte Football League* [1993] 2 All ER 833 may not always be followed. On that basis, the causes of action under judicial review were then considered. Further, it was necessary to examine them because of the possibility that these concepts might be framed within a private law claim, to be discussed later. It would now be prudent to turn to whether human rights claims, at least as they are legislated for in the UK, could be brought against an SGB or ISF.

Human rights and the SGB

It is a misconception that human rights can be relied on to provide a fair outcome in all disputes. Despite being universal rights, the exact format, reach and application of the legislation designed to protect them vary greatly. The United Nations Universal Declaration of Human Rights 1948 (UDHR), for example, is just that: a 'declaration'. This sets out a 'common standard of achievements for all peoples and all nations . . . widely recognised as having inspired, and paved the way for, the adoption of more than seventy human rights treaties'.[54] There is no mechanism by which any nation, body or person can be brought to trial for a breach, however. By contrast, the European Convention on Human Rights 1948 (ECHR)[55] is a treaty drafted in the wake of the horrors of Nazism perpetrated between 1933 and 1945. The geographical scope is more limited in that the signatories are all European. The benefit, however, is that these signatories must answer allegations of human rights abuses against their citizens in a recognised court, the European Court of Human Rights (ECtHR). For instance, despite being widely viewed as a bastion of democracy, the UK has been found to be in breach of the ECHR with respect to its citizens 315 times since 1975 alone.[56] Despite being one of the main authors of the ECHR text, the UK did not adopt a domestic human rights law until the Human Rights Act 1998 (HRA). This came into force in 2000 and was heavily based on the text of the ECHR. The most recent Conservative administration was considering a referendum on withdrawing from the treaty, largely because of the inconvenience it posed with regard to their proposed draconian immigration laws. That threat has receded since they lost power, however. The ECHR and the Human Rights Act are written such that, in general, the only possible defendant is the state itself and its organs. That is to say, not individuals or wholly private entities like companies. In contrast, the US Bill of Rights does allow for individuals, private organisations and the like to be sued on human rights issues, as well as federal and state-level public bodies. The existence of the Human Rights Act does not prevent a UK citizen from taking the UK to the ECtHR, but all possibilities under the HRA must be exhausted first in the British courts.

It is clear then that in UK law, the private nature of SGBs and ISFs may also be a hurdle in establishing a fair outcome through a human rights claim. The position is a little more nuanced than that; however, so it is important to consider the matter further.

The Human Rights Act 1998

Human rights should be a consideration in almost any decision-making process within an SGB. However, this is most true of disciplinary processes. This is because, despite being arbitral processes governed by contract law, their effect can be at least as devastating to reputation and livelihood as criminal proceedings can be. Many disciplinary cases involve allegations of cheating in some form or another, including doping rule breaches. Anti-doping processes themselves involve gross infringements on personal freedoms, but that does not necessarily mean they are a breach of the HRA or Convention. They are, after all, nominally voluntary. For instance, the WADC requires athletes in certain competitions, mostly selected at random, to provide a urine sample. The official requesting the sample must be able to see a stream of urine from the athlete to the bottle provided, and the athlete or player has agreed to participate under the SGB concerned. Therefore, because of the paragraph requiring compliance with the WADC and WADA procedures which will be in the rules, there is no way out of this invasive experience without a severe sanction. Put another way, the athlete or player may have no idea that they will have to urinate into a bottle in the presence of a complete stranger when they accept being under the remit of the SGB. This is true unless they have scrutinised the rule book, the 'small print' of the contract, to an unusual degree. Most people would consider that a significant invasion of their privacy. Article 8 of the ECHR and of the HRA concerns itself with the 'right to respect for your family and private life, your home and your correspondence'. It goes on to say:

> There shall be no interference by a public authority with the exercise of this right except such as is in accordance with the law and is necessary in a democratic society in the interests of national security, public safety or the economic well-being of the country, for the prevention of disorder or crime, for the protection of health or morals, or for the protection of the rights and freedoms of others.[57]

The latter two lines might be stretched to encompass sporting integrity, but in addition, the 'whereabouts rule' has the potential to trigger privacy concerns. WADA holds a Registered Testing Pool (RTP), and members of this group are required to appraise their National Anti-Doping Organisation (NADO) as to where they are during certain timeframes. This is so that athletes and players can be tested out of competition. Each quarter, such athletes are typically expected to provide an address if they stay away overnight, as well as the times, locations and details of regular activities such as work or school. A daily one-hour time slot must also be given to enable such testing to be conducted unannounced. Failure to adhere to this provided schedule could easily result in a sanction for a missed test.[58] Training and competition details must also be provided to the NADO, but to a certain extent, this is public information anyway. Biological passports mean that private medical information is available to NADOs covering a long time period. This allows them to pick up anomalies that might be caused by prohibited substances better than could be achieved by the 'snapshot' of a drugs test. This is also very sensitive and personal information about which sports participants might have concerns regarding sharing, other than with their own doctors.[59] There is, however, no way to compete in a WADA-compliant sport at the elite level without divulging this information. The power imbalance is such that the athlete or player has no choice but to comply with these requests from their SGB.

The ECHR and HRA both assert an individual's right to a fair trial. Article 6(1) of the HRA states inter alia:

> In the determination of his civil rights and obligations or of any criminal charge against him, everyone is entitled to a fair and public hearing within a reasonable time by an independent and impartial tribunal established by law.

Article 6(2) and (3) apply explicitly to criminal proceedings and confer the right to inter alia a defence lawyer and to be promptly informed of the charges against them. It is possible to argue that anti-doping disciplinaries are quasi-criminal, but this has not been done successfully in court as of yet. The issue of a fair trial, under its common law iteration and under judicial review, has been discussed at length in this chapter. When there is bias in the panel, or no hearing is even convened, it is quite possible that this would also be a breach of Article 6(1). As we shall see, though, that hinges on whether SGBs are considered public authorities under UK human rights law.

The public/private question was addressed in *R (Mullins) v Appeal Board of the Jockey Club* [2005] EWHC 2197. It was determined that the test for amenability to judicial review did not differ markedly from the test for a 'functional public authority' required by the Human Rights Act 1998. In *Poplar HARCA v Donaghue* [2001] 4 ALL ER 604, it was stated that 'the courts have acknowledged the need for the definition of a public authority to be given a generous interpretation'. That has, however, not often been proved to be the case except in housing law.[60] Generally, it takes exceptional circumstances for the courts to consider SGBs to be public bodies. *Finnigan v. NZRFU (No. 1)* [1985] 2 NZLR 159, a case under the New Zealand human rights framework, is one example, here the New Zealand Rugby Football Union had decided to accept an invitation to tour South Africa during the apartheid era. This was an issue that sharply divided New Zealand public opinion, and two rugby players challenged the decision. There is more on the relationship of sport more widely, and the South African regime of the time, in Chapter 9. Despite noting the claimants' relationship with NZRFU, a private sports club, was governed by a series of contracts, the court felt there were sufficient political and geo-political issues to warrant allowing the claim and halting the tour. The same flexibility of approach has not been employed by British judges, however.

To examine why the UK courts have generally taken a restrictive view of 'public authority', the first port of call is the wording of the Act. The definition is not explicitly made out but Section 6(1) states that it is 'unlawful for a public authority to act in a way which is incompatible with a Convention right'. Section 6(3) lists two examples of what the term includes, namely, 'a court or tribunal, and . . . any person certain of whose functions are functions of a public nature'. However, in order to persuade a court that a particular SGB or ISF ought to be considered public, it is possible to look behind the wording of the Act. Since *Pepper* v *Hart* [1993] AC 593, Hansard may be consulted to help determine the meaning Parliament intended for a particular provision. During the debate on the Human Rights Bill, Section 6(3)(b) and its wording were considered. Lord Irvine opined that the 'provision is there to include bodies which are not manifestly public authorities, but some of whose functions only are functions of a public nature'. He went on to say that the subsection would assist courts when they are unsure because a body falls into the 'grey area between public and private'.[61] In addition, the then Home Secretary, Jack Straw MP, seemed to indicate that such as the Jockey Club (now the BHA) and the FA might fall into a category where a court could, although does not have to, find there were public elements in their functioning. This would mean that they might fall within Section 6(3)(b).[62] He also noted, though, that similar considerations in judicial review proceedings had not resulted in a finding of 'public' with respect to either SGB. Jack Straw further seemed to express surprise at this regarding the Jockey Club, especially as it was founded by Royal Charter. There is contradictory *dicta* on the Jockey Club example as well. Having overtly dismissed the claim that it was a public body in *R v Jockey Club ex parte Aga Khan* [1993] 1 WLR 909, the court went on to assert that if the club did not exist, the government would have to step in.[63] This is a key criterion to satisfy the 'governmental test' after all.

The 'Horizontal Effect'

In 2022, the ECtHR issued an order which prevents migrants from being taken to Rwanda from the UK to have their asylum claims processed.[64] The issue of whether the UK should withdraw from the Convention that this court enforces has been raised again in response to this.[65] This unpleasant scenario is much less likely after a change in administration, though, and the UK remains fully signed up to the ECHR currently. The treaty explicitly requires courts and tribunals to act in accordance with the Convention, and that is replicated at Section 6(3)(a) of the HRA 1998. Without question, then, a court must make deliberations that are in accordance with the rights protected by the Act. Even if the parties to a claim are private in nature, their human rights must be respected by the court as a public authority. This also means that the common law must be developed by those courts with due regard to human rights. This is known as the 'horizontal effect' of the Convention. Further, there is more latitude in the ECtHR's approach to what constitutes a public authority. This should also provide some support to a legal team seeking to argue that a regulatory system of membership, as an SGB is, could be a public authority. This is especially relevant wording must be interpreted in the light of ECtHR jurisprudence, not just domestic case law. This is despite such arguments having been unsuccessful to date. Such claims came before the court in *RSPCA* v *AG* [2001] 3 All ER 530. However, the finding was that the Royal Society for the Prevention of Cruelty to Animals (RSPCA) was 'not a public authority and has no public functions within the meaning of section 6'. In particular, the court felt that the activity of regulating members was definitely a private one. This would have a direct analogy with an SGB regulating and disciplining its members. As has been discussed, the public/private distinction was considered in *Mullins* and the Jockey Club was ruled to be a private body. This is a regrettable situation as human rights frameworks everywhere have fairness and equity as cornerstones. To only be able to address human rights abuses when they are committed by the state does not reflect the realities of the modern capitalist state. Neoliberalism has been on the ascendancy since the Reagan/Thatcher era of the 1980s. The trend has been towards prioritising entrepreneurialism and the free market together with limiting the remit of the state as much as possible. In the US, this has hopefully reached its apogee in Donald Trump's second term. Fairness is again the casualty when an individual aggrieved cannot sue a transgressor simply because it does not satisfy an artificially narrow definition of a public body. The injury to the wronged party is no less grievous.

The public/private divide going forward

There are challenges under the common law, such as the right to a fair hearing and the right to work, that are not predicated on whether the functions of an SGB or ISF are public. However, the foregoing discussion indicates that currently, under either judicial review or the HRA 1998, jurisprudence holds such bodies to be private in nature. This is fatal to either of such actions. That being said, there is a significant argument that notions such as the rule against bias, the right to a fair trial, the right to privacy and so on, can find their way into private law claims anyway.[66] Private law has always sought to protect the core values of 'individual dignity, autonomy, respect, status and security'.[67] These are encapsulated by the underlying themes in such as the Convention and the judicial review field. These threads include, *inter alia*, proportionality, the right to a fair trial and the right to privacy. The relationship between an SGB and its participants is seen as entirely contractual by judges at the moment. A key facet of contract law is determining which provisions might be implied to exist in the contract, irrespective of its explicit terms; however, a leading test for implied terms is known as that of the 'officious bystander', developed in *Southern Foundries (1926) Ltd v Shirlaw* [1940] AC 701. In the judgement, the test was expressed like this:

> if, while the parties were making their bargain, an officious bystander were to suggest some express provision for it in their agreement, they would testily suppress him with a common 'Oh, of course!'.

The test does require the term to be very apparent to both parties, so obvious that they felt no need to include it in writing.[68] Thus, the term can be regarded as the 'unexpressed intentions of both parties'.[69] If the rulebook of an SGB is the foundation of the contractual relationship between it and the sports participant, then if the question is asked, 'do these provisions take account of human rights law?', the answer must surely be in the affirmative. More specifically, the query might be, 'does this rulebook and associated procedures acknowledge the athlete's "right to a fair trial" under such as the Convention?' Again, in that case, the reply must surely be 'yes'. It would be very difficult for the SGB to say that these concepts should not be implied into the contract as the resulting press would be deeply damaging. Therefore, they can be part of the athlete or player's private law claim against the SGB or ISF (see Figure 3.5). Moreover, the court may simply apply these ideas by virtue of the fact that it is, itself, a public body under the 'horizontal effect' of the ECHR. Admittedly, examples of the courts invoking human rights issues of their own volition are rare. Perhaps the best example is *Bank Mellat v HM Treasury (No 2)* [2014] AC 700; this was a case concerning UK sanctions against an Iranian bank following political tensions at the time. Here, the court raised the issue of the human rights of individual customers of the bank, without that being advocated by either side in the case. It is therefore a possibility rather than a probability.

There are also examples of the Human Rights Act affecting the actions of sports disciplinary bodies despite no litigation being initiated. The boxer Mike Tyson was

Figure 3.5 Public vs private – potential for bringing an action for breach of human rights/judicial review.

alleged to have punched Lennox Lewis after a boxing bout had finished. The British Board of Boxing Control (BBBC), however, restricted itself to a mere censure of Tyson at even the mention of a possible human rights challenge.[70] In terms of judicial review, heads of claim being incorporated through an implied clause, it is also worthy of note that the BHA disciplinary against the trainer Jim Best discussed earlier was suspended pending a report by Christopher Quinlan QC. His remit was specifically to conduct a review to ensure the '[BHA's] disciplinary, licensing and appeal functions remain legally robust and would withstand legal challenge'.[71] This was directly in response to an 'allegation of appearance of bias' on the panel in the *Jim Best* case,[72] it was not because Best made an application to court. Finally, on the international stage, skater Claudia Pechstein and footballer Adrian Mutu jointly took a case under Article 6, 'Right to a Fair Trial' of the Convention to the ECtHR in 2018. Their arguments were, *inter alia*, that they had not been given a fair hearing before the Court of Arbitration for Sport (CAS) in their disciplinary appeals. They were only partially successful, but the fact that their governing bodies, and indeed CAS itself, are private institutions did not prevent them from bringing their case.[73]

Bradley and beyond

There is no doubt that the English courts have long had a policy of not interfering in the running of sporting bodies if such can possibly be avoided. It is also evident from the foregoing discussion that the chances of SGB's decisions being assessed for fairness would be increased if this policy were reversed. In a move in that direction, that judicial reluctance has softened slightly in the years since the turn of this century. As long ago as 1911, a seemingly self-evident statement made its way into caselaw, albeit nothing to do with sport. Specifically, that 'anyone who decides anything' is obligated to apply the principles of natural justice.[74] However, this principle was not overtly applied to an SGB until *Flaherty v National Greyhound Racing Club* [2005] EWCA Civ 1117. Flaherty was a greyhound trainer accused of administering a prohibited drug to a dog and was sanctioned by his SGB. In response, Flaherty asserted in court that he had not been allowed to perform his own tests on the urine sample concerned. Further, CCTV evidence he believed would assist his case was not considered admissible. The Club's findings were therefore invalid, *ultra vires* or otherwise unlawful as the disciplinary procedure had not been fair in the Claimant's view. Flaherty also alleged bias on the part of the stewards. The judgement gave due prominence to the need for natural justice in private disciplinary proceedings just as much as in court. The test is a relatively simple one, namely, 'whether, having regard to the course of the proceedings there has been a fair result . . . The question in every case is the extent to which the deficiency alleged has produced unfairness'. This laid the ground for further expansion of the judiciary's role in overseeing decision-making in SGBs; that change came abruptly in *Bradley v Jockey Club* [2005] EWCA Civ 1056. This case caused marked apprehension in SGBs likely to now be subject to the jurisdiction of English common law. During the preparation for the writing of this book, a lead official in an SGB was asked why so much effort was going into re-writing and restructuring the internal disciplinary rules for that SGB. This was especially if there historically had been clear reservations amongst judges about overturning awards made within sport. The reply was brief, purely anecdotal, but telling, 'because of *Bradley*'.

In the case, the Court of Appeal adopted a proportionality approach in relation to sanctions on athletes and players applied during an internal disciplinary procedure. To adjudge whether the penalty or penalties in question were 'fair', the test formulated by the Court of Appeal looks like the following. Firstly, the object or objectives of the disciplinary procedures must be sufficiently important to justify limiting a fundamental right. Such a right might be the right to work if a period of suspension or ineligibility is to be imposed, for instance. Secondly, the measures designed to meet the objective must be rationally connected to it. Finally, the means used to impair the right or freedom must be no more than is necessary to accomplish the objective (see Figure 3.6). Put another way, if the disciplinary tribunal concerned can clearly demonstrate that these three principles were applied in imposing sanctions on an athlete or player, then a subsequent challenge in the courts would be much easier for the SGB to defend.

European Union law, 'Brexit' and SGBs

Since 1957 and the Treaty of Rome, there has been a supranational body of law which has evolved to the point that athletes and players can seek to enforce their rights under it. The EU was originally named the European Economic Community (EEC). It has within it provisions to protect such as employment rights and 'free movement of persons' within the bloc's borders. These rights have been and still are used by sports persons and stakeholders to challenge perceived overreach by SGBs where *locus standi* exists.

A body of statute and case law has grown up delimiting the rights and duties of SGBs under EU law. The complicating factor in preparing this book is that, despite

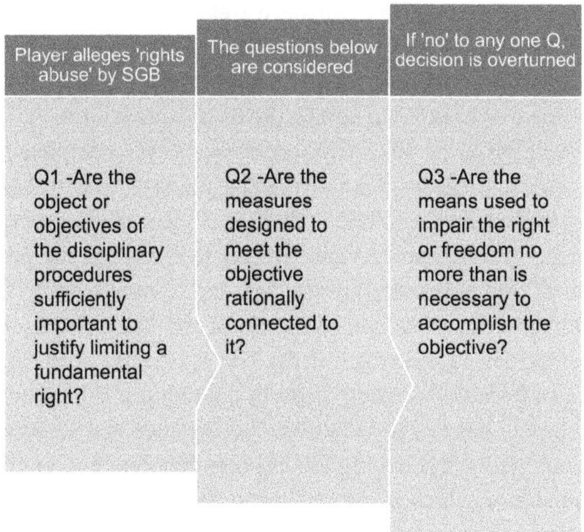

Figure 3.6 The process of bringing an action under *Bradley v Jockey Club.*

the British electorate deciding to leave the EU by 51.89 per cent to 48.11 per cent in 2016, and much political sloganeering since, 'Brexit' cannot yet be considered 'done'. Before considering which, if any, EU law is still useful to mount a challenge with, it is necessary to consider where the UK's relationship with the EU actually is, particularly in the context of sports law.

A brief history of 'Brexit'

The period since the Brexit referendum to the present has been a politically tumultuous one for the UK.[75] The European Communities Act 1972 was the means by which the UK became a member state in 1973. It was essentially this legislation that needed to be repealed as a key part of the process of leaving. The primary legislation of the EU is no longer the Treaty of Rome; it has been replaced by the Treaty on the Functioning of the European Union (TFEU). The provisions of Article 50 TFEU were the mechanism for the UK to leave the bloc, and this was formally done by the UK government as a result of the referendum. The initial date for leaving was 29 March 2019. However, on multiple occasions, Parliament could not reach agreement on the withdrawal deal negotiated by the then Prime Minister, Theresa May. Ultimately, this led to the resignation of May and the controversial tenure of Boris Johnson. Mr Johnson won a convincing victory in the December 2019 general election, not least because he promised to 'Get Brexit Done' as a cornerstone of the manifesto. There were then two further prime ministers since Johnson, over a matter of months, such was the chaos Brexit caused in the ruling party alone. The UK is currently in serious financial difficulty, not helped at all by the Covid-19 epidemic. A thorny problem has been that of the UK's only land border with the EU, that between the north of the Island of Ireland and *Eire*. This has led to one of the countries that make up the UK, Northern Ireland, being at least temporarily still governed, in part, by some rules from the EU. This includes some European Court of Justice (ECJ) jurisdiction remaining under the 'Northern Ireland Protocol'.

The former Prime Minister, Rishi Sunak, pledged to erase all remaining EU-derived laws from the statute book by 2023. This work was never completed, as some 3,400 statutes from 50 years of membership are yet to be analysed to see whether they should be repealed or absorbed into UK law.[76] Thus, it is almost impossible to fully judge the extent to which EU law is still a viable means to challenge the perceived excesses of an SGB or ISF at this point, despite the last day of membership of the EU being 31 January 2020. Nevertheless, a consideration of the key cases brought by athletes and players under EU law is still worthwhile. This is because of the residual influence the EU has, but also because sporting disputes concerning British competitors could still arise where the EU has full jurisdiction. For instance, CAS operates under Swiss law and Switzerland, whilst not having full EU membership, has a number of bilateral agreements with the bloc which bring EU law to bear. Furthermore, UK citizens play for and compete with a number of teams in countries that are still full members, such as France, Italy and Germany. If such a team were sanctioned by an SGB and challenged that under EU law, those citizens would be affected notwithstanding their individual lack of *locus standi* since 2020. Considering the complexities and uncertainties of challenges to the power of SGBs is part of the core purpose of this book, examining unfairness in the administration of sport. Consequently, and because of all the above reasons, considering the jurisdiction of the ECJ is important. Finally, President Trump has an isolationist stance in his second term and has instituted an unprecedented trade tariff regime in early 2025. This is likely to add to a growing dissatisfaction with Brexit from a large sector of the UK population. This in turn has accelerated a desire for a closer legal union of some kind with the EU in the future as an economic defence mechanism.

Key legal principles in ECJ cases

As discussed in Chapter 2 in brief, the EU was conceived as a trading bloc and the bedrock of this project is the easing of trade between member countries. Therefore, the EU has a clear economic focus, and the harmonising of employment law, border controls and consumer protection are all key to that broader aim. Sport straddles two worlds; it is widely accepted that it has social utility, improves health and promotes team playing and social cohesion to name but a few societal benefits. That view is critiqued as merely neoliberalism at work again, and these benefits are hard to substantiate but are perpetuated by sports evangelists using anecdotes and unsystematic observations,[77] however. Nevertheless, sport is also a business, in the case of some sports, billions of pounds worth of trade. EU laws were originally designed mainly to affect the economic activities of a member state, not, for instance, its defence policy or non-trade related foreign policy, although more recently there has been creep in this direction. Sport has therefore gained something of a special position under EU law; this is often referred to as the 'specificity' of sport. That specificity has led to a certain degree of distortion when EU law is applied in sporting disputes. What specificity means was most neatly articulated in Article 165 TFEU and the 2007 White Paper on Sport. These documents espoused the special benefits of sport to society and left room for courts to decide whether EU law is engaged when there is a dispute between a sportsperson and an SGB or between SGBs and other sporting bodies. The leading case in this area is Case 415/93 *Union Royale Belge des Societes de Football Association ASBL* v *Jean-Marc Bosman* [1995] ECR I-4921. In *Bosman*, the courts found that sport has unusual characteristics which make it different from 'normal commercial'[78] operations. This case and earlier, Case C-176/96 *Jyri Lehtonen and Castors Canada Dry Namm-Braine ASBL v Fédération royale belge des sociétés de basket-ball ASBL (FRBSB)*, or the *Lehtonen* case, employ an important distinction. As considered in Chapter 2, sporting rules have different rationales and motivations behind them. In most cases, this is obvious; 'rules of the game', such as the size of the ball, dimensions of the pitch or specifications of equipment, are to do with fair play and safety when playing the game. Other rules, such as restrictions on logos on playing attire, contractual arrangements with clubs and teams and relationships with sponsors, are overtly commercial. Some rules may be considered to have both elements, so-called 'hybrid' regulations. An example of which are the financial fair play regulations, as they are to do with the commercial operation of teams. They also, however, ensure a fair playing field between lesser and better-resourced clubs, benefitting perhaps from ownership by wealthy individuals.[79] It is only the commercial rules and those in the hybrid category that engage EU law because the business element is paramount. *Christelle Deliège v Ligue Francophone de Judo et Disciplines ASBL* (Joined cases C-51/96 and C-191/97), or '*Deliège*' concerned a set of such hybrid rules. The claimant argued that selection rules for international competition had harmed her sporting career, and the ECJ found that there was sufficient economic element to these regulations to warrant intervention by the court. This was because the selection rules were part of how the sport itself was organised. However, paying spectators, and in particular, broadcasters seeking exclusive rights to transmit events, would find international competitions more inviting. This proved the economic element irrespective of the intentions of the original drafters of the rules.

With the foregoing in mind, an athlete or player aggrieved at the decision of an SGB or other sports authority needs to frame the complaint as having an economic basis in order to seek protection from EU law. It is not simply a question of asserting that the participant has been the subject of unfair treatment, thus limiting this avenue of challenge to sportspeople quite significantly. The game of Bridge was in exactly this position when the governing body of the card game challenged Sport England's refusal to officially recognise the game as a sport.[80] Lawyers for the Bridge Union argued that this decision put the game at a disadvantageous position regarding sales tax, which is regulated by EU law. The arguments in court then became about tax, not any allegation of unfair or arbitrary treatment of the game *per se*. To use another example, the 'prohibited association' provisions of the WADC provide for sanctions on sports persons who associate with others placed under a ban, usually for doping infractions. To challenge such an outcome from a tribunal, this would best be argued under a head of claim that the prohibition was a restraint of trade in order to bring it under ECJ jurisdiction, rather than that it was, in and of itself, an unjust or capricious decision, for instance.

Finally, on EU law, just to reiterate, the succinct nature of this analysis of EU law as a means of challenging SGBs is appropriate for the juncture at which this book is written. Older works will go into more detail, but they were written when the UK was still a member state. Right now, the relevance of EU law is of limited importance to UK sports participants. This is unless a UK citizen is part of a European team that is disadvantaged by an SGB decision, or the nascent 'rejoin'[81] movement gains sufficient momentum in the future. It remains an important feature in the legal landscape for other European athletes, however.

Challenging SGBs – concluding remarks

SGBs have been described as 'quasi-states' operating 'discriminatory and injurious policies practices'.[82] Further, the macropolitics of these and sponsor corporations can clash with the micropolitics of athletes, players and their support teams[83] in a myriad of ways. It is important, therefore, that there are adequate means for participants to challenge the fairness of their environment and situation whenever inequity presents itself. That process is, however, far from clear or straightforward. Firstly, there is no one route by which the decision or rule may be challenged. The issue may be a contractual one; *Modahl* notwithstanding, the athlete or player has an agreement with their governing body, and that may have been breached. There are also common law rights such as restraint of trade that could be relied upon. What is particularly unfortunate, though, is that the main bodies of law developed specifically to protect the fundamental rights of citizens are not *per se* available for actions against SGBs and ISFs. Without a future *volte-face* by the courts, a stand-alone judicial review action or a claim under human rights will not succeed in the UK, as SGBs are deemed private entities. Such claims may well succeed in being heard against a government actor such as the sports councils, as they are public authorities, however.

As a glimmer of hope, the relevant tenets of both judicial review and human rights are still useful despite the private nature of SGBs. If these causes of action are embedded in a private law claim, such as breach of contract, it would be difficult for the defending body to convincingly argue that the protection of rights is not at least implied provisions in the athlete or player's contract. For example, if there were potential bias on a disciplinary panel, then it would be self-defeating for the SGB to argue that the disciplinary rules did not inherently take account of the rule against bias. Similarly, it would be unconscionable for an SGB to argue that an athlete's terms and conditions of membership did not accord with principles corresponding to Article 6 ECHR right to a fair trial.

EU law could still be brought to bear if the complaint against the SGB or ISF engaged it, but only if the failure alleged by the SGB related to the sport as an economic activity. In terms of UK sportspeople, however, the relevance of the ECJ has been all but erased by 'Brexit'. However, the main principles of this area of law are included in this chapter by way of completeness as their redundancy is not yet total. These principles remain available to sportspeople who are citizens of any of the remaining member states, as long as the dispute is about sport as a business, not how it is played.

Finally, on a more positive note, the historical reluctance of courts to intervene in sports disputes has been eroded by the *Bradley* case. The judiciary will now accept a supervisory jurisdiction if the athlete or player's 'fundamental rights' have been infringed. There is a test set out in the case for this. In that context, fundamental right does not mean human right as in the ECHR or HRA 1998, although there may be obvious common ground. The increasing commercialisation of sport and the potentially vast sums at stake mean that this is an area of increasing litigation. This case law has increased the vulnerability of SGBs to suits if they make capricious or arbitrary decisions.

The persons of fundamental importance to sport, the participants and fans, need to be able to ensure that they are treated fairly by governing bodies and mega-commercial entities. This is predicated on their ability to 'speak softly but carry a big stick'[84] when approaching the 'rulers' of their sport. That is the only way to redress the power imbalance between the parties. If the means of formal challenge through litigation are opaque, complex and illogically limited, that 'stick' is unfairly lessened in its deterrent power.

Notes

1 Jules Boykoff, 'Glitterati and grit: The perils and possibilities of sports mega-event research', *Journal of Sport and Social Issues* (2024): 75, https://doi.org/10.1177/01937235241247038.

2 Voting Rights Act 1865; see also the fifteenth Amendment to the US Constitution, 1870.

3 Jessica Horton and Jonathan Merritt, '"Show me your horse and I will tell you who you are": Brexit, a chance to acknowledge animal sentience in law', *Denning Law Journal*, 31 (2019): 7–8.

4 Frank Keogh, 'Jockeys to meet horse racing bosses over whip dispute', *BBC*, 16 October 2011, http://www.bbc.co.uk/sport/0/horse-racing/15327053.

5 Paul Michael Brannagan, Nicolas Scelles et al., 'The 2021 European Super League attempt: Motivation, outcome, and the future of football', *International Journal of Sport Policy and Politics*, 14, no. 1 (2022): 169–70.

6 'Lord Hailsham's Dimbleby lecture', *BBC*, 14 October 1976, audio, 21:25, https://www.bbc.co.uk/programmes/p00fr9gh.

7 Mark James and Guy Osborn, 'The Olympics, transnational law and legal transplants: The International Olympic Committee, ambush marketing and ticket touting', *Legal Studies*, 36, no. 1 (March 2016): 93–110.

8 The Psychoactive Substances Act 2016 is also relevant, although this legislation on 'legal highs' focuses on production, supply and importation, not possession.

9 Rebecca Murray, '"No room for these drugs in sport": Showjumper who lost Olympic place banned for two years', *Horse and Hound*, 3 March 2022, https://www.horseandhound.co.uk/news/australian-showjumper-jamie-kermond-banned-for-two-years-779109.
10 British Horse Racing Authority, 'Rules of racing and guides', accessed 5 October 2023, https://www.britishhorseracing.com/regulation/rules-guides/.
11 Boykoff, 'Glitterati and grit', 77.
12 Gibson Burrell and Gareth Morgan, *Sociological Paradigms and Organisational Analysis* (Aldershot: Ashgate, 2005), 1–3.
13 Antonio Gramsci and David Forgacs, *The Gramsci Reader: Selected Writings, 1916–1935* (New York: Schocken Books 1988), 218.
14 Boykoff, 'Glitterati and grit', 71.
15 Jonathan Merritt, *Regulating Sport for the Non-Human Athlete* (Lanham: Rowman and Littlefield, 2019), 123–6.
16 'Sport England – A code for sports governance', accessed 5 October 2023, https://www.sportengland.org/campaigns-and-our-work/code-sports-governance.
17 'Sport England – A code for sports governance – Requirements', accessed 5 October 2023, https://www.sportengland.org/campaigns-and-our-work/code-sports-governance?section=the_requirements.
18 *Re Yenidje Tobacco Co Ltd* [1916] 2 Ch 426.
19 See for instance the creation of the Republic of South Sudan in 2011 after two brutal civil wars in Sudan during the twentieth century, which only ending in 2005.
20 Boykoff, 'Glitterati and grit', 75.
21 Department of Digital, Culture, Media and Sport, *A Sporting Future For All* (London: DCMS, 2000), 6.
22 See *Greig v Insole* [1978] 1 WLR 302, where the ICC and TCCB were unable to prevent players signing for Packer.
23 Boykoff, 'Glitterati and grit', 71–2.
24 Leon Davis, 'From a pub game to a sporting spectacle: The professionalisation of British Darts, 1970–1997', *Sport in History,* 38, no. 4 (2018): 507.
25 Ibid., 527–31.
26 'Professional Darts Players Association – PDC/BDO, "The split,"' accessed 5 October 2023, https://www.pdpa.co.uk/statistics/unique/.
27 See *Dunlop Pneumatic Tyre Co Ltd v Selfridge and Co Ltd* [1915] AC 847 and see also the Contracts (Rights of Third Parties) Act 1999.
28 Rebecca Murray, 'Sir Mark Todd: Update on disciplinary hearing', *Horse and Hound*, 24 March 2022, https://www.horseandhound.co.uk/news/sir-mark-todd-update-on-disciplinary-hearing-781565.
29 Consideration is usually expressed in monetary terms such as a purchase price, but does not have to be. For example, in a sporting context, there may well be a joining fee and certainly a detriment, a loss from having to abide by rules set by the SGB.
30 See for example, the arguments in *Jones v Vernons' Pools Ltd* [1938] 2 All ER 626.
31 This was a type of race essentially across farmers' fields and hedges. These had originally been between the 'steeples', or bell towers of neighbouring country churches, thus providing a course with easily visible landmarks at either end.
32 See for instance, *Greig v Insole* [1978] 1 WLR 302.

33 For example, the Sporting Events (Control of Alcohol etc.) Act 1985 and the Football Spectators Act 1989.

34 'World Cup 2010: FIFA issues ban deadline to Nigeria', *BBC*, 2 July 2010, http://news.bbc.co.uk/sport1/hi/football/world_cup_2010/8780028.stm.

35 Michael Beloff, 'Drugs laws and Versapaks', in *Drugs & Doping in Sports: Socio-legal Perspectives*, by John O'Leary (Abingdon: Cavendish, 2001), 40.

36 Joe Tidy, 'US teenager wins $3m as Fortnite world champion', *BBC*, 28 July 2019, https://www.bbc.co.uk/news/technology-49146644.

37 *R v Bingham Justices ex p Jowitt* (1974) QBD.

38 Kirsty Scott, 'Straw forced to defend Tyson decision', *The Guardian*, 23 May 2000, https://www.theguardian.com/politics/2000/may/23/uk.boxing.

39 *Law v National Greyhound Racing Club Ltd* [1983] 1 WLR 1302.

40 Ibid.

41 Ibid.

42 See John Welsh, 'The European Super League debacle: Why regulation of corporate football is essential', *Soccer & Society*, 24, no. 2 (2022): 172–89.

43 Dan Roan, 'FA reform: Former chiefs say, "elderly white men" block change', *BBC Sport*, 12 December 2016, http://www.bbc.co.uk/sport/football/38274152.

44 Richard Coway, 'FA reform: As MPs debate the issue, is real change a stretch too far?', *BBC Sport*, 8 February 2017, http://www.bbc.co.uk/sport/football/38907978.

45 Peter Walker, Damien Gayle and Jessica Elgot, 'Boris Johnson threatens to use "legislative bomb" to stop European Super League', *Guardian*, 20 April 2021, www.theguardian.com/football/2021/apr/20/uk-government-may-legislate-to-stop-european-super-league-says-minister.

46 See for instance, *Modahl v British Athletic Federation (No 2)* [2002] 1 WLR 1 192, *R (on the application of William Mullins) v Appeal Board of The Jockey Club and The Jockey Club (Interested Party)* [2005] EWHC 2197; [2006] ACD 2.

47 Jack Anderson, 'An accident of history: Why the decisions of sports governing bodies are not amenable to judicial review', *Common Law World Review*, 35, no. 3 (2006): 173.

48 William Steinkraus et al., *The Horse in Sport* (London: Macdonald Orbis, 1987), 223–43.

49 These also have their equivalents in Convention/Human Rights Act provisions but are part of a distinct and separate line of cases. They should not be confused with Article 6 of the Human Rights Act 1998, 'The Right to a Fair Trial'.

50 'Jim Best may seek High Court ruling over rehearing dispute with BHA', *The Guardian*, 28 August 2016, https://www.theguardian.com/sport/2016/aug/28/jim-best-high-court-ruling-rehearing-bha.

51 'Quinlan review 2016 – Terms of reference', accessed 5 October 2023, http://www.britishhorseracing.com/wp-content/uploads/2016/06/TERMS-OF-REFERENCE-Review-of-DP-AB-and-LC-01-06-16.pdf.

52 Simon Gardiner et al., *Sports Law* (London: Routledge 2012), 193–4.

53 Laura Donnellan, 'Dispute resolution in Irish sport: The courts as reluctant interlopers', *Entertainment and Sports Law Journal*, 14, no. 3 (2016): 5.

54 'United Nations – Universal Declaration of Human Rights 1948', accessed 5 October 2023, https://www.un.org/en/about-us/universal-declaration-of-human-rights.

55 This treaty has nothing to do with the European Union, which was not to be founded until nearly another decade had passed.
56 Joanna Dawson, 'UK cases at the European Court of Human Rights since 1975', *House of Commons Briefing Paper*, Number CBP 8049, 19 December 2019, 3, accessed 5 October 2023, https://researchbriefings.files.parliament.uk/documents/CBP-8049/CBP-8049.pdf.
57 Human Rights Act 1998, Article 8(1) and 8(2).
58 'WADA – Whereabouts rule', accessed 5 October 2023, https://www.wada-ama.org/en/athletes-support-personnel/provide-whereabouts.
59 'WADA – Biological passports', accessed 5 October 2023, https://www.wada-ama.org/en/athlete-biological-passport.
60 See *R v Servite Houses ex parte Goldsmith* [2000] 5 WLUK 415, *Donoghue v Poplar Housing & Regeneration Community Association Ltd* [2001] 3 WLR 183, *R (on the application of Weaver) v London and Quadrant Housing Association* [2009] EWCA Civ 587.
61 Hansard HL, 24 November 1997, col. 811.
62 Ibid., 17 June 1998, col. 410.
63 Anderson, 'An accident of history: Why the decisions of sports governing bodies are not amenable to judicial review', 183.
64 *N. S. K. v. the United Kingdom* (application no. 28774/22, formerly *K.N. v. the UK*).
65 Diane Taylor, Rajeev Syal and Emine Sinmaz, 'Rwanda asylum flight cancelled after 11th-hour ECHR intervention', *The Guardian*, 14 June 2022, https://www.theguardian.com/uk-news/2022/jun/14/european-court-humam-right-makes-11th-hour-intervention-in-rwanda-asylum-seeker-plan.
66 Dawn Oliver, *Common Values and the Public – Private Divide* (Oxford: Butterworths, 1999), 27.
67 Ibid., 29, 60–70.
68 An alternative test is the 'business efficacy test' from *The Moorcock* (1889) 14 PD 64. The best use of both tests was helpfully explained in *Marks and Spencer plc v BNP Paribas Securities Services Trust Company (Jersey) Limited and another* [2015] UKSC 72.
69 Andre Naidoo, *Complete Contract Law: Text, Cases, and Materials* (Oxford: Oxford University Press, 2021), 6.5.4.
70 Gardiner et al., *Sports Law*, 217–21.
71 'Quinlan review 2016 – Terms of reference'.
72 Ibid.
73 *Mutu and Pechstein v Switzerland* (Applications nos. 40575/10 and 67474/10).
74 *Board of Education v Rice* [1911] AC 179, Lord.
75 See Horton and Merritt, '"Show me your horse and I will tell you who you are,"'
76 George Parker, 'UK plan to scrap all EU laws suffers new setback', *Financial Times*, 8 November 2022, https://www.ft.com/content/0c0593a3-19f1-45fe-aad1-2ed25e30b5f8.
77 See for instance, Jay Coakley, 'Youth sports: What counts as "positive development?"', *Journal of Sport and Social Issues*, 35, no. 3 (2011): 306–24.
78 Steven Weatherill, '"Fair play please!" – Recent developments in the application of EC law to sport', *Common Market Law Review*, 40 (2003): 53–4.
79 Joe Bray, 'UEFA fine eight clubs for Financial Fair Play breaches and place Man City on watchlist', *Manchester Evening News*, November 22, 2022, https://www.man

chestereveningnews.co.uk/sport/football/football-news/uefa-man-city-ffp-fines-24919263.

80 'CJEU rules bridge card game is not a sport for the purposes of the VAT directive', accessed 5 October 2023, https://eur-lex.europa.eu/content/news/CJ_bridge.html.

81 'Thousands of London protesters call for UK to rejoin EU', *The Guardian*, 22 October 2022, https://www.theguardian.com/politics/2022/oct/22/thousands-of-london-protesters-call-for-uk-to-rejoin-eu.

82 Boykoff, 'Glitterati and grit', 77.

83 Ibid.

84 *Attr.* President Theodore Roosevelt, 26 January 1900, in a letter to Henry Sprague.

4

Doping Control

The status quo – the 'War On Cheats'

Much that has been written about doping proceeds from the unchallenged notion that doping is cheating and that Sports Governing Bodies (SGBs) and International Sports Federations (ISFs), supported by their National Anti-Doping Organizations (NADOs) are waging a tireless, righteous battle against determined, systematic wrongdoing. Part of the purpose of this chapter is to consider whether the people and processes involved in anti-doping are indeed the guardians of truth and justice or whether the situation is more complex and nuanced. In doing so, it will be possible to establish whether the current anti-doping regimes are fair.

Gramsci wrote that 'one of the commonest totems is the belief about everything that exists, that it is "natural" . . . that it could do no other than exist'.[1] He was writing about the acceptance of capitalism manufactured in the populace by the ruling class in twentieth-century societies, but the idea can be applied more widely. Sports governance provides both small societies within the greater whole and is also not divorced from that greater social order. If there are inbuilt structural inequalities in that order, they will be replicated in sport. The current iteration of doping control is presented by the ruling class of sport as if there could be no other effective process. There is a large body of academic literature that critiques doping rules, but despite this, competitors are subtly coerced into thinking there is no other way. Consequently, it would be rare to find anything other than uncritical support among participants for anti-doping as it now is. For instance, strict liability and reverse burdens of proof are defended as having no reasonable alternative. In wider society, the 'war on drugs' uses similarly accepted rhetoric, that all efforts should be directed at eradicating illegal drugs using existing norms, definitions, practices and resources. This is despite the fact that street drugs show no signs of being removed from civilisation at all. It also ignores the experience of countries like Portugal[2] that have adopted a 'public health' rather than an enforcement dynamic, together with a degree of legalisation. These states appear to be doing rather better than those that rely more heavily on law enforcement and 'stiff' penalties. The Scottish administration has even proposed such measures, including widespread decriminalisation, challenging the UK-wide prohibition policy. Although without the approval of Westminster, this is unlikely to become law in all four countries of the UK in the near future.[3]

Returning to doping, there may well be 'another way', but a great many myths and long-entrenched ideas about doping will have to be overcome first.

The stated rationale for doping control

An important part of the rules of any sport, first discussed in Chapter 2, is the anti-doping provisions. The idea is that without these, athletes and players will be able to enhance their performance to such an extent that there will no longer be a 'level playing field' in the competition, and that will not be fair. There will also be no control over substances and procedures that are harmful to competitors, and an undesirable message will be sent to young people, including aspiring players. Doping, along with other forms of cheating, has a long history. However, it was not a human-only sport that first introduced regulation regarding prohibited substances. Horse racing has had doping control the longest. As early as the beginning of the twentieth century, the Jockey Club introduced rules to address evidence that American trainers were giving the horses cocaine when racing in the UK.[4] The British Horse Racing Authority (BHA) still has its own doping control rules and does not subscribe to the World Anti-Doping Code (WADC). In practical terms, there is even a lack of reciprocity, despite there being many examples of owners operating both racing thoroughbreds and other horses used in sports that are subject to the Code, like polo and show jumping. The paradoxes that result from this in these sports are really quite startling.[5]

The anti-doping regulations and processes in use in most other sports date back only to the 1980s. All of these, including bespoke programmes like that of the BHA, have common features like strict liability and reverse burdens of proof where the defendant, to at least some extent, has to prove their own innocence. This is a notion that most democratic legal systems reject. Despite this draconian approach, examples of doping scandals abound. It can seldom get more serious than when there is evidence that the doping may be state-sponsored and widespread, rather than the actions of individuals relying solely on their own judgement. In recent years, the most prominent example is that of Russia, discussed further in Chapter 9. The result was that Russian competitors could only compete as neutrals in international competitions in World Anti-Doping Code (WADC) signatory sports for a period. A blanket ban from the World Anti-Doping Agency (WADA) in 2019 was initially for four years but was reduced to two after an appeal to the Court of Arbitration for Sport (CAS).[6] Russian and, additionally, Belarusian competitors remained under a similar sanction from 2022; however, this was due to the war in Ukraine. Whilst a high-profile doping scandal is poisonous for the public image of any SGB, the effects on competitors involved can be equally devastating. This can be emotionally so, in terms of reputation, and/or in terms of personal finance. There does not even have to be a direct connection between the competitor and the scandal for harm to result. For example, UK multiple Olympic, World and European champion long-distance runner Sir Mo Farah CBE was affected despite no allegation being levelled against him at all. Sir Mo had previously been trained by his coach, Alberto Salazar. Subsequent to this, in 2019, Salazar was banned over doping allegations. Despite there being no suggestion that Sir Mo was involved, he felt it was necessary to issue a statement publicly disassociating himself from his former coach.[7] In 2015, UK three-time London Marathon winner and world-class long-distance athlete, Paula Radcliffe MBE, had been in a similar position. This time, because a Conservative MP, protected by Parliamentary privilege, made certain comments during a House of Commons enquiry into doping. The statement was taken to imply that a UK athlete who had won the London Marathon was 'potentially' implicated in blood doping.[8] Radcliffe had to publicly state that she was not the athlete concerned, despite never being named nor there being any evidence presented that these allegations regarding any athlete were true. It is not even necessary for an athlete or player to supply a positive sample to have their reputation tarnished. The Manchester United and England soccer player Rio Ferdinand was found liable for a doping offence because he did not comply with a testing process, not because he was proven to have used a banned substance. Whether there were actually errors on the part of the testers instead was hotly disputed, however.[9] Nevertheless, a world-renowned football personality had their reputation tainted. The position is similar to that under UK drinking and driving laws. A criminal offence is committed either by a blood alcohol content shown to be over the legal limit or by refusing to submit to testing without a reasonable excuse.[10]

It is clear from the foregoing discussion that doping carries a huge moral stigma. With that in mind, the fact that there need be no guilty mind for liability to be found should be examined at its most fundamental level.

Strict liability, a necessary evil?

Strict liability allows liability to be imposed without proof of fault. This is a concept that sport has borrowed from criminal law in Anglo-American legal systems (see Figure 4.1). Many driving offences and health and safety violations (see Chapter 5) are examples. Strict liability does exist in tort and contract but to a much lesser extent. This type of liability is very rare in the Civil Codes of countries such as France and Germany, however. These systems, not based on common law traditions, reject strict liability in principle, and there are far fewer instances of liability being imposed without fault in continental legal systems than in the UK.[11] Generally, where it is absolutely necessary, such as in environmental pollution cases requiring a clean-up, an administrative penalty can be imposed without proof of fault. This does not carry the stigma of a criminal conviction but is both restorative and deterrent in nature. The Belgian *Milieuhandhavingsdecreet* environmental statute of 2008[12] is an example of such regulation.

Despite threats to withdraw from the European Convention on Human Rights (ECHR) from the previous Conservative administration, the UK is still a signatory. The Human Rights Act 1998 (HRA) is therefore as yet unamended or repealed. It is still important that the provisions of anti-doping regimes, like all sports governing bodies (SGB) rules, are human rights compatible. As discussed in Chapter 3, a direct human rights challenge is not possible, but despite this, there are various legal

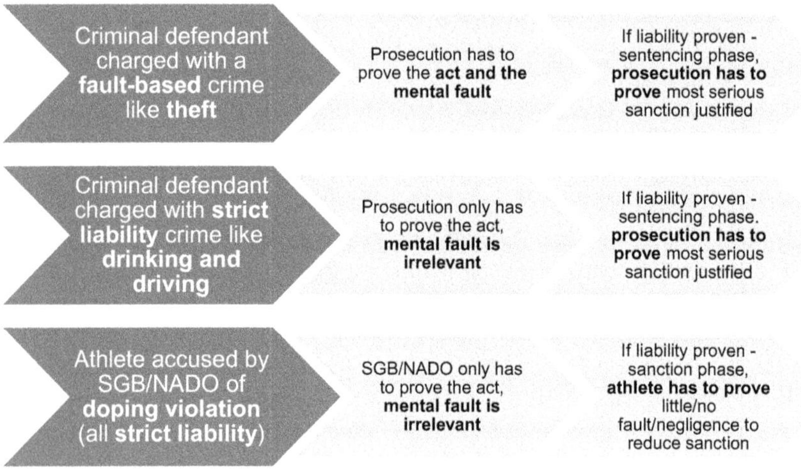

Figure 4.1 Strict and fault-based liability: a comparison of criminal proceedings and anti-doping cases.

mechanisms considered there whereby non-compliance with human rights principles can still be challenged. Nevertheless, the proponents of strict liability have a laudable aim: the preservation of a 'level playing field' for all competitors. The terms used, however, are reminiscent of previous failed attempts to defeat perceived crime waves in wider society. Phrases like 'zero-tolerance' and 'war on cheats' suggest that doping is an blight that can be stamped out by more and more prohibitive measures. As with crime, however, where the rewards are great enough or the alternatives unattractive, determined wrongdoers can sidestep these attempts using technology put to ill use. With street law and order, 'Zero-tolerance policing'[13] disproportionately affects citizens of colour, and the 'war on terror' has led to hundreds of thousands of deaths and suffering amongst people totally unconnected with terrorism.[14] The danger is that the innocent will similarly continue to suffer if such a combative approach is not reviewed in anti-doping. It is clear that the 'unwary' competitor can be caught up in a doping case just as a serial cheat can. Sometimes contamination can happen because of poor procedures during food preparation at the factory, as the late Queen Elizabeth II found in relation to a racehorse she owned.[15] The Queen was not implicated, but this does show that even the most sophisticated sporting procedures, such as those at Her Majesty's stables, cannot always prevent an innocent positive sample. The sanction might vary for positive findings where no intent is found, but the moral stain is little different for the majority of competitors.[16] It is hard to think of something more unfair than a sanction for behaviours that were entirely accidental or the result of third-party acts or omissions.

Strict liability is defended by sportsmen and women themselves. This is unsurprising because it is presented as without alternative by the top echelons in the world of sport. These are the people that Gramsci might have termed the 'rulers'.[17] The unflinching attitude of sport's ruling class is exemplified by former British Olympian Sebastien Coe, now a Life Peer. Lord Coe wrote, '[w]e cannot, without blinding reason and cause, move one millimetre from strict liability – if we do, the battle to save sport is lost'.[18] This statement does not stand up to scrutiny, however, because by this logic, the battle to eradicate street drugs from our towns and cities is already doomed. This is because the Misuse of Drugs Act 1971 is not based on strict liability, yet offenders are routinely successfully prosecuted under it. In fact, strict liability in street drug cases had already been ruled in case law as entirely inappropriate before the Act was passed.[19] The legality of strict liability in sports cases, essentially private arbitrations, has rarely been tested in the national courts but was reviewed in *Gasser v. Stinson* (1988) QBD, (unreported). In the judgement, it was considered that the result of making doping cases fault-based would be a negative one. Specifically, 'the floodgates would be opened and the IAAF's attempts to prevent drug taking by athletes would be rendered futile'.[20] This narrow view simply reflects the paradigm embraced by SGBs. That in itself is unsurprising as the courts have long held a view, considered in Chapter 3, that those running sport know best. Further, that their rules should not be questioned except where there is the most egregious injustice. Indeed, it would be difficult for anyone involved in sport to question the notion of strict liability in doping cases because of the dominance of WADA. This organisation holds that 'the code as a whole, strikes an appropriate balance between the needs of anti-doping and the fair treatment of athletes'.[21] For a participant to publicly diverge from that view would mean that much of elite sport would be closed to them. Furthermore, if an SGB broke ties with WADA, it would not be allowed in the Olympics. WADA is another example of a 'quasi-state' in this regard,[22] with enormous power to determine and delimit the conversation on doping. It is also for this reason that it is not particularly useful to seek the views of career athletes as to the merits of current anti-doping regimes for this book. To speak against the status quo in print would be career limiting at best. The influence of 'gatekeepers'[23] has long been regarded as a limiting factor for primary research with human subjects.

Anti-doping is meant to help ensure a 'level playing field' is maintained, but this in itself is a contested concept. There is commentary to the effect that it does not really exist in the first place, and further, especially at the elite level, the very best competitors sometimes get there because they are genetically irregular. This natural unfairness is tolerated if not actually celebrated. It would be very difficult indeed for a competitive swimmer to match the propulsion gained from a rival having size seventeen feet,[24] essentially natural flippers. Competitive cycling is gruelling enough, but success is bound to come easier for a person with a naturally enlarged heart and lungs.[25] According to the *British Medical Journal*,[26] the 'level playing field' is not really an achievable goal at the moment, and performance-enhancing drugs (PEDs) could actually address this. The use of PEDs is currently constructed as cheating, but it is possible to use approaches borrowed from criminology. This involves investigating rule-breaking in a dispassionate manner and looking at causes, the desirability and efficiency of the rules themselves, and setting the behaviour in a wider context. In that light, the question must be asked as to whether PEDs should be allowed in a controlled manner. This would allow, say, a cyclist with typical physiology to compete fairly against a five-time Tour de France winner with a lung capacity of eight litres when six litres is the norm.[27] The use of PEDs in a monitored way could actually *level* the playing field for those not advantaged by the genetic lottery.

Furthermore, sometimes it is difficult to see the logic employed in banning certain substances. For example, an athlete will benefit from an increase in oxygen-carrying red blood cells. This effect can be achieved either by consistently training at higher altitudes, sleeping in a barometric tent or by taking the drug *Erythropoietin* (EPO). The former two solutions are considered fair and allowed in sport, whereas the drug is not. There may also be different schools of scientific thought about certain PEDs. As an example, in show jumping, Olympic rider Christian Ahlmann competed at the 2008 Games. He was among a number of riders who were penalised for applying a proprietary liniment to their horses, which contained *Capsaicin*, a plant extract. Ultimately, the case went to the Court of Arbitration for Sport (CAS), which had little choice but to apply the rules[28] as they stood. CAS were, however, mindful of the conflicting veterinary opinions about the effects of *Capsaicin*. CAS specifically commented that the *Fédération Equestre Internationale* (FEI) should revisit its list of banned substances to ensure this ingredient really needed to be a banned substance.[29]

Strict liability is a key feature of the UK criminal justice system, together with those of countries like Canada, the United States, Australia and New Zealand. However, it is not universally accepted by academics as fair and adequately serving justice.[30] Further, in Canada at least, the concept has faced the scrutiny of the courts. The Supreme Court applied the Canadian Charter of Fundamental Freedoms (1982) in the reference, *Re BC Motor Vehicle Act* [1985] 2 SCR 486. Albeit this concerned strict liability that resulted in imprisonment, it was held that in such cases, if the accused acted diligently but still broke the law, a conviction would be a breach of human rights. Undoubtedly, a prison term carries a higher moral stigma than, say, a community sentence. Paradoxically, though, one common justification for strict liability is that generally, statutes that allow no proof of fault for a conviction provide for minor offences such as speeding and ignoring traffic signs. These types of offences carry a low moral stigma, so it is argued that any injustice only has a minor effect on the defendant. This argument is predicated on an unjustified certainty as to what will or will not in perpetuity attract public opprobrium. The reality is that much will depend on the sentence, which is entirely independent of the question of liability. A few driving points and a fine will not lower the offender's standing in society for many people. Conversely, a driving ban could well damage a reputation, even if it is for successive minor transgressions under the 'totting up'[31] procedure. This is without considering the potentially crippling financial implications of suddenly not being allowed to drive. Furthermore, public attitudes change and, for example, public tolerance towards drink driving has undoubtedly plummeted as a result of successful government media campaigns.[32] This means that whilst less moral stigma might have attached to a drink driving conviction when the Road Traffic Act 1988 was passed, it is now something to hide through shame, much as a theft conviction might be.

A further argument in support of convicting people without having to prove *mens rea* or moral fault is that gaining convictions can be done more efficiently. This is tied very closely to the previous point about stigma. Convicting for very serious offences like fraud and rape could be achieved more efficiently if they were not based on fault, but no one is seriously suggesting that because of the danger of a wrongful conviction. Nevertheless, the efficiency argument is still a rather cynical approach. It suggests that the most important thing is to secure guilty verdicts, with convictions of the *right people* being secondary. Put another way, the risk of unjust convictions is an acceptable one because the larger evil is the behaviour that is being addressed by the law. This is an odd approach when it is a key maxim of criminal law that it is 'better that ten guilty persons escape than that one innocent person suffers'.[33] Given that the moral stigma attached to doping in elite sport is usually enough to make it headline news, the same principle should apply in sport. The key tribunal case on the fitness of strict liability for anti-doping is *USA Shooting & Quigley v UIT*.[34] However, CAS appears to have had scant regard for the 'one innocent person', preferring 'the promotion of the collective interest of athletes above the "just" treatment of the individual'.[35]

Making anti-doping regimes fairer – what is the alternative to strict liability?

It would be unhelpful to disparage the use of strict liability in doping cases without suggesting alternatives. First of all, it would be useful to address the received truth that PEDs should be prohibited . After all, the prohibition of alcohol in the United States did not work and was abandoned in 1933 with the ratification of the twenty-first Amendment of the Constitution. Since then, as in most Western democracies, the use of this most potent of drugs has been monitored and controlled rather than banned. The concept of an 'anything goes' sports competition may seem fanciful, but the first 'Enhanced Games' is mooted to take place sometime in 2025. There will be competitions in 'track and field, swimming, weightlifting, gymnastics, and combat sports' and there will be no limits on the ingestion of PEDs.[36] There are questions as to whether the legal and logistical barriers can be overcome, but the event's promoter, Australian millionaire Aron D'Souza, is unrepentant and determined.[37] The question of the extreme risk posed to athletes' health by such an approach will be discussed later, however.

In the fight against street drugs, there has been a consistent drift in some major Western democracies towards a 'public health' rather than a prohibition-based approach. This means treating drug takers as those with health and social problems rather than as criminals, much the same as those suffering from addiction to one of the most dangerous yet legal drugs, alcohol.[38] The emphasis is therefore on dissuading the use of drugs whilst aiming to minimise the ill effects of them by providing information, safe spaces and equipment to take these substances. This may well be coupled with vigorously targeting legal action at the suppliers instead. There is some evidence that this is more effective and less resource-intensive than only using the full force of the criminal law. Taking a public health approach presents political difficulties, however. This is because of a likely perception that a particular political party is 'soft' on drugs. By way of example, there was a well-publicised disagreement between the then Labour administration and Professor David Nutt, the government's own chief drug adviser.[39] In 2007, Professor Nutt published his views in an article in *The Lancet*.[40] He opined that taking some drugs, such as *methylenedioxymethamphetamine* (MDMA) or 'ecstasy', was safer than other perfectly legal recreational pursuits such as horse riding. Statistically speaking, Nutt was right; horse riding is more dangerous. However, the UK Home Office, which is responsible for drug policy, sought to distance itself from Nutt's views as they were potentially politically damaging. The Home Secretary did not seek to find scientific evidence that contradicted Professor Nutt, though. Instead, Jack Straw made rather general moral statements that framed 'drugs as menacing not just to health but also to our children, national security, and the moral fabric of society itself'.[41] This is something politicians do when presented with unpopular truths, as do senior sports officials, it would seem, when strict liability is questioned. Despite this, key figures in policing[42] have spoken in favour of the public health approach. They see this as an alternative to the 'War on Drugs' as it would break the drug dealers' business model, make drug taking less exciting because it would not be illicit and reduce accidental overdoses and infections.[43] These views won backing from at least two of the UK's elected Police and Crime Commissioners (PCCs).[44] In further support, an evidence-based international Home Office study[45] suggested that countries that do have at least some degree of drug legalisation, such as Portugal and Uruguay, were having favourable outcomes. In Scotland, serious consideration is now being given to a 'Drug Consumption Room', where a user's own drugs can be injected under medical supervision and without fear of prosecution.[46] It is hoped that this will help combat Scotland's problem with drug deaths, which is the worst in Europe. This is very much an example of an innovative public health-based intervention.

The way that prohibitionist policies regarding PEDs in sport are promoted bears a striking resemblance to the methods used to advance 'just say no' as a response to street drugs. They have in common that they rely on ideals, not pragmatism, are moralistic and partisan views are presented as unassailable truths. This is key to any population being persuaded that certain social conditions, in this case, rules and their enforcement, are inevitable.[47] Yet regarding sport, there is some commentary suggesting an end to the prohibition of PEDs in favour of a regulatory framework which prioritises harm reduction. Monitoring, rather than banning these drugs, could reduce harm, as currently they have to be taken clandestinely without adequate medical oversight. This argument is also used to advocate an end to outright prohibition of street drugs[48] on the basis that there is a direct analogy between controlling the use of PEDs and attempts to stem recreational drug use in wider society.[49]

Harm reduction does need to be a central plank of any new anti-doping policies as the lack of concern of athletes regarding their own health when taking PEDs can be quite frightening. Research indicates that over 50 per cent of elite competitors would take a PED, *even if* it would definitely result in death within five years, provided it was undetectable and success was guaranteed in the sport concerned.[50] Furthermore, moving away from the prohibition of PEDs would acknowledge the proven fact, and the public perception, that the status quo is not working. At the elite professional level, the financial rewards are such that those who dope are highly motivated and innovative.

Attempts to catch such people out with random drug testing, even with biological passports and out-of-competition (see later) dope tests, 'is a costly and ultimately futile pursuit'.[51] It is a common perception that only the 'unlucky or pharmaceutically unsophisticated' get caught, despite an estimated £300 million being spent globally on detecting and punishing transgressors.[52] Committing these enormous resources has not appreciably limited the use of PEDs, nor addressed negative public perceptions of how 'clean' sport is. There are therefore at least the foundations for a serious debate about prohibition versus public health-style regulation. An overt *volte-face* away from prohibition is unlikely, though, not least because those who run sport are as unwilling to be seen to be 'soft' on PEDs. This is just as politicians fear being perceived as the same regarding street drugs.

An alternative solution to the unfairness of strict liability in sports doping cases, which prima facie seems obvious, is to introduce fault-based liability. A key reason why this has not been attempted is similar to one advanced to justify retaining strict liability in crime. The prosecuting authority in each case is operating with limited budgets and resources, severely so in the case of some SGBs. It is argued, therefore, that these limitations preclude fighting on the issue of fault at the liability stage in a doping case. The irony is that with the advent of 'presumed fault' (discussed next), the athlete now has a reverse burden of proof. The accused, not the anti-doping body, must advance and prove arguments that they acted without intent or even negligence in ingesting the banned substances (see Figure 4.1). An example of such a lack of moral fault can be found in CAS 2002/A/376 *Baxter v IOC*, where Baxter checked the ingredients of his medicine allowed under a Therapeutic Use Exemption (TUE) but did not realise the recipes differed by country. In the United States where he was competing, the drug did include a prohibited substance that was not present in the version marketed in the UK. Currently, such arguments can only be used in defending against the sanction and must be countered by the SGB. This involves lawyers, the calling of expert witnesses and detailed consideration of their complex reports and scientific testimony, a costly exercise.[53] It is logical, therefore, that the same costs and time would be expended on the same evidence if it were able to be produced in order to show the athlete or player is not guilty in the first place. It is difficult to see how requiring intent or negligence to be proven for a doping 'conviction' would be any more or less burdensome than it currently is countering the athlete's evidence on moral fault at the sanction stage.

If strict liability must be retained, then there are still ways to mitigate the unfairness of this principle. There have already been some moves in this direction by WADA, and the WADC can now best be described as based on the notion of presumed fault or the 'modified strict liability principle'. Prior to 2003, there was no formal way for the athlete to argue their sanction should be mitigated because of lack of intent or negligence. Legal opinion sought at the time made it clear that the strict liability principle did not violate international law or human rights notions. However, that was only in respect of the fact that an adverse finding led to disqualification, not with respect to the sanctions imposed. As a result of that opinion, provisions adding a reverse burden on the athlete or player to show an absence of intent or negligence at the sanction stage were added to the WADC.[54] For example, the presence of cocaine in the body of the tennis player

Richard Gasquet in 2009 led to him being found liable for a doping offence because it is a strict liability matter. Gasquet successfully argued that this was residual and the result of a kiss on the lips with a woman in a nightclub who was a user of this recreational drug. Gasquet was entitled to reduce his period of ineligibility for competition in this way.[55] Non-WADC SGBs, such as the BHA, have ultimately followed suit with similar reverse burdens. To build on these steps to make strict liability less unfair, it would be possible to add a 'due diligence' defence. In research carried out in 1996, it was found that around 50 per cent of all strict liability criminal offences enacted in England and Wales had a form of due diligence defence written or inferred in.[56] There is similar thinking in Australian law[57] and can be seen in the case of *He Kaw Teh v The Queen* (1985) 157 CLR 523. Here, the defendant was convicted of importing heroin but could show that he had no knowledge of the drug being in his possession. The particular statutory provision was worded as if it was one of strict liability, but the court held that,

> it is unlikely that the Parliament intended the consequences of committing an offence so serious should be visited on a person who had no intention to do anything wrong and no knowledge that he or she was doing so.

This mirrors Canadian jurisprudence already discussed in this chapter. *Re BC Motor Vehicle Act* [1985] 2 SCR 486 shows judicial creativity in reading in a due diligence defence where none has been provided by statute. If the will existed, it would be possible to amend the WADC and other anti-doping codes to include similar due diligence defences. It should be more widely acknowledged that the severity of the outcome for a competitor, whilst not criminal in name, has similarly devastating effects on reputation, finances and career as a criminal record. The construction of doping regulations should reflect this.[58]

The foregoing might be dismissed by some as academic wishful thinking; it is not. These ideas are the product of at least a decade of intensive research, which led to a PhD being awarded to the author and a number of peer-reviewed publications. What follows is a review of anti-doping measures as they are currently constituted; for the foreseeable future, strict liability and reverse burdens are here to stay. This will illustrate just how unfair they can be.

'We are where we are' – WADA and the WADC

Anti-doping rules and procedures have come a long way from the earliest efforts, designed to eradicate cocaine use in racehorses in the UK at the beginning of the twentieth century. The creation of the World Anti-Doping Agency, based in Montreal, Canada, was a major part of that modernisation.

Cases result from an 'adverse analytical finding' from a sample, usually of urine, obtained from the athlete. As encountered in Chapter 3, this testing is conducted randomly at venues and also out of competition. For this reason, athletes at the elite level have to keep their National Anti-Doping Organisation (NADO) informed of their intended whereabouts during a set period of time. These testing visits are unannounced for obvious reasons. The collection of a sample is an intrusive process. The athlete has to provide a sample of urine in such a way that the tester can see a continuous stream of urine from the subject. The tester will be of the same gender as the athlete or player, and privacy will be maintained; however, it does require a competitor to submit to a degree of indignity. This submission is contractual, though, as all such sports have a term in their membership documents that mandates compliance with these testing procedures. As with all contractual documents, a party is deemed to have accepted all the terms, whether or not they have read them. The disciplinary process itself is conducted on the same contractual basis. The athlete has accepted the jurisdiction of the relevant disciplinary body, which therefore sits as an arbitration panel to determine the outcome once an adverse analytical finding has been returned. As discussed previously, both WADC and non-WADC compliant sports rely on anti-doping rules that are strict liability in nature. However, the presumed fault terminology recognises that the athlete or player can present arguments on their degree of moral fault to attempt to mitigate their sanction. These outcomes range from a reprimand where little to no negligence is found to a lifetime ban in the case of the most egregious transgressions, where intent on multiple occasions is evident. Put another way, the liability phase of the case is strict liability, whereas the sanction phase is fault-based.

The law of sports arbitration has grown up in a global context. Many of its constituent parts resemble concepts from common law legal systems like those of the United Kingdom, Canada, and the United States, such as the adversarial system of trial. Other facets, for instance, the 'comfortable satisfaction' standard of proof, have much more in common with continental civil law jurisdictions like France and Germany. Arbitrations do not operate under a precedent system, so whilst leading arbitral awards can be cited in arguments before a tribunal, there is no binding effect. CAS 94/129 *USA Shooting & Quigley v UIT* is a good example. In this case, the concept of strict liability in the WADC was tested and approved. Oddly, despite the lack of a binding precedent system, citing this case would now likely defeat any argument that strict liability is unfair or contrary to justice. It should be possible to invite the panel to depart from strict liability in the interests of justice, but here too the strict liability paradigm holds sway. If liability is to be avoided, all arguments must therefore be on the validity of the testing process. Any other legal submissions would be around the degree of moral fault to influence the sanction once liability has been found.

Anti-doping regimes have three main pillars: to uphold the integrity of competition, legality and to preserve the health of the athlete (see Figure 4.2). Each of these aims will now be discussed in turn.

Integrity of competition

Deliberately ingesting a prohibited substance to obtain enhanced performance is considered a form of cheating and, therefore, not in accordance with generally accepted norms of fair play. In this way of thinking, the athlete concerned is seeking

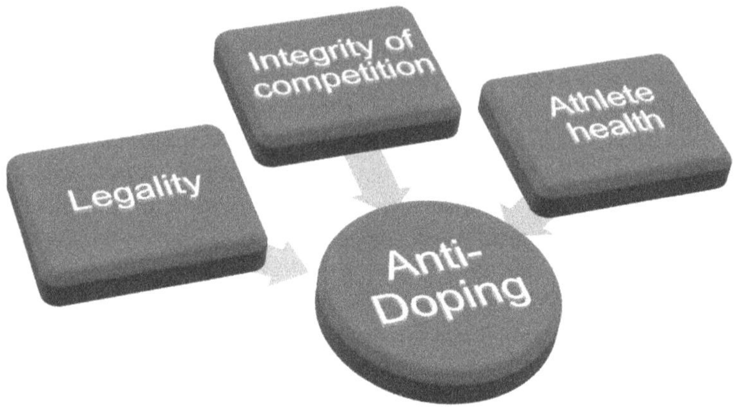

Figure 4.2 The 'Three Pillars' of anti-doping.

to obtain an illicit advantage, and for this to go unchecked would bring the integrity of the competition into question. Because the rules are of strict liability, those who are naïve or careless about what they are taking or eating are caught by this too, however unfair or unjust that might be. A clear example is that the consumption of poppy seeds could trigger a positive finding for opiates. These seeds are found in a number of popular recipes for cakes and breads that are on general sale. An athlete at the elite level must therefore take great care regarding what they eat. That includes with respect to the contents of over-the-counter medications available for coughs, colds and other everyday ailments. Anabolic steroids are in commonly use to treat a number of conditions, including joint pain and inflammatory bowel disease. These drugs are also capable of increasing stamina and endurance and are therefore one of the most infamous banned substances in sport. There are also classes of drugs that are prohibited, not because they enhance performance *per se*, but because they are so-called 'masking agents'. These drugs can make it difficult to detect the presence of the PED. Some drugs can have both functions; diuretics, for example, are useful for achieving significant weight loss quickly because they act on the kidneys, encouraging them to release water through urination. Certain sports require competitors to be at a defined weight to compete, horse racing and boxing, for example. If sufficient weight loss cannot be achieved in time for competition, a diuretic may help, so in that sense, they are PEDs. In addition, a diuretic taken in conjunction with a steroid may mask it because a doping test would reveal the diuretic but not necessarily the steroid. This class of drugs has produced a doping scandal for some notable figures.[59]

Legality

This part of the rationale, as it now stands, is concerned with drugs that would be illegal in many, if not all, jurisdictions. These are so-called 'recreational' or 'street' drugs such as heroin, MDMA or 'ecstasy', and cannabis. These are on the prohibited list despite them having no performance-enhancing effect in most sports. The reason they are banned is to support state policy with regard to illegal drugs. The question is whether this is actually within sport's remit; alternatively, whether the policing of these drugs should be left to international, state and local law enforcement agencies. This is relevant both as a matter of principle, as WADA is not a law enforcement agency, and also regarding the agency's limited resources.[60] The counterargument is that any responsible body has a civic duty to assist the police and to notify them if one of its members has been found to have committed a criminal offence. It should be noted, however, that the presence of such drugs *in the body* of a person does not provide evidence for any offence under the Misuse of Drugs Act 1971. In common with most jurisdictions, these provisions require possession or intent to supply to mount a prosecution. Consequently, the reach of NADOs exceeds that of most law enforcement agencies with respect to street drugs.

Perhaps more solid ground is provided by relying on the notion that SGBs and ISFs have a duty of care towards their younger members and followers of the sport. On these moral or safeguarding rather than legal grounds, sporting bodies should not leave illegal drug taking by elite athletes unsanctioned. This is for fear it sends the wrong message to impressionable fans and young future athletes.

Health of the athlete

SGBs and international sporting federations (ISF) certainly do have to ensure, as far as they are able, the health and well-being of their members. These responsibilities are discussed in detail in Chapter 5. This goes further than trying to prevent or reduce the dangers of addiction to drugs like opiates that are well known for such effects. It is clear from research that athletes will take risks with their health that might be unconscionable to other members of the public. The 'Death in the Locker Room' studies[61] undertaken in 1984 and repeated in 1992 made for some shocking reading. Survey responses showed that at the elite level, more than half of the athletes questioned admitted they would take an undetectable banned substance if sporting success would result, even if death within a five-year period was inevitable. Of course, submitting a survey response and actually carrying out the deed are two different things. However, even if a proportion of these respondents were earnest in their beliefs, that is reason enough to regulate in an attempt to save such competitors from themselves. It also explains why sportsmen and women are also prepared to accept debilitating side effects from PEDS short of death, in the pursuit of winning. Again, anabolic steroids are an example and can cause high blood pressure together with abnormal blood fat levels, which are both significant contributors to heart attacks and strokes. This is not to mention the daily danger posed by increased levels of aggression and other physiological changes.

In practice – SGBs, the WADC and 'In-House' Codes

Not every SGB has signed up to the WADC, preferring instead to develop their own anti-doping rules; horse racing internationally is an example. For sports that have adopted the Code, WADA is the ultimate authority in world anti-doping.[62] It is from this organisation that annually updated lists of proscribed processes and substances emanate. As we have discussed, this is even when the science behind the inclusion of a given substance is questionable. Individual sports are at liberty to adapt the Code to suit their sport where necessary, with WADA's oversight and approval. The addition of a version of the Code applicable to horses in the Olympic equestrian sports is one such example. In addition, sports are free to add, although not remove, substances should that be appropriate. Motor racing has chosen to ban alcohol, for instance. Before WADA came into being on 10 November 1999, there was a degree of inconsistency between sports regarding the rules themselves and also the sanctions imposed for effectively the same transgressions. The first time an athlete or player was caught taking a PED might result in a ban ranging from one year to four years, depending on the sport. WADA set about ensuring harmonisation across all its members. WADA derives its funding partly from governments and also from the International Olympic Committee (IOC). In turn, the IOC is funded in great part by selling the various intellectual property rights in the Olympic Games. The IOC's total comprehensive income for the year ending 2021 was nearly $889m (around £711.5m).[63] Further evidence of the total dominance of the IOC as a 'quasi-state'.

To supplement the Code, WADA must issue a 'List of Prohibited Substances and Methods' annually; these are effective from 1 January each year.[64] It is incumbent on athletes, coaches and other professionals to keep up to date with the most recent restrictions. Simply not reading an email can be disastrous if that message contains such details. In 2016, Maria Sharapova was apparently unaware that the medicinal drug she had been taking for some years had been newly added to the list because she did not check her inbox properly. There were, of course, considerably more details to the story than that.[65] Before WADA, the IOC published a similar list and compliance with that anti-doping programme was a requirement in order to be considered eligible for inclusion in the Olympics. Now, membership of WADA and the application of the Code are mandated. A number of sports have no apparent interest in being part of the Olympic movement, however, and use their own anti-doping procedures. Baseball, American football and polo are examples of these. In some cases, such as in horse racing, the anti-doping measures are slowly developing to have at least a measure of similarity with the WADC.[66]

The myth of privacy – out-of-competition testing and human rights

In the modern world, privacy has never been so difficult to achieve. Government data aside, supermarket chains know a huge amount about us from our loyalty cards, and social media platforms are adept at sniffing out our likes and dislikes, for instance. These intrusions can be avoided by not taking out a loyalty scheme and avoiding social media. The same is not true with elite sport; to compete is to agree to severely limit one's privacy or choose a different career. Testing at competitions is typically carried out on podium finishers and also randomly. The athletes selected must be accompanied by testing personnel from the end of the competition at any post-finish events such as media appearances and award ceremonies, until they can provide their samples. As already discussed in Chapter 3, this has to be done in a way which, in any other circumstances, would be considered a gross violation of privacy by a complete stranger. This is also resource-intensive and, because of its partially random nature, a gamble as to whether the 'right' athlete has been selected. From the deliberate cheat's point of view, doping at or immediately prior to an event with a view to achieving a finish in the top three all but guarantees an adverse analytical finding. The likelihood is that competitors who wish to evade the rules will use prohibited substances between competition dates, therefore. The hope is that a lasting competitive advantage will result, but the substance concerned will no longer be detectable at the venue. 'Out-of-competition testing' has therefore developed in WADA's and NADO's arsenals, designed to defeat such tactics. In order for this system to work, however, the NADO needs to know where an athlete will be so that the testers can arrive unannounced and ensure the subject has no opportunity to conceal their activities. Typically, an elite competitor would be required to submit an itinerary to cover a three-month time span. The requirement is to provide a location during a one-hour time slot, five days of the week. If the athlete or player is not at the stated location when the testing team arrives, then they run the risk of a ban based on this, rather than from any positive sample. Thus, reputations can be tarnished with a doping issue when the athlete is guilty of nothing more than being disorganised or unavoidably delayed. This was the fate of US track athlete, Brianna Rollins, in 2017[67] and an outcome narrowly avoided by cyclist Lizzie Armitstead not long before the 2016 Olympics.[68] Much will depend on the degree to which the NADO alleges the sportsperson was negligent regarding a missed visit; however, these rules have not been without challenge. In Chapter 3, the difficulty of bringing a human rights challenge in the UK against a private body like an SGB was explored. However, moves were taken to enshrine these whereabouts requirements in French national law. As a result, one hundred claimants brought an action in the French courts alleging that the very nature of the whereabouts rules infringed their constitutional rights. The claim was made in the ECtHR by the *Fédération Nationale des associations et des syndicats Sportifs* (FNASS) and ninety-nine other bodies and individuals. These included the *Syndicat National des Joueurs de Rugby, the Union Nationale des Footballeurs Professionnels* (UNFP) and the *Association des Joueurs Professionnels de Handball* (AJPH). Their case was that the rules violated their Right to Privacy under Article 8 of the Convention, amongst other freedoms, such as travel. The ECtHR rejected their claim in 2018 and, in giving judgement, cited the overwhelming public interest in defeating doping in sport. The Court noted that there was no restriction on international travel, just a mandate to provide location information inside France.[69] Unsurprisingly, WADA welcomed the ruling, but it was notable that the Court arrived at this unanimous decision without considering any less obtrusive alternatives at all.

Sample analysis and TUEs

The scientific process used to obtain the adverse analytical finding is sometimes challenged by competitors, and with good cause. Examples include former Liverpool FC player Mamadou Sakho and Chinese swimmer Sun Yang.[70] If there are doubts about the validity of the testing process, chain of custody or laboratory science, then that can completely undermine the case brought against the athlete, as well it should (see Figure 4.3). In criminal law, no one should be convicted of drink driving based on the readings from a faulty

breathalyser after all. Likewise, no athlete should lose their livelihood and reputation based on mistakes made in a laboratory. Most famously, British athlete Diane Modahl successfully challenged her doping finding in court on these very grounds. In *Modahl v British Athletic Federation Ltd* (1997) CA (Unreported), Modahl argued that her urine sample was left unrefrigerated in the Portuguese laboratory charged with analysing it. Therefore, any positive finding was due to chemical reactions facilitated by the heat. These procedural failings are rare though, and WADA has strict protocols to try to avoid allegations of this kind. Once the urine has been provided under supervision, it is then split into an 'A' and a 'B' sample and sealed within direct sight of the donor. These two bottles are then subject to a 'chain of custody' process whereby careful written records are kept of who has possession and where and when the sample is being transported, stored or worked on and so on. The A sample is tested in a WADA-approved laboratory, but the B sample is refrigerated to be tested later if required. This is usually because the athlete requests it or there is some doubt about the process applied to sample A. The results of the test would then be relayed to the NADO concerned; in the case of the UK, United Kingdom Anti-Doping (UKAD). The SGB of the athlete or player then has the results passed to them. In the event of an adverse analytical finding, this will result in (usually) a provisional suspension, followed by an arbitration hearing, at which the competitor is invited to attend. They have the choice whether to be legally represented or not, but any associated costs would be their responsibility. This is unfair because, given the highly technical nature of the evidence itself and the legal arguments to be deployed, it would be foolhardy indeed to choose to defend oneself. Not all athletes or players are particularly wealthy, though, so even to question the validity of a test requires a significant financial commitment by the accused, an impossible burden for some.

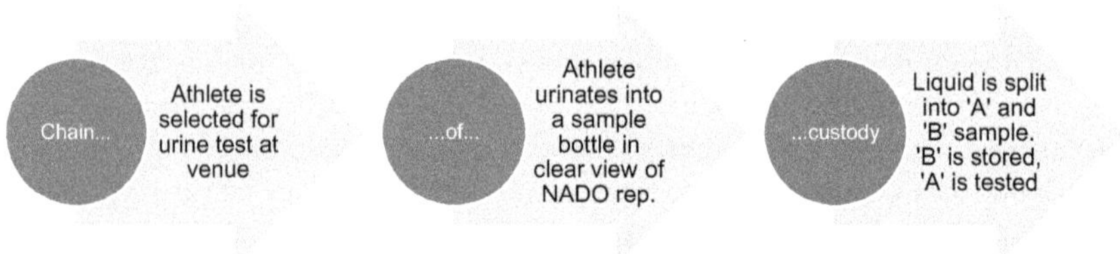

Figure 4.3 NADO testing process and chain of custody.

A provisional suspension is not automatic because the ultimate outcome may be that the competitor successfully defends the case or is given a sanction short of a ban. In such cases, the ineligibility to compete during the suspension would be harsher than the arbitral award made. This is rather like a prisoner who is remanded into custody to await trial but is ultimately found not guilty. Such circumstances do occur in sport but are not in accordance with general notions of justice. SGBs will of course argue that they have a responsibility to the other competitors at the event in question, as well as to maintain the integrity of the sport generally, and they make their decision based on the facts of each case.

The substance discovered and recorded in an adverse analytical finding may be one for which the competitor has an exemption. Therapeutic Use Exemptions (TUEs) must be applied for in advance of any test and are subject to strict conditions. Athletes and players apply to their respective NADOs rather than to WADA, but would only need to do so if their medication contains substances on the prohibited list. Not every athlete can apply for a TUE; the WADC International Standard for TUEs (ISTUE) limits potential applicants to:

> Any Person who competes in sport at the international level (as defined by each International Federation) or the national level (as defined by each National Anti-Doping Organization).[71]

It goes on to say that whilst any Anti-Doping Organisation can apply anti-doping rules to an athlete who is below these rankings, they can apply less stringent testing procedures. This might range from not testing for the full range of substances, not requiring TUEs in advance, or not testing at all. This renders applying for TUEs in advance unnecessary. In certain limited circumstances, a retroactive TUE will be permitted even for international and national level competitors. TUEs are only granted if, on the balance of probabilities, the athlete can show that:

'a) The Prohibited Substance or Prohibited Method in question is needed to treat a diagnosed medical condition supported by relevant clinical evidence.
b) The Therapeutic Use of the Prohibited Substance or Prohibited Method will not, on the balance of probabilities, produce any additional enhancement of performance beyond what might be anticipated by a return to the Athlete's normal state of health following the treatment of the medical condition.
c) The Prohibited Substance or Prohibited Method is an indicated treatment for the medical condition, and there is no reasonable permitted therapeutic alternative.
d) The necessity for the use of the prohibited substance or prohibited method is not a consequence, wholly or in part, of the prior use (without a TUE) of a substance or method which was prohibited at the time of such Use'.[72]

It is evident from the above that the application would need to be supported by the significant involvement of the competitor's attending physician. Even with scrupulous attention being paid to this process, great care is needed by the athlete, however. In

Baxter v IOC, the hapless athlete obtained a TUE for an inhaler as it was formulated in the UK. He did not realise that such inhalers manufactured by the same company in the United States have a different formula, which his TUE did not cover and was therefore the subject of a doping finding. This adds further weight to the argument that strict liability is fundamentally unfair.

Policing the past – retrospective ttesting and biological passports

Technology is advancing at a sometimes bewildering rate across all the sciences. It is therefore unsurprising that not all the substances that are performance-enhancing are yet known. New chemical formulations are created, for medicine or for nefarious purposes, and may not come to the attention of WADA straight away. For this reason, the agency has given itself jurisdiction to act retrospectively and retest samples from previous years if it deems that necessary. This is to test for substances that were either, at the time undetectable by the tests in use or were then not known to be PEDs. This process is mainly restricted to those who competed at the Olympics, but is now possible up to ten years after the Games in question.[73] With respect to London 2012, by 2019, sixty athletes, including seven gold medallists, had been found to have taken a PED using retrospective testing. This compares to only nine testing positive during the games.[74] There is a limit to the deterrent value of the prospect of being stripped of a medal nearly a decade after the event, however. The majority of the benefits from the publicity, fame and sponsorship deals (depending on the robustness of clawback clauses) have long been had.[75]

Retrospective rules are always controversial, and none more so than when enacted into domestic law. The principles of natural justice engaged are the same, however. It is not normally conscionable to expect members of society, or sports competitors for that matter, to conduct their lives based on what might or might not become prohibited in the future. There are occasions when the need for justice is overwhelming and trumps any concerns like these, though. For example, the War Crimes Act 1991 provides for the Crown to prosecute for involvement in behaviour which may well have been quite legal at the time it was committed. German law between 1933 and 1945 did not criminalise even the most heinous acts committed by the Nazis during the Holocaust. The acts concerned are so diabolical, however, that no right-thinking person would commit them even under orders. The use of PEDs in sport hardly even comes close to this extreme, though, so it is surprising that WADA has the power to punish retrospectively. It is argued that taking anything to improve performance is cheating, even if it is not explicitly banned at the time. Retrospective action merely seeks to cater for competitors who are taking advantage of the time-lag before WADA becomes aware of a new PED and the development of the tests required. However, this is a simplistic view as products can be used for thoroughly legitimate purposes for many years, only for medical or veterinary scientists to discover performance-enhancing side effects. The example of *Capsaicin*, a derivative of chilli peppers used for a long time as a legitimate muscle liniment for horses, has already been encountered in Chapter

3. At the 2008 Games, four show jumping horses tested positive.[76] CAS had no choice but to enforce the WADC as it stood but made the award recommending that the SGB concerned should revisit its regulations because the science on this substance was not settled.[77] This did not stop four medallists being branded cheats, however.

Furthermore, from a civil liberties point of view, any act or omission is lawful until there is a law against it. It is not the norm to sanction immoral choices, only illegal ones. On that basis, it is not wrong to take a drug that is not yet prohibited. The argument from those who 'rule' sport, however, is that retrospective testing is proportionate given the pre-eminence of the fight for 'Clean Sport',[78] even if that results in unfairness and injustice.

Biological passports are a more recent addition to the effort to combat doping.[79] This system is available to produce a record of biological variables in a competitor's body over a time span. These readings are recorded in the Athlete Biological Passport (ABP). This monitoring is targeted at the physiological changes in the athlete or player's body that are typically the result of taking PEDs, rather than detecting the ingested substance itself. Having identified potential target athletes, Article 2.2 of the Code empowers NADOs to investigate possible doping based on the analysis of an atypical ABP. The operating guidelines for the latest version were written 2021[80] and allow for the profiling of an individual athlete's haematological (blood) variables. This is better known as the 'Blood Module', and there is also a 'Steroidal Module' that was added in 2014. This is designed, as the name suggests, to monitor steroid concentrations in urine over time. The system operates with the Anti-Doping Administration System (ADAMS), which allows doping data to be shared across different NADOs, SGBs and WADA itself. This helps to standardise and co-ordinate the global anti-doping campaign.

The ABP system necessitates large amounts of personal data being held online about athletes. This will have been contractually agreed to by the competitors, such as through membership in individual SGBs. Nevertheless, the handling and storage of this data would have to accord with national data protection legislation. In the UK, the Data Protection Act 2018; in France, Act No. 2018-493 of 20 June 2018; and so on. Both implement the EU General Data Protection Regulation 2016 (GDPR), standardising data protection across Europe. Data protection in the United States is rather more fragmented. The federal Health Insurance Portability and Accountability Act (HIPAA) 1996 and Gramm-Leach-Bliley Act (GLBA) 1998 regarding financial institutions would be comparable in form, however. state-level legislation in places like California[81] extends protection beyond these sectors somewhat, but some states have no such laws at all. Accordingly, the ability of an athlete or player to challenge the necessity for such sensitive data to be held varies enormously by jurisdiction and can hardly be called a level playing field in itself.

Challenging an adverse analytical finding

The difficulties involved in mounting a legal challenge to the decisions of SGBs and IFs have been considered at length in Chapter 3. Many of these cases have involved attempting to defend a positive test result or mitigate the sanctions flowing from it. It would be useful, therefore, to provide a summary here. Many sports recognise CAS as the supreme appeal panel for their doping cases. CAS can hear cases where the athlete feels that the sanction is too harsh or that the correct procedures have not been followed. Cases have also been brought challenging the human rights compatibility of core parts of the system. Strict liability and the extent to which a fair trial is possible under the existing regulations have been tested, for example. In like vein, an SGB or ISF can appeal to CAS if they think that a sanction applied by a first-instance arbitration panel is too lenient. From CAS, a route of appeal exists to the Swiss Federal Tribunal (SFT)[82] at least in terms of compatibility of CAS findings with Swiss public law. This process has echoes of judicial review in the UK. There have also been limited examples of sports participants bringing their cases before the EU's European Court of Justice (ECJ) or under the Convention which established the ECtHR.[83]

Alternatively, the domestic courts can be utilised to challenge SGBs on procedural grounds. As has been shown previously, the courts are most unlikely to overturn a decision based on the substantive legal issues raised. These are considered the exclusive province of sport itself as the experts in the field. If there has been a decision that manifestly interferes with the fundamental rights of the athlete or player, then a mechanism exists for the court to find it has jurisdiction to overturn the finding. This again is based on the fact that due process has not been followed and emanates from *Bradley v Jockey Club* [2004] EWHC Civ 2164 (QB). It is not currently possible to bring a human rights challenge *per se* in the UK courts because the Human Rights Act 1998 does not apply to private organisations directly. It may be possible to incorporate the same issues in a private law claim, such as alleging a denial of the right to a fair trial as a limb of a breach of contract case, for example.

Some SGBs do not use CAS as an appeal panel, such as horse racing. Some utilise it only in rare circumstances with the agreement of both parties, such as UK Soccer's Football Association (FA). In these circumstances, the appeal will be to the judicial arm of the organisation, or an autonomous branch set up by the SGB to hear such cases. In horse racing, it is the BHA's Judicial Panel/Appeal Board. Any appeal from this body will be to the domestic courts and again be on procedural grounds only. In sum, mounting a legal challenge to an adverse analytical finding is expensive, difficult and time-consuming. Time and money are things that all but the highest-paid competitors do not have.

Future threats – cloning and gene doping

The idea of cloned athletes may seem fantastical, but the technology exists. Cloned animal athletes, horses and quite probably greyhounds, already compete.[84] Accordingly, it seems a little naïve to categorically claim that absolutely no rogue scientists have created a cloned human anywhere in the world.

A quarter of a century has already passed since 'Dolly' the Sheep was cloned and there was a stated intention by other scientists to use the same technology to create a cloned human.[85] 'Dolly' was cloned using adult sheep cells and 'transgenesis'. This involves introducing an external gene into a living animal; there have been experiments on mice using embryonic stem cells dating back as far as the 1980s. Although Dolly was relatively short-lived, she had several offspring, and the science developed is the basis for human cloning, the existence of which has never been fully disproven.[86] The barriers to widespread human cloning, in reality, are moral, not scientific, and the United States was the first to ban government funding for this type of research. The National Bioethics Advisory Commission (NBAC) was also created to consider the ethical, scientific and legal questions that human cloning poses.[87] The American Medical Association (AMA), World Medical Association (WMA) and the World Health Organisation (WHO) had already stated their opposition to human cloning. These, together with most US states, nineteen other countries and the Pope created a significant pushback against the idea, albeit not necessarily based on science or reason.[88] There is, as a result however, little appetite for a legal challenge to the moratorium.[89] Notwithstanding this, there has been interest amongst athletes and their trainers in this new technology.[90] This is because genetics are such a large part of success at the elite level, more so than commitment and quality of training.[91]

There is clearly no need yet for SGBs and IFs to urgently re-write their rulebooks to cater for the prospect of cloned *human* athletes being the norm. This is despite some high-profile sporting organisations having done exactly that in response to contested and incomplete science on a tiny number of elite transgender competitors. This is discussed further in Chapter 5. There are major league sports where a *non-human* athlete is a vital team member, however[92] and the first cloned horse was born in 2003.[93] Since then, a number of clones have been produced for competition in the equestrian Olympic sports as the *Fédération Equestre Internationale* (FEI) does not explicitly ban the use of clones.[94] The BHA does have such a ban with regard to horse racing, although this has not prevented a Chinese consortium reportedly at least planning to clone Thoroughbred horses on an industrial scale.[95] Cloned animals are not prohibited from competing in polo either.[96] This is a paradox as a tiny trace of *Capsaicin*, poppy seed or '*Bute*'[97] can have devastating consequences for the rider if found in a sample. Genetically engineering the animal from hoof to ear tip does not seem to raise any ethical, athlete welfare, integrity or fair play questions, however. Further, it may be that an era where clones are a significant part of some major horse sports may not be far away.[98] In which case, it is here that some of the ethical, moral and legal questions associated with cloning and sport more generally might fall to be addressed. There are also significant intellectual property conundrums that may well arise in using clones to produce valuable competition animals, but discussion of these is beyond the scope of this volume.[99]

SGBs and IFs may not yet be addressing the integrity issues that wholesale cloning will produce, but WADA is alive to the problem of gene doping. This technology involves the introduction of genes or at least genetically modified cells into a human body in order to enhance performance. For instance, tests for the hormone *erythropoietin*

(EPO) have existed for years. This controls the production of red blood cells and is on the Prohibited List. Injecting the *erythropoietin* gene should have the same effect, although the safety of doing this is contested science. The existing tests for the hormone may well not pick up the gene, so WADA produced its first comprehensive testing guidelines in 2021[100] based on a Polymerase Chain Reaction (PCR) test. The term will be familiar as it is the same process involved in more advanced Covid-19 testing than home Lateral Flow Tests (LFT) can provide. No athlete has yet been caught using gene doping techniques, but as long ago as 2002, WADA was making public its awareness of the threat posed by this technology.[101] WADA continues to regularly review scientific developments in an attempt to be one step ahead of competitors and support personnel tempted to utilise this controversial offshoot of gene therapy.[102]

Conclusions on fairness in anti-doping

This chapter has charted the landscape of anti-doping and highlighted how uneven, if not mountainous, its topography is. The logic behind strict liability is flawed and produces manifest injustices, and the anti-doping regimes are fragmented and very difficult to challenge despite a huge 'inequality of arms' between the 'prosecution' and defence teams. There are also paradoxes in the logic behind combatting different forms of cheating and no appetite to go back to the drawing board despite the current system both not catching cheats and unfairly sanctioning well-intentioned people. The system also involves moral choices such as targeting recreational drugs and those who took a 'legal' but enhancing PED in the past. The 'level playing field' that anti-doping seeks to protect is a myth, in addition. There are alternatives, as outlined in this book, but like with street drugs, it would be a brave sports administrator who suggested going against the hegemony to any significant degree. As with drug matters in wider society, this is, in large measure, a political question; therefore, it is left with sports governance politicians. However, a courageous approach to politics is a rare thing in all spheres.

Notes

1 Antonio Gramsci, *Selections from the Prison Notebooks*, trans. Quintin Hoare and Geoffrey Nowell-Smith (New York: International Publishers, 1971), 157.
2 See Sheryl Spithoff and Meldon Kahan, 'Cannabis and Canadian youth – Evidence, not ideology', *Canadian Family Physician*, 60, no. 9 (September 2014): 785–7.
3 Libby Brooks and Severin Carrell, 'Scotland proposes drug decriminalisation in Westminster challenge', *The Guardian*, 7 July 2023, https://www.theguardian.com/uk-news/2023/jul/07/scotland-proposes-drug-decriminalisation-in-westminster-challenge.
4 Neil Carter, 'Testing times', in *Medicine Sport and the Body: A Historical Perspective* (Oxford: Bloomsbury Academic, 2012), 105.
5 Jonathan Merritt, *Regulating Sport for the Non-Human Athlete* (Lanham: Rowman and Littlefield, 2019), 67–70.

6 'WADA Statement on Court of Arbitration decision to declare Russian Anti-Doping Agency as non-compliant', 17 December 2020, accessed 5 October 2023, https://www.wada-ama.org/en/news/wada-statement-court-arbitration-decision-declare-russian-anti-doping-agency-non-compliant.
7 'Mo Farah "Wants answers" over Alberto Salazar doping claims', *BBC*, 6 June 2015, http://www.bbc.co.uk/sport/0/athletics/33034350.
8 Owen Gibsen, 'Paula Radcliffe denies "cheating in any form" after allusions in parliament', *The Guardian*, 8 September 2015, http://www.theguardian.com/sport/2015/sep/08/paula-radcliffe-denies-cheating-parliamentary-committee.
9 Ben Rumsby, 'Rio Ferdinand's "brutal" eight-month drug ban was the fault of incompetent testers according to Alex Ferguson', *The Telegraph*, 22 October 2013, https://www.telegraph.co.uk/sport/football/teams/manchester-united/Sir_Alex_Ferguson/10397197/Rio-Ferdinands-brutal-eight-month-drug-ban-was-the-fault-of-incompetent-testers-according-to-Alex-Ferguson.html.
10 Section 7(6) Road Traffic Act 1988.
11 John Spencer and Antje Pedain, 'Approaches to strict and constructive liability in continental criminal law', in *Appraising Strict Liability*, ed. Andrew Simester (Oxford: Oxford University Press, 2005), 281.
12 Flemish Environmental Enforcement Decree 2008.
13 Especially taking into account institutional racism issues, see for instance, Avram Bornstein, 'Institutional racism, numbers Management, and zero-tolerance policing in New York City', *North American Dialogue*, 18, no. 2 (Fall 2015): 51–62.
14 See Neta C. Crawford, 'Brown University "costs of war" project – Blood and treasure: United States budgetary costs and human costs of 20 years of war in Iraq and Syria, 2003–2023', 15 March 2023, accessed 5 October 2023, https://watson.brown.edu/costsofwar/papers/2023/blood-and-treasure-united-states-budgetary-costs-and-human-costs-20-years-war-iraq-and.
15 Gordon Rayner, 'Queen's gold cup-winning racehorse *Estimate* tests positive for banned drug morphine', *Telegraph*, 22 July 2014, http://www.telegraph.co.uk/news/uknews/queen-elizabeth-II/10984322/Queens-Gold-Cup-winning-racehorse-Estimate-tests-positive-for-banned-drug-morphine.html.
16 Merritt, *Regulating Sport for the Non-Human Athlete*, 181–3.
17 Berch Berberoglu, *An Introduction to Classical and Contemporary Social Theory: A Critical Perspective* (Lanham: Rowman and Littlefield, 2005), 57.
18 Sebastien Coe, 'We cannot move from strict liability rule', *Telegraph*, 25 February 2004, http://www.telegraph.co.uk/sport/othersports/drugsinsport/2373729/We-cannot-move-from-strict-liability-rule.html. See also Jannica Houben, 'Proportionality in the WADC: Is there enough room for flexibility?', *International Sports Law Journal*, 1, no. 2 (2007): 10.
19 *Sweet v Parsley* [1970] AC 132.
20 Paul McCutcheon, 'Sports discipline, natural justice and strict liability', *Anglo-American Law Review*, 28, no. 1 (1999): 45.
21 Simon Gardiner et al., *Sports Law* (London: Routledge, 2012), 375.
22 Jules Boykoff, 'Glitterati and grit: The perils and possibilities of sports mega-event research', *Journal of Sport and Social Issues* (2024): 77, https://doi.org/10.1177/01937235241247038.
23 Mark Israel and Iain Hay, *Research Ethics for Social Scientists* (London: Sage, 2006), 70–3.

24 Jack Anderson, *Modern Sports Law* (Oxford: Hart, 2010), 163.
25 Ibid.
26 See Julian Savulescu et al., 'Should athletes be allowed to use performance enhancing drugs?' *British Medical Journal*, 347 (2013), http://www.bmj.com/content/347/bmj.f6150.
27 Anderson, *Modern Sports Law*, 151.
28 FEI anti-doping rules for humans and horses are based on the WADC and differ little from each other; essentially, horses are treated as 'non-human athletes'. See Merritt, *Regulating Sport for the Non-Human Athlete*, 25–36.
29 CAS 2008/A/1700 *Deutsche Reiterliche Vereinigung v FEI & Christian Ahlmann*.
30 Andrew Simester, 'Is strict liability always wrong?' in *Appraising Strict Liability*, ed. Andrew Simester (Oxford: Oxford University Press, 2005), 49.
31 In the UK, usually twelve points result in a driving ban, and this can be awarded for a single offence. Alternatively, four minor offences across a three-year period, each worth three points, would have the same effect under this procedure.
32 'Department of Transport Press release, November 7th, 2014, – 92% of people feel ashamed to drink and drive as 50th anniversary THINK! campaign is launched', accessed 6 October 2023, https://www.gov.uk/government/news/92-of-people-feel-ashamed-to-drink-and-drive-as-50th-anniversary-think-campaign-is-launched.
33 Attributed to Sir William Blackstone and Benjamin Franklin.
34 CAS 94/129 *USA Shooting & Quigley v UIT* [15].
35 Anderson, *Modern Sports Law*, 124.
36 John William Devine, 'The enhanced games: Letting athletes use drugs could lead to worse problems than cheating', *The Conversation*, 11 July 2023, https://theconversation.com/the-enhanced-games-letting-athletes-use-drugs-could-lead-to-worse-problems-than-cheating-209349.
37 Mike Henson, 'Enhanced games: The mind behind the "doped games"', *BBC*, 28 March 2024. https://www.bbc.co.uk/sport/68672104.
38 Tim Newburn, *Criminology* (London: Routledge, 2007), 520.
39 Mark Tran, 'Government drug adviser David Nutt sacked', *The Guardian*, 30 October 2009, http://www.theguardian.com/politics/2009/oct/30/drugs-adviser-david-nutt-sacked.
40 David Nutt et al., 'Drug harms in the UK: A multicriteria decision analysis', *The Lancet,* 376, no. 9752 (2010): 1558–65.
41 Stephen Rolles, 'An alternative to the war on drugs', *British Medical Journal,* 341 (2010): 127–8.
42 Henry McDonald, 'It's time to end the war on drugs says top UK police chief', *The Guardian*, 28 September 2013, http://www.theguardian.com/society/2013/sep/28/time-end-war-drugs-uk-police-chief.
43 Newburn, *Criminology*, 495.
44 'Chief constable: War on drugs has comprehensively failed', *Northern Echo*, 30 September 2013, http://www.thenorthernecho.co.uk/news/10706142.print/.
45 'Home Office, Drugs: International comparators', accessed 6 October 2023, https://www.gov.uk/government/uploads/system/uploads/attachment_data/file/368489/DrugsInternationalComparators.pdf.
46 'Glasgow drug consumption room could be approved in weeks', *BBC*, 12 September 2023, https://www.bbc.co.uk/news/uk-scotland-66783640.

47 Louis Wolcher, *Law's Task: The Tragic Circle of Law, Justice and Human Suffering* (Oxford: Routledge, 2008), xvi.
48 Rolles, 'An alternative to the war on drugs', 341.
49 Jack Anderson, 'Doping sport and the law: Time for a repeal of prohibition?' *International Journal of Law in Context,* 9 (2013): 9.
50 See Bob Goldman and Ronald Klatz, *Death in the Locker Room: Steroids in Sport* (South Bend: Icarus Press, 1984) and Bob Goldman and Ronald Klatz, *Death in the Locker Room 2* (Chicago: Elite Sports Medicine, 1992).
51 Anderson, 'Doping sport and the law: Time for a repeal of prohibition?' 141.
52 James Connor and Jason Mazanov, 'Would you dope? A general population test of the golden dilemma', *British Journal of Sports Medicine* 43 (2009): 871–2.
53 For an example of the complexity, see the veterinary evidence presented in CAS 2012/A/2807 *Khaled Abdullaziz Al Eid v. Fédération Equestre Internationale*/CAS 2012/A/2808 *Abdullah Waleed Sharbatly v. Fédération Equestre Internationale*, Paras 3.11-3.14. An online version is available at https://arbitrationlaw.com/sites/default/files/free_pdfs/cas_2012.a.2807_kaae_v_fei_-_cas_2012.a.2808_aws_v_fei.pdf (accessed 5 September 2024).
54 Jessica Foschi, 'A constant battle: The evolving challenges in the international fight against doping in sport', *Duke Journal of Comparative International Law*, 16, no. 2 (2006): 477.
55 Mark James, *Sports Law* (Basingstoke: Palgrave Macmillan, 2013), 52.
56 See Andrew Ashworth and Meredith Blake, 'The presumption of innocence in English criminal law', *Criminal Law Review* (1996): 306.
57 McCutcheon, 'Sports discipline, natural justice and strict liability', 53.
58 Further discussion of alternatives to strict liability in anti-doping is outside the scope of this book, but for a detailed debate on these matters, see Merritt, *Regulating Sport for the Non-Human Athlete*, 161–79.
59 'Veronica Campbell-Brown tests positive for banned diuretic', *BBC*, 15 June 2013, https://www.bbc.co.uk/sport/athletics/22919193 and 'On this day in 2003: Shane Warne handed 12-month ban after taking diuretic', 22 February 2022, https://www.independent.co.uk/sport/cricket/shane-warne-australia-the-oval-queensland-victoria-b2020183.html.
60 Ivan Waddington, Ask Vest Christiansen, John Gleaves, John Hoberman and Verner Møller, 'Recreational drug use and sport: Time for a WADA rethink?' *Performance Enhancement & Health,* 2, no. 2 (June 2013): 41–7.
61 Goldman and Klatz, *Death in the Locker Room: Steroids in Sport* and Goldman and Klatz, *Death in the Locker Room 2.*
62 'World anti-doping agency', accessed 6 October 2023, www.wada-ama.org.
63 'IOC Annual Report 2021 – Faster, higher stronger – Together', 184, accessed 6 October 2023, https://stillmed.olympics.com/media/Documents/International-Olympic-Committee/Annual-report/IOC-Annual-Report-2021.pdf?_ga=2.4683184.2092531801.1684250454-1859082748.1684250454.
64 'WADA – Prohibited list 2023', accessed 6 October 2023, https://www.wada-ama.org/en/resources/world-anti-doping-program/prohibited-list.
65 Kevin Mitchell, 'Maria Sharapova receives two-year ban for failing drug test', *The Guardian*, 8 June 2016, https://www.theguardian.com/sport/2016/jun/08/maria-sharapova-banned-two-years-failing-drugs-test-meldonium.

66 Merritt, *Regulating Sport for the Non-Human Athlete*, 52–60.
67 'Olympic gold medallist Brianna Rollins handed year ban for missing drug tests', *The Guardian*, 20 April 2017, https://www.theguardian.com/sport/2017/apr/20/brianna-rollins-olympic-100m-champion-one-year-ban.
68 Gregor Brown, 'How did Lizzie Armitstead miss three anti-doping tests? "Whereabouts" system explained', *Cycling Weekly*, 2 August 2026, https://www.cyclingweekly.com/news/racing/olympics/how-did-lizzie-armitstead-miss-three-antidoping-tests-270214.
69 *Fédération Nationale des Syndicats Sportifs (FNASS) and Others v. France* (application no. 48151/11 and 77769/13) ECHR.
70 Jack Anderson, 'Why drug cheats are still being caught seven years after the 2012 London Olympics', *The Conversation*, 5 August 2019, http://theconversation.com/why-drug-cheats-are-still-being-caught-seven-years-after-the-2012-london-olympics-121123.
71 'World anti-doping code international standard for therapeutic use exemptions 2023', 5, accessed 5 October 2023, https://www.wada-ama.org/sites/default/files/2022-09/international_standard_for_therapeutic_use_exemptions_istue_2023.pdf.
72 Ibid., para 4.2.
73 'WADA Press release January 27, 2022, – WADA publishes testing figures and calls on anti-doping organizations to take full advantage of IOC's long-term sample storage', accessed 6 October 2023, https://www.wada-ama.org/en/news/wada-publishes-testing-figures-and-calls-anti-doping-organizations-take-full-advantage-iocs.
74 Anderson, 'Why drug cheats are still being caught seven years after the 2012 London Olympics?'
75 Ibid.
76 'Ireland's Olympic boss fed up with doping', *Reuters*, 23 August 2008, https://www.reuters.com/article/us-olympics-equestrian-ireland-idUSPEK30997520080823.
77 CAS 2008/A/1700 *Deutsche Reiterliche Vereinigung v FEI & Christian Ahlmann*.
78 Niall Trainor, 'The 2009 WADA code: A more proportionate deal for athletes?' *ESLJ*, 8, no. 1 (2010): para 43–7, https://www.entsportslawjournal.com › articles › eslj.45 › galley › download.
79 'WADA – Biological passports', accessed 6 October 2023, https://www.wada-ama.org/en/athlete-biological-passport.
80 'WADA – Athlete biological passport operating guidelines, 8th Version', accessed 6 October 2023, https://www.wada-ama.org/sites/default/files/resources/files/guidelines_abp_v8_final.pdf.
81 California Consumer Privacy Act (CCPA) 2018.
82 The Swiss Supreme Court.
83 Unrelated to the European Union and therefore for UK competitors, it is unaffected by Brexit.
84 Jonathan Merritt, '"Attack of the clones": Problematising equine sports integrity regulation on the ascendancy of the genetically copied athlete', *Contemporary Issues in Law*, 14, no. 3 (2018): 191–216.
85 Lori Andrews, 'Is there a right to clone? Constitutional challenges to bans on human cloning', *Harvard Journal of Law and Technology*, 11, no. 3 (1998): 644.
86 Andrew Miah, *Genetically Modified Athletes: Biomedical Ethics, Gene Doping and Sport* (Oxford: Routledge, 2004), 3.
87 Ibid.

88 See for instance Russell Blackford, 'Human cloning and "posthuman" society', *Monash Bioethics Review*, 24, no. 1 (2005): 10–26.

89 Andrews, 'Is there a right to clone? Constitutional challenges to bans on human cloning', 676.

90 Stephen Holland, *Arguing about Bioethics* (Oxford: Routledge, 2012), 94.

91 Ross Tucker, 'What makes champions? A review of the relative contribution of genes and training to sporting success', *British Journal of Sports Medicine*, 46 (2012): 560.

92 Merritt, *Regulating Sport for the Non-Human Athlete*, 25–37.

93 'World's first cloned horse is born', *New Scientist*, 6 August 2003, https://www.newscientist.com/article/dn4026-worlds-first-cloned-horse-is-born/.

94 Pippa Cuckson, 'Clone of "best ever horse" Gem Twist is bought by Olympic show jumping owner', *Telegraph*, 7 July 2012, www.telegraph.co.uk/sport/olympics/equestrianism/9383567/Clone-of-best-ever-horse-Gem-Twist-is-bought-by-Olympic-show-jumping-owner.html.

95 Neil Connor, 'China "cloning factory" to produce cattle, racehorses and pets', *Telegraph*, 24 November 2015, http://www.telegraph.co.uk/news/worldnews/asia/china/12013158/China-cloning-factory-to-produce-cattle-racehorses-and-pets.html.

96 Gareth Davies, 'Cloning in polo has arrived and set to be talk of the town in Argentine season', *Telegraph*, 21 October 2016, http://www.telegraph.co.uk/polo/2016/10/21/cloning-in-polo-has-arrived-and-set-to-be-talk-of-the-town-in-ar/.

97 A drug commonly used with horses, it has similar effects to paracetamol in humans.

98 Andrew Read, 'Cloning for gold', *British Journal of Sports Medicine*, 31 (1997): 174.

99 Merritt, '"Attack of the clones": Problematising equine sports integrity regulation on the ascendancy of the genetically copied athlete'.

100 'WADA Laboratory Guidelines – Gene Doping Detection based on Polymerase Chain Reaction (PCR)', Version 1, January 2021, accessed 6 October 2023, https://www.wada-ama.org/sites/default/files/resources/files/wada_guidelines_for_gene_doping_pcr_test_v1_jan_2021_eng.pdf.

101 See generally, Miah, *Genetically Modified Athletes: Biomedical Ethics, Gene Doping and Sport*.

102 See Rebeca Araujo Cantelmo et al., 'Gene doping: Present and future', *European Journal of Sport Science*, 20, no. 8 (2020): 1093–101.

5

Athlete Welfare

Fair treatment – on and off the field

Caring for the welfare of those who compete is a vast subject. It encompasses not just the duties and responsibilities of those who manage sport, but also the legal routes that individuals can use to trigger both criminal sanctions against, and compensation from, those who wrong them. It is also important to understand the causes of unfair and harmful conduct; these are not limited to sport, after all. The theme of this book is how unfairness also permeates the structures and processes used in administering sport. There are plentiful examples of that in this chapter.

Welfare as fairness – a broad spectrum

Discussing athlete and player welfare requires consideration of a wide range of themes. The press regularly carries stories about discrimination in one sport or another, yet this is not a problem unique to sport but reflects flaws in society generally. Discrimination is unfair, but it is particularly difficult to unpick in the world of sport because sport is inherently discriminatory. Sport discriminates between persons of different skill levels and abilities, and in certain sports at least, between genders on the basis that males are physiologically stronger than females. Society has tolerated these discriminations when it would not in any other sphere. This is because, up to now, the question has been a rhetorical one: How could it be otherwise?[1] The debate is further complicated by the issues of transgender athletes and, separately, women athletes who naturally have a higher level of testosterone.

The welfare of athletes also requires that they can obtain redress if they unlawfully suffer harm because of the wrongs of another. In turn, that process has the effect of deterring unfair or unjust conduct, potentially making sport fairer in the future. The criminal law provides for violence, sexual offending and health and safety breaches amongst many other things. The civil law is there to provide compensation, primarily for assaults and negligence in this context. The sums paid out and attendant negative publicity also have a *de facto* deterrent effect even if that is not the primary aim. It is particularly important to gauge the effectiveness of both civil and criminal law in tackling the abuse of child and vulnerable athletes by those in positions of authority. Closely tied to this conversation is the issue of the duties that the sports governing bodies (SGB) and international sporting federations (ISF) have to safeguard the mental and physical well-being of their competitors. The further question being what liabilities may fall on whom if those duties are not met, hence the link with the discussion of civil law remedies. Athlete welfare generally has become an issue of ever greater importance with the increasing commercialisation of sport and the prominence, therefore, placed on 'medalling'. Enormous strains are put on the bodies and minds of athletes and players in this context, and there is a balance to be struck.

It would be less than useful to consider the foregoing issues in sport alone; there are strong undercurrents, particularly in western society, that bear heavily on what goes on in sport. In terms of discrimination, the most controversial men's soccer World Cup in recent memory took place in 2022. Concerns ranged from alleged corruption in how the country of Qatar was awarded the competition in the first place to allegations about the treatment of migrant workers used to build the required infrastructure. Very prominent, though, was the issue of discrimination in the country, both towards LGBTQ+ citizens and women.[2] This is addressed again in Chapter 9. Qatar is a Muslim country, and the legal rights of women and LGBTQ+ people are derived from majority (although not universal) interpretations of the Qur'an and related holy texts. Other Abrahamic religions are also still a significant influence on the legal systems of many countries. Much law in Israel can be traced back to verses in the Torah, and Christian fundamentalist ideology seems to be holding increasing sway over legal developments in the United States. In 2022, the religious right undoubtedly influenced the US Supreme Court to overturn[3] the countrywide legalisation of abortion that was introduced by *Roe v Wade* 410 US 113 (1973). It is now up to individual states to tighten legislation on abortion and a number did so radically as soon as *Roe v Wade* was overruled. There is concern from some commentators that issues such as gay marriage and perhaps even the legalisation of homosexual acts may be challenged in the same way, driven by the same reactionary forces.[4] The overturning of *Roe v Wade* is described by the political left as part of a wider attack on hard-won women's rights. There are even fringe voices calling for the removal of a woman's right to vote.[5] The fact that gender discrimination in sport is reflective of wider societal attitudes came to the fore in the scandal that unfolded following Spain's victory over England in the final in 2023. The Spanish soccer executive Luis Rubiales ultimately resigned over a non-consensual kiss he gave Jenny Hermoso of the national team on the podium. Rubiales was also the subject of a criminal complaint. Many female, and some male, soccer players came out in support of Hermoso. They claimed that the matter was representative of wider patriarchal and even misogynistic attitudes in Spanish soccer. Moreover, much was made of the sexism that still pervades society and which gave rise to this sort of behaviour. For instance, a senior female Spanish politician was quoted as saying, 'The feminist country is advancing faster and faster . . . The transformation and improvement of our lives is inevitable. We are with you, Jenni, and with all women'.[6] This affair followed a United Nations (UN) report published earlier in the year, which revealed nine out of ten men and women still hold gender-biased attitudes worldwide.[7] Against that global background, it is unsurprising that sport is not isolated from unfair attitudes towards women.

Conversely, some societal attitudes to the treatment of athletes appear to have taken a more progressive tack. From many quarters, although not all, there was considerable sympathy for tennis players such as Naomi Osaka, amongst others,[8] and Olympic gymnast Simone Biles, who withdrew from the Tokyo Games for the sake of her mental health.[9] Concerns about the levels of injuries in professional rugby are routinely voiced now, and a group legal action has been commenced regarding concussion in the game.[10] Further, the injuries that can be caused by heading the ball in soccer have led the Scottish Football Association (SFA) to introduce some of the most stringent controls on heading anywhere. Players under twelve have been banned from the practice altogether, and there are now restrictions on heading in adult training sessions, if not yet the game itself.[11]

These changes mirror a greater intolerance in wider society for harm. For example, domestic abuse is now taken more seriously by the criminal justice system and the physical chastisement of children has been severely restricted, if not outlawed altogether, by many jurisdictions.[12] What used to be called road traffic accidents are now referred to as 'road traffic collisions'.[13] This is an acknowledgement that there is almost always an identifiable cause and blame to attribute. This reduces the tendency to put the traffic incident down to pure accident or 'Act of God', which cannot be learned from or prevented in the future. In like vein, physical and sexual abuse or harassment of the vulnerable has never been acknowledged to the extent that it is now. Allegations and convictions against famous names from Rolf Harris to Jimmy Savile, Harvey Weinstein to Jeffrey Epstein and Ghislaine Maxwell have received much media commentary. These cases have been a product of a societal shift towards tending to believe complainants. This has encouraged more historical claims to be made. In tandem with this, the greater litigiousness of western societies generally has encouraged complainants to seek redress through the civil courts for physical and sexual abuse as well. Sport, existing as it does within the political and social framework of society, has been forced to confront its own issues of discrimination, abuse and harassment. The main legal levers for dealing with all these issues shall be discussed here.

Unlawful discrimination in sport

Sport in the UK has been increasingly in the spotlight over discrimination allegations in recent years. English Soccer's Football Association (FA) has been accused of having an overly white, predominantly male, middle-aged leadership that cannot adapt to the inclusivity agenda.[14] In a similar way, horse racing has drawn criticism for a gross under-representation of females in the jockey role and an even worse reputation in terms of racial diversity.[15] In addition, the Welsh Rugby Union had to react to a report which found sexism and misogyny in its organisation.[16] These are but three examples of issues that actually affect a range of sports. This is not a UK-specific problem of course and sport is a global phenomenon. In March 2023, Nelson Piquet, who was a Formula One Champion three times in his career, was ordered to pay the equivalent of

£780,000 in damages by a Brazilian court. This was because of racist and homophobic comments he publicly made about seven-time champion, Sir Lewis Hamilton. The judge was quoted as saying the award was made so 'society can be free' of prejudice, acknowledging the interplay between sport and the wider world. Piquet asserts his words were mistranslated however.[17]

One problem is that, as well as mental abilities like stamina and tactical thinking, sport relies on physical attributes to a very great degree. Traditionally, men have justified a separation of men's and women's competitions in sports like tennis and soccer based on physiological differences.[18] This argument is easier to justify in sports where brawn is a major factor, like rugby, but would be unsustainable and unfair where skill and judgement are paramount, like show jumping and darts. In sports where skill and strength are more evenly weighted, like soccer and horse racing, the point is still hotly contested, however. A further issue is that sport is inherently discriminatory; the very process of selection, as well as segregation, discriminates on ability. There are of course divisions between para and able-bodied sports too.[19]

Into this controversial area has recently arrived the debate around transgender athletes. In society as a whole, the religious right, such as its formulation in the United States, is least accepting of the notion that one can choose one's own gender. As the Qatar World Cup 2022 has raised, many Muslim countries are unwilling to depart from scripture in this regard too. Even without religion as a consideration, though, some of the most visceral opposition to transgender athletes has come from women's sport. The position being that a person born as a biological male, who transitions to female, may still possess enough male physiology and testosterone to make it unfair for them to compete against athletes born as females. In 2022, swimming's world body, FINA, effectively banned transgender athletes,[20] this only a little after Tokyo 2020 (2021) was the first Games in which a transgender athlete, a New Zealand weightlifter, competed. By March 2023, World Athletics had followed World Rugby in banning transgender women who had gone through male puberty from competing at the elite level. This was pending a review by a working group which will include such athletes.[21] Former prime minister Sunak's government was considering a change to the Equality Act 2010 to define sex as biological, although the incoming Labour administration has shelved this idea. This was ostensibly because the UK's Equality and Human Rights Commission (EHRC) recommended the clarification to make it easier for SGBs to exclude transgender athletes from women-only sport. That criterion was amongst others, like preserving women-only spaces such as toilets. Set against this, the EHRC has also said that such an amendment would possibly make it more difficult to protect the vulnerable in other areas of discrimination.[22] The matter was 'clarified' in April of 2025 in *For Women Scotland Ltd v The Scottish Ministers* [2025] UKSC 16. The Supreme Court was asked to rule on the definition of 'woman' considering the provisions of the Equality Act 2010 and the Gender Recognition Act 2004. In summary, the latter provides for a certificate which recognises the sex the person has transitioned to 'for all purposes' unless a statute provides otherwise. The 2010 Act was held to be read as referring to 'woman' as 'biological woman', which effectively means that the certificate does not allow a trans woman to be treated as a woman purely on the basis of that certificate. Consequently, trans women should not use women's toilets, pending NHS policy changes; they probably cannot be treated on female hospital wards either. Crucially for this book, they also cannot compete in UK women's sports. Amnesty International has called the decision 'disappointing . . . [and with] potentially concerning consequences for trans people'.[23] However, it should be noted that the court emphasised trans people are fully protected in a category of their own in the Equality Act 2010 and that this case was not a victory for any group in society. It is baffling, though, how this ruling can be said to bring clarity. If fully enforced, a person presenting as a man, who looks male and has lived as a man for many years, will have to be treated in a female ward because they are a 'biological woman'. It is difficult to see how that will not cause distress to that person and the other patients and families on the ward. They must also always use female restrooms, and that must cause concerns to the cis women already in there. Further, it is open to any man to go into a female public lavatory for the purpose of offending, declaring that they are a biological woman. The question arises as to whether the police would be called to check this matter on every occasion or only when it is too late and a sexual offence has been committed. The first sport to implement the judgement was the Ultimate Pool Group (UPG), the professional body for 8-ball pool, so that only 'biologically born' women can compete in women's events.[24] They do have an open category for trans competitors, but it does beg the question as to why pool is gender-segregated at all. The game is not predicated on physiological strength, but the SGB maintains that based on scientific evidence, men have an advantage over women when playing the game. These are undoubtedly the opening salvos in a long-running battle, and to indicate that sporting attitudes are not yet settled on this, Paralympic rules do not ban transgender athletes.[25] Fairness and equity once again not extending to the running of all sport.

A final layer of complexity is the issue of biological females who have abnormally high testosterone levels, such as the athlete, Caster Semenya. This 'Differences in Sex Development' (DSD) athlete has lost her legal fight to compete in women's sport without medication.[26] This is unfair as it is at odds with logic; a swimmer with abnormally large feet or a cyclist with an unusually enlarged heart and lungs[27] would not be required to have surgery to reduce the size of those. Their genetic aberration is deemed a stroke of luck, and they are allowed to compete. Unsurprisingly, this CAS ruling has all but decimated Semenya's career.

Given these issues, it is important to know what UK law does and does not seek to regulate with regard to sport. One of the most important pieces of legislation for this discussion is the Equality Act 2010. This statute is designed to provide recourse across a number of sectors where discrimination may occur. Many, but not all, such actions have been in the field of employment, and professional sport can, but does not always, fall under this heading. The Act incorporates previous legislation such as the Equal Pay Act 1970, the Sex Discrimination Act 1975 and the Race Relations Act 1976 into one statute. Further, it enshrines a number of characteristics on the basis of which unfavourable or favourable treatment cannot be lawful. The better policy is prevention, and therefore a number of organisations[28] provide guidance, advice and conciliation services in an effort to prevent discrimination. Alternatively, at least prevent disputes from becoming adversarial if possible.

Discrimination as a legal concept

Discrimination is mostly legislated against within civil law, however, certain criminal acts can be deemed more serious if the motive is discrimination. These are often referred to as 'hate crimes'. Initially, the police documented and categorised these crimes according to their own perception of whether discrimination was a factor. More recently, however, the authorities have moved to allow the victim to categorise the matter as fuelled by bigotry in some form or another.

'Hate Crimes'

A good example of a racially aggravated offence is the charge that the then captain of Chelsea FC soccer club, John Terry, faced in court in 2011. The basic offence is one of public order and could apply, with some qualifications, anywhere in a public or private space. Section 5 of the Public Order Act 1984 prohibits the use of:

> threatening or abusive words or behaviour, or disorderly behaviour, or . . . displays any writing, sign or other visible representation which is threatening or abusive, within the hearing or sight of a person likely to be caused harassment, alarm or distress.

This is considered aggravated and a hate crime by virtue of Section 31 of the Crime and Disorder Act 1998, but only applies to racial discrimination. Other legislation provides for a sentencing uplift in respect of any crime motivated by prejudice regarding religion, disability, sexual orientation or transgender identity, however.[29] The matter concerned an altercation with another player on the pitch, Anton Ferdinand. The allegation was that Terry had used a racist slur in the argument. Terry maintained that he had said the words but had merely repeated back what he thought he had been accused of saying earlier in the exchange. There was no intent to insult in what he said. Terry was acquitted based on the fact that lip-reading experts could not disprove his version of events, amongst other evidential points.[30]

Discrimination under the civil law

Discrimination can be direct, such as refusing to employ or select someone on the grounds of their skin colour, for instance. Indirect discrimination involves stipulating certain criteria for a post or position that cannot be fulfilled as easily or at all by a protected group of people. Examples include stipulating a taller height requirement for a job when mostly, only men can reach such a height.

The 2010 Act lays out the cornerstone definition of discrimination. Section 13(1) stipulates that a 'person (A) discriminates against another (B) if, because of a protected characteristic, A treats B less favourably than A treats or would treat others'. The protected characteristics list is contained in Section 4. These are: age, disability, gender reassignment, marriage and civil partnership, pregnancy and maternity, race, religion or belief, sex, and sexual orientation (see Figure 5.1).

Indirect discrimination has a separate definition in the 2010 Act, and this is defined in Section 19(1). Specifically, a 'person (A) discriminates against another (B) if A

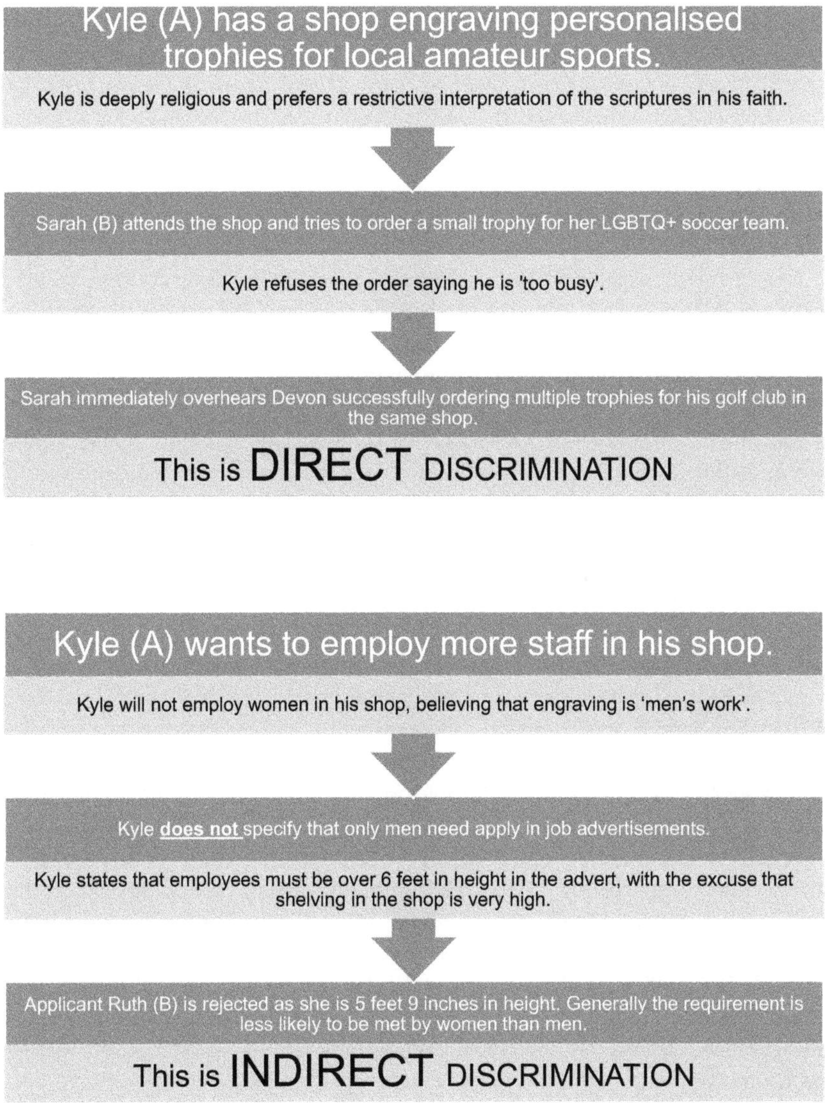

Figure 5.1 A comparison of direct and indirect discrimination under the Equality Act 2010.

applies to B a provision, criterion or practice which is discriminatory in relation to a relevant protected characteristic of B's' (see Figure 5.1).

With respect to either type of discrimination, the motive is unimportant. This means that positive discrimination is also unlawful, even where it is aimed at assisting disadvantaged people. This might happen if a well-meaning employer, noticing they do not have a very diverse workforce, states in their job advertisement that persons of an ethnic background other than 'White British' will be guaranteed an interview. In *James v Eastleigh Borough Council* [1990] IRLR 288, the defendant Council offered free swimming to 'persons of pensionable age'. At the time, the national pension age was sixty-five for men and sixty for women. Both Mr and Mrs James, each aged sixty-one, attended their local swimming baths, and Mrs James obtained free entry, but Mr James did not. There was no discriminatory motive in the Council's actions; they were simply respecting the differing pension ages in place at the time. Ultimately, the Council was found liable for direct discrimination under previous similar legislation to the Equality Act, but not before the case had gone all the way to the Supreme Court.

One of the drawbacks of the Act which can lead to unfairness is that, whilst it applies to employees and such as consumers or service users, it is not always easy to apply to sports participants. Much will turn on whether players or athletes are deemed employees in their particular sport. For instance, since *Walker v Crystal Palace* [1910] 1 KB 87, footballers are deemed to be employed directly by their club. Consequently, in 2001, in *Hussaney v Chester City Football Club and Ratcliffe* EAT 203/98,[31] racial discrimination in employment was found under the forerunning legislation to the Equality Act. This was because of a comment about the claimant by the manager. It was alleged Hussaney was called a 'Black ****' as overheard by other players. More recently, in 2016, Jonás Gutiérrez, once considered one of Newcastle United's most valuable players, sued his club under the Equality Act 2010 for disability discrimination at work. In an unreported Industrial Tribunal case, Gutiérrez was awarded a purported £2m in compensation because he was dropped from his team only two months after cancer surgery.[32] Conversely, the employment status of professional cyclists was tested in 2020. Jess Varnish, a former world silver medallist, claimed that the then technical director for British Cycling, Shane Sutton, had said to her 'go and have a baby' when she lost Sports Council funding in 2016. An enquiry ordered by British Cycling found Sutton to have used sexist language and he resigned. Varnish subsequently took a claim for sex discrimination and bullying to the Industrial Tribunal. The first point of contention was whether cyclists had an employment relationship with British Cycling. That matter had to be settled before the discrimination case could be heard. The Employment Appeal Tribunal in *Varnish v British Cycling Federation t/a British Cycling* UKEAT/0022/20/LA ruled against the claimant on the basis that the particular contractual relationship adopted in that sport did not fit the definition of employment in English law. Varnish was 'integrated' into the organisation, worked closely with her coach and wore team clothing at practice and events[33] and these are important aspects of the employment test in *Ready Mixed Concrete (South East) Ltd v Minister of Pensions and National Insurance* [1968] 2 QB 497.[34] However, other criteria from that case were not met. In like vein, Varnish did not have an employment relationship with UK Sport, the second defendant in the case. Consequently, the sex discrimination issue was never heard. Whether a participant can take advantage of employment legislation to protect themselves from discrimination is therefore a lottery based on which sporting discipline they are skilled at.

There is little doubt, however, that other activities carried out by SGBs would be covered by the Act. These include the provision of goods or services, licences, training, qualifications and membership of sports bodies, clubs and societies, and the like.

Wider anti-discriminatory legal themes

Anti-discrimination is also the subject of international law. These are heavily influential, but not all treaties have the same binding force. For instance, United Nations declarations do not have a court in which breaches could be tried. The European Convention on Human Rights (ECHR) does have a judicial body, as does the European Union (EU), however.

The United Nations

The Universal Declaration of Human Rights (UNDHR)[35] was adopted in 1948 as a response to the cataclysm that was the Second World War. It is a treaty to which all the member nations are bound. The UNDHR is a milestone document drafted by probably the most diverse range of people from vastly different legal systems across the globe. The Declaration has also been translated into over five hundred languages and is credited with having inspired over seventy other human rights treaties.[36] The breadth of coverage is also very wide. Article 2 states: 'Everyone is entitled to all the rights and freedoms set forth in this Declaration, without distinction of any kind, such as race, colour, sex, language, religion, political or other opinion, national or social origin, property, birth or other status'. The words 'such as' have been interpreted widely; for instance, the United Nations (UN) welcomed the decision of the Supreme Court of India when it overturned a 137-year ban on gay sex, the case being brought on behalf of gay men and one transgender woman.[37]

Despite its worthy aims, the UNDHR, unlike the ECHR, to be discussed later in the chapter, unfortunately lacks an enforcement mechanism. Even states that are members of the Security Council, such as Russia currently, can deviate from it without fear of any real sanction apart from condemnation from other members.[38] The Declaration may be useful and persuasive as part of an argument in a discrimination case, but that is about the extent to which the document can be used to counter discrimination in sport.

The European Union

The limitations of EU law being applied to cases in sport solely within the UK have been discussed more fully in Chapter 3. However, it is still worth recounting the position for the purposes of this chapter. In summary, the UK has left the EU and the influence of the European Court of Justice (ECJ) is significantly reduced. Specifically, only in relation to some matters within the 'Northern Ireland Protocol', some vestiges of EU law remain. Such principles originally emanating from EU law that are to stay have, in theory, all been absorbed into UK law as of 31 January 2020 when 'Brexit' officially occurred. That said, a further 'cull' of remaining EU-generated laws is mooted but has yet to be carried out. Coupled with this, it may be that UK stakeholders will still have an interest in teams and players that belong to one or more of the remaining twenty-seven member states. Finally, there is a 'rejoin' movement in its infancy but gaining ground. In any event, short of re-entry, it may well be that closer alignment with the laws of the UK's nearest large trading partner becomes inevitable. This is because, *inter alia*, exiting the bloc continues to do harm to the UK's economy[39] and trading relations with the United States have begun to sour in President Trump's second term. 'Brexit' most certainly is not 'done' despite the much-trumpeted political slogan. For these reasons, a brief summary of the EU's anti-discrimination measures will still be useful.

The foundation statute of the EU is the Treaty on the Functioning of the European Union (TFEU) or Lisbon Treaty. Human rights principles are set out in that document, but there is also the EU Charter of Fundamental Rights. This must not be confused with the ECHR, though. The treaties involved, institutions and legal framework are completely separate and being a signatory to the ECHR is unaffected by Brexit. The secondary legislation of the EU is in the form of Directives and Regulations. The former are only binding on individual citizens once they have been enacted by their member state. However, Regulations have effect on all five hundred and fifty million citizens of the EU as soon as passed. There are anti-discriminatory Directives, such as on employment and consumer law, which are central to the trading bloc's purpose. Indeed, one of the central pillars of the EU has always been 'free movement of persons' between member states, which in itself prevents discrimination on the basis of nationality.

Applying EU anti-discriminatory provisions to sport, the ECJ in Case 36/74 *Walrave and Koch v Union Cycliste Internationale* (1974) ECR 140536/74 considered Article 7 of the Lisbon Treaty's original forerunner, The Treaty of Rome 1957. This was what is now Article 18 of the TFEU. That article prohibits 'any discrimination on grounds of nationality'. The case concerned the Cycling Union's insistence that pacemakers in a cycling race, who operate on motorcycles, must be of the same nationality as the 'stayer'. This is a competitor who cycles in the immediate wake of the motorcycle. Walrave and Koch were Dutch pacemakers and they brought an action arguing that this requirement was discriminatory on the grounds of nationality and in breach of the Treaty. The ECJ agreed, further holding that the Treaty did apply to the Cycling Union because, although it was not a public body, it regulated gainful employment and the provision of services. A further case, centred around the free movement of persons, was Case 415/93 *Union Royale Belge des Societes de Football Association ASBL* v *Jean-Marc Bosman* [1995] ECR I-4921. Bosman played for RFC Liège, a Belgian club which is ultimately governed by soccer's world governing body, *Fédération Internationale de Football Association* (FIFA). Bosman was to be transferred to French club, Dunkerque, but they would not pay the transfer fee requested. Bosman was therefore forced to stay with his club even though he now faced a 70 per cent reduction in salary as he was no longer a first team player. This was despite being out of contract with Liège. This was quite within FIFA rules as they stood at the time. Bosman took his case to the ECJ and won. Firstly, the court ruled that rules restricting the employment opportunities of a player (employee) who was no longer under contract were in restraint of trade. Thus, all such players are entitled to a free transfer between clubs based within the EU.[40] Secondly, and most importantly for this chapter, it ruled that there can be no restrictions on the number of foreign players from another EU country in a team based within the EU. This further entrenches the notion that discrimination on the basis of nationality is fundamentally in opposition to the TFEU. As detailed in Chapter 3, however, for an athlete to challenge discrimination under EU law, as with any dispute, the matter has to be under EU jurisdiction. The cause of action must be to do with how the sport operates as a business and not how the game is played. This route of challenge is not guaranteed to be open to all sports participants in all circumstances, therefore.

European Convention On Human Rights (ECHR)

The ECHR, or Convention for the Protection of Human Rights and Fundamental Freedoms, to use its full title, has no connection at all with the EU. This treaty was written in response to the flagrant abuse of human rights by the Axis powers, particularly Germany, during the Second World War. It was written in 1948, adopted in 1950 and has a court as a venue for disputes to be heard under the treaty. This is the European Court of Human Rights (ECtHR), based in Strasbourg, France. Ironically, despite the document being influenced in great part by British lawyers, it was not until 1998 that the terms of this treaty were passed into UK law with the Human Rights Act 1998 (HRA). This came into force in 2000, some fifty-two years after the ECHR was drafted. Even then, the Act has no special protection from repeal or amendment. In the UK's 'unwritten' constitution, Parliament has the power to 'make or unmake any law whatsoever'. This is in stark contrast to the US Bill of Rights, which is considered inviolate and requires a special majority to amend. Any domestic legislation may be struck down by the US Supreme Court if it conflicts with the Bill of Rights. The UK Supreme Court has no such power. In recent years, the previous Conservative administration made repeated threats to repeal the HRA and leave the ECHR, especially as both are regularly used in the courts to thwart the deportation of refugees.[41] Dealing with the numbers of asylum seekers and illegal immigration is a thorny problem for most of Europe, but mass deportation *in order for asylum claims to be processed overseas* was never in accordance with the ECHR.

The HRA articles replicate most of those in the ECHR; Article 6 is still the Right to a Fair Trial and Article 8 is the Right to Privacy as in the Convention and so on, the wording is unchanged. The main article that renders discrimination unlawful, however, is Article 14, which states:

> The enjoyment of the rights and freedoms set forth in this convention shall be secured without discrimination on any ground such as sex, race, colour, language, religion, political or other opinion, national or social origin, association with a national minority, property, birth or other status.

Now that the HRA is enacted, the Convention rights can be asserted directly in a court in the UK, most usually the High Court. Prior to 2000, however, cases of this nature had to be taken to the ECtHR in Strasbourg. That is still possible for a claimant, but the appeal routes within the UK must be exhausted first. The list of rights contained in Article 14 is not exhaustive, and such as a claim for abuse of rights based on a person's transgender status would also be possible.

In Chapter 3, it was explained how there are limits to claims that can be brought under the HRA in domestic courts. Firstly, there is no difficulty if the sports organisation accused is part of the state or an organ of the state, such as a Sports Council. As discussed in Chapter 3, however, the unfairness here is that it is not currently possible to bring a direct human rights claim against a private organisation, which the courts currently deem an SGB to be. Consequently, a discrimination claim framed as a breach of human rights cannot be brought against UK Athletics or the Football Association, for instance. This again is in direct contrast to the US Constitution, under which a human rights claim can even be brought against a private individual. However, there are ways to incorporate human rights themes in private law claims, which Chapter 3 explores in depth. That discussion should be consulted as it is equally applicable to Article 14 claims. Secondly, where the claim is that legislation is not compatible with the Convention, here on discrimination grounds, the Court is only able to issue a 'Declaration of Incompatibility', and it is up to Parliament to decide whether to amend or repeal the statute concerned. There is no power to strike down the legislation, such as the US Supreme Court or French *Conseil Constitutionnel* have.

Lawful discrimination in sport

The title of this section may seem to be an oxymoron but, as discussed previously, sport is exempt from being bound by some of the Equality Act 2010. This is because, for instance, not segregating some sports by gender would be deemed unfair in itself, given the physiological differences between men and women on average. Where physical power is paramount, such as in weightlifting, there is logic to that. That is often not the case in sports where skill and tactics are every bit as important as physical attributes, such as in horse racing and motorsport. Section 195 of the Act renders discrimination in sport on the grounds of gender, transsexuality, nationality and age, legal in certain limited circumstances.

Segregation on the grounds of gender

Section 195(3) covers gender-affected activities; this separates out what are currently perceived to be sports where physique is the dominant factor:

> a sport, game or other activity of a competitive nature in circumstances in which the physical strength, stamina or physique of average persons of one sex would put them at a disadvantage compared to average persons of the other sex as competitors.

Section 195(1) states that '[a] person does not contravene this Act, so far as relating to sex, only by doing anything in relation to the participation of another as a competitor in a gender-affected activity'. Therefore, there is *permission* from the Act to segregate certain sports relying heavily on physical strength into men-only and women-only sections. There is no obligation to do so. It is therefore in the gift of sports administrators to decide whether to segregate their sport. Given the reactionary, traditional nature of sports governance bodies already established in this book, the view taken is rarely a progressive one. Nor is it always based on clear science, as would be just and fair. The fear that failure to segregate in such sports might prompt complaints from female competitors that they are at a physical disadvantage seems paramount instead.

It is also important to note that whether an *individual* woman would be at a disadvantage is irrelevant. The subsection refers specifically to a comparison between 'average persons' of each sex. In 1998, there was an Appeal Court case on this point, *Bennett v Football Association* (unreported), an action brought under the forerunner of s195, namely Section 44 of the Sex Discrimination Act 1975.[42] An eleven-year-old girl had been a star player for her mixed North Muskham Primary School team. She was dismayed when she was selected for the Muskham United under-twelve boys' team, but the Nottinghamshire FA and the national governing body refused to register her as a player. She was undoubtedly capable of competing on equal terms with her male counterparts, but she lost the case because the 'average' eleven-year-old girl would not be. Section 195 of the 2010 Act goes further than Section 44 did; however, S195(4) allows for the 'age and stage of development of children who are likely to be competitors' in determining whether a sport is gender-affected when children play it. At Paragraph 616 of the explanatory notes to the Act, the example is given that '[i] t would be lawful to have men and women, though not necessarily younger boys and girls, compete in separate 100 metre races'. Therefore, it is now possible to compare the average girl to the average boy in the relevant age range. If it is arguable that the 'average' physiological differences are not so marked in that bracket as they might be in adulthood, then that would pave the way for mixed teams or competitions for juniors. This is of course scant comfort to the individual female athlete or player, like in *Bennett*, who is perfectly capable of competing against males but is barred. The exemption is limited to competitors; however, it is absolutely permissible to allow a woman to umpire a men-only tennis match or a female referee in a Premiership soccer match. There are in fact over fifty female officials operating at that level in soccer.

As a final thought, it is open to litigants to argue whether a sport really does fit the Section 195(3) definition. A sport may be widely considered as relying on physical strength and the like, but that may be a social construction reliant on traditional notions. This is very likely given the aforesaid typical traditional makeup of sports' ruling councils. These might be because a view is widely held in society but with little to no evidential basis. This is especially so as sport develops, sometimes techniques in a sport evolve such that skill may defeat brute strength, the increased use of spin bowling in cricket, for instance. Interestingly, tennis is still regarded as a gender-affected sport. Famously though, as long ago as 1973, Billie Jean King challenged Bobby Riggs to a one-off inter-sex singles match and won the $100,000 prize money. The story is retold in 'Battle of the Sexes', a 2017 film starring Emma Stone and Steve Carell. Whilst this may be a case of 'the exception that proves the rule', modern moves to equalise prize money between the men's and women's games might be a step towards eventual mixed singles tennis. There are, after all precedents; this is a journey that horse racing has already made enormous progress on.

Transgender sports participants

With regard to transgender players and athletes, Section 195 again goes further than Section 44. Section 195(2) allows discrimination against such competitors, 'if it is necessary to do so to secure in relation to the activity . . . fair competition, or . . . the safety of competitors'. For the meaning of this section in practice to be anything close to robust, it will need to be fully tested in litigation, a process which has only just begun. In June 2022, the world governing body for swimming ruled that transgender women could not compete in women's swimming unless they had transitioned before experiencing male puberty. The stated reasons were again to preserve a level playing field. To successfully challenge this rule change under Section 195(3), it would be necessary to test the science behind these assertions to start with. This science would be the only way to justify any ban on the grounds of 'fair competition'. It is hoped that transgender athletes will litigate to determine if such a ban is really fair instead of simply a reaction to public opinion. It has to be said that the numbers of trans athletes are tiny and the notion that mediocre sportsmen will choose to transition, with all that involves, *solely* to win in women's sports is risible. Further, a person who needs to transition has gender dysphoria which only treatment can correct. The condition once treated may leave some competitors with a physiological advantage in women's sports. They were, however, born with the body of the wrong gender. This begs the question as to how this is any different from a participant born with an abnormally large heart and lungs or a swimmer with size 17 feet. They also have a competitive advantage through genetics, yet no one is suggesting banning them. Put another way, athletes with large lung capacity are born with that advantage; female athletes born with a male body are born with that advantage. On that construction of the argument, it can only be public disquiet about the whole notion of trans rights that means one is treated differently from the other. Fairness is the casualty again.

It is unclear what the legislators were informed by when including a provision allowing discrimination against transgender athletes on the grounds of 'safety of competitors'. Recently, though, in wider society, there have been some less than edifying exchanges about transgender people being able to use certain toilets and changing spaces.[43] Those discussions have been around places reserved for those with a particular gender assigned at birth. The issue of transgender prisoners in single-sex prisons has also been raised.[44] This discourse has been heard both in legislatures and in other places in both the United States and UK, at least. It is to be hoped that the thinking behind the wording in Section 195(c) was a little more sophisticated than those discussions. Paragraph 614 of the explanatory notes no more than repeats the wording of the section. It does, however, go on to emphasise that safety and fairness represent a closed list; there are no other lawful reasons. Again, this section refers to participants only; transgender officials could not be lawfully discriminated against under this provision.

Finally, it is worthy of note that, even though this is a complex and contested area, SGBs have the choice between restricting eligibility and widening participation. This latter approach is encouraged by the Sports Councils[45] and can be achieved by having open categories as well as segregation by gender. This solution was selected by British Cycling, after some indecision. The UK's highest profile transgender cyclist, Emily Bridges, was impacted by the debate in her sport. Bridges reacted with some vigour, saying that:

> cycling is still one of the whitest, straightest sports out there . . . there needs to be a nuanced policy discussion and continue to conduct research [but] . . . [r]esearch isn't being viewed critically, or any discussion about the relevance of the data to specific sports . . . I've given my body up to science for the last two years . . ., [but the debate is] 'inherently political . . . framed by the media who are driven through engagement by hate [and I am] terrified to exist'.[46]

These are powerful words and resonate with the content of much wider debates than those on sport. These are about the position and experience of transgender people in society generally.[47] If transgender people are not treated fairly in the wider world, that will undoubtedly affect how they are considered in sport.

Nationality, the Equality Act and sport

This and the following sub-heading consider aspects of anti-discrimination processes relevant to sport that are difficult to critique. It is obviously a feature of international sport that teams, players and athletes are selected to represent their nationality or region. It would be strange indeed if selection for the England soccer team or the Welsh rugby team could not be restricted on the grounds of nationality. The Equality Act makes provision for such discrimination in Section 196(5). Specifically, when selecting for a sport or competition, an SGB will not 'contravene this Act only because of the nationality or place of birth of another or because of the length of time the other has been resident in a particular area or place'. Section 195(6) clarifies that this relates to'selecting one or more persons to represent a country, place or area or a related association'. Again, para. 616 of the explanatory notes gives an example, 'It would be lawful to require participants in a county tennis championship to have been born in that county or to have lived there for a minimum period prior to the event'.

Age banded activities

In 2012, Subsections (7) and (8) were added to Section 195 by statutory instrument to allow for sports to be lawfully segregated into categories such as 'junior' and 'senior' brackets. Like segregation on grounds of gender, this is limited to activities where mental acuity (rather than mental stamina) is not overwhelmingly important compared to physical attributes. Section 195(8) states that the sport must be one where competitors:

> physical or mental strength, agility, stamina, physique, mobility, maturity or manual dexterity of average persons of a particular age group would put them at a disadvantage compared to average persons of another age group.

The explanatory notes do not expand on these paragraphs, but an extreme example might be to say that rules preventing under-10s from competing in a 100-metre sprint competition with adults would not be unlawful. There might be more avenues for challenge if, for instance, a crown green bowls competition rule book prevented over 60s from competing with younger adults, however.

Practical anti-discrimination issues

Discrimination still exists in all sectors; cases are still brought in industry, government employment, financial services, the armed forces and by emergency or health workers. This is despite laws explicitly banning discrimination, with exemptions, on the basis of a wide range of criteria. In many instances, the reasons that discrimination still happens have more to do with practical rather than legal issues. It is, for instance, widely accepted that despite laws dating back to 1970 on equal pay regardless of gender, women are still, on average, paid less than men for like work. The EHRC monitors compliance with the Equality Act 2010, but in most cases, it falls to victims of unlawful acts and processes to bring a complaint. This can be hampered by, for example, not being aware of the pay scale that one's male colleagues enjoy if the pay structure is not transparent. Further, a victim may not wish to be seen as a troublemaker and thereby harm their prospects with the organisation. Fear of legal processes and their associated costs can further inhibit potential claimants. Some of these difficulties are amplified in sport, and this may contribute to discrimination in this sector continuing to make headlines.[48] It can be a difficult decision for a sports participant to fight his or her SGB on discrimination grounds. All SGBs and ISFs have internal mechanisms to allow such claims to be made.[49] However, if the athlete or player deems these to have not fully addressed the issues, they have to consider whether going to law might unofficially affect their chances of team selection. Further, many aspiring sportspeople are juggling training, work, family and not all are generously funded. In such circumstances, there may be little energy or will to take on a legal battle as well. An athlete's main focus is to train and compete in their chosen sport, and a court case is going to be an unwelcome distraction from that. This is especially true if it comes with unwanted media attention. This can result in discrimination going unchallenged, even when a good case can be made out and fairness, justice and equity are again not apparent.

Fair justice for competitors – the criminal law

It is quite possible for a sports participant, spectator or other stakeholder to commit a crime whilst in a competition. Crimes such as assaults, sex offences and frauds committed away from the sport by competitors are outside the remit of this book. In any event, these are treated no differently from crimes committed by any member of the public. This is save that media interest is likely to be piqued by the fact that a sports celebrity is involved. Any good criminal law textbook is therefore a better resource.

The study of crimes and torts that occur in competition or in connection with training and preparation largely relies on careful consideration of the appropriate level of consent to the risks inherent in the sport. For instance, a boxer consents to the risk of serious brain injury, which can sometimes can be fatal, in the pursuit of their sport. Table tennis players quite obviously do not consent to such a possibility. It is the risks that are allowed for within sporting rules and conventions for competitors, officials, and spectators that make the study of crime in sport different.

Homicide

Murder on a sports field is thankfully something that is so unlikely that it warrants very little discussion here. Suffice it to say that the age-old common law definition can be distilled to 'Unlawfully killing a human being under the King's peace,[50] with intent, death occurring within a year and a day'.[51] The intent need not be to cause death; it can be to commit grievous bodily harm (see later in the chapter), and a murder conviction will still result. Consequently, a player or athlete must have had serious harm as their aim or purpose or at least have foreseen it as virtually certain such that a jury can infer intent to risk a conviction for such a heinous crime.

Manslaughter, on the other hand, has been the subject of proceedings from acts and omissions committed on and around the sports field. Quite recently, David Duckenfield, the police superintendent in charge at a football stadium on matchday when ninety-seven fans died, was tried for gross negligence manslaughter. This was some thirty years after the event and resulted in an acquittal. The prosecution only came about after significant public pressure,[52] however. *Voluntary* manslaughter only arises as a partial defence if, and only if, there is a murder charge, so need not be discussed here. There are two variants of *involuntary* manslaughter (see Figure 5.2) and the term refers to either gross negligence manslaughter or unlawful dangerous act manslaughter, also referred to as constructive manslaughter. These are common law offences, and gross negligence manslaughter was the charge that Duckenfield faced. The principles were developed from civil law notions of negligence and operate when the level of such is too severe for a compensation claim in the civil courts to represent sufficient justice. Note, though, that it remains possible to be liable for death through negligence under civil law and for this not to trigger a criminal charge. It is the level of lack of care that brings about a Crown Court trial, not the fact of the death. *R v Adomako* [1994] 3 WLR 288 provides a very useful definition of the offence: specifically, there has been

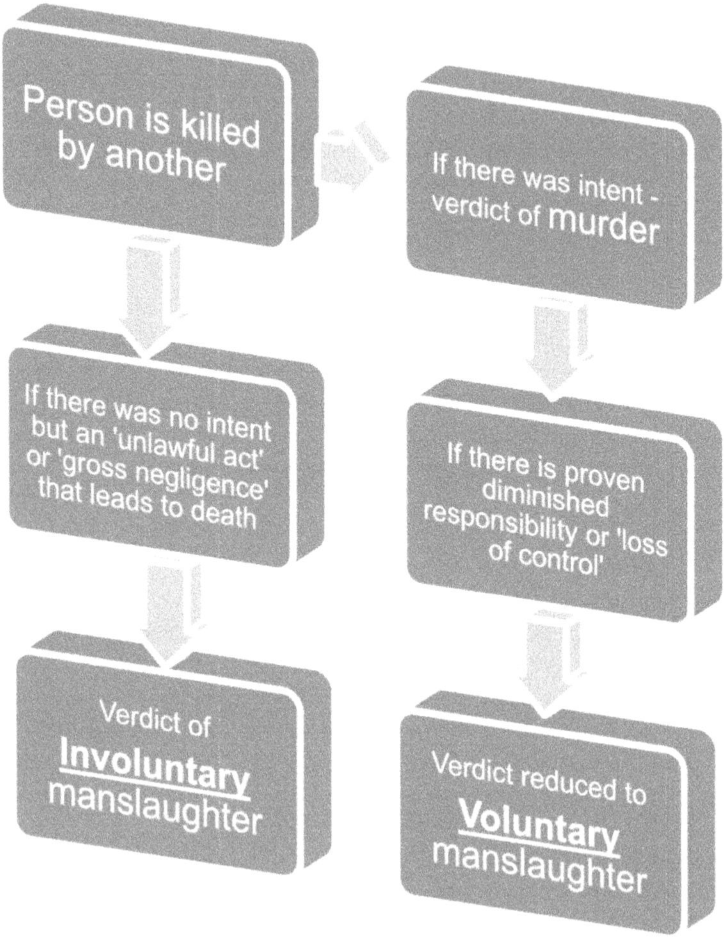

Figure 5.2 Murder, voluntary manslaughter and involuntary manslaughter compared.

a breach of a duty of care, that breach was grossly negligent, and caused death. Two things are noteworthy about this test: firstly, that the first part is simply a conflation of the principles found in the civil negligence case of *Donoghue v Stevenson* [1932] AC 562, which will be discussed again later in this chapter. The second issue is that this is a fairly circular definition in that it does not actually define what 'gross' means in the context of negligence. For assistance with understanding that term, case law must be consulted further, starting with *Adomako* itself. The process of determining if there was a duty of care and if the loss (in this case, death) is caused by the breach of duty differs little from the civil law. In terms of a 'gross' breach, however, Adomako was a qualified anaesthetist, which requires many years of training and experience to hold the post. Despite this, Adomako failed to notice a number of clear signs that his patient could not respirate properly. For instance, the patient's oxygen mask was not connected to a supply, the machine monitoring his breathing was not switched on, there were no outward signs of respiration, and, on the contrary, evidence of cyanosis was present. The lips were blue rather than a healthy pink. These are signs that might well have been evident to a first aid-trained person, so should have been obvious to a trained doctor. Adomako was convicted of gross negligence manslaughter, therefore.

An athlete or player could play dangerously enough to breach the duty of care they owed to other players to such an extent that their negligence was deemed gross. If this act or omission led to a death, then manslaughter under this head might be an appropriate charge. It is also possible for a corporation, such as an SGB or a company owning a sports venue, to commit the same crime. When a corporation is alleged to be at fault, however, the same charge is laid but under the Corporate Manslaughter and Corporate Homicide Act 2007. There were repeated difficulties in the 1980s and 1990s when it came to prosecuting manslaughter cases against corporate bodies. This is because, in common law gross negligence manslaughter, a clear chain of errors through a distinct line of command to a senior figure at the company would be necessary to secure a conviction of the corporation. For example, this proved an obstacle when a ferry company operating a ship out of Zeebrugge in Belgium was prosecuted because 193 passengers and crew drowned when the 'Herald of Free Enterprise' capsized.[53] The 'Zeebrugge Ferry Disaster' occurred on 6 March 1987 when the bow loading doors were not closed on leaving the harbour, causing tonnes of sea water to flood the vehicle deck. It was not clear, however, whether the fault lay with the crew member responsible, the design of the ship, or factors to do with scheduling unrealistically tight turnaround times. As a result, the prosecution could not proceed. The Act came about partly in response to this tragedy and could now be used to prosecute organisations rather than individuals. Sports clubs, SGBs and ISFs would be examples of such bodies should their breach of duty be adjudged 'gross' and death result. In January 2014, there was a successful prosecution of a water sports company under the Act. This was only the fifth guilty verdict since the legislation was passed. Princes Sporting Club was found guilty over the death of an eleven-year-old girl who was hit by a speedboat operated by the business in September 2010.[54]

Unlawful dangerous act, or 'constructive', is the other type of involuntary manslaughter and is proved quite differently. So-called 'one punch manslaughter' cases are prosecuted under this head. The criminal offence which leads to the death can be very minor indeed; it need not even be an assault at all. This common law offence is committed when an act, not an omission,[55] is criminal and there is a clear chain of causation to the death. A widely cited definition can be found in *DPP v Newbury and Jones* [1977] AC 500. Firstly, there must be an unlawful act; in this case, it was children causing criminal damage to a train. In others, it has been such as burglary or robbery as well as minor assault. Secondly, that act must be dangerous to a 'reasonable sober person', as was held in *R v Church* [1966] 1 QB 59. The word 'sober' can be ignored as this is really a version of the historic 'reasonable man' used in both civil and criminal law for more than 100 years to denote an objective test. Finally, the act must have caused the death in both a factual and legal sense. In *R v Bradshaw* (1878) 14 Cox

CC 83, the defendant was playing soccer. Bradshaw performed a tackle which was ill-judged when his knees impacted the abdominal area of another player. This caused injuries from which the victim later died, and Bradshaw was charged with unlawful dangerous act manslaughter. This was on the basis that if the tackle was not within the rules of the game, it would constitute a criminal assault which caused death. The rationale here is one that is also vitally important for the discussion of assaults which is to follow later. Specifically, if the injury occurs during an act which is within the rules of the game, then it can be inferred that the victim consented to the risk of it. This in turn means that the act cannot be unlawful. Accordingly, Bradshaw was acquitted of manslaughter. The Australian case of *R v Natera* [1995] QSC 1 involved a manslaughter definition which is similar to that in the UK. Natera was a teenage soccer player who struck one of the opposing team on the field so hard that a fatal brain haemorrhage occurred. The accused was acquitted, however, because not all of the elements of the charge could be proved beyond a reasonable doubt. It is clear that manslaughter in sport under this head will very likely turn on a close examination of the rules of the particular competition concerned. Participants, officials and spectators consent to a far greater level of risk at a motorsport rally than they do when a tennis match is played and so on.

Other violence in sport – criminal assaults

This chapter is about athlete welfare and clearly homicide law can do little more than provide a sense of justice for families, friends, colleagues and perhaps a degree of deterrence. Assault law can and does bring some redress for sports participants, officials and spectators, however. There are difficulties in achieving a fair result, however, that derive from the fact that the main UK statute in this area dates from 1861 and has been updated only piecemeal via case law.

There have been convictions for assaults occurring during the playing of sport that have drawn attention because of their newsworthiness. Now a TV sports commentator, Chris Kamara was prosecuted for Grievous Bodily Harm (GBH) in 1988 whilst he was a player at Swindon FC.[56] Famously, in 1995, Eric Cantona performed a flying kick on a rival fan after being sent off when he played for Manchester United FC[57] and was found guilty of common assault. In 2004, amateur soccer player Mark Barnes inflicted a serious injury to the leg of another player during a tackle for which he was sent off. He was charged with GBH contrary to Section 20 of the Offences Against the Person Act 1861 (OAPA) and convicted. On appeal in *R v Barnes* [2004] EWCA Crim 3246, he was acquitted; however, whilst the tackle breached FA rules, this did not mean that there was sufficient evidence of intent or recklessness as to serious harm as required by Section 20. More recently, a fan, Joseph Watts, was sentenced for battery against Arsenal goalkeeper, Aaron Ramsdale, by kicking him during a match in 2023.[58]

A detailed discussion of the development of the law of assaults and the major legislation that was passed some 160 years ago is outside the scope of this book, but there follows a summary of the major offences. The impact of consent when the alleged assault occurs on the field of play is of considerable importance, though, and merits careful analysis after that synopsis. There are four groupings of offences under this heading: common assault, which is common law, and the statutory offences of actual bodily harm (ABH), GBH and wounding. With the exception of ABH, these can be committed in a number of ways, however, depending on the method of infliction and the *mens rea* or guilty mind of the accused (see Figure 5.3).

Common assault requires an act, not a mere omission[59] and was the charge Cantona and Watts faced. It is the most minor of the offences discussed here. It should be noted, though, that it is also the foundation of ABH and a number of sexual offences which will be encountered later. Common assault can be committed as 'psychic' or technical assault. Here, there is no physical contact with the victim. Alternatively, it can be a battery, often referred to as 'assault by beating'. This is a common law offence, but the penalties are prescribed in Section 39 of the Criminal Justice Act 1988. There are no definitions of the offence in this statute, but despite this, a further term of 'Section 39

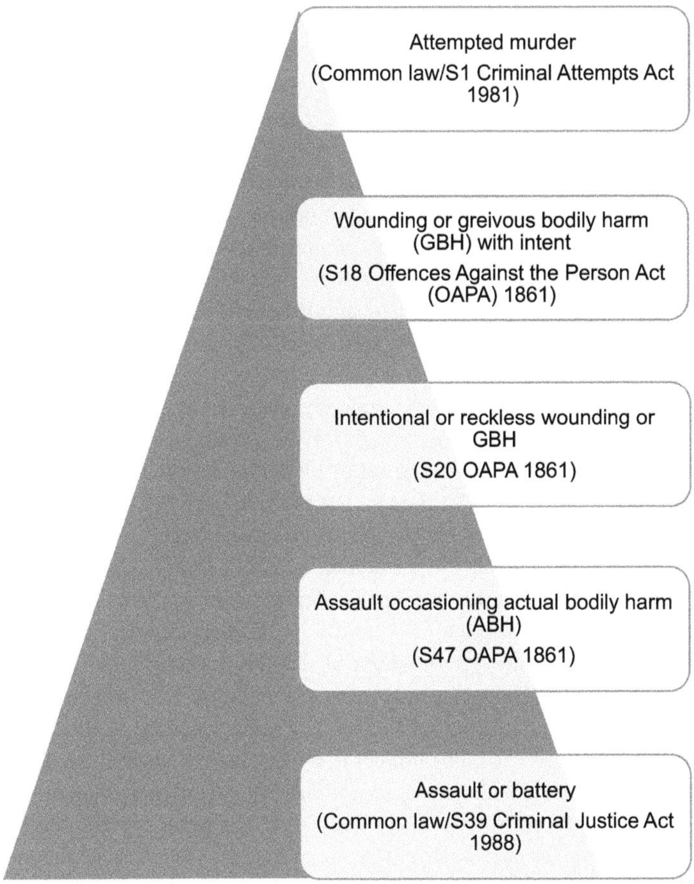

Figure 5.3 Assaults ranked from most to least serious.

assault' has developed to describe common assault. A technical assault occurs when the accused does not touch the victim but 'intentionally or recklessly causes another to apprehend immediate unlawful force'. This definition, rather like murder, comes not from a single case but is so old its origin is unclear. This is nevertheless the definition currently in use and would normally be committed by using threatening words and/or gestures. This is behaviour that might alternatively trigger Sections 4, 4A or 5 of the Public Order Act 1986,[60] causing 'alarm, harassment or distress' to the victim. It is conceivable then that players and athletes who lunge toward one another during a competition, outside the rules, could be guilty of this offence even if restrained by colleagues from actually touching each other. It should be remembered, though, that a successful prosecution requires a complainant, or at least witnesses, to co-operate with the police. Aggressive behaviour is common in certain sports, such as the 'trash talk' which often peppers boxing news conferences, and it is hard to imagine either fighter making a complaint to the police. This is despite the words and actions potentially being, in a strict sense, unlawful.

The words intention and reckless have their own specific legal meanings. Intention is best defined as a decision to bring about a prohibited consequence, sometimes referred to as a person's aim or purpose. These meanings can be distilled from the judgement in *R v Mohan* [1976] QB 1 but have since been extended to *allow a jury to infer* intent if the defendant appreciated that 'death or serious bodily harm was a virtual certainty'. This was in the case of *R v Matthews and Alleyne* [2003] EWCA Crim 192, but so far this wider definition has only been applied to murder cases. Recklessness is defined as deliberate risk taking per the case of *R v Cunningham* [1957] 2 QB 396. 'Cunningham Recklessness' requires that the defendant knew they were taking a risk irrespective of whether anyone else would have done so, and is therefore a subjective test.

The behaviour complained of, which has even been held to include silent staring in the right circumstances,[61] must be the cause of the apprehension in both a factual and legal sense. Therefore, technically, even a tense stand-off between, say, a player and an official might be enough for the offence to be made out. It would be necessary for the aggressor to intend or be deliberately reckless that the official apprehends physical violence, however. The word apprehend does not mean 'fear' in this context. The meaning here is closer to the word 'expect', and the expectation must be that the force would be immediate and not merely likely to occur later, such as in the changing rooms or car park. This was the outcome of the delightfully old case of *Tuberville v Savage* (1669) 1 Mod Rep 3 King's Bench Division. Implied threats to stab the victim were qualified by a reference to law enforcement being nearby, so the threat could not be held to be immediate.[62] The force expected can be the most minor of physical contact and has the same meaning as when the word is used in battery. The force must be unlawful; for instance, a steward having reason to eject a spectator from a stadium would not commit the offence of technical assault even as they move forward to grab the fan's arm. The force apprehended could be rendered lawful by consent during *playing* sport, however. This is true of all the assaults discussed here, so the complex issue of consent has a section of its own below.

Battery or 'assault by beating' is what many people think of when the word assault is mentioned. There are some similarities with the civil 'trespass to the person', which will be discussed later. Some very early cases are on the civil version of assault but can be used as precedents for criminal battery because they predated the creation of a distinct criminal law. For this offence, the accused must intentionally or recklessly apply unlawful force to another. Intention and recklessness have the same meaning as already discussed above. Any touching at all will suffice for a conviction. As per *R v Thomas (Emyrs)* (1985) 81 Cr App R 331, this can include clothing the victim is wearing, even if the victim is unaware of the touch. This may seem minor, but as in *Thomas*, when there is a sexual element, it is easy to see why such behaviour might be adjudged criminal. Thus, grabbing a player's shirt would be enough for the offence, as indeed would even spitting on them from *R v Misalati* [2017] EWCA 2226. This case involved only spitting *towards* the victim, but the Court of Appeal made it clear that such conduct is an assault whether the saliva makes contact or not. The force can be direct or indirect, so deliberately obstructing a horse during a race such that it swerves, collides with, and unseats another rider could be battery. This point was affirmed in *Haystead v Chief Constable of Derbyshire* [2000] 3 All E.R. 890.[63] The force must be unlawful and so would be justified if, say, a referee or umpire were trying to break up a brawl on the pitch. Like technical assault, in sport much will again turn on the issue of consent.

The remaining assaults are statutory and are contained in the wonderfully recent statute, Offences Against the Person Act 1861 (OAPA). The legislature has not seen fit to update these offences with more contemporary wording. This means that a proliferation of case law must be consulted to decipher the true meaning of the sections. Actual Bodily Harm (ABH) is defined in Section 47, which states:

> Whosoever shall be convicted upon an indictment of any assault occasioning actual bodily harm shall be liable . . . to imprisonment for not more than five years.

The assault referred to is a common assault of either the technical or battery variety, but for this offence, the assault must have occasioned (caused, both factually and legally) actual bodily harm. Per the conjoined appeals in *R v Savage; Parmenter* [1992] 1 AC 699, it was held that the *mens rea* for this offence is the same as that for common assault. For that offence, it is intention or recklessness. Only intention or recklessness as to the initial common assault need be proved, whatever further harm may have been caused. Put another way, if an athlete pushed a fellow competitor in an altercation after a race, that would be battery. If the victim fell and hit their head on a trackside obstacle as a result of the push, that could be ABH. This would be despite the fact that it did not occur to the accused that anything other than the initial pushing and shoving would happen.

It is important to understand what actual bodily harm is as a legal term, however. In other words, what the level of injury is that the common assault must cause to trigger a prosecution under this section. A useful definition is provided by *R v Miller* [1954] 2 QB 282 which is 'any hurt or injury calculated to interfere with health or comfort [of the victim]'. This need not be permanent but, as in *R v Donovan* [1934] 2 KB 498, must more than 'transient or trifling'. The Crown Prosecution Service (CPS) guidance on charging standards currently lists 'grazes, scratches, abrasions, minor bruising, swellings, reddening of the skin and superficial cuts'[64] as too trivial for an ABH indictment. This is unless there are aggravating circumstances, such as repeated instances causing extreme fear, as in *R v Langford* [2017] EWCA Crim 498. Diagnosable mental illness resulting from, usually repeated, common assaults is also added to the list per the charging standard, as was held in *R v Chan-Fook* [1993] EWCA Crim 1. Substantial damage to a person's hair can result in a conviction of ABH, as in *DPP v Smith* [2006] EWHC 94 (Admin), although it was acknowledged that this was very much on the borderline between battery and ABH. As an outline guide then, in sport, the injury would normally have to be such that some medical treatment was required, and that could include therapy for mental trauma.

Grievous Bodily Harm (GBH) is, as the name suggests, the most serious assault. It is contained in two sections of the OAPA, Section 20 and Section 18. Both sections have an alternative of wounding, but the two are quite different offences. Firstly, the Section 20 offence is defined as to:

> unlawfully and maliciously wound or inflict any grievous bodily harm upon any other person, either with or without any weapon or instrument.

This is the offence that both Chris Kamara and Mark Barnes were charged with, mentioned in the opening paragraphs of this section. Both were convicted, but Barnes was successful on appeal. He proved that he was neither reckless nor did he intend harm to the opposing player. His intention was merely to perform a tackle, which was against FA rules. This is reprehensible but not illegal. The word 'unlawfully' appears in this definition again and, whilst such as self-defence can render a serious injury lawful, it is consent that is most relevant to sport. That issue will be discussed shortly in the context of all the assaults. The meaning of maliciously was considered in *Savage*; *Parmenter*, encountered in the discussion on ABH and was again held to mean either intention or recklessness. The defendant need not have intended or been reckless as to the level of injury that happens, only to 'some harm' per *R v Mowatt* [1968] 1 QB 421. In other words, if a tennis player punches a line judge, only intending to bruise her, that is sufficient for a conviction even if the ultimate injury was in fact a fractured skull.

'Inflict' is synonymous with the term 'cause', but wound and GBH are best dealt with entirely separately. A wound has been determined to mean a cut to the skin which penetrates both the dermis and epidermis; that is to say, a full thickness cut. This was held in *Moriarty v Brookes* (1834) 172 ER 1419. Further clarification came in *JJC v Eisenhower* [1984] 3 All ER 23, in that some tissue which is at or near the outside of the body does not meet this definition. For instance, as in this case, the blood vessels in the eye. The urethra and the surface tissue inside the mouth would similarly not qualify for a charge of wounding. The term GBH was considered in *DPP v Smith* [1960] 3 W.L.R. 546 and further clarified in *R v Saunders* [1985] Crim LR 230. Taking those cases together, the injury must constitute 'serious harm'. Such harm need not be permanent or dangerous per *R v Golding* [2014] EWCA Crim 889. The CPS charging standard states that:

> [l]ife-changing injuries should be charged as GBH . . . significant or sustained medical treatment (for instance, intensive care or a blood transfusion) may indicate GBH injuries, even if a full or relatively full recovery follows.[65]

R v Burstow [1997] UKHL 34 held that serious psychiatric illness resulting from the attack would also constitute GBH.

GBH or wounding contrary to Section 18 OAPA is often referred to as 'GBH with intent' and is the most serious assault. It is defined as to:

> unlawfully and maliciously . . . wound or cause any grievous bodily harm to any person, with intent to do some grievous bodily harm . . . or with intent to resist or prevent the lawful apprehension or detainer of any person.

The words GBH and wound carry the same meaning as those in Section 20, but the *mens rea* is what makes this offence carry a discretionary life sentence, as opposed to five years for Sections 20 and 47. Only intention to commit the level of injury actually inflicted will suffice, which makes the distinction between this and attempted murder (S1 Criminal Attempts Act 1981) very fine indeed. There is an additional factor in this definition; however, if the attack happens to resist lawful detention taking place, the offence is also made out. For instance, if a sports spectator is being held by stewards pending the arrival of the police and intentionally injures one of his captors seriously, then a Section 18 charge might be appropriate. The injury does not have to be caused to a police officer. As with all the assaults discussed, consent could render the injury lawful. For example, in a boxing match, a knockout could, in almost any other circumstances, be the foundation of a Section 18 conviction.

Consent, criminal assaults and sport

There are a number of circumstances in everyday life where the consent of the recipient of the injury renders lawful what would otherwise be an assault. Dentistry and surgery could be GBH and/or wounding without the patient having consented. The law does restrict the validity of some consents, however. Sexual touching of a person under sixteen would be a battery and thus a sexual assault, irrespective of the even genuine consent of the victim. One cannot consent to death as that would be euthanasia. This is currently unlawful in the UK but not, in limited circumstances, in the Netherlands or Switzerland. For consent to be valid, the activity concerned needs to be a legitimate regulated sport. In *R v Coney* (1882) 8 QBD 534 injuries were sustained during illegal 'underground' prize fighting. Undoubtedly the participants agreed to fight; however, as it was an unregulated activity, the fight was treated as if a 'punch-up' outside a public house because the consent was not valid in law. In such circumstances, each party is deemed to have assaulted the other irrespective of their having tacitly agreed to fight. Consent can sometimes be valid even in unregulated activities, but much will depend on common practice and the 'social utility' of the pursuit. If the activity is widely considered harmful to society, in either a tangible or moral sense, then it is less likely that consent will be valid in law. Violence within consensual adult sexual relations, for example, might be considered a matter of private conscience. However, *R v Brown* [1993] UKHL 19 considered the validity of consent in sado-masochistic sexual encounters and determined that consent in such circumstances is not valid beyond a battery. This is because the court felt consent ought to be limited on the grounds of public morality and because there was no social utility in these incidents. Contrast this with what might be termed 'rough and tumble' or youngsters 'larking' around. An informal soccer kick about in a park might descend into this. In *R v Jones* [1987] Crim LR 123, the young people were throwing each other in the air and catching them as a game. Injury resulted, and whether this was a reckless assault turned on whether the injured party could consent to the risk of harm in law. The court termed this 'rough and undisciplined horseplay'. Although the social utility of this practice might be considered only a few degrees more socially useful than that in *Brown*, the court held that in these circumstances consent would be valid. In *R v Aitken* [1992] 1 WLR 1006, the Courts Marshall considered servicemen engaging in 'hazing', despite the risk of severe burns. Here again, consent was held to be valid.

In regulated sport, a great deal turns on the rules of the game. Violence can be something to be expected in the game, such as the impact of a tackle in rugby. The player being tackled, if injured, impliedly consents by playing. If the violence happens other than in accordance with the rules but within the bounds of what might be expected, then consent might still operate. For instance, scuffles in ice hockey are not allowed but remain common. In soccer, in *R v Barnes* [2004] EWCA Crim 3246, the tackle Barnes executed was bad enough for him to receive a red card and an early exit from the game. That did not amount to conduct that had not been consented to by the victim, however. In *R v Billinghurst* [1978] Crim LR 553, the conduct complained of was a punch in a rugby game. This is certainly not within the rules but at the time a common sight in rugby matches. This was adjudged to be behaviour to which there was no implied consent. The difference between the two sets of facts might at first glance be slight. However, Barnes was executing a move within the rules, a tackle, but very badly. Billinghurst was engaging in conduct not allowed for in the rules at all. In general, the more severe an application of force that is inherent in a sport, the more risk that the participants have impliedly agreed to. Consequently, if adhering to the rules, the level of injury that will *not* constitute assault will be much higher in boxing than it would be in cricket. Similarly, it will be higher in field hockey than it would be in table tennis and so on.

Assaults on vulnerable athletes, including children, and where there is a sexual motive, will be dealt with under the following section on safeguarding.

Safeguarding in sport

Safeguarding has various definitions, but they all have a common theme. For the National Health Service (NHS), the term denotes 'protecting a citizen's health, wellbeing and human rights; enabling them to live free from harm, abuse and neglect'.[66] The UK Government's Office for Standards in Education (OFSTED), in the context of vulnerable adults, defines it as 'protecting the rights of adults to live in safety, free from abuse and neglect'.[67] Sport England, one of the four sports councils of the UK, uses the designation 'the process of protecting children and adults from harm by providing a safe space in which to play sport and be active'.[68] The Sports Councils are responsible for distributing National Lottery funding to individual sports. As a condition of that funding, they require SGBs to have a clear and robust set of safeguarding policies, procedures and practices. Those developed by British Gymnastics[69] are an example, and the policy notes that there is a statutory framework for safeguarding. There is also statutory guidance for all individuals and organisations involved with children and vulnerable adults, and sport is explicitly included.[70]

In sum, safeguarding is largely about preventing harm. This includes making sure that only suitable adults are in charge of children and the vulnerable. In addition, it is emphasised that it is everyone's responsibility to intervene in and/or report instances of abuse or neglect to the appropriate authorities. This should be done by using standard procedures designed to minimise instances of wrongdoing being overlooked or ignored. Neglect can include unsafe facilities or inadequate supervision. Abuse can take the form of behaviour that might not quite tip over into the unlawful. An example might be bullying, whether face to face or online, but which is nevertheless unacceptable. Criminal violence, including verbal assaults and sexual molestation are also targets of safeguarding policies, and it is important to understand how the law deals with these behaviours, as well as how sometimes the civil law might provide redress.

Assaults on vulnerable athletes

The assaults that can be suffered by child athletes and vulnerable adults playing sport generally do not occur on the sports field. Unscrupulous coaches and other support personnel, as well as older team members, are in a position to physically abuse their charges in various situations. These vary from changing rooms to training venues and overnight accommodation. Those assaults would need to satisfy the definitions analysed in the section 'Other Violence In Sport – Criminal Assaults' to bring about a prosecution. The sole difference being that in such situations the implied or even actual consent of the victim would not have any weight as a defence. Similarly, neither would a discussion of what sports rules or unwritten conventions allow for. When considering 'off the pitch' violent incidents, reference should be made to the above section of this book, ignoring the discussion of consent.

If a criminal assault is proven, or even if the standard of proof of 'beyond reasonable doubt' is not quite reached, a civil action for trespass to the person can still be initiated. This is true of sexual assaults too and is the subject of a section later in this chapter. There follows a discussion of the sexual offending to which an athlete or player could be victim.

Sexual offending

As with criminal assaults in a safeguarding context, obviously sexual molestation is not likely to take place during a game. Therefore, sexual offending against athletes, especially children and vulnerable adults, would be investigated in a way that is not changed by the fact that it occurred in a sporting context. As with criminal assaults away from the pitch or track, the fact that the offence was connected with sport should make no difference to how the accused is proceeded against. Whether the behaviour meets the various definitions of sexual assault, rape etc. should be paramount, as it would be with any sexual offence allegation in any walk of life. The statistics for successful prosecutions in society generally are woefully low, however, and similar factors that inhibit investigations and prevent guilty verdicts are present both from wider society and in sport.

Criminologists refer to crimes that are committed but are either unreported or unrecorded as the 'dark figure' of crime. Sexual offending as a category has a particularly poor record of having a larger dark figure than most crimes. These statistics are gathered by comparing the number of crimes reported to the police with the number reported to, but not recorded as such by them. The reasons for a lack of recording range from officers being under pressure to improve their 'clear-up' statistics to a witness withdrawing their co-operation. There can also be too little evidence for the police to even consider the matter to be a crime.[71] With regard to sex crimes, unrecorded offences were found to be as high as 71 per cent.[72] Finally, these numbers are compared with the number of crimes ascertained by the use of 'victimization surveys',[73] the first of which were carried out as research projects starting in 1972. Now, these surveys are carried out by the Crime Survey for England and Wales (CSEW). These, together with the police figures and other sources, form the official crime statistics for the UK published by the Office for National Statistics (ONS). Since 1972, the United States has carried out such victimisation surveys from 49,000 households or about 100,000 people twice a year. This is called the National Crime Victimization Survey (NCVS) under the direction of the US Census Bureau.[74] Until quite recently, the CSEW did not include figures for under 16s and, being a household survey, did not capture data from the homeless. It has been criticised for such gaps amongst others. Nevertheless, it still contains many more offences than the police figures do. There are many reasons why victims do not report crimes, even sexual offences. These range from fear of the offender to deeming the matter too trivial, from distrust of the police to a lack of understanding that an offence has taken place.[75] These factors are just as prevalent in offending within sport, especially given the sway that sports officials and organisations hold over individual competitors. Here, it is the regulator/participant unequal power dynamic, already much discussed in this book, that compounds the unfairness.

Generally, there is further attrition within the criminal justice system on all offences. This comes from factors such as withdrawal of witness statements, offences being 'taken into consideration' in sentencing and offences being dealt with by way of a caution. In one study, for every hundred crimes committed, forty-five were reported, twenty-four were recorded and two resulted in a conviction.[76] This is a snapshot of why there is a dark figure of crime in the UK, and all the indications are that sexual offending fares particularly badly in that picture. It has a larger dark figure than assaults and thefts, for instance.[77] The charity Rape Crisis found that in 2021, only one in a hundred reported rapes resulted in a conviction.[78] In December 2022, *Operation Soteria Bluestone* produced its first-year report.[79] This is a study across a range of police forces in England and Wales, led by American criminologist Betsy Stanko OBE. She led a team of over fifty analysts researching in the field to why the clear-up rate for sexual offences, in particular rape, is so low. Interim findings include a lack of specialist knowledge and training amongst officers, together with too much focus on the credibility of the victim. High workloads leading to impossible caseloads and officer burnout were also identified. This assumes that the allegations make it through an individual sport's 'internal procedures' of course and are reported to law enforcement.

The real effects of the gap between reported and recorded crime figures can be catastrophic. For example, former police officer Wayne Couzens is serving a life term without the possibility of parole for the rape and murder of Sarah Everard. Couzens has been further sentenced for a series of indecent exposure incidents. These are contrary to Section 66 of the Sexual Offences Act 2003 and date from the months prior to the murder. In court, it became evident that these offences were immediately reported to the police and had good evidence to support them. A car registration and even credit card details were supplied but were not acted upon. Had the police taken these reports seriously instead of effectively ignoring them, Couzens might not have been free to kill his victim.[80]

In sport, often the offender is in a position of authority, such as a manager or trainer, and minor offences may initially seem too trivial for the victim to pursue. Further, this behaviour tends to happen in private with no witnesses, leading to a belief that the police will not be able to act. In practice, it takes the corroboration of a number of people victimised over several years to bring about a successful prosecution. Such was the case with UK soccer coach Barry Bennell[81] and US Gymnastics doctor Larry Nassar.[82]

It would be useful now to turn to a summary of the main sexual offences under UK law. This will be a relatively brief synopsis as the definitions are not affected by the sport context within which they may be committed. As such, a good general criminal law textbook should be consulted if further detail is required. Unlike assaults, sexual offences have a mercifully recent statutory basis. The Sexual Offences Act 2003 has made considerable changes to its predecessor, the Sexual Offences Act 1956. In some ways, the law is stricter now; for instance, some predatory activity is now prohibited that was not the subject of the 1956 Act. This is not least because the technology being misused did not exist then. Further, if sexual activity occurs between minors, then both commit the offence, whereas under the old Act, the presumption was that the boy was the offender. In other ways, there have been some relaxations; for example, prior to 2003, sexual activity with a child under sixteen, the age of consent in the UK, was a strict liability offence. Since that date, a genuine error as to a person's age, provided they are thirteen or over, can found a defence. Sexual molestation of a minor of twelve and under remains strict liability, however. Legislation from 1978 deals with child pornography.

The sexual offences that will be considered in this chapter are rape, sexual assault, underage sexual activity and indecent photographs of children. Rape is defined in s1(1) of the Sexual offences Act 2003 as when:

> [a] person (A) . . . intentionally penetrates the vagina, anus or mouth of another person (B) with his penis . . . B does not consent to the penetration, and . . . A does not reasonably believe that B consents.

This wording confirms that the test for whether the victim consents or not is an objective one. It considers both whether the accused believed there was consent and, crucially, if there was a reasonable basis for such a belief. The accused should have carried out some steps to ascertain consent, and all the circumstances will be taken into account. It also means that under the 2003 Act the victim can be male. Whilst a woman[83] cannot commit the offence, it has always been possible for a woman to 'aid and abet' a rape. Also, under the 'joint enterprise' rules in evidence law, a woman could commit the offence if she were an accomplice who was directly involved in carrying out the attack. This might be by holding the victim down, for instance. As it is such a pivotal point, Section 74 of the Act defines consent in relation to all the offences where the word appears in the definition. Specifically, 'a person consents if he agrees by choice, and has the freedom and capacity to make that choice'. With this in mind, a seriously intoxicated person would lack such capacity, as would a person with limited intellectual abilities, such as many of the athletes competing in the Special Olympics.

Many victims of sexual offending in sport are children, and the rape of a child is a separate offence. If the child is under thirteen, the offence is one of strict liability, and therefore no *mens rea* need be proven. Per Section 5(1), '[a] person commits an offence if . . . he intentionally penetrates the vagina, anus or mouth of another person with his penis, and . . . the other person is under 13'. There is no need to prove *mens rea* as to either consent or age, therefore. For victims aged thirteen and over but under sixteen, *mens rea* as to the age of the victim would need to be proved, as well as with respect to consent. Thus, sexual intercourse with a fifteen-year-old who genuinely consented would not result in a conviction if the accused honestly believed the victim to be sixteen or over. The age is increased to eighteen or over, however, if the other party is in a position of trust, such as a soccer coach. The offence of sexual assault by penetration is the most serious sexual offence other than rape. It caters for instances when a foreign object or another body part is used in the penetration rather than a penis. Section 2(1) states that this will be an offence if:

> [a] person (A) . . . intentionally penetrates the vagina or anus of another person (B) with a part of his body or anything else . . . the penetration is sexual . . . B does not consent to the penetration, and . . . A does not reasonably believe that B consents.

This would mean that genuine and appropriate treatment by a team doctor would be lawful by virtue of its non-sexual nature and the consent. There is a corresponding offence regarding children under thirteen in Section 6(1) which is strict liability regarding age. However, under this section, proper medical treatment by team medics would not be an offence because it would lack a sexual element. Lack of genuine informed consent can turn even a medical procedure into an assault. This was the case in *R v Tabassum* [2000] 2 Cr App R 328 where the consent was fraudulently obtained. An underappreciated fact is that many sexual offences are not about gratification but about exerting power over the victim. Sometimes objects are used in a sexual way to assert dominance and as a way of humiliating the victim. Such behaviour is captured by the definition of the offences in Sections 2(1) and 6(1).

Sexual assault can occur without any penetration. Even the victim being touched against their will can be devastatingly traumatic. Section 3(1) provides the definition of sexual assault. If a person '(A) . . . intentionally touches another person (B) . . . the touching is sexual . . . B does not consent . . . and . . . A does not reasonably believe that B consents', they commit the offence. As mentioned in the discussion of criminal assaults in this chapter, the above offence borrows heavily from common assault (battery) case law definitions. This save that the touching cannot be committed recklessly for a conviction. The definition of consent from Section 74 would be applicable here as in all the aforementioned sexual offences.

With respect to underage sexual activity, that term refers to being under the age of consent. That age differs around the world and even within the borders of a country. For instance, unless there is a significant age gap between the parties, the age of consent in the Netherlands is twelve. In Iran, it is also twelve, raised relatively recently from nine. In Germany, it is fourteen. In some states in the United States, bearing in mind each state has its own legislature, it is fourteen and in others, eighteen. That being said, it is a federal offence to take a young person across a state boundary to take advantage of a lower age of consent. In Dubai, sexual activity is never lawful unless the parties are married irrespective of age. In the UK, the age of consent was raised to its current level of sixteen from thirteen in Victorian times. The social attitudes, norms and traditions of the relevant society will have an effect here, and issues like high infant mortality will tend to apply pressure to lower the age. Conversely, generally speaking, the more progressive a society is, the higher the age is likely to be, although there are exceptions. The law responds to changes in these societal views at varying rates of speed. For instance, the age of consent for homosexual sex was twenty-one in the UK. In a very short space of time in the 1990s, it was legislated down to eighteen then sixteen to give parity with heterosexual sexual relations. This movement is not necessarily always to liberalise the law; for instance, in 2022, the minimum age for marriage was raised from sixteen to eighteen. Cumulatively, this illustrates that moral codes are not necessarily constant across all societies or across time. The law has to try to accommodate changing attitudes whilst providing clarity. The age of consent is now set at sixteen in the UK, and thus, underage sexual activity means relations with a person of fifteen years or less. There are two separate offences: one committed by an adult and the other by a person under eighteen.

Whilst an offence might be committed by a teammate in a youth team, the overwhelming majority of offences in sport are committed by adults in charge of children. Section 9(1) provides that:

> [a] person aged 18 or over (A) commits an offence if . . . he intentionally touches another person (B) . . . the touching is sexual, and . . . B is under 16 and A does not reasonably believe that B is 16 or over, or . . . B is under 13.

Again, the age of eighteen would be substituted for sixteen if the accused is in a position of trust or authority, and many sports support personnel would fall into that category. The distinction between a victim aged twelve or under and one aged thirteen to fifteen remains. Thus, any offence against someone under thirteen will be one of strict liability. As with common law battery, the touching can be of the most minor kind, but, coupled here with the sexual motive, it triggers the statutory offence. Where the touching is on the body and what the circumstances are will have an effect on sentencing, however. Full intercourse is viewed as the most serious offence in this context and is prosecuted under Section 10 of the Act. In that provision, 'touches' is replaced by 'causes or incites another person . . . to engage in sexual activity'. The section goes on to define this activity as various forms of penetration. Whether the victim consents or not has no effect, as the consent of a person under sixteen in this context is not valid in law.

An alternative offence is one committed by a person who has not yet reached eighteen. This could include both parties, neither of whom have reached the age of consent, being charged as a result of consensual sexual activity. In these circumstances, the offence is the same but charged under Section 13 rather than Section 9. The maximum penalty is also limited to five years rather than fourteen years for adults. CPS guidance on whether to charge an offence where both parties are under age will be affected by wider factors. This includes such matters as whether the parties are in a genuine relationship, whether a child has resulted or alternatively whether there was a degree of coercion or grooming and the like.[84]

For people who commit sex offences, it is common for there to be a pattern of behaviour that escalates. That trajectory can begin with a fascination with pornography. Even during the commission of such offences, offenders may take photographic images for distribution or for their own later gratification. Child pornography is legislated against by the Protection of Children Act 1978. Section 1(1) makes it an offence to:

> take, or permit to be taken or to make, any indecent photograph . . . of a child or . . . distribute or show such photographs . . . or . . . have in his possession such indecent photographs . . . with a view to their being distributed.

The section also prohibits advertising such services. This renders the taking, distributing or publishing the material criminal. Very often today, however, these images will be on an offender's computer or device for their sole use. This behaviour is addressed by Section 160(1) of the Criminal Justice Act 1988 in that it 'is an offence for a person to have any indecent photograph or pseudo-photograph of a child in his possession'. Law enforcement may have these images on their devices for work purposes, so there is a defence that the accused had a legitimate reason for having the images. Unsolicited images are not included if it can be proved that the recipient had not seen the material and did not know, or even suspect, that it was indecent. Furthermore, there will be no offence if he made no request for the images and, having seen them, he did not keep them for an unreasonable time.

There are further sexual offences, mostly in the 2003 Act, such as grooming and meeting a child subsequent to grooming them. The foregoing discussion has been limited to those offences most likely to be committed in a sporting context, however. It is now possible to turn to less emotive but nevertheless important criminal liability that can be utilised to protect athlete welfare as well as that of other sport stakeholders.

Health and safety in sport

'Health and safety', rather like 'data protection', is an often-used phrase but one for which the legal detail is rarely accurately or clearly understood by non-lawyers. Just like offices, building sites, factories and the like, sports venues and facilities are places of work. It is essential they are safe and healthy for their users, from athletes to spectators, employees and other visitors. The leading legislation which imposes criminal liability for unsafe practices is the Health and Safety at Work Act 1974. As with all criminal law, the standard of proof bar is high at 'beyond reasonable doubt'. However, investigations and prosecutions are not led by the police but are carried out by the Health and Safety Executive (HSE). This is the government body responsible for enforcing the Act. It is possible that an incident that triggers an HSE investigation may also be a cause of action in civil law where harm is caused. This could be either for breach of contract or negligence, for example. Civil law remedies will be discussed later in the chapter. Many of the offences that can be committed under this Act are strict liability, which means that there is no need to prove *mens rea* for a conviction. This makes convictions easier to obtain, but for a critique of the concept of strict liability, see Chapter 4. Section 3(1) of the Act makes it clear that it is not just employees who are protected under the legislation; it states that:

> It shall be the duty of every employer to conduct his undertaking in such a way as to ensure, so far as is reasonably practicable, that persons not in his employment who may be affected thereby are not thereby exposed to risks to their health or safety.

Thus, a stadium owner or racetrack operator would also owe such duties to sports participants, support personnel, spectators, third-party vendors and other visitors on their property. Some of the offences are corporate ones, so the entity responsible for the venue would be liable. Some place liability on individuals, separate corporate personality notwithstanding.

The duty mentioned is laid out in Section 2(1); the employer must ensure 'as far as reasonably practicable the health, safety and welfare at work of his employees'. The category of employee includes government trainees and work experience students. In *Coult v Szouba* (1982) ICR 380 it was made clear, however, that such persons must have 'clocked in' at the time of the incident to be classed as employees. The section specifically states that the employer must ensure safe plant and systems of work, safe handling, storage and transport of articles and substances, provision of information, instruction, training and supervision. In addition, there must be a safe working environment within a safe place of work and a satisfactory safety policy. This must be in writing for businesses with five or more employees.

Section 4 of the Act explains the duties that pertain to occupiers of premises. This is wider than owners and leaseholders, as less formal and temporary occupants are covered too. The latter would be termed in law as having a 'licence' to be on the land. There is some parity with the position under civil law regarding occupiers' liability, which will be discussed in the next sections. Therefore, even the informal use of another team's training facility by permission could render the person in control on the ground liable under the Act. This assumes that the usual occupant and/or owner is not present or represented. For liability to arise, the temporary occupant would need to have contractual obligations regarding maintenance and entry or egress. If such a contract does not exist, then it would be a duty to take steps that are reasonable in the circumstances to ensure health, safety and well-being. The Act places the responsibility to ensure health and safety on everybody to some degree. Consequently, the employees, and by extension, athletes, players and so on are expected, under Section 7(1), to take reasonable care for themselves and others likely to be affected by their actions or want of care. Section 37 of the Act provides that personal criminal liability can fall on directors and senior managers. Therefore, it is possible that management removed from the day-to-day running of a sports venue could still find themselves indicted if their connivance or neglect as a senior officer can be proved. For instance, in *Armour v Skeen (Procurator Fiscal, Glasgow)* (1977) IRLR 310, a worker died from a fall on a major construction project. The Director of Roads for Strathclyde Council was held liable in that they did not safely manage the site despite not being responsible for directing daily operations at the location.

It is unusual to find vicarious liability in criminal law, being more commonly found in civil matters. However, under the Act, this type of liability attaches to a business for the criminal actions of its employees. There are restrictions, in that the individual must be directly employed and not engaged in activities wholly outside their employment contract at the time. In *R v Gateway Foodmarkets Ltd* [1997] 3 All ER 78, an employee died from falling whilst trying to free a lift that had jammed. Safety rules at the store regarding the lift were routinely flouted by store managers, but the company management was unaware of this malpractice. The company was nevertheless held vicariously liable for a criminal offence. In like vein, many sporting premises are owned by corporate entities. Provided an employee is doing their job badly, rather than not doing the activities they were employed to do at all, then the business entity could be held criminally liable because sports venue staff neglected health and safety rules.

Welfare as fair reparation for harm to athletes – the civil law

The civil courts of first instance are the County Court and High Court, from which the Court of Appeal and Supreme Court can hear appeals. The purpose of civil law is not to impose punishment. The civil courts are a venue for people, including juristic persons, to obtain redress if a civil wrong has been committed. The purpose of civil law, then, is to procure a rebalancing between the parties that represents a fair and just solution to a dispute. It is not uncommon for a criminal prosecution to give rise to a separate legal action for damages. For instance, if a coach is convicted of one of the sexual offences discussed in the last section, it would be open to the victims to sue the SGB that employed or authorised them for compensation. This would be under either the tort of negligence or of trespass to the person, both of which form part of the forthcoming discussion. The standard of proof required in civil actions is much lower than that in criminal proceedings, which is *beyond reasonable doubt*. It is only necessary to prove an issue 'on the balance of probabilities' or that it is *more likely than not* true (see Figure 5.4).

If harm or loss is caused, this may be the result of a breach of contract. For instance, if a competitor is injured in an avoidable way at a sporting event, they will have paid a fee to enter and the organisation running the event has agreed to their participation. There is at the very least an implied term in the contract that the competitor will not be injured by the acts or omissions of the organisers. Such a claim may be separate to, or

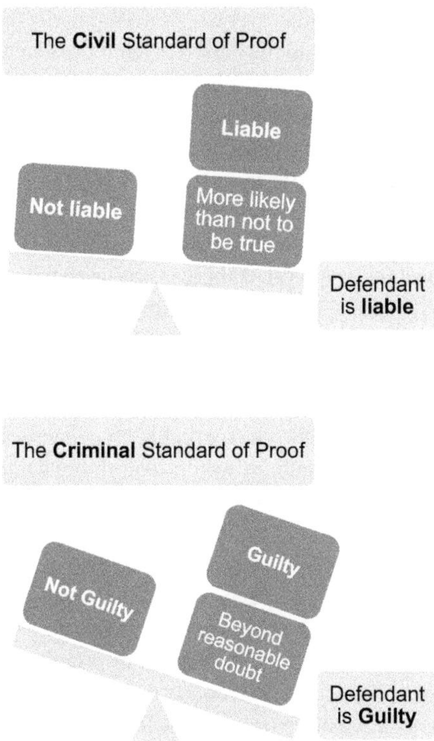

Figure 5.4 Civil and criminal standards of proof compared.

run in conjunction with a claim in tort. The focus of this part of the chapter is tortious claims. Tort simply means 'civil wrong' and the most important topics for discussion in a sporting context are trespass to the person (civil battery), negligence, vicarious liability and occupiers' liability. A sports person may also suffer defamation. This is outside the scope of what is already a very large chapter. Suffice it to say here though, that this is common law based and has the components of libel and slander. Libel is the permanent form, usually written, whereas slander is the spoken form. Both essentially concern information not based on fact that would have the tendency to damage the reputation of an individual in the minds of 'right-thinking' members of the public.

Trespass to the person – battery

Every person's body is to be considered inviolate; *Collins v Willcock* [1984] 1 WLR 1172 affirms that the slightest unwarranted touch is enough to claim for trespass to the person. There is a significant overlap between the criminal offence of battery and the civil version. The earliest cases make no real distinction, as a fully developed criminal legal system with state institutions to enforce and prosecute it did not exist. Individuals were left to bring an action before the courts themselves. Therefore, the definition of 'to intentionally or recklessly apply unlawful force to another', previously encountered in the discussion of criminal assaults, is equally relevant here. The action for damages will have to be brought as trespass to the person, even if the touching was sexual, up to and including an alleged rape. This might happen if the police or CPS consider there is insufficient evidence for a successful prosecution or if there is a trial and a not guilty verdict is returned. Further, upon a finding of guilty in an assault or sexual offence criminal trial, it is open to the victim to separately sue for damages if the offender is wealthy enough to make that worthwhile. This might well be the case for an offender who was a Premiership soccer player, for instance. Even if the offender is impecunious, it may be possible to sue the employer, if there is one, in vicarious liability. In *Vasey v Surrey Free Inns* [1996] PIQR P373, two nightclub doormen and a manager attacked a man who had previously damaged the nightclub door. One of the doormen was convicted of GBH. Subsequently, the owner of the nightclub was held vicariously liable for this trespass to the person. The precise limitations on this type of liability in civil law will be discussed later, but suffice it to say that an overzealous steward ejecting a troublesome fan from a soccer stadium would be a direct analogy with *Surrey* in a sporting context. If more than reasonable force were used, liability could fall on the employer for civil battery.

Furthermore, given the increase in reporting of sexual violence against young people in sport in recent years,[85] it is open to any victim to attempt to sue the employer of the offender, whether a criminal prosecution has been successful or not. In the case of a not guilty verdict, this is because the standard of proof is so much lower in civil courts. The action would have to be in trespass to the person, but the level of harm from sexual offending would tend to increase the level of damages significantly over a mere physical battery. It is worth pointing out that in such a scenario, alternatively, a compensation claim against an SGB or other employer could be made under the tort of negligence. This is because the employer of the coach, manager, trainer, physiotherapist or team doctor, owes a duty of care to the victim. This is especially pertinent in a culture of safeguarding, and that duty may well have been breached if they have failed to prevent the abuse.

Negligence

Negligence is the basis of personal injury law, although claims can be made under breach of contract, battery and breach of statutory duty in addition or as an alternative. The aim is redress for physical, psychological or financial loss, sometimes a combination of those harms. In sport, the issue of concussion and related brain injuries has been worrisome where impact with the head can be expected as part of the game. This is especially so in American football, soccer and rugby but could be an issue for a number of other sports in years to come. This is because as sport becomes more commercial and with higher stakes, players take greater risks to win.[86] Professional rugby is a sport particularly affected by injury statistics. As the rewards for winning increase with attendant sponsorship and merchandising deals and the like, the size and level of fitness of rugby players that make it to the top level have increased. This has led to greater forces being exerted during tackles.[87] As discussed in Chapter 2, the rules are set by the sport governing body. Accordingly, if it be proven, on the balance of probabilities, that those rules did not account for the modern understanding of brain injuries, then the result could be class-action negligence claims. Leaving aside extreme sports like base jumping and cave diving, there is a high incidence of injury in some less well-followed sports. Boxing is dangerous but, depending on the statistics consulted, competitive cheerleading is riskier than boxing in terms of injury. Also, well within the top five comes horse riding, especially competitive jumping. Rules aiming to prevent injury, the provision of adequate medical facilities as well as timely intervention by officials are all important to avoid the possibility of negligence claims.

The tort of negligence is almost entirely case law based. Before the advent of this cause of action, the only way for an injured party to sue was if there was a contract in place. In *Priest v Last* [1903] 2 KB 148, the claimant bought a hot water bottle which was used by his wife, and on the fifth use, it burst through a defect, scalding her. The lady did not have a contract with the seller, and the husband did but was not injured. This meant that the only way that any redress could flow to the husband was to claim for medical expenses and the cost of hiring services to cover what his wife would have done if not injured. At the time, this would not have been questioned as meaning childcare, cooking, cleaning and the like. The difficulties that this strict approach caused were well recognised by the inter-war period and were the reason for the creation of effectively a wholly new tort, that of negligence. That occurred as a result of *Donoghue v Stevenson* [1932] AC 562. Here, instead of a contractual set of obligations, the court substituted a relationship denoted by the 'neighbour principle'. This delimits the classes of persons to whom the wrongdoer owes a 'duty of care'. As applied in the case, this showed that the manufacturer of a product owes a duty to the ultimate consumer even if there is no contract. Therefore, had *Priest v Last* been decided even thirty-five years later, Mrs Priest could have sued in her own right. The neighbour principle in *Donoghue* means that everyone owes a duty of care to 'persons who are so closely and directly affected by [their] act that [they] ought reasonably to have them in contemplation as being so affected [by their] acts or omissions'. The duty of care is only one part of the definition of negligence; however, the claimant must show that the duty was breached and that the breach of duty caused the loss complained of. Each of the three components will be discussed in turn.

The test for duty of care was also first formulated in *Donoghue v Stevenson*, but after several versions from cases in the intervening years, the current interpretation can be found in *Caparo Industries PLC v Dickman* [1990] 1 All ER 568. In this case, it was held that for a duty of care to be owed to another, that person or those persons firstly must be 'proximate'. This is not necessarily in the sense of close in time or space but can mean in terms of a business relationship. For example, in *Caparo*, the proximity was argued to be with potential investors who might read the negligently prepared document. Those of course could be anywhere in the world. That claim was unsuccessful on those particular facts, however. Secondly, the person must be foreseeable, in that the defendant should have thought about them as likely to be affected by their acts or omissions. Finally, it must be just and reasonable to impose a duty of care. This is not to be taken as 'just' *vis-à-vis* the claimant but takes into account much wider principles. It is designed to prevent undesirable precedents, particularly when the imposition of a duty of care might cause difficulty in public policy terms. For instance, in *Hill v Chief Constable of West Yorkshire* [1987] UKHL 12, the mother of a murder victim sued the police for releasing a serial murderer after an inconclusive investigation over previous deaths. This allowed him to go on to kill her daughter. Among other issues, it was held that it would not be just and reasonable for the police to be held to have a duty of care to the victims of crime. This is because it would unduly restrict how they investigated offences.

Caparo simply added the last criterion to what had been a two-stage test in *Donoghue*. Another way of looking at this third requirement is that it can be used to prevent opening the 'floodgates' to a large number of claims. In a sporting context, *Alcock v Chief Constable of South Yorkshire Police* [1992] 1 AC 310 came out of the 'Hillsborough Tragedy'. There, ninety-seven soccer fans lost their lives due to police negligence in not managing the crowd properly, causing a crush. Relatives of the victims mounted the claim because they had been diagnosed with mental health conditions from witnessing events via live television or radio broadcasts. It was held that as they were not present in the stadium, on policy grounds, the police owed them no duty of care. Those who were in the stadium at the time of the incident were able to claim for their mental health conditions, grouped together under the legal term 'psychiatric shock'. This was largely because of the additional factor that they were in physical danger themselves on that day. Discussions have also been around the existence or otherwise of a duty of care on the playing field. Specifically, the duty owed by players and athletes to each other, duties owed by such participants to spectators and also by match referees, umpires and other officials to players and athletes. It has also been necessary to establish the duty of care that SGBs owe to their participating members in terms of at-venue medical facilities.

In *Condon v Basi* [1985] 1 WLR 866, the test formulated in *Donoghue* was adjudged equally applicable to soccer players, and therefore, they owe a duty of care to one another. In *Caldwell v Maguire* [2001] EWCA Civ 1054, it was held that this test also applied to jockeys in a horse race; therefore, in a range of sports, participants owe a duty of care to other competitors. In *Woolridge v Sumner* [1963] 2 QB 43, a photographer was injured due to the riding of a professional showjumper. It was held that sports participants owe a duty of care to spectators, of whom a photographer is merely a professional version. These latter two cases will be the subject of further discussion in a later section on breach of duty.

Officials, referees and the like also owe a duty of care to the competitors that they oversee. In *Smoldon v Nolan and Whitworth* [1997] ELR 249, the referee did not intervene to prevent a dangerous scrum which collapsed, causing injury. In *Vowles v Evans* [2003] EWCA Civ 318, a rugby referee failed to check the suitability of a substitute player for a particular position as he came onto the field. This was against the rules, and subsequently the player was injured. In both cases, the *Donoghue* test, in its new formulation since *Caparo*, was used to establish such a duty. In *Vowles*, arguments were employed unsuccessfully by the defence that the third limb of the test applied so that there were good policy reasons to deny the existence of a duty.

The question has also arisen as to whether SGBs owe a duty of care if they are responsible for competition facilities in any way. *Watson v BBBC and Others* [2001] QB 1134 concerned a boxing match between Michael Watson and Chris Eubank in 1991. Eubank applied a within-the-rules uppercut that caused Watson brain damage, leaving him to have to learn to walk and talk again. There were no suitable medical facilities on site despite it being a title fight, and the British Board of Boxing Control (BBBC) was responsible for such fixtures. Had Watson received earlier medical intervention, the injury would have had less severe long-term effects. Consequently, the Board was found to have a duty of care and to have breached that duty in this instance. Much will depend on the jurisdiction, however, as Australian cases have not followed this UK precedent. In the conjoined case of *Agar v Hyde; Agar v Worsley* (2000) 201 CLR 552, two rugby players suffered injuries which they attributed to failings in the rules set by the SGB of the time. However, no duty of care was held to apply in that context. The same was decided in *McCracken v Melbourne Storm Rugby League Football Club* [2005] NSWSC 107, when a player was allowed only to sue fellow players for his injury, not the SGB.

As considered earlier, sexual abuse claims can be dealt with by way of civil battery litigation as well as a criminal case. A negligence action against the SGB or another employer could be brought as an alternative. This is particularly true as they will be insured against such claims, whereas the offender may well be in prison and may not have sufficient funds to be worth pursuing. The claim would be that the sports organisation did not meet its duty of care in selecting, training and monitoring the support personnel who offended. It would be very difficult for an SGB to allege it did not owe a duty of care under *Caparo* in such circumstances. A claim in vicarious liability could also be possible if the employment relationship and so on is clear enough. Vicarious liability will be considered in more detail towards the end of this chapter.

There is legislation in place that automatically provides for a duty of care between the occupiers of a premises and lawful visitors. This would apply to the occupiers of sporting stadia, racetracks, athletics or swimming venues, and the like. Such occupiers would owe a duty of care to spectators, officials, athletes, players, support personnel and so on. This duty has been extended to include trespassers as well in certain circumstances. The social policy reasons behind this are not to provide a 'burglars' charter,' as some less than balanced media and other commentary have alleged. This is to acknowledge that many trespassers are in fact children. The Occupiers Liability Act 1957 stipulates that a duty of care is owed to lawful visitors by anyone owning, leasing, controlling or otherwise occupying premises. Thus, it may not be the owner of a sports ground who owes this duty but the club leasing it from them. Much will depend on who has the duty of maintenance and who controls entry and egress to the ground. The Occupiers Liability Act 1984 extends this duty to cover trespassers. Essentially, if a hazard would be a danger to a lawful visitor, then if it injures a trespasser, the fact that the injured party is not there lawfully will not prevent them from claiming. It does not mean that a trespasser will succeed in all circumstances, however. Depending on what the intruder is on the premises for, the defences of *ex turpi causa* (illegality), *volenti* (knowingly volunteering for the risk) or contributory negligence might well apply. How these might fully or partially defeat a claim is covered later in the chapter. The best way to help counter such a claim is to have well-placed, clear and maintained signs. These might say things such as 'enter at own risk' or 'danger of death or injury – no entry'. If a guard dog is in use, 'beware of the dog' in prominent places may suffice and so on. These signs will have limited effect if, however, the injured party has to ignore them. This would occur if they are placed at the only point they can enter or leave a space, irrespective of the notified risk. It is also important to have adequate fences and good physical security at any sports venue. It is equally vital that the playing surface and facilities for spectators, vendors and the like are safe. In one horse racing case, the judge castigated Doncaster Racecourse as being so badly maintained that the jockeys effectively played 'Russian Roulette' when they rode there.[88]

Once a duty of care is proven, the next stage for an injured athlete is to show that this duty has been breached; in other words, that an unacceptably low level of care was applied. How the law addresses this in sport is important and will be discussed next.

Sporting standards of care

In negligence cases outside a sporting context, the rules on breach are relatively clear. Cases have established tests in relation to everyday activities and those that require a certain level of professional skill. For unskilled and semi-skilled undertakings, the test is referred to as the 'man on the Clapham omnibus'.[89] This is a phrase originating in the pre-*Donoghue* case of *Blythe v Birmingham Waterworks* (1856) 11Ex 781 and the defamation claim, *Maguire v Western Morning News* [1903] 2 KB 100 (CA). In other words, the test tries to establish what level of care would be expected to be applied by the reasonable man or woman in everyday activities and is therefore objective. Such activities might include salting an icy street or placing signage warning of unsafe steps and the like. If the job is skilled, such as cancer surgery or captaining a container ship, this test would not be effective as the reasonable person would not be able to make a judgement. With such activities, the test is still objective but refers to the 'ordinary competent professional' or 'Bolam' test. This term was coined in *Bolam v Friern Hospital Management Committee* [1957] 1 WLR 582, where it fell to be determined whether or not it was negligent to intubate a very small baby. Obviously, only a body of opinion from ordinary, competent paediatric specialists could determine that. The standard has been held to be a higher one where victims are particularly vulnerable in that they have a pre-existing injury. An example would be if the claimant had already lost an eye, as in *Paris v Stepney Borough Council* [1951] AC 367. Eye protection for industrial workers was not standard at the time, and not providing some was held to be a breach of the duty of care. However, this was only because Paris' good eye was harmed, leaving him blind. The courts have also lowered the threshold in emergency situations, such as in *Watt v Hertfordshire County Council* [1954] 1 WLR 835. Here, crush injuries occurred in a fire truck responding to a life-threatening situation. The claim was disallowed as the 'normal' standard of care cannot necessarily be reached in such circumstances.

Utilising these tests in sports injury cases is problematic, however. If the standard of care expected were set too high, then for the athlete, the desire to push the limits of their ability and skill might be tempered by the fear of litigation. This could impact the level of excitement from watching the sport and, in turn, reduce gate receipts and viewing figures. These losses could be disastrous for professional sport. In addition to protecting sporting endeavour, many decisions are made in a split second and in 'the agony of the game'. Therefore, it might be unfair to expect the same standard of care as outside sport. For example, asking a Formula One driver to exercise the same level of care in overtaking a rival as should a commuter making the same manoeuvre on the highway is unrealistic. Set against this, it is important that injured players and athletes are compensated adequately when the incident is not their fault. For instance, a horse racing jockey should be able to receive adequate damages for injury whether they are barged off their horse by a negligent competitor or if they are hit by an incompetent driver whilst cycling to the track. The court considered this conundrum in *Woolridge v Sumner* and in *Caldwell v Maguire*, as well as the existence of a duty of care. It was held that a sports participant would not breach the duty of care owed to another player or athlete as long as they did not display 'reckless disregard' for the health and safety of others. This means that less care can be taken and yet litigation still avoided, but not without limit.

Unfortunately, the opportunity for clarity has been missed as there is still controversy over the true meaning of 'reckless disregard'. On the one hand, the phrase could be taken as a substitute test for breach of duty of care in sports injury cases. This would mean that the 'reasonable person' and 'ordinary competent professional' tests do not apply. Alternatively, reckless disregard for the injured party's welfare could be merely an evidential standard that must be used in sporting cases. In other words, specific evidence of 'reckless disregard' would be needed to prove that the ordinary competent professional competitor would not have behaved as the defendant did, leaving the test itself still applicable. More opacity is added when the *obiter* comments in *Condon v Basi* are considered. The soccer match where the incident occurred was part of the Leamington Local League. In the judgement, it was stated that the standard of care in such a game might be lower than that expected in a First Division, or nowadays a Premiership playoff. The FA Cup competition is such that lower league, even part-time sides can be drawn against top-flight clubs. For instance, Oxford United in the Second Division beat Premiership side Swansea City 3-2 in 2016. This feature of the competition brings about the somewhat nonsensical situation where a different standard of care would have to be applied to players on one side compared to their opponents. Other sports will have these 'giant killing' traditions as well, where comparative unknowns can compete against champions and the same problem could arise.

In an earlier discussion, it was pointed out that sexual molestation could give rise to a civil battery claim as well as a criminal case. Such a case could alternatively be mounted by a negligence action against those responsible for selecting, training and monitoring the support personnel who offend. In such an action, the test for breach would not involve consideration of 'reckless disregard' but would be that of the 'reasonable person' or 'ordinary competent professional'. This is because these decisions are not made in the heat of competition.

Causation of loss and remoteness

The final hurdle for a claimant in a sports injury case is to prove the third element of the *Donoghue* negligence definition, that the loss was caused by the defendant. This does not differ from the same considerations in an ordinary negligence case, and the 'But For' test would be applied. This was established in the *Barnett v Chelsea & Kensington Hospital* [1969] 1 QB 428 case and would be phrased as 'but for the breach of duty of player X would player Y have suffered injury?'. If the answer is no, then damages are payable. Compensation may only be claimed for effects of the negligence that are not too remote. That is to say, too far removed to be properly attributable in law to the incident. These losses must be 'reasonably foreseeable', as was held in *Overseas Tankship (UK) Ltd v The Miller Steamship Co (The Wagon Mound) (No. 2)* [1967] 1 AC 617. To put this into a sporting context, an athlete who was wheelchair-bound after negligence might expect to receive lost earnings. They could also expect to be reimbursed for the cost of adaptations to accommodation and ongoing medical costs. Most of the treatment would be provided free by the NHS, but there could still be certain private treatments that it would be reasonable to access in addition. Lucrative contracts that the same person might have obtained in later years, had they been uninjured, could be deemed too remote, however.

There are legal principles that can defeat a negligence claim or possibly mitigate the financial effect of one for a defendant, and those shall be considered in the next section.

Defeating a sports negligence claim

The focus of this section is on defences which can be complete or partial. A complete defence will defeat the claim entirely, whereas a partial defence would merely reduce the amount of damages to be paid. In some circumstances, though, the reduction could be substantial.

Contributory negligence

Contributory negligence, if proven, holds the injured party partly to blame for the injuries they suffered. This is never awarded at 100% and is only possible if the defendant is held liable for the injury in the first place. This apportionment of blame has only been possible since the Law Reform (Contributory Negligence) Act 1945. Prior to this, any negligence by the claimant would result in no damages at all. In *Froom v Butcher* [1976] 1 QB 286, the claimant was not wearing a seatbelt when he was hit by a negligent driver. The court took the opportunity to give guidance on the amount of reduction to be applied. It held that a decrease of between 15 per cent and 25 per cent would be appropriate depending on the extent to which the claimant's behaviour was a contributing factor to their injuries. Thus, a claim for £100,000 could be reduced to £75,000 in most instances of contributory negligence. If the injuries are considered to be the fault of the claimant to a much higher degree than this, then alternatively the full defence of *volenti non fit injuria* should be employed, which will be discussed next. This is illustrated in the sport of powered flying. In *Morris v Murray* [1991] 2 QB 6 at first instance, the court awarded 80 per cent contributory negligence to the injured passenger, which was overturned on appeal and a finding of *Volenti* substituted, meaning there was no compensation available at all. The passenger had got into a private plane for a joyride with a pilot he knew was drunk, and the plane crashed.

Consent and the civil law

Both consent and *volenti non fit injuria*, if raised successfully, will defeat the claim entirely. *Volenti* is used in negligence cases, however, whereas consent would be appropriate for battery cases. This Latin phrase is best understood as 'he who volunteers for a risk cannot complain of a wrong'. Consent is equally important in both criminal and civil actions for sports injuries, particularly arising on the field of play. Also, to a more limited extent, when seeking compensation for battery off the pitch or track. In such a case, if the claimant is capable of valid consent in law, then proof of such consent could defeat even a sexual battery suit. This will be in the minority of cases, however, as the age of consent is eighteen when the defendant is in a responsible position regarding the claimant. This would be such as a coach or trainer. Furthermore, the standard of proof is much lower in civil cases, making it considerably easier to show that the consent was vitiated or not present at all. In battery cases arising from the field of play, like criminal law, much will depend on what the injured competitor has consented to. This consent can be implied from engaging in the game. The risks that are inherent in the particular sport will be important, rugby being much more likely to produce injury than, for instance, snooker. Therefore, the level of injury impliedly consented to will vary. In each case, though, risks over and above those that can be so expected will be easier to show as outside the level of consent the injured competitor had given.

In both consent and *volenti*, it is important that acquiescing to the risks is freely done and not subject to any pressure. This can be the economic pressure of being employed or from undue influence from a team manager or coach. Most commonly nowadays, the defence of *volenti* is rarely successful as contributory negligence and the consequent reduction, not elimination, of compensation is deemed a fairer outcome. It did succeed in *Imperial Chemical Industries Ltd v Shatwell* [1965] AC 656, where demolition explosives contractors were injured when they operated outside existing safety rules. This was held to be their own unfettered decision; however, they lost their case. Whether a claimant is aware of the risk and its extent is a subjective question. It matters not whether the reasonable person would have appreciated the risk. Employment cases pose a particular problem, and it must be remembered that soccer players are employees of their clubs per *Walker v Crystal Palace Football Club* [1910] 1 KB 87. This is also true of members of teams in other sports, but not all. In such situations, it is easy for an employer to assert that the employee consented to the risk, whereas in fact, that happened under the implied or express pressure of being in an employment situation. In both *Smith v Baker and Sons* [1891] AC 325 and *Woodley v Metropolitan District Rly* (1877) 18 QBD it was pointed out that concerning employees, true consent was hard to show. This is due to the economic pressure that inevitably flowed from that natural desire to remain employed and/or advance in career terms. Furthermore, knowledge of the risk does not equate to consenting to the lack of care. These issues are coming to the fore with discussions about the long-term effects of heading a soccer ball. Mostly, these were in former times very heavy leather examples made even more weighty by rain, but there are still concerns about modern designs. Also, the sheer toll that professional rugby takes on its players today, compared to the past, engages this area of law.[90] There is no doubt there is an assumption of risk by playing at the top level. Further, the rules currently do not mandate anything close to the level of body protection that the rules of American Football do. However, merely consenting to the sport's inherent risk is not the same as being *volenti* to the lack of care of players and officials, nor the drafting of rules that may no longer be fit for purpose.

A case from sport where *volenti* was successfully employed was *Morris v Murray*; however, encountered under contributory negligence, the two parties had been drinking excessively, and one of the parties had a pilot's licence and owned a small private plane. Both agreed to take a flight in this machine, and due to mistakes made under intoxication, the plane crashed shortly after take-off. The pilot was killed, and the passenger was seriously injured, subsequently suing the estate of the deceased pilot. On appeal, it was held that getting into a plane with an obviously drunk pilot triggered the defence of *volenti*, which meant the injured party recovered nothing. This was a blatant case of fully and unreservedly volunteering for the risk, but other situations in sport may not be so clear-cut. Sometimes, similar considerations may be required in assessing whether the standard of care has been breached at all. That is to say, the same facts and arguments might be part of the defendant's case that there is no negligence in the first place. In the alternative, these same points might be employed to help determine whether the injured party was *volenti* or not. By way of example, if a spectator is injured standing close to the track in a motocross event or car rally, there may be little in the way of substantial safety barriers. The sports fan impliedly accepts this risk but also that the riders or drivers owe them a lower standard of care, as *Woolridge* and *Caldwell* seem to say. There will first be a discussion as to whether there has been a breach of the duty of care in those circumstances. If so, the same facts might be used to argue '*volenti*' or at least contributory negligence.

What this all collectively may mean is that *volenti* has limited application in sports injury cases. In summary, contributory negligence may be preferred as more equitable. Secondly, the level of assumption of risk by the claimant may well have been dealt with earlier in the case. This would be when the appropriate standard of care that the defendant should have adhered to, and therefore whether they are negligent at all, was considered.

Illigality – ex turpi causa

This defence operates to defeat the claim entirely if the claimant was engaged in illegal activity. In *Pitts v Hunt* [1991] 3 All ER 344, the claimant was a pillion passenger on a motorcycle being erratically ridden by the drunk, unlicensed and uninsured defendant. There was an inevitable accident and the passenger sued the deceased rider's estate. Given the circumstances, several crimes were committed on this journey and because of his jeering and encouragement, the passenger was held to be part of a criminal joint enterprise. As such, *ex turpi causa* operated to make it impossible to establish a duty of care between the rider and passenger, and the claim failed. This defence would have limited applicability in sporting injury cases as well. However, if two competitors injured each other in a brawl on the track or pitch, this might well result in both receiving assault convictions. In such circumstances, *ex turpi causa* might prevent a successful civil action by either one against the other.

Liability for a player's torts – vicarious liability

Vicarious liability is commonly found in civil actions; essentially, the employer is held liable for the employee's torts. There are several reasons why this is deemed fair and just. For one thing, the employer has to carry insurance against this event by law. This reduces the chances of an injured party being left without compensation simply because the defendant is impecunious. Secondly, the employer is responsible for the selection, training and supervision of the employee, and thus bears some responsibility for the acts and omissions of its staff. Also, vicarious liability gives the employer a financial incentive to ensure, as far as possible, that employees operate safely.

For a soccer club, tennis or cycling team, or SGB to be made vicariously liable for the torts of its employees, a number of hurdles need to be overcome. First of all, it must be established that the sports team member or support person is in fact an employee in law. The position is clear in soccer since *Walker v Crystal Palace* held all such players to be employees of their club. In cycling, much more recently in 2020, the opposite was held to be true between a professional cyclist and her SGB.[91] Thus, the precise relationship in each sport will depend on the particular contractual arrangements and judicial precedent, irrespective of what the parties think the relationship can be characterised as. This has led to an inequality between sports persons as to whether they can have employee protection, which will depend on what sport they engage in. The Employment Rights Act 1996, section 230 defines an employee as 'an individual who has entered into or works under . . . a contract of employment'. In other words, a person who is not self-employed, but this is hardly a complete test that reflects the realities of twenty-first-century workplaces. The most comprehensive test to determine if a person is an employee or not comes from *Ready Mixed Concrete (South East) Ltd v Minister of Pensions and National Insurance* [1968] 2 QB 497. The test considers matters like whether the person has to carry out the work personally and who is responsible for tax and National Insurance payments, together with any requirement to use a certain livery or uniform. Section 230 also defines a 'worker' who is not directly employed. This may be an agency employee or a self-employed person, but who has a sufficiently close relationship with the employer that it is compulsory for them to carry out the work in person and not subcontract it. Examples might include a specialist IT consultant or engineer and actions or omissions by workers may also bring vicarious liability on an employer in some cases.

Once an employment relationship has been established, a further issue must be addressed. In *Poland v John Parr & Sons* [1927] 1 KB 236, the question was posed like this:

> was [the act or omission complained of] merely a wrong method of doing an authorised act . . . [or] . . ., was the act one which was done for the servant's own purposes and not in his master's interest?

Put another way, was the employee doing their job but badly, or were they engaged in something that did not form part of their employment at all? This might include using the company truck to collect groceries for home during work time. In fact, even unauthorised acts that are nevertheless in furtherance of the employer's interest will still potentially leave the employer vicariously liable. An example could be not using 'compulsory' safety equipment because it would slow down the production rate. In sports cases where battery or sexual battery by support personnel, including volunteers, is alleged, the SGB or club concerned may argue that the act was not one done in the interests of the employer at all. This may yet, however, be a case of an employee doing their job but doing it badly, very badly indeed. This issue was considered in *Vasey v Surrey Free Inns*, discussed earlier under civil battery. Essentially, three nightclub employees, including two bouncers, followed a customer they believed to be troublesome to a car park where they beat him severely. The defendant was held vicariously liable. More recently, in *Mohamud v Wm Morrison Supermarkets PLC* [2016] UKSC 11, a customer attended a supermarket-owned petrol station and was berated with foul and racist language by the Morrisons employee in the kiosk. This man then followed Mohamud to his car and beat him. This was also a case of the act being so closely associated with the employment relationship that social justice required that the employer be held responsible. Given the foregoing, there is little doubt that violence meted out by employed athletes and players in a competition or in immediate proximity to it could make their employers vicariously liable for their torts. In the United States, this can even extend to acts of personal vengeance if the club or other employer is aware of the defendant's tendency towards violence.[92]

Countering the threat from fans – crowd control and sport

Athletes' welfare can be undermined by the very people there to support them. However, such measures as there are to deal with large numbers of spectators are contained in legislation. This was mostly enacted in response to soccer violence and disruption that reached a peak in Europe and particularly the UK in the late 1980s. These statutes provide for a range of criminal offences or civil prevention orders and relate to UK soccer with little wider application. That said, soccer hooliganism is a worldwide problem with many complex social causes.[93] The difficulties that were the genesis of these statutory provisions can impact on players. For instance, the risk of being hit by a missile thrown from the stands or from drunken behaviour, including pitch invasions, was much higher before enactment. These statutes warrant a brief discussion here; therefore, this is limited though as a detailed debate would be outside the scope of this book.

The Sporting Events (Control of Alcohol etc.) Act 1985 provides that spectators cannot consume alcohol within view of the soccer pitch within a time period. This begins fifteen minutes before kick-off and ends a quarter of an hour after the final whistle. Drunk and disorderly fans may also not enter the ground. With regard to designated matches, alcohol may not be consumed on certain modes of transport, including coaches and trains, travelling to the match. Possession of fireworks or flares at the ground is prohibited as well.

The Football Spectators Act 1989 created a licensing body, the Sports Grounds Safety Authority. This regulates which soccer stadia will be able to issue tickets to view matches in England and Wales. Breach of the licensing conditions can constitute a criminal offence. The Act applies to international matches and all Premier League and English Football League grounds. It is difficult to know whether the Act has had an effect or whether societal pressures and changes in attitude have driven down the incidences of hooliganism by themselves, though. There were up to 55 per cent fewer arrests for football-related disorder between the 2010/11 and the 2018/19 seasons. There has, however, been a significant spike in the figures during the first post-Covid-19 season for which there are complete records, 2021/22.[94] There are football-specific offences listed in the Act. Most importantly, there are provisions for both these offences and for various public order offences committed in a soccer context to potentially lead to a civil sanction. These preventative Football Banning Orders (FBOs) prevent an offender attending matches or even travelling abroad to attend games for a specified period of time.

A note on the 'Non-Human Athlete'

Not all participants in sport are human, and there are welfare concerns to be addressed with horses, greyhounds and the like too. Such sport needs a 'social licence' to operate,[95] by which is meant that the use of these animals in sport must have public support to continue. For example, this social licence has been lost with regard to hunting with dogs in the UK and for bullfighting outside Spain, Portugal and a handful of other countries. Such public distaste leading to legislation[96] banning the activity was, at one time unheard of. However, the change in public attitudes there should be a warning that ensuring the welfare of animals in sport is not just necessary on the grounds of humanity. The fragility of this licence has been shown by public reaction to welfare-related incidents more recently. In respect of the show jumping phase of the Modern Pentathlon at the Tokyo Games in 2021[97] for instance. Poor treatment of the horses has led to a major change in that sport; the show jumping phase has been removed. Pentathlon can survive this change as it only affects one phase of the competition. Olympic equestrian sport and horse racing could not overcome such a ban on horses for obvious reasons. In a similar vein, perennial concern about the welfare of horses in jumps racing comes to a head every year with horse fatalities at the UK premier event, the Grand National. At the 2023 race, over one hundred animal rights protesters were arrested, three horses died and the Royal Society for the Prevention of Cruelty to Animals (RSPCA) has voiced its concerns about welfare in the horse racing industry.[98] The controversy here is very much live.

There are also doping and cheating concerns that pertain particularly to horses. Both horse racing and the Olympic equestrian sports use strict liability-based doping rules with many similarities to those used for human athletes. To these are added further rules that prevent doping on welfare, not necessarily cheating grounds. There is a myriad of problems associated with using strict liability when the athlete is not human. Many paradoxes and much unfairness result. However, a full discussion of these issues is outside the scope of this book, but a full treatment of the horse *qua* athlete and associated doping and welfare issues can be found in another work from this author, 'Regulating Sport for the Non-Human Athlete'.[99]

Addressing the question – is their fairness in athlete welfare terms?

The central question for this book has been to assess the fairness in sport's structures, policies and governance, irrespective of what happens on the playing surface. Athlete welfare is a large and diverse topic, so this section attempts to summarise some of the key points of tension.

With respect to discrimination, there are fairly comprehensive statutes and even treaties to help prevent prejudicial behaviour and provide redress for unfair treatment in many forms. The difficulty in pursuing claims, though, rests on barriers that exist in wider society but may, in some instances, be exacerbated in sport. Athletes and players who are not recognised as employees due to the nature of their sport cannot rely on employment law, for example. In addition, some discrimination is normalised in society, and this, more than science, may influence the differential treatment of female competitors in sports where physique is not the only determining factor. In Chapter 3, it was argued that challenges of all kinds against sports bodies require taking the risk that a competitor's career will be harmed, and the same is true of discrimination allegations. Further, fighting a discrimination case requires time and mental energy away from training and competing, and the financial cost may be beyond many athletes in the less well-funded sports. Transgender competitors are in a particularly difficult position. Even when the above problems have been surmounted, what is or what is not discrimination on grounds of gender transition is not by any means clear or consistent across the sports. In this area too, public perception or received wisdom appears to be of greater importance than science and statistics. This is in a similar vein to the 'culture wars' that politicians and commentators tend to engage in outside sport.

With regard to criminal law, again, there are statutes (albeit archaic and cumbersome on assaults) and a myriad of cases to determine what is and what is not a crime. However, in everyday life, that body of law loses effectiveness because of perception. A victim has to interpret behaviour as a crime against them. This in turn may be deeply affected by what they regard as unexceptional behaviour from their lived experience. If this were not true, the figures for reporting domestic violence and sexual offending would not be so low. In sport, there are added factors. On the pitch, what is considered a crime as opposed to a breach of the rules of the game turns on the wording of those rules and the unwritten culture of the game in question, particularly on the issue of consent. As examples, some physical altercations would go unreported in ice hockey, rugby and soccer whereas they absolutely would not in tennis or athletics. Not only does the victim have to categorise what has happened as a crime, but the 'gatekeepers' in the apparatus of the SGB concerned need to view the matter in that light too, unless the victim goes straight to the police. This is much less likely to happen with vulnerable and child victims. Sexual offending almost always happens in private, and in sport, the reporting of that will be further hindered by such factors as fear of reprisals from the offender and worry about not being believed. This is exaggerated in sport when retribution can come in the form of deliberate harm to an already precarious career. Coupled with this, there has been the historical tendency for claims being ignored by the sports hierarchy until the problem becomes undeniable. With health and safety crimes, the important requirement for redress is that athletes realise their space is in fact a workplace. That is not a given.

The main purpose of the civil law is to provide a means to rebalance the fortunes of the parties after a wrong has occurred. It also has the function of sharing with, or even passing accountability to any structure that can be held responsible for the wrongdoer through the widespread use of vicarious liability. The negatives are powerful, though; the civil law requires individuals and corporations to fight it out in an adversarial fashion, with the state merely providing the venue. The athlete has to instigate the proceedings and must have the financial muscle and mental energy, away from competing and training, to do so. Also, other than a possible deterrent effect, civil matters are not preventative and merely try to put the parties back to the position they were in before the incident. Once embroiled in court proceedings, there is the added hurdle that determining the appropriate level of consent brings. This is together with a less than clear standard of care in sports competitions compared to everyday activities.

There is a common theme: law which ensures fairness in athlete welfare terms has largely been created and/or refined through adjudication, although flaws and lacunae still remain. The barriers to protecting athlete welfare through those laws are mostly significant practical and societal obstacles, however.

Notes

1 For commentary on obstructive totems like this, see Antonio Gramsci, *Selections from the Prison Notebooks*, trans. Quintin Hoare and Geoffrey Nowell-Smith (New York: International Publishers, 1971), 157.

2 See Sarath K. Ganji, 'Leveraging the World Cup: Mega sporting events, human rights in Qatar, risk, and worker welfare reform', *Journal on Migration and Human Security*, 4, no. 4 (2016): 221–59.

3 See *Dobbs v. Jackson Women's Health Organization*, No. 19-1392, 597 US (2022).

4 Joan Greve, 'Contraception, gay marriage: Clarence Thomas signals new targets for supreme court', *The Guardian*, 24 June 2022, https://www.theguardian.com/world/2022/jun/24/clarence-thomas-roe-gay-marriage-contraception-lgbtq.

5 Peter Baker, 'Trump's far-right embrace – Why it's important to know more about Nick Fuentes', *New York Times*, 29 November 2022, https://www.nytimes.com/2022/11/29/briefing/nick-fuentes-trump.html.

6 'Luis Rubiales resigns as president of Spanish FA over Jenni Hermoso kiss', *BBC*, 9 September 2023, https://www.bbc.co.uk/sport/football/66637879.

7 'United Nations – New UN report reveals chronic bias against women over last decade', June 12, 2023, accessed 6 October 2023, https://news.un.org/en/story/2023/06/1137532.

8 Cindy Schmerler, 'The mental health of tennis players is no longer in the shadows', *New York Times*, 15 January 2022, https://www.nytimes.com/2022/01/15/sports/tennis/mental-health-players.html.

9 Sean Ingle, 'Simone Biles pulls out of Olympics all-around gymnastics final to focus on mental health', *The Guardian*, 28 July 2021, https://www.theguardian.com/sport/2021/jul/28/simone-biles-withdraws-from-tokyo-olympics-all-around-gymnastics-final.

10 Chris McLaughlin, 'Steve Thompson in group of ex-rugby union internationals to sue for brain damage', *BBC*, 8 December 2020, https://www.bbc.co.uk/sport/rugby-union/55201237.

11 'Scottish football to ban heading on days before and after matches', *ITV News*, 28 November 2022, https://www.itv.com/news/2022-11-28/scottish-football-to-ban-heading-on-days-before-and-after-matches.

12 Section 58 Children Act 2004.
13 For instance, compare the terminology in Section 170 of the Road Traffic Act 1988 with that of current police professional practice guidance: 'College of policing – Investigation of fatal and serious injury road collisions', accessed 6 October 2023, https://www.college.police.uk/app/roads-policing/investigation-fatal-and-serious-injury-road-collisions.
14 See Dan Roan, 'FA reform: Former chiefs say, "elderly white men" block change', *BBC*, 12 December 2016, http://www.bbc.co.uk/sport/football/38274152 and Richard Coway, 'FA reform: As MPs debate the issue, is real change a stretch too far?' *BBC*, 8 February 2017, http://www.bbc.co.uk/sport/football/38907978.
15 Bridie Jabour, '"Get stuffed": How Michelle Payne and family beat odds to win Melbourne Cup', *The Guardian*, 3 November 2015, https://www.theguardian.com/sport/2015/nov/03/get-stuffed-how-michelle-payne-and-family-beat-odds-to-win-melbourne-cup and Greg Wood, 'Khadijah Mellah becomes first UK jockey to wear hijab – And wins race', *The Guardian*, 1 August 2019, https://www.theguardian.com/sport/2019/aug/01/khadijah-mellah-first-uk-jockey-to-wear-hijab-wins-race-goodwood-horse-racing.
16 'Welsh rugby: WRU was in denial on sexism – Acting chief exec.', *BBC*, 2 February 2023, https://www.bbc.co.uk/news/uk-wales-politics-64497272.
17 'Nelson Piquet fined £780k for racist and homophobic comments about Lewis Hamilton', *Reuters*, 25 March 2023, https://www.theguardian.com/sport/2023/mar/25/nelson-piquet-fined-lewis-hamilton-comments-f1.
18 The issue in tennis has been addressed so far by equalising the prize money despite fewer sets being required of female players. This has not been without controversy, see 'Novak Djokovic questions equal prize money in tennis', *BBC*, 21 March 2016, https://www.bbc.co.uk/news/world-us-canada-35859791.
19 See CAS 2008/A/1480 *Pistorius v IAAF*, award of 16 May 2008, the now disgraced Oscar Pistorius won the right to compete against able-bodied athletes.
20 Matthew Futterman, 'FINA restricts transgender women from competing at elite level', *New York Times*, 19 June 2022, https://www.nytimes.com/2022/06/19/sports/fina-transgender-women-elite-swimming.html.
21 Katie Falkingham, 'World Athletics bans transgender women from competing in female world ranking events', *BBC*, 23 March 2023, https://www.bbc.co.uk/sport/athletics/65051900.
22 Kate Devlin, 'Rishi Sunak to consider law change to protect "biological women"', *The Independent*, 5 April 2023, https://www.independent.co.uk/news/uk/politics/kemi-badenoch-trans-women-biological-b2314144.html.
23 'UK: Supreme Court outcome "disappointing" but court affirms the right of trans people to protection from discrimination and harassment', Amnesty International Press Release, 16 April 2025, https://www.amnesty.org.uk/press-releases/uk-supreme-court-outcome-disappointing-court-affirms-right-trans-people-protection.
24 Dan Roan, 'Transgender women banned from female pool category', *BBC*, 24 April 2025, https://www.bbc.co.uk/sport/articles/c1k4gd2vge9o.
25 '"I hope my son is proud" – Transgender sprinter Valentina Petrillo misses out on Paralympics final', *New York Times*, 16 September 2023, https://www.nytimes.com/athletic/5740197/2024/09/02/transgender-valentina-petrillo-paralympics/.

26 Sean Ingle, 'Semenya loses landmark legal case against IAAF over testosterone levels', *The Guardian*, 1 May 2019, https://www.theguardian.com/sport/2019/may/01/caster-semenya-loses-landmark-legal-case-iaaf-athletics.
27 Jack Anderson, *Modern Sports Law* (Oxford: Hart, 2010), 163.
28 See 'Advisory, Conciliation and Arbitration Service – ACAS', accessed 6 October 2023, www.acas.org.uk, 'The Government Equalities Office', accessed 6 October 2023, www.equalities.gov.uk and 'The Equality and Human Rights Commission', accessed 6 October 2023, www.equalityhumanrights.com, which can bring actions under the Act as well as, or instead of, individuals.
29 'Crown Prosecution Service – Hate crime guidance', accessed 6 October 2023, https://www.cps.gov.uk/crime-info/hate-crime.
30 Dominic Casciani, 'The John Terry verdict explained', *BBC*, 13 July 2012, https://www.bbc.co.uk/news/uk-18835915.
31 See also *Sterling v Leeds Rugby League Cup* [2001] ISLR 201.
32 Nazia Parveen, 'Jonás Gutiérrez wins case against Newcastle over cancer reatment', *The Guardian*, 14 April 2016, https://www.theguardian.com/football/2016/apr/14/jonas-gutierrez-wins-discrimination-claim-against-newcastle-utd.
33 James Brown, 'The icarious liability of sports governing bodies and competition organisers', *Legal Studies*, 43, no. 2 (2023): 225.
34 See also *Nethermere (St. Neots) Ltd v Gardiner and Another* [1984] ICR 612.
35 United Nations General Assembly Resolution 217A.
36 'United Nations – Universal Declaration of Human Rights', accessed 6 October 2023, https://www.un.org/en/about-us/universal-declaration-of-human-rights.
37 *Anwesh Pokkuluri v Union of India W.P.*(Crl.) No. 000121 - / 2018.
38 'United Nations – UN General Assembly votes to suspend Russia from the Human Rights Council', 7 April 2022, accessed 6 October 2023, https://news.un.org/en/story/2022/04/1115782.
39 'Centre for European Reform – Hot topics, Brexit', accessed 6 October 2023, https://www.cer.eu/hot-topics/brexit.
40 The *Kolpak* case extends this to countries, such as Switzerland, that have bilateral agreements with the EU.
41 See for instance, Martin Kettle, 'Suella Braverman is spoiling for a fight on human rights – One that undermines this whole government', *The Guardian*, 8 December 2022, https://www.theguardian.com/commentisfree/2022/dec/08/suella-braverman-human-rights-undermines-rishi-sunak.
42 See a discussion of *Bennett v Football Association* (1978) Court of Appeal, 28 July, Transcript No. 591 in Seema Patel, *Inclusion and Exclusion in Competitive Sport: Socio-legal and Regulatory Perspectives* (Oxford: Routledge, 2015), 73–4.
43 Emanuella Grinberg and Dani Stewart, '3 myths that shape the transgender bathroom debate', *CNN*, 7 March 2013, https://edition.cnn.com/2017/03/07/health/transgender-bathroom-law-facts-myths/index.html and Aletha Adu and Aubrey Allegretti, 'Tory MP under fire for transphobic comments about Eddie Izzard', 26 October 2022, https://www.theguardian.com/culture/2022/oct/26/tory-mp-under-fire-for-transphobic-comments-about-eddie-izzard.
44 'Nicola Sturgeon: No apology over transgender prisoner row', *BBC*, 30 January 2023, https://www.bbc.co.uk/news/uk-scotland-scotland-politics-64431383.

45 See for instance, 'Equality in sport – SCEG project for review and redraft of guidance for transgender inclusion in domestic sport 2020', accessed 6 October 2023, https://equalityinsport.org/docs/300921/Project%20Report%20on%20the%20Review%20of%20the%20Guidance%20for%20Transgender%20Inclusion%20in%20Domestic%20Sport%202021.pdf.

46 Dan Roan, 'British Cycling to ban transgender women from competing in female category', *BBC*, 26 May 2023, https://www.bbc.co.uk/sport/cycling/65718748.

47 See Elaine Dunkley and Christine McSorley, 'Oxford split over Kathleen Stock's invite to Union debate', *BBC*, 28 May 2023, https://www.bbc.co.uk/news/education-65722845 and Roan McClean, 'I was so fraid of coming out as transgender that I struggled with OCD and psychosis as a teenager', *Independent*, 13 May 2021, https://www.independent.co.uk/voices/transgender-mental-health-lgbt-b1846149.html.

48 See Matt Slater, 'Eni Aluko feels "vindicated" by FA apology but accuses chief xecutive Martin Glenn of blackmail', *Independent*, 18 October 2017, http://www.independent.co.uk/sport/football/news-and-comment/eni-aluko-football-association-hearing-martin-glenn-conduct-like-blackmail-a8007111.html, Sean Ingle, 'Lizzie Armitstead becomes latest rider to accuse British Cycling of sexism', *The Guardian*, 31 March 2017, www.theguardian.com/sport/2017/mar/31/lizzie-armitstead-becomes-latest-rider-to-accuse-british-cycling-of-sexism and Jabour, '"Get stuffed": How Michelle Payne and family beat odds to win Melbourne Cup'.

49 'The Legal 500 – Discrimination in footall, its most famous cases, the evolution of its regulations and remedies', accessed 6 October 2023, https://www.legal500.com/developments/thought-leadership/discrimination-in-football-its-most-famous-casesthe-evolution-of-its-regulationsand-its-remedies/.

50 Essentially, wherever the UK has jurisdiction, including certain territories, ships, embassies and places occupied by UK troops.

51 In effect, this has been extended to an unlimited time by the Law Reform (Year and a Day Rule) Act 1996.

52 David Conn, 'Hillsborough: David Duckenfield found not guilty of manslaughter', 28 November 2019, https://www.theguardian.com/uk-news/2019/nov/28/hillsborough-david-duckenfield-verdict.

53 Geraint Vincent, 'Zeebrugge: Britain's worst peacetime maritime disaster explained', *ITV News*, 6 March 2017, https://www.itv.com/news/2017-03-06/zeebrugge-britains-worst-peacetime-maritime-disaster-explained.

54 'Water sports firm pleads guilty to Mari-Simon Cronje death charge', *BBC*, 22 November 2013, https://www.bbc.co.uk/news/uk-england-london-25056230.

55 *R v Lowe* [1973] QB 702.

56 *R v Kamara* (1988), Times Law Reports, 15 April.

57 *R v Cantona* (1995), Times Law Reports, 25 March.

58 Aine Fox, 'Man charged with attack on Arsenal goalkeeper Aaron Ramsdale', *Independent*, 17 January 2023, https://www.independent.co.uk/sport/football/aaron-ramsdale-arsenal-tottenham-metropolitan-police-b2263927.html.

59 Although *DPP v K* [1990] 1 WLR 1067 and *DPP v Santana-Bermudez* [2003] EWHC 298 would seem to suggest otherwise.

60 See the earlier discussion of John Terry's racially aggravated Section 5 charge under 'Discrimination' in this chapter.

61 *Smith v Chief Superintendent of Woking Police Station* [1983] Crim LR 323.

62 Much will depend on the weightiness of the threat versus the vulnerability of the victim; however, as per *R v Light* (1857) D & B 332.
63 See also *R v Martin* (1881) 8 QBD 54 and *DPP v K* [1990] 1 WLR 1067.
64 'Crown Prosecution Service – Offences against the person, incorporating the charging standard', accessed 6 October 2023, https://www.cps.gov.uk/legal-guidance/offences-against-person-incorporating-charging-standard.
65 Ibid.
66 'NHS England – About NHS England safeguarding', accessed 6 October 2023, https://www.england.nhs.uk/safeguarding/about/.
67 'Office for Standards in Education (OFSTED) – Safeguarding policy', accessed 6 October 2023, https://www.gov.uk/government/publications/ofsted-safeguarding-policy/ofsted-safeguarding-policy.
68 'Sport England – Safeguarding', accessed 6 October 2023, https://www.sportengland.org/guidance-and-support/safeguarding.
69 'British Gymnastics – Safeguarding policy and procedures', accessed 6 October 2023, https://www.british-gymnastics.org/documents/regions-and-home-countries/london/policies-and-procedures-1/12382-safeguarding-policy-september-2021/file.
70 The statutory guidance can be found at 'HM Government – Working together to safeguard children', accessed 6 October 2023, https://www.gov.uk/government/publications/working-together-to-safeguard-children--2. The statutes that underpin safeguarding include The Children Acts 1989 and 2004, the Legal Aid, Sentencing and Punishment of Offenders Act 2012, and the Care Act 2014.
71 Tim Newburn, *Criminology* (London: Routledge, 2007), 52.
72 Ibid., 53.
73 Ibid., 56.
74 Ibid.
75 Ibid., 61.
76 Ibid., 54.
77 Ibid., 52.
78 'Rape crisis – Rape and sexual assault statistics', accessed 6 October 2023, https://rapecrisis.org.uk/get-informed/statistics-sexual-violence/.
79 'Home Office – Operation *Soteria Bluestone*, year one report', https://www.gov.uk/government/publications/operation-soteria-year-one-report/operation-soteria-bluestone-year-one-report-accessible-version.
80 'Wayne Couzens sentenced to 19 months in prison for indecent exposure', *The Guardian*, 6 March 2023, https://www.theguardian.com/uk-news/2023/mar/06/wayne-couzens-sentenced-to-19-months-in-prison-for-indecent-exposure.
81 'Ex-football coach Barry Bennell pleads guilty to nine sexual offences', *The Guardian*, 31 July 2020, https://www.theguardian.com/uk-news/2020/jul/31/former-football-barry-bennell-coach-pleads-guilty-to-nine-sexual-offences.
82 See Heather Udowitch, 'The Larry Nassar nightmare: Athletic organizational failures to address sexual assault allegations and a call for corrective action', *DePaul Journal of Sports Law & Contemporary Problems*, 16 (2020).
83 In the context of this specific discussion only, the word 'woman' is used to mean a person without male reproductive organs at birth. In general, though, the book is written from the position that a person's gender is what they identify as.

84 'Crown Prosecution Service – Rape and sexual offences – Chapter 7: Key legislation and offences, legal guidance, sexual offences', accessed 7 October 2023, https://www.cps.gov.uk/legal-guidance/rape-and-sexual-offences-chapter-7-key-legislation-and-offences#.

85 'Football abuse hotline receives "staggering surge" in calls', *BBC*, 1 December 2016, http://www.bbc.co.uk/news/uk-38161301.

86 Danile Taylor, 'Football is heading for trouble over brain injuries caused by the ball', *The Guardian*, 30 September 2017, https://www.theguardian.com/football/blog/2017/sep/30/football-heading-brain-injuries-ball-kevin-doyle.

87 Chris Jones, 'Premiership rugby: Impossible to draw conclusions from injury crisis', *BBC*, 4 October 2017, http://www.bbc.co.uk/sport/rugby-union/41498498.

88 Mark Popham, 'Racing: Court paves way for Cook compensation: Judge says jockeys were playing Russian roulette when riding at Doncaster', *The Independent*, 15 July 1993, http://www.independent.co.uk/sport/racing-court-paves-way-for-cook-compensation-judge-says-jockeys-were-playing-russian-roulette-when-1485240.html.

89 This is rather archaic language for 'the man on the street'. Clapham is a district of London, and 'omnibus' is the original term from which the word 'bus' is derived.

90 For context, see Michael Aylwin, 'Rugby union's brutal reality: The physical and mental toll of an elite playing career', *Guardian*, 5 May 2016, https://www.theguardian.com/sport/2016/may/05/rugby-union-brutal-reality-elite-player-welfare.

91 *Varnish v British Cycling Federation t/a British Cycling* UKEAT/0022/20/LA.

92 Howard Bluver, 'Owner liability for intentional torts committed by professional athletes against spectators', *Buffalo Law Review*, 30, no. 3 (July 1981): 567–8.

93 See Eric Dunning, 'Towards a sociological understanding of football hooliganism as a world phenomenon', *European Journal on Criminal Policy and Research*, 8 (2000): 141–62.

94 'Home Office – Football-related arrests and banning orders, England and Wales: 2021 to 2022 season', accessed 7 October 2023, https://www.gov.uk/government/statistics/football-related-arrests-and-banning-orders-england-and-wales-2021-to-2022-season/football-related-arrests-and-banning-orders-england-and-wales-2021-to-2022-season.

95 Julie Fiedler and Paul D. McGreevy, 'Reconciling horse welfare, worker safety, and public expectations: Horse event incident management systems in Australia', *Animals*, 6, no. 3 (2016): 1–2.

96 For instance, the Hunting Act 2004.

97 'Modern Pentathlon: Vote goes in favour of replacing show jumping with obstacle racing', *BBC*, 12 November 2022, https://www.bbc.co.uk/sport/modern-pentathlon/63611122.

98 'Grand National 2023: Trainer blames delays caused by protesters for horse death', *BBC*, 12 November 2022, https://www.bbc.co.uk/sport/horse-racing/65296693.

99 Jonathan Merritt, *Regulating Sport for the Non-Human Athlete* (Lanham: Rowman and Littlefield, 2019).

6

Sport and Intellectual Property

What is a fair price?

There is no doubt that the world of sport would be unrecognisable to Nicholas 'Pa' Jackson, the founder of English soccer club Corinthian FC in 1882. The club was built on the amateur principles of playing for the love of the game and promoting fair play, as discussed at the end of Chapter 2. At its inception, the club was even constitutionally prohibited from entering any matches where trophies or shields might be won. It therefore initially limited itself to friendly matches. Nowadays, sport is a multi-billion-dollar global industry. Broadcast rights alone for the Rio Olympics in 2016 are estimated to have been in excess of £3.5bn. Similar arrangements raised around £8.5bn for soccer's Premier League between 2016 and 2019.[1] Sport has not built this worth through gate receipts alone; intellectual property (IP) rights are central to the revenue streams of most elite sports. The ownership of copyright, trademarks, broadcasting rights and patents means that the most popular sports can now leverage their brand to raise eye-watering sums. The absorption of sport into capitalist hegemony is not to everyone's liking, however, and sports purists lament the way that 'money rules'. For instance, there is much disquiet about the involvement of Saudi Arabian wealth in international golf. There is growing apprehension that similar things are happening in soccer and cricket, with phrases like sport 'being repackaged as investment vehicles, advertising boards [and] weapons of geopolitical power'[2] being used. These debates will feature in Chapter 9 as well. The fact is, though, professional sport has commercialised rapidly over the last half-century or more, and IP has been key to that. The main ways that IP can be packaged and sold are through merchandising, sponsorship, patents, broadcasting and database rights. The latter two are considered in most depth in Chapter 7, but merchandising and sponsorship, two often-confused terms, are explained here.

Patent law is outside the scope of this book; it is a large topic in and of itself, and not all sports routinely develop new technology to the extent that, for instance, Formula One does. In any event, where new sporting equipment is developed and patented, this really only benefits the manufacturer and does not exist in a sporting context per se. Consequently, any good patent law text will assist in understanding this area of law. Interestingly, though, patenting new technology in the cloning of racehorses and other competition animals may become a burgeoning area of litigation.[3]

An introduction to intellectual property rights and their rationale

There is some overlap between entertainment and sports law in this context. Modern elite sportsmen and women are often media stars as well. For instance, the legal principles around protecting the IP in a celebrity wedding may apply directly to a sports event. In *Douglas v Hello! Ltd* [2001] QB 967, Michael Douglas and Catherine Zeta-Jones were unable to prevent the use of unauthorised photography at their nuptial event because of inadequate entry restrictions that did not bar photography. There might have also been doubt about whether being invited to a wedding constituted a contract in UK law anyway. The case was partially won by the couple on another contractual basis, however.

Know your limits

It may come as a surprise to know that, unlike jurisdictions such as the United States and France, the law in the UK does allow image rights to attach to a 'spectacle'. This includes a sporting event in itself, as was held in *Sports and General Press Agency v 'Our Dogs' Publishing Co.* [1917] KB 125 CA. This case was followed in Australia in *Victoria Park Racing & Recreation Grounds Co Ltd v Taylor* (1937) 58 CLR 479. Together, these cases mean that no one in the UK or much of the Commonwealth, including sports personalities, owns image rights in their own face and likeness. Therefore, under domestic IP law, any person may photograph or film a sporting event they are present at without restriction. This applies to free-playing competitions where there is no element of pre-planned movements, such as a rugby or baseball match. Dance is an official sport in the UK, and choreographed routines,might be subject to copyright, so that would be a different matter. This could possibly also apply to cheerleading ancillary to a match or as a distinct competitive event. However, none of this prevents the IP in a sports event or a person's likeness from being monetised. For instance, by operation of contract, the Football Association (FA) shares the rights to its players images. This is enforced by conditions of entry to venues, another contract, between the photographer and the ground at which they wish to take pictures. Similarly, ordinary spectators can be prohibited from filming the event on pain of ejection from the ground. Professional photographers are allowed in only on condition that they assign to the FA the copyright they have as creators of the photographic images. If the playing surface can be viewed from outside the area controlled by the venue or the SGB, then there is little that either can do to restrict the taking of images, though, per *Victoria Park v Taylor*. In this case, it was held that horse races could be lawfully filmed from a platform on adjoining land. This may now also apply to drone footage from above adjoining land.

There are also ways that data protection legislation can apply to a person's likeness insofar as they are identifiable as a data subject. This would require the sportsperson to make a complaint under relevant legislation and so is not really IP law at all. It could, however, be used to restrict the circumstances where unauthorised images may be taken. Also, although the field of play, the people on it and the overall spectacle do not become IP, there may be images displayed there that do. For instance, club crests and logos may be trademarked, and any music played may be subject to copyright. Enforcing these rules might well render any photographs and filming almost useless.[4]

In summary, IP in sport can be packaged and sold in the UK, but in many instances, this is achieved by cobbling together enforceable rights from the law of contract, trespass and so on. However, merchandising and sponsorship can fully engage with copyright and trademark law, where human creativity and design are involved.

Owning ideas – moral and practical points

In fact, it is not the idea itself that is protected by law; it is the manifestation of that idea. For instance, a photographer deciding that an image of Tiger Woods or Lewis Hamilton would have artistic merit is not protected by copyright, but the resulting photograph is. Therefore, anyone can take a photograph of the same subject without considering other photographers' IP rights. The original photograph may not be copied without permission, however. In turn, the themes and colours in a graphic artist's mind cannot be trademarked, but a new club logo can be. That said, the rationale for attaching a monetary value to creativity should be explored as it was not always so. Not all societies throughout time have embraced this idea. In China, for instance, before the well-crafted, if not consistently enforced, modern laws on IP were enacted, cultural notions held more sway. Those prevailing attitudes to IP rights date back more than 2000 years to Confucianism. In this way of thinking, copying earlier works is done to be accurate about and to pay due homage to the intellectual effort involved.[5] The term 'intellectual property' seldom invites a critique in and of itself, but in fact, determining that intellect is ownable ought to warrant further thought. This monetisation is a feature of modern capitalism and anything that can be commodified will be. That stretches from owning land to arranging security for persons and property, from manufactured products to a picturesque view that is only available by purchasing an overlooking hotel room. The hotel itself is probably blocking the same view from the land behind as might have been enjoyed free for centuries. Little is immune from this process, and so it is with creative skills. The argument goes, however, that the mental and physical efforts of the creators should be rewarded, and in our society, that means in terms of wealth rather than creative stature. This means that, ironically for capitalism, fair competition must be eradicated to allow a period wherein the creator can fully benefit from their labours.

Merchandising

In simple terms, merchandising in the sporting and entertainment sector involves producing and selling branded products that rely on a *bona fide* relationship with personalities, teams, clubs, leagues and the like. Examples would include items such as replica team shirts, hats and scarves with team logos embroidered on. Also in the list would be ceramic wear such as plates and mugs bearing the faces of sports personalities, representations of motor racing drivers and their cars made as toys, and posters or sticker books featuring a team brand. High street clothing, from shoes to hoodies, t-shirts and outer coats that bear a team name or brand, would also fall under this bracket. The possibilities are almost inexhaustible. Maximising the revenue from these items depends almost entirely on restricting who is permitted to produce and sell them. If anyone could manufacture and sell these without legal sanction, then the permission to do so would have no value to the owner of the brand. If only one or a narrow range of businesses can lawfully deal in these items, then the law of supply and demand means that the value increases. This is why IP agreements can have such a high monetary value.

Criminal breach of IP law

Each year, law enforcement the world over seizes 'counterfeit' goods.[6] In some cases, these goods are unlawful because they do not meet safety and other consumer standards. In many instances, though, the issue is that the goods are produced without a valid IP agreement between the manufacturer and/or distributor. Yet the items bear branding that purports to rely on an official merchandising agreement. Regarding these counterfeits, it is important to understand that in the UK, the criminal law only gets involved if the unlawful operation is organised and commercial. Generally, it must also involve a significant volume of material that is produced with the intention of making a profit. That area of law is outside the scope of this book. The concern here is IP within the civil branch of the law. In most situations, a breach of IP law has to be addressed by the party alleging the wrong. Breach of such as copyright is not 'theft', no matter how much commercial entities would like to persuade the public that it is. The exception is where IP is protected by statute and breaches are criminalised in relation to major sporting events. The World Cup and the Olympics[7] are examples of the level of elite sport that can be the subject of such legislation.

IP and the civil law

Whether the breach is considered criminal or not, the main ways that IP is protected in this sector are through trademarks and copyright. Copyright is also a key feature of broadcasting, covered in Chapter 7, and trademarks can feature here as well. It is perhaps most useful to begin with a discussion of trademarks under the general heading of merchandising. This is because so much of 'branding' is about images and logos that can be legitimately trademarked. There are both registered and unregistered trademarks to be understood. Registered trademarks are protected in the UK by statute and by international treaty. Unregistered trademarks are protected under English common law. The tort of 'passing off' offers a cause of action if a brand that has not been registered is used without permission. This is a little more problematic than being able to rely on statute, however.

Registered trademarks

Unregistered trademarks can be marked in the UK with a ™ symbol. This carries no legal significance as the IP rights in the brand concerned already exist by operation of law, as shall be discussed later. However, the letters do assert that the owner is aware that they own IP rights in the logo, design or form of words signified. Registered trademarks are formally protected, though, by a successful application under the Trade Marks Act 1994. Such brands have the ® symbol displayed on them.

It is worth noting that whilst the primary function of a trademark is to protect the owner's investment in creating the design, there is a secondary purpose which has much more to do with how a capitalist, consumerist society operates. The producer will hope that the logos and designs that adorn consumer goods are associated with quality or even a certain lifestyle. Decisions to purchase, such as a t-shirt, may be made on the basis that it bears a well-known trademarked sports logo. This is also, to a certain extent, a badge of quality, as it would be unwise for a sports team or any other commercial entity to allow their name to be associated with poorly manufactured items. In turn, businesses may, from time to time, find themselves associated with a sportsman or woman who has fallen into disgrace, perhaps through a doping finding. In that event, the relationship is likely to be terminated by the commercial entity. To take the quality assurance point further, the trademarked item is likely to have a higher price than other non-branded clothing. This is often justified by the seller on the basis that it is a stamp of distinction, but in reality, the purchase price may contain a very high profit margin that is hard to justify, especially as the branded and non-branded items may be made in the same 'sweatshops' in the developing world. What this all rather underscores is that in capitalism, ownership of goods and other signs of material wealth have become perhaps the only acceptable measure of success. It is unsurprising that parents routinely complain about 'having' to buy their sports-mad children the latest team strip, despite its exorbitant price. The clubs could even be accused of having 'adopted the system of planned obsolescence used by car manufacturers, [changing] the design of their strips every couple of years in order to stimulate new sales'.[8] Sometimes this problem has been exacerbated by unlawful anti-competitive practices between sports clubs and retailers uncovered by the Competition and Markets Authority (CMA).[9]

The Trade Marks Act 1994

The Act defines what a registered trademark is, and this is the basis upon which a register of such marks is maintained. It is also under this legislation that enforcement by rights holders in respect of these types of brands is conducted. The Act defines a trademark as 'any sign which is capable . . . of being represented in the register in a manner which enables the registrar . . . and the public to determine the clear and precise subject matter of the protection afforded to the proprietor' in Section 1(1)(a). Perhaps most importantly, the mark must allow for goods from one business to be distinguished from those of another. By Section 1(1)(b), it may 'consist of words (including personal names), designs, letters, numerals, colours, sounds or the shape of goods or their packaging'. Trademarks are granted only for the types of goods or services applied for. The registry is divided into classes: one for ceramic goods and the like, another for clothing and so on. It is therefore important to note that registering a club emblem solely in the class related to clothing will not prevent its use on toys or paper goods, for instance. Multiple classes need to be specified in any application.

It is worth remembering that sometimes the brand of the product is more memorable than the product itself. In the UK, vacuuming the carpet might well be described as 'hoovering' despite the fact that many other manufacturers besides Hoover manufacture vacuum cleaners. The same analogy might be used in the United States, where the word 'kibble' is used to describe a type of dry dog food but is also a specific brand name. The most important feature, though, is that the mark must refer to something with an element of graphic design to it, and this includes packaging. Some containers are so iconic that they themselves represent the contents, and the Coca-Cola bottle is an example. This waisted glass container is synonymous with that particular drink, even though many similarly tasting drinks are available with more or less the same colour. It was only after the Act was passed that this glassware could be registered. Certain aftershaves, perfumes or *eaux de toilette* have distinctive bottles as well that are capable of registration, although smells cannot be trademarked in the EU.[10] It remains to be seen whether case law develops that allows 'olfactory signs' to be protected now that the UK has left the bloc, however. Currently, this might explain the proliferation of copies of famous scents on the market, though. These are quite lawful provided that neither the brand nor the packaging is copied.

The need for there to be a graphic design element means that simple forms of words may not be protected (See Figure 6.1). The words 'Formula One' can be used without restriction, for instance. 'Formula 1' or 'F1' in the particular font, style and colour that the sport has registered as a logo is protected, however. Photographic images cannot be trademarked under this legislation, and both these and forms of words without additional stylising would need to rely on the law of copyright discussed later in this chapter. Sports personalities have, however, been able to register graphic representations of themselves. Former England, Manchester United and LA Galaxy player David Beckham had an instantly recognisable pose as he took a free kick in a soccer game. This was reproduced as a graphic design and registered as a trademark in 2004, although it has since expired.[11] There are two main criteria by which an application for a trademark may be refused. These are on 'absolute' or 'relative' grounds. The absolute grounds in Section 3 start with a restatement of the obvious: that the mark does not meet the definition in Section 1 of the Act. There follows, though, a list including in Section 3(1)(b), 'signs which are devoid of any distinctive character . . . [or which indicate] . . . quality, quantity, intended purpose, purpose, geographical origin or the time of production of goods [or services]', from Section 3(1)(c). Thus, prices, 'best before' dates and 'Made in Portugal', amongst other things, would not be registrable. Under Section 3(1)(d), signs or indications which have become genuinely customary in the established practices of the trade, such as 'Buy One Get One Free' or 'Summer Sale', are similarly excluded. This is unless they have a distinctive character through common usage. This latter provision, along with much of this section, is not particularly clear. It is difficult to establish what was in the minds of the legislators, but the purpose appears to be to provide some detail to augment Section 1, especially that the mark must be distinctive in nature. Under Section 3, other absolute grounds

Trade Marks Act 1994 Sections	Provision:	Examples:
Definition		
S1(1)(a)	A trademark is '...any sign which is capable...of being represented in the register...to determine the clear and precise subject matter of the protection afforded to the proprietor...'	'Formula 1' (in the style and format F1 uses)
S1(1)(b)	It may '...consist of words (including personal names), designs, letters, numerals, colours, sounds or the shape of goods or their packaging'	Coca Cola bottle
Absolute grounds for refusal		
S3(1)(a)	'Signs which do not satisfy the requirements of section 1(1)'	
S3(1)(b)	'...signs which are devoid of any distinctive character...'	Generic picture of a cat
S3(1)(c)	Signs which indicate '...quality, quantity, intended purpose, purpose, geographical origin or the time of production of goods [or services]...'	'Made in Portugal'
S3(1)(d)	Signs '... which have become customary in the current language' of the trade	'Summer Sale'
	Other grounds for absolute refusal in S3 include that the mark must not be immoral, prohibited by national law or treaty or applied for in bad faith.	Nazi emblems
	Furthermore, marks that may be deceptive or that give the incorrect impression they are associated with the patronage of the British Royal Family. Trademarks such as the Union Jack, any of the four national flags of the UK, coats of arms and the like. The Olympic symbol.	'Royal Supermarket'
Relative grounds for refusal		
S5(1)	A '...trade mark shall not be registered if it is identical with an earlier trade mark and the goods or services...are identical [or too similar] with the goods or services for which the earlier trade mark is protected...'	'H and S Trading' could not be registered if there is a 'Hands Trading' on the register.
S5(2)	If there '...exists a likelihood of confusion on the part of the public'.	A Miss Marks and a Mr Spencer could not register M and S Stores, because Marks and Spencer is a household retail name in the UK.

Figure 6.1 A summary of the main provisions of the Trade Marks Act 1994.

include that the mark must not be immoral, prohibited by national law or treaty, or applied for in bad faith. Immorality is a notoriously difficult area, especially as societies become ever more culturally diverse. Signs and symbols which are inoffensive under 'public policy or . . . accepted principles of morality', as the Act puts it, may not be acceptable at all to large sections of the population with a different ethnic or religious background. Section 4 of the Act deals with prohibitions relating to marks that may be deceptive or that give the impression that the product receives the patronage of the British Royal Family without authority. It also prevents the trademarking of national symbols such as the Union Jack, any of the four national flags of the UK, coats of arms and the like. Importantly for sport, the Olympic symbol may also not be trademarked by anyone else but the IOC under Section 4(5).

Relative grounds are covered in Section 5, and the main purpose is to prevent identical or too similar marks from existing side by side for entirely different products. Under Section 5(1), a 'trade mark shall not be registered if it is identical with an earlier trade mark and the goods or services . . . are identical with the goods or services for which the earlier trade mark is protected'. An application will also be refused if the mark is identical or similar to an earlier mark or if the goods and services are identical or too similar, and per Section 5(2), there 'exists a likelihood of confusion on the part of the public.'

Litigation relating to sport has arisen with respect to the prohibition of national symbols. In *RFU & Nike v Cotton Traders Limited* [2002] EWHC 467 (Ch), clothing manufacturer Cotton Traders created a range of shirts with the English rose, otherwise known as the Tudor or Union rose, as an emblem on them. This heraldic symbol is part of English cultural heritage. The rose was created in red and white to symbolise the union of the Houses of Lancaster and York in peace after the bloody Wars of the Roses in the fifteenth century. The Rugby Football Union (RFU) had a merchandising deal with Nike, and the trademarked symbol of the RFU is a red and white rose with lettering. However, the flower was not identical to the heraldic image. Both litigants alleged that Cotton Traders had infringed their trade marks inter alia by producing these shirts. The claim failed because Nike and the RFU could not claim to have a trademark that included a national symbol. There was also the problem that this image could not be proven to be associated closely enough with the RFU in the minds of the public. As is quite common, the claim also had a separate head that alleged 'passing off'. This is a tort that does not require the brand to be registered as a trademark and which will be discussed further, later in the chapter. The case on these grounds was dismissed for the same reasons.

Another case which involved both registered trademarks together with unregistered marks under a 'passing off' claim was *Arsenal Football Club PLC v Matthew Reed* [2014] EWHC 781 (Ch). The litigation actually commenced in 2002 and concerned the activities of Mr Reed, a market trader selling hats, scarves and other memorabilia outside Arsenal's home stadium. The case began in the High Court, was referred to the European Court of Justice (ECJ) for a ruling and, based on that, was finally heard in the Court of Appeal. The crux of the matter was that, amongst other brandings, Arsenal registered the soccer club's name within a crest and its famous cannon logo.[12] The merchandise on Mr Reed's stall was carefully separated into 'licensed' and 'unlicensed' products to make it clear that only some of the items were 'official' merchandise. Mr Reed maintained that the remainder were simply 'badges of allegiance' and that he had no intention of representing them as being authorised by the club. Despite this, Arsenal brought an action under the Act for 'passing off'. This latter claim was disallowed, but the Court of Appeal held that there had been an infringement of the Act. This protracted and expensive legal action highlighted the importance of registering club logos and the like as trademarks for all sports clubs and societies wishing to protect the IP in their brand. It also emphasised how enthusiastic large sports corporations can be in pursuing an individual, notwithstanding that they were merely a market trader trying to make a living. It is worth noting, however, that the use of protected logos and so on would need to be integral to the reproduction to trigger protection under the Act. In *Trebor Bassett Limited v The Football Association Limited* [1997] FSR 211, the confectionery company included cards with photographs of England players as promotional items in packets of sweets. These players had the 'Three Lions' emblem on their shirts, and the FA sought protection for its trademark registered on this image. The court held that the use of the image was purely 'incidental' and not on the packaging itself. Thus, a 'paparazzi' capturing an image of a person wearing a football shirt in the street probably need not 'blur out' any visible commercial branding. If such an unauthorised photo were taken of a player on the field of play or in training, the safest course might be to digitally erase these motifs, however.

The economy is a global one, so there is a limit to the jurisdiction of IP legislation enacted in any one country. A trademark protected under the Trade Marks Act 1994 would have no protection in France, India or China, for instance. It is, however, perfectly possible for goods to be manufactured in those countries that are identical to protected goods in the UK and exported to the same markets. Consequently, there are treaties between certain countries that geographically extend the protection that the signatories' domestic laws have given. Details of all of these are outside the scope of this book. Nonetheless, the most important of these are those emanating from the EU, United Nations (UN) and the Trade Related Aspects of Intellectual Property Rights Law (TRIPs) of 1994. This latter being signed by all members of the World Trade Organisation (WTO). Being a member state of the EU allows for IP laws to be harmonised, and it is possible to apply for protection throughout the bloc in addition to anything the home country's laws provide for. This, of course, no longer applies in the UK. These marks are referred to as Community Trade Marks (CTM).[13] The UN has an agency, the World Intellectual Property Organisation (WIPO), which allows for protections in member states to be applied globally. TRIPs, based on the earlier Paris Convention, offers the widest and most detailed opportunities for international IP protection.

Unregistered trademarks and the tort of 'passing off'

This type of IP protection, which operates in substantially the same area as registered trademarks, is based on common law, not statute. Case law has long allowed for the owner of a brand to take legal action in tort for the civil wrong of 'passing off' by another of goods or services as if they were from the brand owner. It might be described as the unlawful appropriation of another business's 'goodwill' and reputation. Another way of putting that is 'brand awareness', as it is possible to have a reputation in a particular location where you do not have significant trade, and therefore no goodwill.[14] The protection of a brand using a case framed in tort is not as straightforward as relying on trademark legislation, however. This begs the question as to why all brands are not protected by statute. There can be many reasons; there is a cost in time and money in applying for registration. Alternatively, the brand owner may not think of their goodwill and reputation as something that can be protected by trademarking logos and so on. Further, the designs and images may not satisfy the precise requirements of Section 1 of the Trade Marks Act either. They may still represent a much-respected brand and reputation, however.

The pitfalls of taking action over an unregistered mark are considerable. Firstly, it must be proven to the court's satisfaction that there is a well-established brand awareness to be protected. Conversely, with an action under the Act, that aspect is already shown by the existence of a registered trademark. In *Reckitt & Coleman Products v Borden* [1990] 1 All ER 873, the appellants were seeking to protect the brand they had in selling lemon juice in life-sized yellow plastic lemon-shaped containers, 'Jif Lemons'. Other manufacturers had begun marketing lemon juice in similar packaging, and Reckitt and Coleman alleged 'passing off'. The claim was rejected on the basis that the plastic lemons were more of an indicator of the contents of the packaging, that is, the juice of lemons, than they were of the appellants' goodwill. There was an opportunity in the case, however, to set out the requirements for a successful passing off claim. Firstly, the claimant's goods or services must have acquired 'goodwill or reputation in the mind of the purchasing public and [be] known by some distinguishing feature'. Secondly, there must have been a 'misrepresentation' by the defendant, whether intentional or not, that leads, or is likely to lead, customers to believe that the goods or services offered are those of the claimant. Finally, it must be shown that damage to the claimant's goodwill is or is likely to result 'as a consequence of the misrepresentation'.

An important passing off case with a sporting dimension is *Irvine and another v Talksport Ltd* [2002] EWHC 367 (Ch). Eddie Irvine drove for the Ferrari Formula One team. Talksport had obtained the rights to broadcast races in the 1999 season and began a promotional campaign. Talksport used a photograph they had licensed but altered it. They removed the mobile phone from Irvine's hand and substituted it with an image of a radio bearing Talksport's branding. This, according to Irvine, falsely associated his personal brand image with the radio broadcaster, creating a false endorsement. Irvine alleged that his goodwill was harmed by this misrepresentation. The court held that Irvine's achievements meant he was a recognisable individual and so had goodwill to protect. Further, members of the public had, or were likely to have, been misled into believing the claimant had an endorsement deal with the defendant. Finally, although negligible in commercial terms, there was damage. This was finally assessed at £25,000, and the point of the case, to require cessation of the defendant's activities, was achieved. *Arsenal v Reed*, discussed earlier under registered trademarks, had a passing off strand to the case as well. In addition to the Trade Marks Act allegation, Arsenal claimed that Reed had been passing off goods as official Arsenal merchandise when they were not. The case had an extended period of back and forth between the ECJ and the English Courts, but the final judgement concentrated on the legislative provision, not the common law claim. It is unclear why passing off was ultimately never fully addressed, but Arsenal was content with proving a statutory violation.

Sport and copyright

There is no need to register copyright; ownership of 'artistic' work subsists from the point of inception of the work and belongs to the creator. In this context, 'artistic' is not a qualitative term. A creation can objectively have no artistic merit at all, yet be the intellectual property of the painter, writer and so on. There must be a perceptible element of intellectual effort in creating the work, however. For this reason, databases, despite having considerable potential value in sport, have to be considered separately from other IP rights that attach to words, figures and pictures.

Copyright also applies to computer-generated images and lines of code. As such, it is an important part of the framework that esports is built on. As discussed in Chapter 2, the games publishing houses in effect 'own' the sport because they cannot be played without using the IP belonging to the creators. A hypothetical parallel would be if soccer could only be played using footballs manufactured by Nike. This structure will make it very difficult for the emerging esports national and international governing bodies for this multi-billion-dollar sector to gain total control in the way that is common in traditional sports. It also remains to be seen what the rapid rise in sophistication experienced by artificial intelligence (AI) will mean for copyright law. If a machine is programmed by a human but then develops its own skills in creating imagery, the question will be whether the copyright in those images vests in any human at all. This point will be returned to in Chapter 7. Having said that, copyright exists from the moment of manifestation of the idea, and that right is transferable. The words on this page, be they ever so humble, are the intellectual property of the author as they are being written. That right is then transferred to the book's publisher by the terms of the publishing contract and indicated by the © symbol found in the first leaves of this book. In the same way, photographers have the copyright in the photographs they take at sporting events. However, it may be a condition of the contract for their entry into a secure venue, that copyright is transferred to the relevant SGB. Examples would be Wembley Stadium for soccer or Madison Square Garden for an ice hockey match. In the UK, for instance, copyright in the image of a soccer player in a match is transferred to the FA, which then transfers it to the player's club and the player. Which of these is able to monetise that image depends on whether it is the player alone who is in the photograph, or whether other players are in the shot. It also depends on their footballing stature relative to the main subject. The details of these arrangements are published in the FA regulations.

Ultimately, the transfer by contract is the only way that the athlete or player can own the image rights in their own face and likeness. At the head of the chapter, it was established that in UK law there is no IP in a 'spectacle', per *Sports and General Press Agency v 'Our Dogs' Publishing Co.* and *Victoria Park Racing & Recreation Grounds Co Ltd v Taylor*. Copyright law vests ownership in the photograph in the photographer unless they agree to transfer it. Once the sportsperson owns the image rights by this means, however, they can charge for its use and with top-flight individuals and clubs, this can be lucrative. Many top players set up image rights companies for the income from such deals. This keeps the payments separate from their playing contract and also means that His Majesty's Revenue and Customs (HMRC) can only require tax at the corporation rate. This is currently 19 per cent rather than the 45 per cent likely to be applicable on such high earners. It is interesting to note that this receives little media attention compared to the tax-minimising activities of mega-corporations, yet in all cases, this simply means less funds for vital public services.

The Copyright Designs And Patents Act 1988

This legislation regulates matters such as how long the copyright can last and what exceptions there are, whereby works can be used without authorisation for limited purposes. The Act also covers design rights, which might be applicable to sport. These rights are outside the scope of this book but are typically functional designs rather than emblems, logos or forms of words that could be possible to trademark. The period of time before copyright ceases to apply differs depending on the type of work. For instance, for literary, dramatic, musical or artistic works, Section 12 delimits the timeframe as 70 years from the end of the year of the death of the creator. For films, there is a specified list of who is to be regarded as the creator from the principal director onwards. Section 13A applies a period of 50 years for sound recordings; however, that period is from the end of the year that the recording is made. Section 14 extends that cover to broadcasts. A more detailed discussion of these provisions appears in Chapter 7. From Section 16, the author or creator of the work is the only person who can, without restriction:

> copy the work . . . issue copies of the work to the public . . . rent or lend the work to the public . . . perform, show or play the work in public . . . communicate the work to the public [or] . . . make an adaptation of the work or do any of the above in relation to an adaptation.

There are exceptions; however, Section 28A allows temporary copies, as do personal ones for private use per Section 28B. Copies for research and private study are provided for in Section 29 and for text and data analysis for non-commercial research by Section 29A. Section 30 provides for copies to be used in criticism, review, quotation and news reporting. Parody or caricature is also permissible under Section 30A (see Figure 6.2). Incidental use of copyrighted work, such as a quote on an advertising billboard happening to be behind the main subject of a photograph, will not be prohibited either. In the event of infringement, the usual course of events will be for an author to issue a 'cease and desist' instruction to the perpetrator. If this is not heeded, damages at least equating to any lost revenue can be sought. Examples of copyright infringement being part of an action in a sporting context can be found in Cases C-403/08, *Football Association Premier League and Others v QC Leisure and Others* and C-429/08, *Karen Murphy v Media Protection Services Ltd*. Both cases involved the lawfulness of transmitting Premier League soccer games to receivers in sports bars and pubs in the UK. The copyright element primarily involved the commentary of the match. These were essentially broadcasting cases and will be dealt with in more depth in Chapter 7.

Copyright, Designs and Patents Act 1988 Sections	Purpose:
S12	Delimits the timeframe of protection as 70 years from the end of the year of the death of the creator. For films, there is a specified list of who is to be regarded as the creator from the principal director onwards.
S13A	Applies a period of 50 years protection for sound recordings, from the end of the year that the recording is made.
S14	Extends the cover in S13A to broadcastings
S16	Provides that the author or creator of the work is the only person who can, without restriction: '...copy the work...issue copies of the work to the public...rent or lend the work to the public...perform, show or play the work in public...communicate the work to the public [or]...make an adaptation of the work or do any of the above in relation to an adaptation'.
S28A	Allows temporary copies.
S28B	Allows personal copies for private use.
S29	Allows copies for research and private study
S29A	Allows copies for text and data analysis for non-commercial research.
S30	Allows copies for criticism, review, quotation and news reporting
S30A	Allows copies for parody or caricature

Figure 6.2 A summary of the main provisions of the Copyright Designs and Patents Act 1988.

Sports databases, fixture lists and copyright

This is not especially related to merchandising, but it has a natural place in this chapter after the introduction of the issue of copyright. This material will be discussed again in relation to broadcasting in Chapter 7. The Copyright Designs and Patents Act 1988 did not cover databases in a satisfactory way, so the Copyright and Rights in Databases Regulations 1997 were brought into force. This Statutory Instrument was the result of an EU Directive and inserted provisions into the Act to ensure certain databases were adequately protected. By virtue of a new Section 3A, a database is defined as 'a collection of independent works, data or other materials which . . . are arranged in a systematic or methodical way, and . . . are individually accessible by electronic or other means'. Crucially, the section goes on to limit the types of databases that can have copyright protection. By Section 3A(1)(2), databases are only included 'if, by reason of the selection or arrangement of the contents of the database the database constitutes the author's own intellectual creation'. This means that databases which involve some element of skill and artistry in compiling them will be protected as if they were any literary work. Section 13 of the Regulations further provides for other databases. A 'database right' exists if there has been a 'substantial investment in obtaining, verifying or presenting the contents of the database'. The term investment includes 'of financial, human or technical resources' per Section 12 of the Regulations. Such databases are protected for fifteen years, and this period starts again every time the database is substantially altered. Databases that satisfy neither definition, those that are mere lists of facts and figures relatively easily compiled, are not considered to have IP rights in them at all.

Sport obviously makes great use of fixture lists, databases of statistics and so on. To be protected, these databases must be capable of meeting one of the two above definitions. In *British Horseracing Board v William Hill Organisation* [2005] EWCA Civ 863, the betting company had been using the databases on racehorses produced by the Board (one of the forerunners of the BHA), on its websites and so on without permission. William Hill argued that the databases were mere lists and did not meet the criteria for protection under the Act or Regulations because they did not require enough effort and/or skill to produce. The matter was referred to the ECJ for a decision as the law here emanates from EU Directive 96/9/EC. In Case C-203/02, *The British Horseracing Board Ltd and Others v William Hill Organization Ltd*, the ECJ was not convinced that there was any basis for protection of the databases concerned. Therefore, William Hill did not need permission to reproduce them. In a 2015 non-sport related but applicable case, Ryan Air sought to test the legality of applying contractual terms and conditions to lists of flight departures and arrivals. It was settled law that this type of database was not sophisticated enough to attract protection per *BRB v William Hill*. Nevertheless, the question was whether Directive 96/9/EC itself prevented databases from being subject to contractual terms that limited or prevented their use by third parties without permission. In Case C-30/14, *Ryanair Ltd v PR Aviation BV*, the ECJ confirmed that such terms did not infringe the Directive. For sport, this provides an alternative to copyright or database rights. Relatively simple compiled databases can be accompanied by contractual terms specifying agreement to a charge. This will be enforceable even if there is no IP in the list itself.

Sport on the web – domain names

The internet dominates the commercial world, and many business entities not only use the internet to market and sell their goods and services but also make '.com' and so on part of their overall brand. 'Sportsdirect.com', the clothing and sporting goods retailer, is one example, 'amazon.com' is another. By virtue of the technology, registering a domain name that is the same as a competitor's is impossible. Each is unique, and if the domain name is taken, then it cannot be registered to someone else. That said, 'lookalike' domain names are not unknown. It would be possible to register the very similar 'αmαzon.com' because here, the two letter 'a' components are in fact the letter 'alpha' from the Greek alphabet. This is not immediately apparent to the unwary and is a tactic regularly used by scammers. The registration software at a web hosting company may not pick up on the issue either, as the use of the Greek letter renders the new application unique. The use of a domain name obtained by this sort of trickery would therefore have to be addressed by taking action under the Trade Marks Act 1994. Alternatively, a passing off claim may be made.

Endorsement and sponsorship

Endorsement and sponsorship are essentially the same thing, but they can conflict with one another. Endorsement is the term used when a celebrity, in this context a sports star, agrees as an individual to be associated with a certain product or service. Sponsorship is the same type of agreement but refers to a team, club, league or even SGB instead. The conflict occurs when an individual has an endorsement arrangement in their own name with a particular brand and then wishes to move to another team or club that is sponsored by a competitor. Put another way, manufacturer 'A' may have spent a lot of money having their brand associated with elite player 'X'. If 'X' moves to 'Team Y', which is sponsored by manufacturer 'B', then neither manufacturer will be happy to have lost the exclusivity they paid so much for. They will instead see both brands advertised side by side. Transfer deals can fall at the last hurdle over issues like this, irrespective of whether the competitor and new team are a good fit for each other in sporting terms; that takes second place to financial concerns. As an example, manager José Mourinho had personal endorsements with the car manufacturer Jaguar and the watch company Hublot. The 2016 appointment of Mourinho as the new Manchester United FC manager was held up because of the soccer club's existing sponsorship by Chevrolet and watch producer Bulova. This was until a compromise could be achieved.[15]

Both sponsorship and endorsement, like merchandising, rely on brands. The individual or team, club or ISF has a recognisable brand, reputation and/or goodwill. A commercial enterprise may consider that its own brand will be enhanced by association with a particular sports personality. In which case, it will be prepared to have its trademarked or common law-protected images, logos and emblems associated with this competitor. Often this will be at considerable expense as it is, after all a form of advertising. Problems occur, though, when either brand is perceived to damage the other. Most commonly, this occurs when the competitor or team starts to lose form. For this reason, the agreement may be subject to defined periods after which the sponsor can decide whether it wishes to continue sponsorship. Alternatively, there may be a clause allowing the arrangement to lapse if the team or competitor drops below a certain ranking or is relegated from their current league.

Sometimes these tensions occur because of controversial acts or omissions by the sports star on or off the field. Unsurprisingly, all of the sponsors previously associated with Lance Armstrong and Oscar Pistorius wanted to disassociate themselves fairly rapidly from the doping and legal catastrophes that each was respectively embroiled in. Doing so requires a well-crafted 'morality clause' in the sponsorship or endorsement contract. This allows the sponsor to take a view as to whether the incidents or behaviour warrant ending the agreement early. In some cases, the decision is not a foregone conclusion. In 2016, Maria Sharapova received a doping ban as discussed in Chapter 4, but it was the result of negligence rather than intent. On this basis, her sponsors TAG Heuer (watches) and Avon (beauty products) immediately ceased their contracts. Nike (sportswear), Head (racquets) and Porsche (cars) stood by her, at least initially, however.[16] This may have been loyalty or something a little more cynical. As Sharapova went through the drug case and the subsequent appeal, she was in the media spotlight; therefore, so were her remaining sponsors.

Sometimes, the position may be reversed. In less common situations, the commercial company may be receiving public opprobrium, perhaps on ethical grounds. The sports star or team may feel that it is their brand image that is being tarnished in those circumstances and wishes to sever ties. Well-drafted endorsement contracts would contain a term referred to as a 'reverse morality clause' whereby this separation could be achieved. For example, concerns about the use of sweatshops to produce sporting goods for companies such as Nike and Adidas first surfaced in 1996. These companies and others finally got around to addressing the issue of working conditions in subcontractor factories in Asia and the Pacific after that. It is true that this was largely due to consumer activism rather than individual sponsorship deals being terminated by athletes and players. However, undoubtedly had the public backlash been ignored, then sports stars with commercial ties to these brands might have voted with their feet to a greater degree. Nevertheless, even as late as the eve of the 2012 London Games, criticisms were still being levelled at these types of companies. Chiefly, this was for not being as open as they might be on their Third World labour issues, despite having apparently been working on them since the 1990s.[17] These and environmental concerns[18] are the kinds of factors that might cause a sports celebrity to trigger a reverse morality clause. In 2023, for instance, the All England Tennis Club (AELTC), responsible for the Wimbledon tennis tournament, was under pressure to reconsider its sponsorship by Barclays Bank PLC. This was because the bank is the largest European funder of fossil fuels, which has drawn the ire of environmentalists.[19] This point will be further addressed in Chapter 9.

'It's an ambush' – guerrilla marketing and sport

Ambush or guerrilla marketing is not generally illegal unless specifically prohibited by statute in respect of major global sporting events. However, for the rest of the sporting calendar, if these kind of marketing steps outside certain bounds, it may transgress IP laws. It is always a controversial strategy; however, the aim for those tasked with designing these marketing campaigns is to stay just inside the law. Not for nothing has the term 'guerrilla' been coined. Where smaller businesses use it against mega-corporations, it can be a form of fight back against the stranglehold these monoliths have on trade in a 'free' market world.

This type of marketing occurs when a business entity, that is not an authorised commercial partner of a sporting event, seeks to take advantage of the brand image or goodwill of that competition or venue in any way. An example might be a fast-food company running advertising campaigns on television around the time of coverage of a major soccer tournament or other global sporting competition. If that company is not an official sponsor, then logos or themes protected as IP, the way that the IOC protects the Olympic Rings symbol, cannot be used in the transmission. Clever use of general sporting themes linked to the disciplines that are competing can suggest a link in the mind of the viewer without triggering an action to protect IP. For example, whistles, supporters chanting, children playing the sport in the street and so on. In the case of major events like the Olympics, soccer's World Cup and the Commonwealth Games, these rights are mostly protected by statutory criminal sanctions as already discussed. Advertisement designers, therefore, need to tread very carefully.

The organisers of major sporting events do all they can to limit these tactics of course. They and the main sponsors have expended perhaps millions of dollars on an exclusive rights package. Consequently, they take a dim view of what are often quite inventive and resourceful advertising campaigns. Much of the work around protecting IP with regard to major international tournaments has taken place since perhaps the most famous example of an ambush marketing 'war'. This erupted in the 1980s between photographic film companies Fuji and Kodak regarding the Olympics. Various methods used included billboards strategically placed around venues sponsored by the rival and even flying an airship above, emblazoned with the logos of the competitor firm. Tight laws on such activities enacted since make anything as unsubtle as that fraught with legal difficulties. Despite this, at the 2012 London Games, a major betting operator still got away with billboards across the city proclaiming that they were the 'official sponsor of the largest athletics event in London this year'. They were not a commercial partner of the Games but had secured the sponsorship of a minor sporting event in London, France. This 'detail' appeared only in print, a little way away from the main headline.[20]

Is IP law fair?

The first point must be a general one. It is generally accepted without question that ideas should be monetised; that is part of the capitalist hegemony. This is a modern development and very much a product of Western free market economics. Again, there is the Gramscian assumption evident: 'the belief about everything that exists, that it is "natural" . . . that it could do no other than exist'.[21] In this context, the monetisation of ideas is seen as essential and unquestionable. It has not always been so. In terms of sport, the narrower question is whether sport is better for the commodification of intellectual creativity. Sport is better funded and organised because of the income streams from IP, but only at the elite level. However, the money is unfairly distributed, with top clubs in soccer failing to allow the funds to filter down to the grassroots adequately for instance. Also, less popular sports are unable to access these arrangements as they do not suit the brands' needs in terms of reach into the population. Further, there is little pushback when, for example, Premiership clubs are using clever marketing tactics to extract money from fans who merely want to show their allegiance. Too often, this involves children being persuaded to pressure their parents. Fans bemoan that 'money rules', and there is clear evidence of this when successful transfers can depend on conflicting endorsements rather than the quality of the player or manager. Furthermore, litigation can be used as a cudgel against individuals and small businesses just trying to make a living and who often do not have the resources to fight. Whatever benefits commercialisation has brought to sport in the last fifty years, it is evident that the Corinthian ideals take a back seat compared to the need to monetise a sport's success.

Notes

1 Mark James, *Sports Law* (London: Palgrave, 2017), 317.
2 Jonathan Liew, 'Saudi golf takeover is blueprint for what they want to do everywhere else', *The Guardian*, 13 June 2023, https://www.theguardian.com/sport/blog/2023/jun/13/saudi-arabia-golf-pga-tour-public-investment-fund.
3 See Jonathan Merritt, '"Attack of the clones": Problematising equine sports integrity regulation on the ascendancy of the genetically copied athlete', *Contemporary Issues in Law*, 14, no. 3 (2018): 207–8.
4 See Cases C-403/08, *Football Association Premier League and Others v QC Leisure* and Others and C-429/08, *Karen Murphy v Media Protection Services Ltd.*
5 Michael Peng et al., 'History and the debate over intellectual property', *Management and Organization Review*, 13, no. 1 (March 2017): 18 and see generally Peter K. Yu, 'The confucian challenge to intellectual property reforms', *WIPO Journal*, 4, no. 1 (2012).
6 'Cheetham Hill raids: Largest haul of fake goods in UK history, say GMP', *BBC*, 4 July 2023, https://www.bbc.co.uk/news/uk-england-manchester-66093295.
7 See for instance the London Olympic Games and Paralympic Games Act 2006.
8 Ian Kilbey, 'The ironies of Arsenal v Reed', *EIPR*, 26 (2004): 481.

9 Henry Saker-Clark, 'JD sports, rangers and elite sports fined £2m over football kit price fixing', *The Independent*, 27 September 2022, https://www.independent.co.uk/sport/football/jd-sports-cma-belfast-glasgow-b2176025.html.
10 Case C273/00 [2002] ECR I-11737 *Ralf Sieckmann v Deutsches Patent- und Markenamt*.
11 'Intellectual Property Office – Trademark No. UK00002302590", accessed 7 October 2023, https://trademarks.ipo.gov.uk/ipo-tmcase/page/Results/1/UK00002302590.
12 'Intellectual Property Office – Trademark No. UK00001387589', accessed 7 October 2023, https://trademarks.ipo.gov.uk/ipo-tmowner/page/search?id=1748596&domain=1.
13 Council Regulation (EC) No 40/94 of 20 December 1993.
14 For an indication of how 'reputation' and 'goodwill' in this context may have subtle differences, see *Anheuser-Busch v Budejovicky Budvar Narodni Podnik* [1984] FSR 413 and *Hotel Cipriani v Cipriani (Grosvenor Street) Ltd.* [2010] EWCA Civ 110.
15 James Ducker, 'Jose Mourinho to Manchester United Q&A: What is delaying the deal?' *Telegraph*, 25 May 2016, https://www.telegraph.co.uk/football/2016/05/25/jose-mourinho-to-manchester-united-qa-what-is-delaying-the-deal/.
16 'Sharapova's sponsors divided after two-year tennis ban', *BBC*, 9 June 2016, https://www.bbc.co.uk/news/business-36485320.
17 Simon Birch, 'How activism forced Nike to change its ethical game', *The Guardian*, 6 July 2012, https://www.theguardian.com/environment/green-living-blog/2012/jul/06/activism-nike.
18 Ibid.
19 Jemma Dempsey, 'Wimbledon: Stars call on championships to end Barclays sponsorship', *BBC*, 3 July 2023, https://www.bbc.co.uk/news/business-66084764.
20 Mark Sweney, 'London 2012: Paddy Power wins poster campaign battle', *The Guardian*, 25 July 2012, https://www.theguardian.com/media/2012/jul/25/london-2012-paddy-power.
21 Antonio Gramsci, *Selections from the Prison Notebooks*, trans. Quintin Hoare and Geoffrey Nowell-Smith (New York: International Publishers, 1971), 157.

7

Sports Broadcasting

'As soon as you take money for playing sport, it isn't sport, it's work'[1]

Professional sport is very much driven and supported by financial success, and at the elite level, a great deal of that comes from broadcasting deals. In the 2021/22 season, European top-flight soccer generated €17.2 billion across the 'big five' leagues in England, France, Spain, Italy and Germany. The UK's Premier League leads the way with a total sum of €6.4 billion, and 55 per cent of that, or €3.5billion, was from broadcasting contracts.[2] By comparison, a mere 14 per cent of the UK total came from matchday receipts, such as tickets. Sport at that level is very much 'work' and not just for the players and athletes. It provides employment on a large scale in the broadcasting and associated industries. Player wage costs and broadcasting revenues are inextricably linked, and not everyone feels that the sums involved are necessarily good for the game at its heart. In 2021, twelve clubs from across the 'big five' leagues formed a new league very much against the wishes of their respective national governing bodies (NGB) and international sporting federations (ISF). The European Super League (ESL) was also not a popular prospect with the fan base. This was largely because broadcasting money had driven the project rather than the needs and wants of the fans themselves. It was this groundswell of opposition, amplified by politicians, that brought about the ESL's downfall within days of its launch.[3] There is still, therefore, some power left in the hands of spectators and other such stakeholders. However, it is likely that a variant of the scheme will reappear, and its proponents will have learned a lot from the 2021 debacle, so success is more likely.

The politics of sports broadcasting

Sport, effectively becoming a branch of the entertainment industry, has a political dimension as well. Capitalism requires commodification, and economic growth has come to rely on consumerism, often in terms of 'false needs'. The masses are persuaded very effectively that it is important to replace consumer goods, not because the existing purchase has worn out, but because the new model possesses desirable aesthetic and functional improvements. In other words, owning the latest iPhone or Samsung is a status symbol. Culture has become commodified as well and having access to the best satellite sports viewing package is a similar measure of personal financial success.[4] In fact, possession of any of the above will not necessarily guarantee an increase in human happiness. The acquisition of expensive pay-per-view packages is only available to those with a good income; it is nevertheless a false need generated by the owners of broadcasting to boost their own revenues. Being efficient about convincing the population that these superficial commodities are 'necessary' does bring about compliance with capitalist ideology, however. This is nothing new in one sense, in that historically, distraction from the daily grind has always been a part of sport. The word 'sport' comes from Latin; the verb 'dēportō' is translated as 'to carry away or banish', in this sense being carried away from the daily grind and banishing the associated worries. In Roman times, obsession with gladiatorial combat and chariot races was useful to the ruling elite when political instability, bread shortages and other economic woes threatened.[5] The widely available and heavily packaged broadcasts of sport have taken this phenomenon to a new level in the twenty-first century, however. The distraction provided by televised sport is a much more efficient means to ensure the populace displays more passion about, say, football or baseball than politics. Rather than think about the exploitative nature of the workplace dynamics, it is far more comfortable to sit down in front of the television and become lost in the passion of the game. In this way, the 'major belief systems of the society are sufficiently accepted by the populace that the ruling class can be said to have the consent of the governed'.[6] Put another way, packaged and branded broadcasts of sport en masse are not just 'work' for the competitors and the broadcast industry. They also distracts from the poor quality of many of the decisions made by the political class and make their work easier, or at least make it less open to scrutiny.

Sports broadcasting and 'Brexit'

It is again necessary to explain why elements of European Union (EU) law are still pertinent post-Brexit. The UK's membership of the EU from 1973 to 2021 brought considerable EU-wide alignment for broadcasting. The Audiovisual Media Services Directive 2010/13/EU (AVMS) was instrumental in regulating this arena together with the Broadcasting Acts 1990, 1996[7] and the Communications Act 2003. Further changes have come about by virtue of later Directives up to and including AVMS Directive 2018/1808. These have been achieved by statutory instruments rather than primary legislation. The 2018 Directive was brought into law to take account of 'market realities', chiefly the convergence of televisual and internet services. On leaving the bloc, large tranches of EU law were absorbed into domestic UK law through the European Union (Withdrawal) Act 2018. This ended the direct applicability of EU law. It also made it easier for the amendment or repeal of such laws at a later date, as the UK Parliament sees fit. In the intervening period, the Covid-19 pandemic and periods of political instability have meant that little has been achieved with regard to the body of 'retained law'. On the contrary, there have been difficulties in ensuring a frictionless border with the EU between Northern Ireland and Eire. Due to this, EU law and institutions will continue to have influence over that part of the UK for much longer than originally envisaged. As of 2023, the problems arising from the 'Northern Ireland Protocol' of the Withdrawal Agreement show little sign of being resolved. Partly for this reason, the Northern Ireland political parties, such as the loyalist Democratic Unionist Party (DUP) and the republican *Sinn Féin* were unable to agree on resuming government of the country for two years up until 2024. Northern Ireland was effectively ruled directly from Westminster during that time. Further, after numerous delays, mostly requested by the UK, greater implementation of post-withdrawal trading arrangements has yet to be put in place anywhere in the UK. For example, full import controls on EU food. Finally, media broadcasting is very much an international undertaking. Consequently, there may not be much enthusiasm within the broadcasting industry for diverging from standardisation across Europe for some time to come, possibly ever. Many of the points made about EU law in this chapter therefore remain valid. Albeit this is mostly on the basis that the principles therein have now found themselves part of the UK domestic framework for broadcasting regulation, rather than being directly applicable EU law *per se*.

What are broadcasting rights?

The term 'broadcasting rights' is often used relatively indiscriminately. Firstly, it is important to differentiate between the rights that are necessary to lawfully make the footage, as distinct from the rights that attach to the broadcast itself once it is finalised and aired. It will be obvious from the discussion in Chapter 6 that UK law does not attach any intellectual property (IP) rights to a 'spectacle'. It is therefore necessary to rely on a patchwork of legal rights and duties that arise from different branches of domestic law. These principles are from contract and tort, intellectual property rights in images or artistic works and so on. The broadcast itself is a little easier to protect, being an artistic work in its own right and therefore capable of attracting copyright. Practical problems have definitely increased, however, with the proliferation of social media platforms. Further complications arise from the degree to which these and more traditional forms of media are now integrated. It is the norm for a TV broadcast to have an associated X (formerly Twitter) feed, for instance. By attaching a link, an unofficial release of licensed footage can thus occur on a proliferation of social media channels originating anywhere in the world. In large part, social media giants like Meta and X have to be coerced and persuaded to police themselves for this kind of illicit content. It is very difficult to bring the law to bear across several international boundaries. In addition to the above complexities, Artificial Intelligence (AI) poses further legal conundrums. In Chapter 6, the question was posed as to whether copyright could attach to designs and written or spoken materials that are the result of AI, not a human creator. In 2023, there was commentary for some of the initial rounds of the Wimbledon tennis tournament provided exclusively by AI,[8] and this trend is likely to continue. Although the broadcast itself will be protected by copyright owned by the British Broadcasting Corporation (BBC), there is a legal question yet to be settled.

Specifically, who owns the original copyright in the words themselves, given that there was no human involved at the time of creation of that artistic work.

Broadcasting itself does have a legal definition; however, the provision in the Communications Act 2003 was updated by the Electronic Communications and Wireless Telegraphy (Amendment) (European Electronic Communications Code and EU Exit) Regulations 2020, or S.I. 2020/1419. This was to ensure that the wording took account of the manifold ways that pictures and sound can now reach the consumer. This was achieved by subsuming it within a broader definition of an 'electronic communications service'. Section 32(2A) now prescribes that term to mean:

> 'an internet access service, . . . a number-based interpersonal communications service; and any other service consisting in . . . the conveyance of signals, such as . . . for broadcasting'.

In other words, this means the internet, telephone services and broadcasting. The Television Without Frontiers Directive (89/552 EEC), Article 1(a), contained the original definition upon which the Section 32(2A) version was based. This defined a broadcast as, 'the initial transmission by wire or over the air, including that by satellite . . . of television programmes intended for reception by the public'. Together, these definitions cover a broad array of technologies used to transmit sound and vision to a wide audience.

Unlike in the United States, a UK event organiser does not 'own' the event in an IP sense. In 1938, that question was settled in the US courts with *Pittsburgh Athletic Co v KQV Broadcasting Co*, 24 F Supp 490. It was held that the Pittsburgh Pirates baseball team, together with all of the National League sides, owned a property right in the games they organised. This meant, therefore, that unauthorised broadcasts of games were prohibited. As discussed in Chapter 6, though, UK law recognises no such right in a 'spectacle', sporting or otherwise. *Sports and General Press Agency v 'Our Dogs' Publishing Co.* [1917] KB 125 CA and *Douglas v Hello! Ltd* [2001] QB 967 together indicated another way of ensuring exclusivity of access. This was with regard to photographers, and by extension, broadcasters. The method is to use conditions of entry to bar any rival broadcasters from the venue. Anyone breaching these conditions once they have surreptitiously entered could be removed as a trespasser. In *Douglas v Hello!*, the court went further and awarded damages to Michael Douglas and Catherine Zeta-Jones. This was on the basis that taking unauthorised recordings at an event was a 'breach of confidence'. This arises because of the confidential nature of the exclusive contractual agreement that the event organiser has with the official photographer. In turn, this would also apply to a broadcaster. This may be the only recourse when unofficial images have been taken, when it is possible to view the event without entering a secure stadium. In *Victoria Park Racing & Recreation Ground Company v Taylor* (1938) 58 CLR 479, filming of horse races was taking place. This was from temporary towers erected on land not owned by the claimant but neighbouring their horse racing track. Entry conditions would obviously, therefore, be irrelevant, and the venue lost the case because they owned no IP rights in the event, as such rights did not exist. In recent times, drones have become synonymous with technological advances in warfare. In the civilian sector too, they are also increasing in sophistication, decreasing in size and difficulty to pilot. In effect, using these to film sports events unlawfully is analogous to the methods complained of in *Victoria Park Racing*, albeit using greater sophistication. These machines pose a threat to event organisers because of the degree to which they can be used by a relatively untrained individual and flown from land that is outside the control of the venue concerned. This not only has implications for broadcasting exclusivity but also for gambling. The transmissions from these drones can beat those of the official broadcaster by up to 2 seconds, enough to give a betting advantage to those viewing the sports event this way.[9]

In summary, in the UK, it is perfectly possible to ensure exclusivity in a sports broadcasting agreement. This is not achieved by asserting any IP right attaching to the event itself, however. Instead, a patchwork of legal rights is utilised. These are from areas such as contract and tort. Alternatively, trademarks or copyright in any of the objects visible or audible in the illicit broadcast can be protected in their own right.

Broadcasting, an ever-changing concept

The precise details of the changing technologies and markets in broadcasting are outside the scope of this book. Nevertheless, having a broad grasp of the broadcasting landscape of the UK will be helpful in understanding some of the later discussions around case law and statute.

Terrestrial or 'Over the Air' (OTA) television (TV) was originally the only way that sound and vision were transmitted into people's homes. These broadcasts are transmitted from towers by radio signals that are received by an aerial attached to the building in which the recipient is located. The range of these signals is limited, and often they have to be relayed and boosted by a series of transmitters. This process also accounts for the curvature of the Earth, which would otherwise further limit the reach of these signals. Programmes transmitted this way are free to watch, and this remains the default package in the UK if no purchases of internet-based or satellite services are made (see Figure 7.1). The UK is unique in one respect, though: Section 363 of the Communications Act 2003 makes it a criminal offence, in the absence of a TV licence, to watch live on any channel, TV service or stream TV content. This refers to any device and includes the BBC's on-demand catch-up service. Section 365 of the Act requires a fee to be paid to the BBC for this licence. This is because all TVs are capable of receiving programmes made by the BBC, which is a public service broadcaster, the largest in the world, and set up by Royal Charter. The licence fee is almost the sole way that the BBC is funded, as it has no commercial arrangements whatsoever. Albeit there is pressure for this funding model to change.[10] There are no advertisements on either of the two BBC channels or the national and local radio services that it operates. This licence fee is in effect a tax because it applies to all persons who own or operate a TV, and that is the overwhelming majority of the adult population. It is no defence

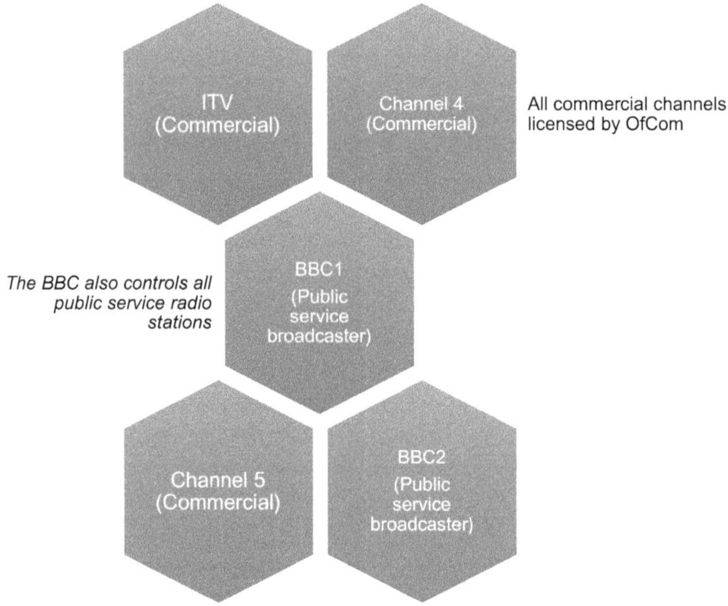

Figure 7.1 The 'free-to-air' channels in the UK.

to prove no BBC content is consumed. The BBC, therefore, has a dominant position in the broadcasting environment. Consequently, this provider, as well as other large commercial 'free-to-air' broadcasters, has effectively 'first refusal' over broadcast rights on certain sporting events of national and international significance. These are the so-called 'crown jewel' events to be discussed in more detail later. The rationale is that it would be unfair if the financial 'muscle' of pay-per-view providers prevented less affluent viewers from being able to see these sporting occasions.

There are three commercial but free-to-air terrestrial channels licensed to broadcast in the UK. These licences are issued by the Office of Communications (Ofcom), which is also the regulatory body for standards in the industry (see Figure 7.1). The first of these three is Independent Television (ITV), which holds the licence for most of the regional TV services in almost all of the UK. ITV derives its revenue from selling advertising space, sponsorships and other contractual arrangements between ITV and its commercial partners. Secondly, there is the Channel Four Television Corporation, set up by the Broadcasting Act 1990. This operates 'Channel 4', which is a national broadcaster. It is a condition of its Ofcom licence that it also provides content that ITV does not generally provide. Channel 4 is particularly known for its association with major sports, most notably horse racing. Finally, Channel 5 is a relative newcomer, being launched in 1997. This channel was the last of the analogue terrestrial channels before the sector was revolutionised with digital technology. Both Channels 4 and 5 carry advertising and sponsorship and are commercial channels like ITV. Despite this, like the BBC, commercial channels in the UK seek to enjoy complete editorial independence from commercial pressure due to the oversight of Ofcom.

Households in the UK nowadays also have access to a proliferation of digital channels on payment of a subscription. These programmes are for the most part delivered by the same technology that provides broadband services to consumers. Fibre optic cables bring the signal to the home through the network that provides telephone services. The terminus in the home is the broadband router, and consumers' mobile phones, mobile devices and televisions alike receive Wi-Fi signals from this. The advances in fibre optic technology allow increasing specialisation, such that channels dedicated to a particular sport, such as Formula One, or even a specific sports club, like Manchester United FC, can be obtained via subscription. The other major player in broadcasting licensed by Ofcom is satellite television. This, like the broadband-based services described above, is subscription-based. It also carries advertising and derives revenue through sponsorship and other commercial arrangements. The market leader is Sky Group Ltd, founded by controversial media tycoon Rupert Murdoch[11] and known as Sky.com or simply as 'Sky'. Sky also has a large presence internationally. The satellites needed to operate this service orbit at the same speed as the Earth's rotation so sit above a particular spot on the equator all the time. Consumers must purchase a 'box' with their subscription which decodes the signal. This ensures that only subscribers receive it in usable form. The international nature of satellite transmission has led to legal wrangles when cheaper decoders from other countries are imported and used in the UK. Primarily, this has been done in order to watch sports events. This is often in sports bars and other leisure facilities, of which more later in the chapter. Increasingly, social media has entered the sector in recent years. It is quite usual for platforms like X, Facebook and Instagram to carry both official and unofficial clips of sporting events posted by individual and corporate accounts. The latter two platforms are owned by Meta, the social media giant run by Mark Zuckerberg, which has now also launched Threads. This is a provision similar to X in how it is operated by users. Threads has gained significant popularity very soon after its inception, because of its easy interface with Instagram. Zuckerberg and X's owner Elon Musk have faced their own controversies in building their social media empires as well,[12] however. This was long before Musk's divisive appointment to the US Government's Department of Government Efficiency in 2025.

UK broadcasting's 'Crown Jewels'

The formal term for these sporting fixtures is 'Listed Events'. These are competitions that are considered of national or international importance. It is considered that there is, therefore, a moral right for everyone to be able to watch these without paying an additional subscription beyond the licence fee. This 'right' is enshrined in statute by Section 97 of the Broadcasting Act 1996, together with subsequent legislative amendments. The term used is 'sporting or other event of national interest', although there is no definition for that phrase in the Act. Instead, the Secretary of State responsible for sport is charged with drawing up a list and amending it from time to time. The EU has a similar regime for its twenty-seven member states provided by the Television Without Frontiers Directive (89/552/EEC). This was amended by Article fourteen of the AVMS Directive (2010/13/EU), although each member state is free to decide whether to have a list and what is on it if they do. The definition of these 'special' sporting events contained there was influential in developing the List in the UK, which at the time was still a member of the EU. To qualify as a Listed Event, the sporting fixture must:

> have a special general resonance and are not simply of significance to those who ordinarily follow the sport or are activity concerned, [or] . . . a generally recognised, distinct cultural importance for the population . . . as a catalyst of its cultural identity. [Alternatively] . . ., the event involves the national team . . . in a major international event, [or] . . . has traditionally been broadcast free-to-air and has commanded large TV audiences.[13]

Per Article 15, short news reporting by pay-per-view providers is allowed; however, it is subject to certain restrictions. The UK List itself, and whether it is still part of a useful regime, is under periodic review, and a White Paper on modernisation was published in April 2022.[14] There are currently two groups of events, Group A and Group B. Group A events are those where full live coverage must be available without subscription on free-to-air channels. This means the BBC, ITV, Channel 4 or Channel 5, and these are designated by the Act as '*Category* A' broadcasters.[15] Events in this part of the List include the Football Association (FA) Cup Final, the Olympic and Paralympic Games, and the Women's Football World Cup European Championships. Live coverage of Group B fixtures, on the other hand, can be offered to pay-per-view broadcasters like Sky or BT Sport or '*Category* B' broadcasters. This is provided that secondary coverage, such as non-live broadcasts or highlights, is available to the BBC and so on. Examples of competitions in this group are the Six Nations rugby union tournament, Golf's Ryder Cup, and all cricket Test matches played in England. As of 2023, there are thirteen Group A events and nine in Group B[16] (see Figure 7.2). Understandably, this arrangement is not popular with those in sport and commerce who want to maximise the revenue they can draw from such major dates in the sporting calendar. They are less concerned with whether those of lesser means should still be able to follow national sporting events. Inevitably, the subscription channels can offer the best deals for sport but are prevented from doing so by this statutory intervention. Legal challenges by FIFA and UEFA have so far been unsuccessful, however.[17] The system is one of 'first refusal', so it is not a total ban on subscription channels screening live premier events. If the free-to-air channels do not wish to offer live coverage of the event in question, the event organisers can then approach the subscription channels. Ofcom, the broadcasting industry regulator, now has Listed Events within its remit and has produced the 'Code on sports and other listed and designated events'. Broadcasters must adhere to this as a condition of their broadcasting licence.

Category A Broadcasters	Category B Broadcasters
'Free to air' broadcasters	'Pay per view' broadcasters
BBC1, BBC2, ITV, Channel 4 and Channel 5	Sky, BT Sport etc.
Must be offered 'Group A' fixtures first before they are offered to Category B broadcasters.	'Group B' fixtures can be offered to pay per view 'Category B' broadcasters, provided that secondary coverage, such as non-live broadcasts or highlights, are available to the BBC.
Examples: The FA Cup Final, the Olympic and Paralympic Games, and the Women's Football World Cup European Championships.	Examples: Six Nations rugby union tournament, Golf's Ryder Cup, and all cricket test matches played in England.

Figure 7.2 The 'Listed Events' regime under the Broadcasting Act 1998.

The notion of restricting sport's ability to derive maximum revenue from its top-flight events seems at odds with free market capitalism, but there is nothing new in that. Free marketeers from the right of politics may see this statutory intervention as a sin, not a virtue, but the reality is that, to an extent, '[w]e are all Marxists now'.[18] There have been various social and economic reforms that can be attributed to Marx, albeit these have been, in large part, brought in to head off the possibility of socialist revolution. Without Marx, there would have been little incentive for the ruling class to instigate free education systems, such as in the UK and United States. This is also true of medical treatment that is free or heavily subsidised at the point of use, such as in Canada and much of Europe. Also, workers' rights, such as the minimum wage in the United States and United Kingdom, are examples of this. Further, guaranteed paid holidays and paid maternity leave, state pensions and welfare benefits, common in advanced democracies the world over, are also concessions to workers' movements. These socialist developments are examples of Gramsci's 'reformist corrosion'[19] that capitalism has suffered during the twentieth and twenty-first centuries. Protection of viewing rights for people of all incomes at the expense of wealth creation by big sporting corporations fits into this narrative perfectly.

'Footprints', satellites and the law

Satellite transmissions, the 'downlink', are produced in the form of a cone shape, with its point in orbit at the spacecraft down to a large elliptical shape at its base when it makes contact with the Earth's surface. It is evident from this that the footprint of the satellite will not be coterminous with any country border anywhere. In the case of Europe, it will straddle several legal jurisdictions. There will therefore be areas of overspill where transmissions intended for one country, and regulated by its laws, will be receivable, with the right decoder, in another (see Figure 7.3). Unsurprisingly, this phenomenon has given rise to some legal disputes in a sporting context. The primary motive for the viewer is cost saving. It is possible to import a decoder that can receive a subscription service from a foreign supplier that is cheaper than that

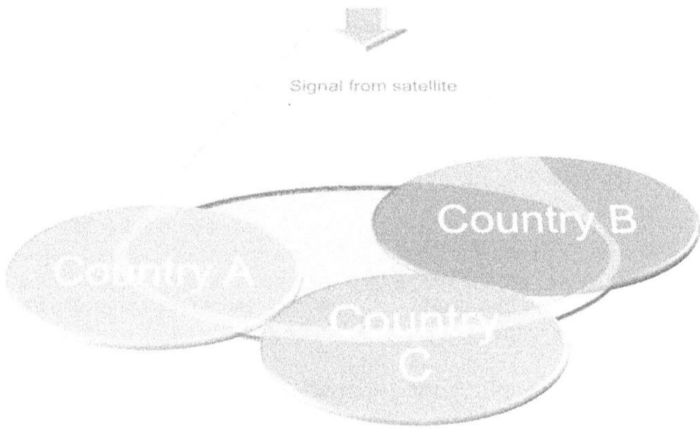

Figure 7.3 A satellite downlink straddles several jurisdictions.

offered in the consumer's home territory. For the subscription service in the home territory that has purchased exclusive rights to broadcast these premier events at great expense, this represents lost revenue. Both these and the clubs and leagues that want to be able to rely on this exclusivity to maximise their broadcast rights income in the future naturally want to have legal recourse to stop this practice. This is, however, quite different from piracy, which is using black market decoders to obtain the service unlawfully. Leading cases have been brought against sports bars, pubs and clubs that saw significant savings over commercial subscription fees by using these decoders in the UK. They were sourced predominantly from Greece. In *Murphy v Media Protection Services Ltd* [2012] EWHC 466 (Admin), Mrs Murphy had previously been convicted under Section 297(1) of the Copyright Designs and Patents Act 1988 (CDPA). She had bought a decoder for her public house so that patrons could view Premier League matches. This decoder was imported, and she was able to provide this service to her customers substantially more cheaply than had she purchased a UK subscription. The conviction was for dishonestly receiving broadcasting without paying the appropriate charge. Mrs Murphy had her conviction quashed, and the prosecution was ordered to pay the costs. This was the end of a long-running legal dispute that involved referrals to the ECJ on points of law. The prosecution was made to pay the costs of the EU cases as well. The Defendant had argued, inter alia, that the definition of dishonesty had not been met. Furthermore, as a citizen of the EU, her activities were compatible with a key provision of EU membership, the free movement of goods and services. The Defendant also argued that under Article 101 of the Treaty on the Functioning of the European Union (TFEU), preventing her from using the Greek decoder was unlawful. This was on the basis that it would represent a trade practice between EU countries which could prevent, restrict or distort competition.

Alongside the above developments, another case was making its way through the courts. In *FA Premier League Ltd v QC Leisure & Ors.* [2008] EWHC 1411 (Ch), the Claimant maintained that the use of imported decoders, such as those featured in *Murphy*, infringed their rights under Section 298 of the CDPA 1988. It was argued that in the coverage of a soccer match, there are individual components that are subject to copyright. This is irrespective of the fact that the overall event cannot attract IP, per *Sports and General Press Agency v 'Our Dogs' Publishing Co.* Any music used to introduce the event, the commentary itself and various other spoken and written phrases may be subject to such copyright. Section 298 allows a broadcaster to essentially have the same copyright protection over these artistic works as is provided to the creator by the Act. This is against any person who 'makes, imports or sells or lets for hire any apparatus or device designed . . . to enable . . . persons to receive the programmes . . . when they are not entitled to do so', from Section 298(1) and (2). The Defendants, owners of venues using these decoders much as Karen Murphy had done, argued that there was no breach of Section 298. Furthermore, like Ms Murphy, their case was also that the contractual arrangements between the Premier League and such as Sky were anti-competitive and therefore a breach of, inter alia, Article 101 TFEU. Ultimately, given that both cases required the application of EU law, they were referred to the ECJ. In 2011, the conjoined case of *Football Association Premier League Ltd and Others v QC Leisure and Others* (C-403/08) and *Karen Murphy v Media Protection Services Ltd* (C-429/08) was heard. The ECJ ruled that the restrictions on the use of foreign decoders were a breach of Articles 101 and 56 TFEU (on the freedom to provide services) and were thus unlawful. However, the court agreed that there was copyright in the anthems and commentary and other such content used in the broadcast. The result was something of a pyrrhic victory for Murphy and for QC Leisure. This was because to continue to broadcast the Premier League games, these would have to be without the voice-over commentary. Further, certain sentences and phrases that appeared on screen, where they were subject to copyright, would have to be digitally obscured or 'blurred out'. The resulting coverage would likely be quite inadequate for patrons of the sports bars where they were aired. At least Karen Murphy did not suffer the ignominy of a criminal record, however. Had these cases gone the other way, many pub landlords and leisure concerns might have also been criminally liable because of the Conditional Access (Unauthorized Decoders) Regulations 2000. This added Section 297A and amended Section 298 of the CDPA 1988. 297A(1)(b) makes it an offence for anyone to have 'in his possession for commercial purposes any unauthorised decoder'. If the decoders in question had been ruled unlawful per se, further prosecutions could have followed under this head. This would have exposed the defendants to penalties of up to ten years in prison.

The outcome of these cases is still relevant post 'Brexit' because the principles of Article 101 and Article 102 are subsumed in the Competition Act 1998, which is still on the statute books irrespective of 'Brexit'. Article 102 prevents any abuse of a dominant trading position in a given market, examples being the imposing, whether directly or indirectly, of unfair prices or trading conditions.

Sports broadcasting and competition law

Whilst capitalism is predicated on maximising individual wealth, there are some brakes on that process allowed in most Western democracies. Competition law, called antitrust legislation in the United States, seeks to ensure that monopolies do not thrive. Further, the dynamics within the market that fall short of an outright monopoly are also controlled. Examples would include situations where a dominant market position is abused. For instance, in the UK, the Competition and Markets Authority (CMA) is charged with enforcing competition law. In 2016, the CMA intervened in the proposed merger of high street and online gambling provider Ladbrokes PLC and part of Gala Coral Group Limited, its erstwhile competitor. In its final report,[20] the CMA stated that the resulting dominating presence of some 4000 betting shops in close proximity would result in a Significant Loss of Competition (SLC). The remedy specified was the sale of some 360 of those Licensed Betting Offices (LBOs) to rival operators.[21] As discussed in relation to *Murphy* earlier, when the UK was a member of the EU, the overall competition regulatory regime stemmed from Articles 101 and 102 of the TFEU. The principles in those provisions are reflected in the Competition Act 1998. Section 2(1)(b) prohibits agreements or practices which 'have as their object or effect the prevention, restriction or distortion of competition within the United Kingdom'. This would include monopolies as per Article 101. Section 18 prohibits the same behaviour which amounts to an 'abuse of a dominant position in a market', as does Article 102. An example might be a mega supermarket conglomerate using its immense bulk buying power to undercut the price of certain staple goods, such that smaller local retailers could not compete. This would be to the detriment of consumers. Chapter III of the Act covers the investigative and enforcement powers of the CMA. In Chapter 3, the near absolute dominance of the British Horseracing Authority (BHA) in all aspects of the world of horse racing was discussed. In *Atheraces v British Horseracing Board Ltd* ([2007] EWCA Civ 38), the High Court found that the Board (one of the forerunners of the BHA) had abused its dominant market position. It did this by charging excessive amounts for the use of its database information by the claimant. The Court of Appeal overturned this finding, but the matter was ultimately settled by negotiation before any further appeals.

Collective purchasing and competition law

The broadcasting companies in Europe can and do operate in concert to buy up all the TV rights for coverage of elite soccer, Formula One and other sports. The European Broadcasting Union (EBU) is an 'alliance of public service media organisations' based in Switzerland. It has 112 member organisations in fifty-six countries and associates in Asia, Africa, Australasia and North and South America. Together, this represents around 2,000 services including television, radio and online channels.[22] The EBU purchases TV rights on behalf of its members in the form of 'collective purchasing'. Potentially, this does create a dominant market position. In terms of soccer, the other party in these negotiations is UEFA, representing all its member soccer clubs wishing to sell their rights. Thus, there is only one undertaking wishing to sell, and one wishing to buy. This does not seem to accord with the principles of a free market with its emphasis on free and fair competition. Despite various legal challenges, however, this arrangement appears to be exempt from EU competition law provisions. The final word appears to be from the European Commission Statement in 'the matter of joint selling arrangements by the European soccer organisation, UEFA'.[23] The document acknowledges that competition is restricted by the collective selling procedures. However, it also recognised that satisfactory changes had been made by UEFA to allow for the creation of various rights packages to be sold separately. In this way, it was argued that collective selling of TV sports broadcast packages would be beneficial to consumers and not contrary to Article 101. Specifically, they would be 'improving the production or distribution of goods or promoting technical or economic progress, whilst allowing consumers a fair share of the benefit'.[24] The Commission felt that, for instance, viewers would be able to purchase one subscription channel for all of the soccer Premiership, instead of having to subscribe to multiple channels, depending on which had the rights to what games. It was felt that this meant simplicity and cost savings to the consumer. The overarching aim of preventing even potential harm to consumers by monopolistic and like behaviour appears to have been lost in this debate, however.

The role of copyright and trademarks in maintaining exclusivity

It is well established that in UK law, there is no IP vested in the sporting spectacle itself. Consequently, as the *Murphy* cases indicate, exclusivity would have to be maintained by employing the IP rights that subsist as components of a TV broadcast. These copyrighted and trademarked features are visible on screen cannot be broadcast without the creator or assignor's permission. Copyright and trademark law have been considered in Chapter 6 already, but it is nevertheless worth revisiting these topics in the context of broadcasting.

Copyright in a sound or vision broadcast

The entire finished TV programme is an artistic work and subject to copyright belonging to the broadcaster. The © symbol will appear on screen next to the BBC, Sky, etc. logo, usually after the credits roll at the end of the broadcast. S1(1)(b) of the CDPA 1988 specifically covers 'sound recordings, films or broadcasts', adding to the 'original literary, dramatic, musical or artistic works' in Section 1(a). Copyright does not subsist in the programme until the recording is made, however. Section 3(1) of the Act assists with definitions of the terms in Section 1. Therefore, 'literary work means any work, other than a dramatic or musical work, which is written, spoken or sung'. This may well cover the commentary on a sporting event. As the use of AI in producing sports commentary expands, however, this may lead to copyright problems. In most legal systems, copyright can only be given to the fruits of the intellectual labour and creativity of a human being.[25] That said, it might be possible, as some jurisdictions are leaning towards, to attribute the copyright to the creator of the AI programme. That would be 'the person by whom the arrangements necessary for the creation of the work are undertaken', according to Section 9 of the CDPA 1998. That is still problematic as it may be seen to be akin to attributing copyright in a handwritten work to the creator of the pen.[26] No doubt this will be a prodigious source of litigation for years to come.

Sports commentary often refers to information produced in a tabular form or artistic representations of where the players will be on the field of play or the race, the 'starting line-up'. Section (3)(a) stipulates that a literary work 'includes . . . a table or compilation . . . and a database'. Some of these tabular representations may constitute such a database, and that will be addressed later in the chapter. It is, however, likely that even a table of results or statistics on screen with colourful graphics would be caught by the Act. As long ago as the 1950s, football fixture lists were held to be literary works in *Football League Limited v Littlewoods Pools* [1959] 1 Ch 637 (ChD). In a similar vein, choreographed dance moves by any cheerleaders or even marching bands before kick-off or at half-time could be covered. These may fall under Section 3(d) covering dance as a dramatic work. All music employed in the broadcast would be protected too.

Sports broadcasting may, of course, be via radio, and even television broadcasts will sometimes carry only voiceovers with no pictures for some interviews. These may be telephone conversations with sports personalities and pundits, players, and managers, with just a still picture of the speaker as visual content. These 'sounds' are not music and are therefore covered under Section 5A(1)(a), as 'a recording of sounds, from which the sounds may be reproduced'. Alternatively, per 5A(1)(b), they would be 'a recording of the whole or any part of a literary, dramatic or musical work, from which sounds reproducing the work or part may be produced'. A direct copy of the recording does not ascribe copyright to the copier, however. These provisions could attach to such as a radio interview with a sportsperson or the commentary on a match or race. Section 11 stipulates that the copyright owner of a sound recording is the producer. Of course, like any copyright, this can be assigned by contract to anyone else. The duration of the protection is 70 years from the last day of the calendar year in which the recording was made. The visual element of the TV broadcast of a sporting event would be classified as a film, and thus, Section 5B applies. Per 5B(1), films are 'a recording on any medium from which a moving image may by any means be produced'. Section 5B(2) stipulates that the soundtrack is treated as part of the film. Again, copies do not confer copyright to the copier. The creation of a film is seldom the work of one person; a team is required with a director, a producer and so on. Section 13B(2)(a)-(d) assists here. The copyright in a film expires 70 years after the last day of the year in which the last of the following dies: 'the principal director . . . the author of the screenplay . . . the author of the dialogue, or . . . the composer of [the] music'. For most sports broadcasts, only the former and the latter would be relevant.

Broadcasts are specifically covered in the Act as a separate entity. Section 6(1)(a) of the CDPA provides for those. Broadcasts are 'an electronic transmission of visual images, sounds or other information which . . . is transmitted for simultaneous reception by members of the public and is capable of being lawfully received by them'. Thus, both radio and TV transmissions are covered, regardless of the means of transmission or the technology used. Alternatively, a broadcast is such an electronic transmission, 'transmitted at a time determined solely by the person making the transmission for presentation to members of the public', per Section 6(1)(b). Section 6(1)A grants an exception to internet transmissions, unless they are available on a website 'simultaneously' with a sports broadcast on TV. This means that audio-visual footage of a sporting event is available on a website after the competition closes and is not being broadcast on TV or radio is not a broadcast. It would constitute a 'film' for the purposes of the Act, though. The duration of copyright here is fifty years from the last day of the calendar year which the broadcast was made. The owner of the copyright is the person or corporation making the broadcast.

In Chapter 6, the unique position in IP rights of databases received initial consideration. There is potential protection under the CDPA and also a separate database right instead, or as well. Much depends on the degree to which there is either intellectual creative effort in creating the database, or alternatively, whether significant resources were employed in making it. These databases, or extracts from them, may well form part of a broadcast, perhaps to illustrate a point that the commentator is making about sporting statistics or the like. Section 3A(1)(a) brings some databases within copyright protection. Specifically, those that 'by reason of the selection or arrangement of the contents of the database . . . constitute the author's own intellectual creation' per Section 3A(2), thus constitutes a literary work. This is provided the database is 'arranged in a systematic or methodical way' and is individually accessible, electronically, or otherwise. The arrangement of the data in the database must require mental effort but also skill, judgement and creativity to be protected under the CDPA. If the entries in the database are literary works in themselves, then they would also attract copyright. Short extracts from sports rulebooks entered into a database for research purposes would be one such example. There is also a separate 'database right' which does not emanate from the CDPA 1988 but from a statutory instrument implementing EU law. The EU Directive on the Legal Protection of Databases of 11 March 1996 (96/9/EC)[27] was implemented in the UK by the Copyright and Rights in Databases Regulations 1997. Section 13 mandates that a 'database right' exists when there has been a 'substantial investment in obtaining, verifying or presenting the contents of the database'. Section 12 explains that '[i]nvestment' includes 'of financial, human or technical resources'. Thus, the creator must have expended considerable capital, either financial or human, for the database right to attach. There are fifteen years of protection under these regulations, from creation or from each substantial alteration. In *Football Dataco Ltd and Others v Sportradar GmbH and Others Same v Stan James Plc and Others* [2012] EWHC 1185 (Ch), it was held that such a database right was owned by Football Dataco Ltd. Thus, Stan James, the gambling provider, was liable for its unauthorised use in their business.

It is possible for a database to fit both the definition in Section 3A of the Act and Section 13 of the Regulations. It is equally possible that a database would not be sophisticated enough to meet either criterion and so would not have any IP protection. As discussed in Chapter 6, this was the conclusion reached in *British Horseracing Board v William Hill Organisation* [2005] EWCA Civ 863. The racing SGB of the time had been publishing databases on thoroughbred horses on its website. William Hill had been utilising these for its betting customers without authorisation. The matter ultimately went before the ECJ as Case C-203/02 *British Horseracing Board v William Hill Organisation*, which ruled that there was insufficient creativity or investment for protection under either the Act or the Regulations. However, one alternative way to protect such databases is to attach contractual terms and conditions of payment to the display. This would discourage copying or at least ensure there is remuneration for their commercial use.[28]

In summary, in sports broadcasting, the protection of a database would depend on the nature of the information in each entry or the intellectual work that went into arranging those entries. Otherwise, the level of investment in time and/or money required to compile it could attract a stand-alone database IP right. Finally, it may be possible to attach legal rights to even a very simple database with terms and conditions that limit its unauthorised use without payment.

Trademarks caught in the broadcasts

In Chapter 6, the notion of registered and unregistered trademarks was addressed in more detail. To recap, registered trademarks are those for which a successful application to the Intellectual Property Office has been made to register a mark. This would require the bid to satisfy primarily Sections 1, 3, 4 and 5 of the Trade Marks Act 1994.

Section 1(a) defines a trademark as 'any sign which is capable . . . of being represented in the register in a manner which enables the registrar . . . and the public to determine the clear and precise subject matter of the protection afforded to the proprietor'. Additionally, the mark must be distinguishable from that of another brand and may have 'words, designs, letters, numerals, colours or sounds'. The shape of goods or their packaging can be trademarked if distinctive enough per Section 1(b). There are absolute grounds for refusal of an application and also relative grounds. Section 3 deals with absolute grounds, beginning with non-compliance with Section 1. Further, such grounds are under Section 3(1)(b), marks lacking 'any distinctive character' or, by Section 3(1)(c), which merely refer to 'quality, quantity, intended purpose, purpose, geographical origin or the time of production'. Under the same section, absolute grounds would include immorality, prohibition by national or international law, offensiveness, or bad faith. Per Section 4, a mark may be prohibited if it is deceptive or purports an association with the British Royal Family if this is not true. Section 4(5) specifically marks out national symbols such as the Union Jack, coats of arms and so on as not capable of registration. By the same provision, the Olympic symbol cannot be registered, or form part of a design submitted for registration. Section 5 clarifies what relative grounds there may be for refusal to register a mark. Under Section 5(1), an application will be unsuccessful if it refers to a mark that is 'is identical with an earlier trade mark' and the goods or services to which it relates. Even if there is enough similarity, such that there 'exists a likelihood of confusion on the part of the public', the application will not be granted per Section 5(2).

In sport, many logos, including club emblems, have been registered under the Act. Sponsors' brands regularly appear on the shirts and equipment of players and athletes.

That is indeed the point of the sponsorship agreement: to advertise the products or services concerned to the spectators and viewing public. As discussed more fully in Chapter 6, it is possible to assert IP rights in a logo and so on, without registering it. Registration can be expensive, and success is not guaranteed. Sometimes, if the market for a good or service is not large enough, the resources for making and maintaining a registration may not be warranted. For example, the name of the English soccer club 'Arsenal FC' is protected in a wide range of classes of products as a registered trademark. The 'New York Yankees' baseball team name is also protected in a smaller number of classes, but not for bathing products. Thus, shower gel and soap bearing the Yankees' name and logo, marketed in the UK, are not protected with registered trademarks (®) but with a ™ to indicate an unregistered mark. This is because the market for this product is much smaller than in the United States, as baseball is not nearly as popular in the UK. Unregistered trademarks are protected by asserting the right through a 'passing off' action in tort. *Reckitt & Coleman Products v Borden* [1990] 1 All ER 873 was a case concerning the production and sale of lemon juice in 'Jif Lemons'. These were lemon replicas made from plastic that operated as squeezable bottles. When other producers of this fruit juice began to copy the idea, Reckitt and Coleman sued, alleging that the defendant was trying to utilise the claimant's 'goodwill' or 'brand awareness' unfairly. The requirements for the tort of passing off to be proved were at least clarified, even if the claim was unsuccessful. From the case, the claimant must prove that their goods are distinguishable and have acquired 'goodwill or reputation in the mind of the purchasing public'. A 'misrepresentation' by the defendant must also have occurred because of which customers were or might have been confused as to the goods' origin. Further, the claimant must prove that their goodwill has or is likely to be damaged because of the misrepresentation.

Two cases illustrate how to apply the above principles in a broadcasting context. The Formula One racing driver Eddie Irvine sought relief when he believed his brand had suffered damage because of the actions of sports broadcaster Talksport. *Irvine and another v Talksport Ltd* [2002] EWHC 367 (Ch) concerned the 1999 racing season and Talksport's purchase of the rights to broadcast it on the radio. In their promotional campaign, they altered a picture of Irvine without his permission. The original showed a mobile phone in Irvine's hand, but this was replaced by a Talksport-branded radio when published. Irvine had a personal brand, as many sports personalities do, which was separate from that of Formula One or his Ferrari team. Irvine's case was that his brand was damaged by the false association with Talksport that this 'passing off' achieved. Irvine won and was ultimately awarded £25,000, a reasonable sum at the time. In *BBC v Talksport Ltd* [2001] FSR 53, however, the issue concerned 'off-tube' coverage. This was a reference to the fact that older TVs relied on a 'cathode ray tube' to project the images onto the screen from the back. This was rather different from today's flat screen technology and the reason why TVs used to be so bulky. The salient facts were that the BBC had won the rights to broadcast the Euro 2004 soccer games live on the radio. Talksport was a commercial radio station, and their presenters were watching the games on TV screens entirely away from the matches and producing radio commentary by that means. This was advertised as live coverage and even included dubbed-in crowd noises to make listeners believe the commentators were present at the venues. The problem for the BBC was that although they had goodwill in their own brand, they had insufficient goodwill in their association with the Euro Championships. Thus, although Talksport was guilty of the required misrepresentation, there was no goodwill for the BBC to seek protection for. Ultimately, this type of commentary could go ahead, as long as Talksport made it clear their presenters were not actually at the matches.

Concluding remarks on the exclusivity of a broadcast

The broadcast itself will be protected by Section 6 of the CDPA. However, there is no IP in a spectacle in UK law, meaning that many broadcasters could attend and record the event. Therefore, ensuring that the commercial partner who wins the sole rights to broadcast has the exclusivity they paid for is achieved through a number of different legal channels.

Firstly, where possible, the venue needs to be accessible by ticket only, and there must be clear conditions of contract for entry that prohibit audio and/or visual recording. The only broadcasting equipment allowed on the ground should be that of the rights holders. Those entry restrictions may, however, not always be possible. The sport could perhaps take place in relatively open ground that is overlooked, like a car rally, cycling or running road race, or even a horse racing track. In such circumstances, any elements of the image or sound that are subject to copyright, such as the commentary, musical score, or forms of words on advertising hoardings, have stand-alone protection as 'literary works' under the CDPA. Databases visible on screen will be similarly protected and could attract the database right. Per Section 16(1), in the UK, only the copyright owner can copy the work, issue copies of the work to the public, rent or lend the work to the public, perform, show or play the work in public, communicate the work to the public or make an adaptation of the work. Thus, if a broadcast showed any images or played any sounds that are under copyright protection, action can be taken in the courts under Section 16(2) for injunctive relief and/or damages. If the copying were done as a commercial operation, then the criminal sanctions in Sections 22–6 could apply. There are exceptions, however – the most important ones for sports broadcasting being for criticism, review, quotation and news reporting under Section 30. It was also apparent in *Football Association Premier League Ltd and Others v QC Leisure and Others* (C-403/08) and *Karen Murphy v Media Protection Services Ltd* (C-429/08) how copyright in individual images and sounds can effectively block unauthorised broadcasting. In a similar manner, any logos or emblems on the competitors' sportswear or on advertising around the venue may be protected by a registered trademark or be a brand capable of protection by a passing off action. The illicit broadcast carrying these images could be the subject of actions for infringing the Trade Marks Act 1994 or in tort, therefore. This is provided that the owners of the brands in question are prepared to take up such litigation. This is highly likely as all parties in that situation would have a vested interest in safeguarding the exclusivity of the broadcasting deal.

It is possible to prevent unauthorised broadcasts by means of a web of contracts. This prevents authorised brands and copyrighted literary works from being published through the broadcast. What is more difficult is barring unauthorised brands from appearing on authorised broadcasts illicitly. In Chapter 6, the concept of 'ambush' or 'guerrilla' marketing was introduced. Such techniques are considered parasitic in that they seek to take advantage of an event for which the 'offending' commercial enterprise is not an official sponsor. A crude example would be infiltrating the crowd with spectators paid to wear clothing bearing indicators for a rival brand to the main sponsor. Bavaria Beer infamously used such tactics at the 2006 and 2010 soccer World Cup series.[29] The intention was that broadcasting would inevitably feature these spectators in the footage, ultimately much to the anger of the paid-up sponsors. Under normal circumstances, such actions are not unlawful despite deliberately seeking to take advantage of the brand image or goodwill in the competitions or venues in an unauthorised way. They are considered unethical and 'akin to theft' or alternatively ingenious and resourceful, depending on the point of view. For events such as the Olympics, Commonwealth Games and Soccer World Cup, however, there is a difference. The territory winning the bid to host the tournament must enact legislation to introduce criminal and civil measures to combat ambush marketing. This will be a requirement for winning the bid. Consequently, arrests and civil actions can follow such attempts at these types of world-class competitions. Even here, innovative ways are found to get around the legislation. For instance, in 1996, Linford Christie wore contact lenses with the Puma logo on them to a press conference at the Atlanta games. This was much to the chagrin of the sponsor, Reebok, who had paid $25m for the exclusive rights.[30]

At a lower level, even at that of nationals, there are no statutory legal remedies as such. Another tactic is for advertisers to buy up advertising space around the time that the event will be broadcast. As long as these do not bear any indication that the company is an official sponsor, there is no illegality. Advertisers must also be careful not to include any words, symbols and the like, related to the event or the participants, that are subject to copyright or trademark laws. Strict conditions of entry that even refer to clothing that can be worn by spectators can also be used, although rightly, opprobrium can fall on venues that take this to an extreme.[31] It is most difficult to prevent advertising hoardings and other indicators of brands being visible in broadcasts of events where the adjoining land is visible. There is nothing to stop a company placing its marketing on hoardings adjoining a horse racing venue or cross-country event in any sport, as long as it is on land not controlled by the venue.

Returning to the main theme, preventing unauthorised broadcasts, there is one further way that exclusivity can be protected. In *Douglas v Hello! Ltd* [2001] QB 967, many of the heads of claim failed when a photographer from Hello! Magazine gate-crashed the Douglas' wedding. A contract guaranteeing exclusivity of photography rights had been entered into with OK magazine, however. The argument that succeeded was that Hello! had committed a breach of the confidence that was inherent in the original contract. This creates a precedent that could be used in TV or radio broadcasting of sporting events as well.

Regulating broadcasting by code

Law is about social coercion; the state desires that a certain set of behaviours be encouraged or, alternatively, eradicated. This is achieved by engendering in the population a concern about the criminal or civil consequences of not complying. Enacting statutes and the evolution of case law are not the only, or even sometimes the best, ways in which such control can be exercised. Major industrial and commercial sectors, as well as elements of daily life, are governed instead by a 'code'. This will usually have a statutory basis, but breach of its provisions does not normally result in litigation. Instead, there can be sanctions under the code, or transgressions can act as an aggravating factor if litigation for more egregious harms is contemplated. For example, in the corporate governance sector, the behaviours of company directors towards their companies and various stakeholders are governed by the Companies Act 2006. These matters are further regulated via the UK Corporate Governance Code (UKCGC). Whilst not law, proof of breaches of that code would not go well for an errant company officer facing proceedings under the Act. Conversely, some poor management will only breach the code and not reach the threshold in the Act at all. Similarly, driving on UK roads is the province of the Road Traffic Act 1988 and associated Regulations. Contravening a red traffic light will therefore fall under the ambit of criminal law. However, ignoring an amber traffic signal is dangerous, but there is no penalty in the Act. Instead, this is a breach of the Highway Code, established to advise on and recommend the best driving practices. If there is an accident after a driver commits this act, however, the breach of the code will be admissible evidence against them if it is relevant and an aggravating factor in sentencing.

Detractors of the use of codes instead of legislation often complain that they have no 'teeth' and therefore there is no deterrent effect or sense of justice when wrongs are done. Large commercial sectors are often in a good position to lobby Parliament to regulate in the form of a code rather than legislation, and that is to their advantage. However, there is expediency in allowing an industry to regulate itself, especially when the area is technically complex. Broadcasting standards are made and enforced in the UK by a set of codes, and the responsibility for these vests in Ofcom. Complaints from viewers about alleged inappropriate content or misleading advertisements, including regarding the time of day they are transmitted, can be investigated. For example, in 2020, 27,000 complaints were filed about a dance routine on a prime-time Saturday night family entertainment show.[32] Membership of the code is a requirement for obtaining a broadcasting licence,[33] so the code is not really voluntary. The sanctions that can be imposed under it are not always considered to be sufficient, however. This is because these outcomes do not carry the stigma of reprimand by a court and rarely fall on individuals, mainly the corporations. The Communications Act 2003 established Ofcom, and as the name suggests, its brief is much wider than just broadcasting. Ofcom also covers 'broadband, home phone and mobile services, [and] . . . the universal postal service, [by] . . . Royal Mail'.[34] There are further services, such as regulating the airwaves used by 'wireless devices like cordless phones, "walkie talkies" and even some car keys and doorbells'.[35] Ofcom would also get involved in investigating scams and bad practices targeting vulnerable people. Section 3(1)(a) charges Ofcom to always seek to 'further the interests of citizens in relation to communications matters'. Section 3(1)(b) places a further requirement 'to further the interests of consumers in relevant markets, where appropriate by promoting competition', in everything it does.

The broadcasting code

Section 319(1) of the Act requires Ofcom 'to set, and from time to time to review and revise, such standards for the content of programmes to be included in television and radio services'. This is the basis of the main code mentioned in Section 319(3). There are other codes, such as for services to those who are deaf, partially sighted or blind. There is also a code for sports broadcasting, which will be discussed later. The standards and objectives that the code should support are laid out in Section 319(2). There are fourteen of these and include ensuring that viewers and listeners under the age of eighteen are suitably protected. Furthermore, news items are to be presented with due impartiality and harmful or offensive material is to be excluded from programmes. Political advertising is also prohibited, except under strict limits, and protection from misleading and/or unlawful commercial advertising is further covered.

The Broadcasting Code operates under a series of principles that correspond with those in Section 319(2). For instance, the first paragraphs refer to protecting those under 18, and children are defined as under 15 years. It reads, 'Principle: To ensure that people under eighteen are protected' and goes on:

> Rules
> Scheduling and content information
> 1.1: Material that might seriously impair the physical, mental or moral development of people under eighteen must not be broadcast.
> 1.2: In the provision of services, broadcasters must take all reasonable steps to protect people under eighteen.
> 1.3: Children must also be protected by appropriate scheduling from material that is unsuitable for them.[36]

There are equivalent sections for news impartiality, prevention of harmful or offensive material and so on. The code covers radio and television broadcasts, not those released via the internet. In applying the rules, context is all important; thus, material that might be considered offensive on a daytime talk show might not necessarily be so in a late-night comedy panel quiz game. As a result, warnings about potentially offensive language or scenes are routinely broadcast before programmes intended for mature audiences. The code is prepared in accordance with relevant legislation, which is listed as Sections '3(4)(h) and 319(2)(a) and (f) of the Communications Act 2003, Article 27 of the AVMS Directive, Article 10 of the European Convention on Human Rights, and the BBC Charter and Agreement'.[37] The BBC is therefore regulated by the Code but is further subject to standards provisions in its own Royal Charter and Framework Agreement. The inclusion of rules as 'principles' rather than as regulations allows Ofcom to look at whether the spirit as well as the letter of the code has been broken. This is one of the great advantages over legislation because there is more opportunity for a 'purposive' interpretation of the wording rather than concentrating on the literal wording, which is the traditional and usual way that statutes are interpreted by judges. Thus, there is less possibility that an offending broadcaster would be able to escape sanction on a 'technicality'. This is similar to the way other regulatory systems work. For example, the UK solicitors' regulatory and disciplinary body, the Solicitors Regulation Authority (SRA), writes its rules based on principles. Even some statutes, particularly those governing such a nebulous quality as integrity or probity, have adopted a principles-based approach. One such example is the Bribery Act 2010. Ofcom works on the basis that it does not vet material before broadcast but investigates complaints afterwards. Fines can follow a successful complaint or even the withdrawal of a broadcasting licence or both. As an example, Russia Today (RT) can no longer broadcast in the UK because it did not show due impartiality in its coverage of the early stages of the Ukraine War in 2022.[38]

Sports broadcasters obviously have to abide by the general code above. They face particular challenges when interviewing competitors who may not have due regard for their language, fresh from the emotionally charged arena. Furthermore, sometimes quite terrible injuries, even fatalities, cannot be predicted and are sometimes caught in live coverage of a fast-paced game or race. For this reason, Ofcom places emphasis on what has been done to ameliorate the effect of the footage. Usually, an apology from the interviewer or quickly pulling the camera angle away from an incident will suffice. Together with this, The Code on Sports and Other Listed Events obviously has relevance for sports broadcasts. The genesis for this code was the Broadcasting Act 1996, and it deals primarily with listed events. The concept of these 'Crown Jewel' sporting dates has already been covered in this chapter.

Fair play in broadcasting

The very concept of IP is central to this chapter just as it was in Chapter 6. In Chapter 6, the moral, ethical, practical and legal paradoxes inherent in commodifying ideas were considered; to revisit them here would be repetitious, though. Given that so much of elite sport's funding is reliant on broadcasting revenue streams, it is inevitable that the dominance of money will tend towards inequity. It seems absurd that fans are prohibited from taking photographs or film to record an event they are entitled to enjoy, or indeed have what they wear dictated by sponsors worried about rival brands being aired. However, this is the norm when the revenue streams from broadcasters, intertwined with sponsors' needs as they are, take precedence. There is no doubt that elite sport, particularly soccer, rugby, cricket and horse racing, would not be as well funded or well organised if funding were not drawn down this way. That said, there is a vast divide between the top flight in these sports and the amateur and grassroots levels, as the money does not trickle down in the way it should. There is also great inequality between sports that are perceived to be popular enough to be worth televising and those that are not. Fashions change in this regard, as during the seventies and eighties, show jumping was a staple Saturday afternoon viewing but is rarely now televised except in an Olympic year. Conversely, some sports have been arguably saved by being suitable for broadcast. Cricket would not be as prominent a sport without the newer formats that were devised very much with sponsors and broadcasters in mind. A monopoly is the anathema of fairness, but when broadcasting deals are made for soccer in Europe, worth eye-watering sums, there is only one buyer and one seller. This is tolerated by the EU, a body which is founded on principles designed to facilitate as free a market as possible, on the grounds that it will ultimately benefit the consumer. By this is meant the consumer of broadcasts, but this does not take into account the overall detrimental effect of broadcasting rights being held by such a narrow group of people wielding so much power, especially if it sidelines the spectators and the interests of smaller businesses.

There are positives to be discussed as well; however, these mainly emanate from the fact that broadcasting standards are largely governed by codes and not statutes. There is something to the argument that codes are beneficial to big business, and they lobby for them on the grounds of 'flexibility' and a reduction in 'red tape' that would slow their growth. It is true that a code can seem to lack 'teeth' compared to a statute with criminal or even civil sanctions attached. However, the ultimate penalty under the code is quite draconian, as a serious breach will mean the loss of the licence to broadcast, effectively ending the business. Despite those criticisms, there is more scope for fair outcomes under the code. Live broadcasting, especially of sports, is unpredictable, and genuine efforts to compensate when unsuitable material is broadcast before there is fully time to mitigate it will be taken into account. This can take place in a way that clumsy, expensive and literal-based court proceedings could not match. The fact that there is a code rather than a statute also means that there is likely to be more buy-in to abide by it. Governance by code 'feels' more like a collegiate effort to maintain standards than it does law to be feared. Perhaps the best example of the code reflecting fairness, though, is the concept of the 'Listed Event'. That has created a situation where, at last, money cannot buy everything, as the rights to broadcast certain 'Crown Jewel' sporting events cannot be sold to the highest bidder. Consequently, despite the chagrin of the broadcasting mega-corporations, being able to watch the key events like the FA Cup and Grand National does not depend on the financial means of the viewer.

Notes

1 Avery Brundage, fifth president of the International Olympic Committee (1952 to 1972).

2 Deloitte, 'A balancing act – Annual Review of Football Finance 2023', 6, accessed 9 October 2023, https://www2.deloitte.com/content/dam/Deloitte/uk/Documents/sports-business-group/deloitte-uk-annual-review-of-football-finance-2023.pdf.

3 Jonathan Merritt and Genevieve Gordon-Thomson, 'European Super League: What can its opponents legally do?' *The Conversation*, 20 April 2021, https://theconversation.com/european-super-league-what-can-its-opponents-legally-do-159393.
4 Simon Gardiner et al., *Sports Law* (London: Cavendish, 2011), 13.
5 Chien-Yu Lin, Ping-Chao Lee and Hui-Fang Nai, 'Theorizing the role of sport in state-politics', *International Journal of Sport and Exercise Science*, 1, no. 1 (2008): 23–4.
6 David Karen and Richard Washington, eds, *Sociological Perspectives on Sport – The Games Outside the Games* (London: Routledge, 2015), 21.
7 The Broadcasting Act 1996 extends statutory provision to digital broadcasting.
8 Dan Milmo and Alex Hern, 'Wimbledon to introduce AI-powered commentary to coverage this year', *The Guardian*, 21 June 2023, https://www.theguardian.com/sport/2023/jun/21/wimbledon-introduce-ai-powered-commentary-to-coverage-this-year.
9 '"Betting drones" frustrating UK racecourses', *BBC*, 17 January 2019, https://www.bbc.co.uk/news/uk-england-nottinghamshire-46905905.
10 Jim Waterson, 'BBC licence fee to be abolished in 2027 and funding frozen', *The Guardian*, 16 January 2022, https://www.theguardian.com/media/2022/jan/16/bbc-licence-fee-to-be-abolished-in-2027-and-funding-frozen.
11 Meg James, 'Murdoch has survived scandal after scandal. Will Dominion-Fox News lawsuit be different?' *LA Times*, 4 March 2023, https://www.latimes.com/entertainment-arts/business/story/2023-03-04/rupert-murdoch-fox-new-accused-spreading-election-lies.
12 See for instance, Julia Carrie Wong, 'Zuckerberg says Facebook is pivoting to privacy after year of controversies', *The Guardian*, 6 March 2019, https://www.theguardian.com/technology/2019/mar/06/mark-zuckerberg-facebook-privacy-vision and Kari Paul, 'Chaotic and crass: A brief timeline of Elon Musk's history with Twitter', *The Guardian*, 25 April 2022, https://www.theguardian.com/technology/2022/apr/25/timeline-elon-musks-history-twitter.
13 'European Parliament, Briefing Paper – "Audiovisual rights in sports events, an EU perspective"', March 2017, 9–10, accessed 9 October 2023, https://www.europarl.europa.eu/RegData/etudes/BRIE/2017/599320/EPRS_BRI(2017)599320_EN.pdf.
14 See John Woodhouse, 'House of Commons Library – Research Briefing: Broadcasting: Listed sporting events', May 3, 2022, https://researchbriefings.files.parliament.uk/documents/SN00802/SN00802.pdf.
15 Section 98 Broadcasting Act 1996.
16 Woodhouse, 'House of Commons Library – Research Briefing: Broadcasting: Listed sporting events', 6–7.
17 Case C-201/11 P, C-204/11 P and C-205/11 P, *UEFA and FIFA v Commission* (2013).
18 Louis Wolcher, *Law's Task: The Tragic Circle of Law, Justice and Human Suffering* (Oxford: Routledge, 2008), xvi.
19 Antonio Gramsci, *Selections from the Prison Notebooks*, trans. Quintin Hoare and Geoffrey Nowell-Smith (New York: International Publishers, 1971), 44.
20 'Competition and Markets Authority – Ladbrokes and Coral – A report on the anticipated merger between Ladbrokes plc and certain businesses of Gala Coral Group Limited', July 26, 2016, accessed 9 October 2023, https://assets.publishing.service.gov.uk/media/5797818ce5274a27b2000004/ladbrokes-coral-final-report.pdf.

21 Ibid., 4–16.
22 'European Broadcasting Union', accessed 9 October 2023, https://www.ebu.ch/home.
23 European Commission Statement IP/03/1105, dated 24 July 2003.
24 Ibid., 185.
25 See, in the United States, *Feist Publications v Rural Telephone Service Company, Inc.* 499 US 340 (1991), in the EU, C-5/08 *Infopaq International A/S v Danske Dagbaldes Forening and in Australia, Acohs Pty Ltd v Ucorp Pty Ltd* [2012] FCAFC 16.
26 Andres Guadamuz, 'Artificial intelligence and copyright', *WIPO Magazine*, 1 October 2017, https://www.wipo.int/wipo_magazine/en/2017/05/article_0003.html.
27 EU Directive 2019/790 (17 April 2019) on copyright and related rights in the Digital Single Market amends Directive 96/9/EC, so database protection in the remaining twenty-seven member states has continued to develop.
28 See Case C-30/14, *Ryanair Ltd v PR Aviation BV*.
29 Jon Kelly, 'How ambush marketing ambushed sport', *BBC*, 17 June 2010, http://news.bbc.co.uk/1/hi/8743881.stm.
30 Nick Collins, 'Famous and infamous sports marketing stunts', *Telegraph*, 16 June 2020, https://www.telegraph.co.uk/news/picturegalleries/7831901/Famous-and-infamous-sports-marketing-stunts.html?image=2.
31 'Mo Farah and his wife in "Fly Mo" flag kerfuffle', *Telegraph*, 13 August 2012, https://www.telegraph.co.uk/sport/olympics/news/9471720/Mo-Farah-and-his-wife-in-Fly-Mo-flag-kerfuffle.html.
32 'Britain's Got Talent: Ofcom will not investigate diversity performance', *BBC*, 17 September 2020, https://www.bbc.co.uk/news/entertainment-arts-54188788.
33 The most notable exception to this is the BBC, as it is established by Royal Charter. All commercial stations must have a broadcasting licence.
34 'Ofcom – What is Ofcom', accessed 9 October 2023, https://www.ofcom.org.uk/about-ofcom/what-is-ofcom.
35 Ibid.
36 'Ofcom – The Broadcasting Code, section one, protecting the under eighteens', accessed 9 October 2023, https://www.ofcom.org.uk/tv-radio-and-on-demand/broadcast-codes/broadcast-code/section-one-protecting-under-eighteens.
37 Ibid.
38 'Ofcom – Press release: Ofcom revokes RT's broadcast licence', March 18, 2022, https://www.ofcom.org.uk/news-centre/2022/ofcom-revokes-rt-broadcast-licence.

8

Sports Gambling

The rules of the game, the stakes and the quitting time[1]

It is possible to mount a defence of gambling on the basis that it is fair because it entirely revolves around chance. Alternatively, it matters not the background or skillset that the gambler has, irrespective of their background or social standing. Unfortunately, news headlines do not regularly provide ammunition for this argument. The Gambling Commission handed out its biggest ever fine to a gambling company in 2023.[2] William Hill PLC, the world's largest gambling provider, narrowly avoided losing its licence. This was after being found to have serious and 'alarming' shortcomings in its consumer protection and money laundering controls. In one case, a new customer was able to spend £23,000 in twenty minutes. In another instance, a gambler bet £276,942 in total, without any checks as to the source of these funds required under money laundering rules. Gambling accounts for £14.3 billion[3] of the UK economy and is a controversial activity to many. The above instances illustrate what can happen; this is an addictive pastime and is a problem that goes beyond sport and into the heart of society and the economy.

It must be remembered that not all cultures accept gambling as part of everyday life, and there are cogent reasons for that. Western capitalism is predicated on the primacy of increasing individual wealth, and at first glance, gambling may seem to be another way to make money quickly. This is seen as achievable from an innate skill set rather than one gained through education or privilege of birth. Gambling has these first impressions in common with trading on the stock market and other speculative business enterprises. On a more detailed analysis, though, the closer cousin to gambling is not commerce but other forms of addiction. The placing of a bet is the purchase of a drug—an entirely legal one produced quite naturally: adrenalin. Potential financial gain is usually the driver of that 'buzz', so the two are nevertheless inextricably linked. The world of gambling, rather like the entertainment sector, is much wider than sport, so much of the law and regulation to be considered is applicable outside sport gambling. In the UK, gambling has many games of chance to offer. These vary from the outcome of a sporting contest and the minutiae of that encounter, such as the first red card and so on, to casino gambling, both in person and increasingly online. Even the humble game of Bingo is now a multi-million-pound earner for the online gambling industry. 'Loot boxes' or 'skins' in online gaming are increasingly coming under scrutiny as a form of gambling too.[4] It is even possible to bet on the next US president or UK political party likely to take power at the next election. Whether the outcome is produced by the vagaries of two sports teams pitted against each other, the electorate or a computer algorithm, though, the result must be uncertain to produce the risk and therefore the excitement. Adrenalin is addictive,[5] so the regulation of gambling and the public policy response generally is better understood in a 'health' context rather than regarding financial services.

With the above in mind, the gambling sector and its attendant laws, attitudes and public perception in the UK and much of the Western world are specific to those diverse societies. For instance, until recently, few US states allowed gambling at all, and it is still heavily restricted compared to the UK. Many Muslim countries forbid gambling outright as it is contrary to the teachings of the Qur'an.[6] Consequently, not all immigrant communities in Western countries will accept gambling, and this must have an impact on the degree of reporting from those groups regarding problem gambling. This is a topic to be covered later in this chapter. What this illustrates is that a study of gambling and sport is wide-ranging, covering economics, sociology, politics, religion, culture and psychology as well as law and industry self-regulation. These academic disciplines can be used to study both sport and non-sport gambling. Very often, the same conglomerates offer services in both sectors. For this chapter, there are four main initial discussions to be had regarding gambling in the UK. Specifically, the potentially addictive and therefore controversial nature of this human activity, as well as the absolute reliance on 'suspense and anticipation'. Following on from this, therefore, the particular threat posed by 'fixing' and the significance of the interdependence of certain sports and betting.

Addiction and controversy

Gambling has much in common with other popular recreational pursuits that are actually the purchase of excitement, even in the form of fear or dread. Horror movies and suspenseful films fall into essentially the same category, as do rollercoasters and escape rooms. The experience produces a 'buzz' from the production of adrenaline in the consumer's body. Given its addictive nature, 'withdrawal' symptoms can occur if this hormone is reduced in some circumstances. Examples include if a committed runner cannot take their morning jog for a period of time, although the precise chemical action that causes this is more complex than is required for this discussion.[7] This is the source of problem gambling and, in contrast to alcohol or street drug addiction, there is often very little indication that there is a problem until the gambling debts are out of control.[8] When considering problem gambling, it is therefore more useful to think of the number of families affected rather than individuals. If the mortgage cannot be paid and the family home is repossessed, then the effect is much wider than just on the addicted person themselves.

Definitions

Like other large commercial sectors in the UK, such as broadcasting and corporate governance, there are different types of state coercion applied to the practice of gambling. In common with those sectors, there is an overarching statutory provision, but also a regulating and licensing body and other measures of control that are more in the soft law category. There is more on soft versus hard law generally in Chapters 1 and 9. The statutory basis is provided by the Gambling Act 2005, although a successor Act is making its way through Parliament.[9] Section 3 of the 2005 Act recognises three terms: 'gaming', 'betting' and 'participating in a lottery'. These terms are further defined in Section 6(1); gaming is a 'a game of chance for a prize', and per Section 6(2), a 'game of chance' includes:

> a game that involves both an element of chance and an element of skill . . . involves an element of chance that can be eliminated by superlative skill, and . . . a game that is presented as involving an element of chance, but . . . does not include a sport.

Thus, betting always involves chance, but not always solely that. For example, a good knowledge of football team performance or racehorse form is a skill and does mitigate the unpredictability of the outcome to a degree. These legal provisions also cover casino games, but the relevance to this chapter is that some gaming machines do not bet on sport per se; their profitability is inextricably linked with the funding of sport. So-called 'Fixed Odds Betting Terminals' (FOB-T) involve placing a stake at the press of a button on the randomised lining up of certain images. They are alternatively and colloquially referred to as 'fruit machines' and 'one-armed bandits'. These machines are prevalent in betting shops, and legislative changes regarding these have had a significant knock-on effect on sport, as we shall discuss later in this chapter in more detail.

The Act goes on to define 'betting'. Section 9 has it as 'making or accepting a bet on . . . the outcome of a race, competition or other event or process . . . the likelihood of anything occurring or not occurring or whether anything is or is not true'. It is clear that the drafters of this definition had traditional trackside and high street gambling in mind. There is, however, a growing awareness that 'in-game' or 'in-app' purchases in online gaming ought also to be construed as a game of chance.[10] Typically, a gamer will be presented with the opportunity to purchase a 'loot box' or 'skin' containing special powers for their game character, or tools and equipment that give them a potential advantage. The player will often not know the nature and quality of the contents of this loot box until after the purchase, which gives the element of suspense. Online gaming can otherwise be referred to as esports, a growing and very well-funded activity. This is not yet a true 'sport', not having International Olympic Committee (IOC) or Sports Council recognition. It does have a nascent sports governing body[11] and operates very much like a traditional international sport, and may yet become one. It remains to be seen whether the revisions to the Gambling Act, currently in Parliament, will include loot boxes as gambling or not.

As much of UK sport funding is derived ultimately from the National Lottery, it is worth noting that, per Section 14, the Act defines lotteries too. This is further evidence of the interdependence of sport and gambling. Critics note the irony of funding activities that promote health and well-being using the proceeds from a potentially addictive pastime.

Regulating gambling

Many of the offences that can be committed under the Gambling Act are regulatory in nature. There are potentially harmful effects of uncontrolled gambling, not to mention the possibility of unscrupulous betting providers operating. It is therefore important to licence and control the activities of betting offices. An example of one of these offences is providing 'facilities for gambling' in the UK without the relevant licence or exemption, under Section 33. Furthermore, under Section 46(1) a person 'commits an offence if he invites, causes or permits a child or young person to gamble'. These and similar offences are not under the purview of the police but are investigated and enforced by The Gambling Commission (GC),[12] which was set up under the 2005 Act. The Commission's main functions are to provide a licensing framework for betting activities. These include the National Lottery, casinos, arcades and bingo halls, betting shops and online gambling operators. The GC also sets conditions and requirements for licence holders[13] and carries out assessments to ensure those are met. Where they are not, and/or offences are discovered, action up to and including enforcement is taken. Outcomes can range from a warning to revocation of a licence with a financial penalty. On occasion, a case can be 'settled' where a public statement, together with other mitigating actions, a payment in lieu of a penalty and reimbursement of the state's costs can occur. An example is the package of measures awarded against Ladbrokes/Coral in 2019. This included a £4.8m payment to the National Strategy to Reduce Gambling Harms and other reparation.[14] Finally, the GC has a responsibility to take action to try to protect vulnerable gamblers, a subject discussed in more detail later in this chapter. For instance, gambling with credit cards has been banned, and there are stricter rules around advertising gambling products. There are also tighter regulations on identity and age checks for online gambling operators.

Industries and sectors with self-regulation mechanisms or at least regulation that is at 'arm's length' from the state must face the criticism that wrongdoing is not taken seriously enough, though. Specifically, the ability to avoid convictions in court by agreeing to a financial settlement is not enough of a deterrent. It is even alleged that the potential cost of such a payment can be factored in as a 'business loss' against huge profits. Large corporations in other areas, from broadcasting companies to water treatment firms[15] operate under the same kind of soft regulation. This is defended as a more flexible and less confrontational approach that better lends itself to ensuring wrongdoing is sanctioned. Furthermore, social and economic damage is repaired. This latter is something that courts are ill-equipped to enforce. The same thinking is applied to controlling the gambling sector. The reason why gambling is regulated at all is that

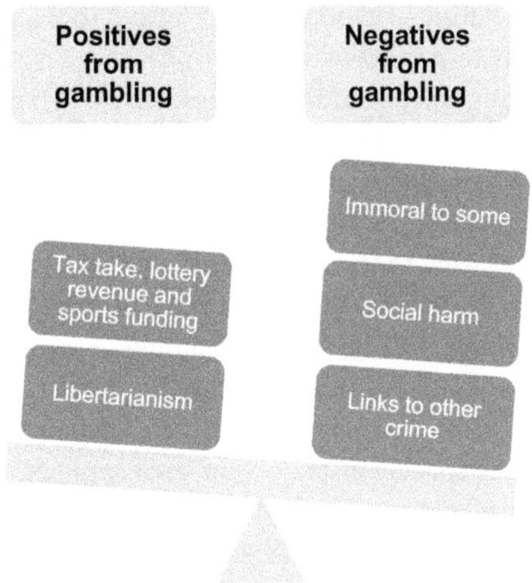

Figure 8.1 The gambling social policy conundrum.

betting is not universally regarded as morally right. Some scripture from the major religions describes it as a sin, and it carries the stigma of being, at best morally dubious to some of the public. The existence of legal gambling in this country, therefore, requires a delicate balance (see Figure 8.1). This is between citizens' rights to pursue a pastime of their choice, added to the significant tax revenue raised by this industry, versus the potential for abuse, crime and addiction problems. The current regime attempts to find that middle ground, and it is in the best interests of the betting providers to be seen to be co-operating with those aims. Accordingly, betting advertising now focuses on the 'safer gambling' tools available and promotes the phrase 'when the fun stops . . . stop'[16] as much as advertising the gambling services on offer. There are commentators who say that the sector is still not regulated sufficiently, however. Furthermore, the betting companies are not doing enough regarding problem gamblers. These critics cite the negative financial, social and health outcomes associated with the activity and the near doubling of active online betting accounts from 2009 to 2019 as drivers for legislative change.[17] This is only one side of the argument, though, as opponents of greater statutory intervention argue that civil liberties are at stake and that financial devastation may ensue for certain sports.[18] There have, however, already been tighter controls enacted for gaming machines, and in a case study later in this chapter, it will be possible to gauge some of the real effects this has had on gambling and sport.

Cheating and gambling

There is no debate about the moral status of cheating in sport; it runs counter to the very ethos of it. Cheating is more than just unethical; it can strike at the very lifeblood of professional sport: funding. A little later in the chapter, the notions of suspense and anticipation will be examined for their specific importance to gambling. It is these factors that drive the spectating of sport as well. Without these, there is little remaining motivation to buy tickets to a sporting event or purchase a sports television channel subscription. Undermining the uncertainty of outcome that true sport has within it is very dangerous indeed for the future of sport as we know it. The lack of faith in Chinese football from its indigenous fans is an example of what can happen if corruption is allowed to take root.[19] Essentially, Chinese soccer is a laughingstock despite the jailing of officials, referees and players to try to address the fixing.

Under the 2005 Act, there is a specific offence of cheating at gambling, under Section 42(1)(a). Section 42(1)(b) adds that 'enabling or assisting another person to cheat at gambling' will also be punishable. There is no need for the person to have won anything through their subterfuge. This would include match or race fixing, and influencing the outcome of specific in-play events that spot betting relies on. Typically, this might be such as the player awarded the first red card in a match. It should also be remembered that such activity, or something connected with it, may also be a breach of the Fraud Act 2006. For instance, Section 3(a), where a person 'dishonestly fails to disclose to another person information which he is under a legal duty to disclose'. Section 3(b) goes on to add the proviso that the person must also intend 'by failing to disclose the information . . . to make a gain for himself or another, or . . . to cause loss to another or to expose another to a risk of loss'. Dishonesty must be proved using the same test as for theft,[20] but there is no need to prove that the victim was actually deceived or that property changed hands. The advantage here over the Gambling Act offence is that the offence is complete as soon as there is a dishonest failure to disclose. It may therefore be of use if the cheating is interrupted at a very early stage. However, all the above offences require proof beyond a reasonable doubt and that is not always achievable. Much cheating is therefore dealt with using sports governing bodies' (SGB) internal disciplinary mechanisms, which will require a lower standard to be met. This is sometimes as low as the civil law's 'on the balance of probabilities' and this is the standard used in horse race fixing disciplinaries for example.[21] The British Horse Racing Authority's (BHA) Integrity Unit is very experienced at spotting irregular betting patterns and soccer's European governing body, Union of European Football Associations (UEFA), has a sophisticated investigations operation too.[22] These internal measures are capable of being triggered if the evidence reaches the civil standard of proof although the investigation may uncover information which also merits an investigation by the police. They and the Crown Prosecution Service (CPS) will judge whether the criminal standard has been met. This is what happened with regard to allegations that jockey Kieran Fallon and others engaged in race fixing. However the 2007 Crown Court trial. In addition, the internal disciplinary that led to it was challenged in the High Court[23] under the rules developed in *Bradley v Jockey Club* [2004] EWHC Civ 2164 (QB). This case was discussed at length in Chapter 3 and gives the High Court supervisory jurisdiction over disciplinaries such as this. The entire affair was hardly a model of a perfect interface between internal regulation and the state criminal justice systems. This led to calls for better co-operation between the two in future.[24] A greater degree of success against criminal corruption has been seen in professional cricket in recent years, though. Players such as Nasir Jamshed, the former batsman, who had represented Pakistan over sixty times, were prosecuted, for example. Jamshed received a custodial sentence at Manchester Crown Court for his role in a spot fixing affair after cricket officials alerted police to the activity.[25]

Reliance on 'Suspense And Anticipation'

The foregoing discussion of cheating and the upcoming specific analysis of fixing in this chapter are linked by betting's reliance on sufficient suspense and anticipation to be an attractive pastime at all. If gambling is essentially the purchase of an adrenaline 'buzz', this is not without precedent in the human condition. Consider the popularity of skiing holidays; participants are not travelling by ski to a destination; they ascend the slope purely in order to experience the thrill of the downhill run. This is made all the more exciting by the real possibility of injury. In the same vein, rollercoaster rides at Disneyland are effectively a form of transport that runs on tracks. They arrive precisely at the point from where they left; however, the purchase is not one of transportation to a destination. Therefore, the price is paid to feel at least apprehension, if not fear, and the adrenaline that comes with that. The same is true of a thriller movie or a novel full of intrigue and suspense. If the thrill-seeker were to know for sure that the skiing or rides are without even the suggestion of danger, then there is no fun. The same is true if one knows the intricacies of the plot or the ending before a movie or book starts. The purchase is one of 'suspense and anticipation'. Thus, it is the danger of financial loss and the unknown outcome of a sporting fixture,[26] which are essential for gambling to thrive. Betting aside, if the outcome of the sporting event is known, or reasonably easily predicted, it is not going to be exciting to watch. This in turn will hit viewing figures as well as betting revenues. It is for these reasons, as much as the desire to protect sporting integrity for its own sake, that SGBs invest so much in trying to catch cheats and fixers. With some sports more than others, widespread predictability through fixing would be nothing short of catastrophic for revenues, as shall be discussed next.

The interdependence of certain sports and betting

Among major sports, horse racing is uniquely dependent on betting. With the exception of some Middle Eastern venues, professional racing has never survived without betting as a significant factor, much of it on-course. For example, at different times during the early twentieth century, public concerns about the moral turpitude of gambling led local legislators in several US states to prohibit on-track betting. Even where those states did not explicitly outlaw the racing itself, the gambling prohibition forced the closure of most tracks in those jurisdictions.[27] Race-going is a different experience from following a team sport, such as soccer or rugby, however. There is an affiliation with a place, team or culture that is often lifelong with these team sports. With racing, there is a changing cast of jockeys and horses, and affinity ties are limited. In order to create sufficient 'suspense' and emotional investment in a race, followers of racing who are not equine enthusiasts *per se* (the majority of racegoers) need to make themselves stakeholders in the outcome of the race by betting. Thus, gambling becomes what economists refer to as 'entertainment goods' and has much in common with attending a casino or even watching a suspenseful television drama. Betting is therefore not as necessary in team sports for that emotional connection to be present. For the most part, spectators at an ice hockey or baseball match are already invested in the game because of their partisan allegiance to a team. Any gambling on the outcome is an added thrill rather than integral to the experience.

The reasons discussed above are why, historically, gambling and horse racing, to a certain extent, greyhound racing and trap racing as well, have come to be so much more reliant on gambling than other sports. This is not to understate the benefits that sports from the Indian Premier League Cricket to Major League Baseball derive from their relationships with the gambling industry. This is in terms of the sale of intellectual property (IP) rights to stream matches in betting venues, to name only one source of revenue. Horse racing and the like are in a league of their own in this context, however.

Some horse racing betting facts

In 2014, HMRC commissioned Frontier Economics to produce a report[28] in which it was found that the Gross Gaming Yield (GGY) from betting on British races was £1.1bn. Of this, 92.1 per cent was terrestrial betting, that is to say, not online. That position may of course have changed since then, particularly considering the Covid-19 pandemic. However, the statistics available for the lockdowns in 2020 and 2021 are difficult to factor in, as the period was so exceptional. Further, just over half of racecourse revenue derives directly from betting, and probably much of the remaining revenue is also betting-dependent. For example, race-day ticket sales would not be as great for the venues without betting being available at the track. In this research, the total costs of all British racecourses that year were found to be £549m, and racecourses received £227m in betting-related revenue streams. Of this, on-course betting revenue was £12.2m, bookmaker sponsorship and advertising made up £17.1m, media rights accounted for £127.8m and Levy Board payments came to £70.3m (see Figure 8.2). The UK's Levy Board is a unique institution more correctly referred to as The Horserace Betting Levy Board (HBLB).[29] This is a statutory body and was established by the Betting Levy Act 1961 and operates under the Betting, Gaming and Lotteries Act 1963 (as amended). It is a public body and is linked to the Department for Digital, Culture, Media and Sport (DCMS). The HBLB does not receive any government funding, nor any from the National Lottery, and it is required to collect a statutory levy from the horseracing business of bookmakers. This is then paid to the horse racing industry to provide a supplementary income.

High Street betting shops still provide a great deal of revenue for the betting industry, and therefore their profitability as retail outlets is very important. These shops may have up to four FOB-T gaming machines in them, in addition to any betting transactions taking place over the counter. These used to be very profitable for the betting shops, and in 2019, they provided £2.5bn GGY.[30] However, there were concerns

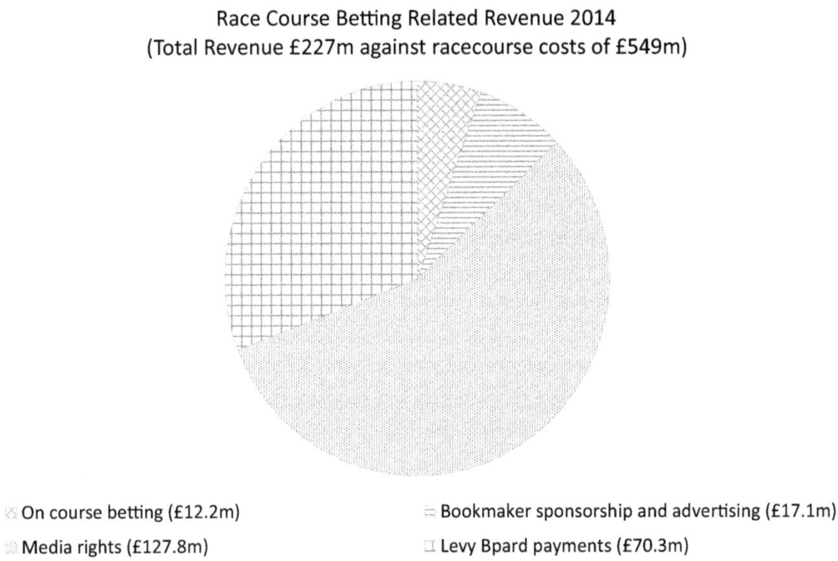

Figure 8.2 Race course betting-related revenue 2014.

fuelled by the tabloid press about the maximum stake allowed on these machines, the possible losses within a short space of time[31] and the difficulty in banning problem gamblers from them. Consequently, the maximum stake was reduced by legislation from £100 to £2. This is not necessarily all media hysteria though; GC figures do show that losses on these machines by UK gamblers reached an all-time high in the year ending September 2016 at £1.82bn.[32] The stake reduction had a profound effect on retail gambling and was likely a factor in many betting companies' decision to cut stores and jobs.[33] This trend is likely to have been accelerated by the pandemic, as both crises have seen providers pushing bettors to go online in a bid to cut their losses. The knock-on effect is that there is likely to be a reduction in the amount that the HRLB can collect and pass on to racing, which will in turn affect the ability of certain races, and even venues, to continue. The pandemic aside, the major impact here is from the legislative changes to regulating gaming machines that ironically have nothing directly to do with horse racing.

The social policy problem

Formulating a public policy response to gambling in a permissive society is problematic. The objections are not all purely moral; there are real harms to take into account. For instance, Dr Declan Jordan of Cork University Business School, Ireland, considers:

> There can be no doubt that the gambling industry, and the sport of horse racing that relies on gambling to exist, has negative social external effects. The effects are

> more significant because they are highly concentrated, in that the damage done to individuals and families is catastrophic.[34]

This is of course a point of view that is hotly contested by the gambling industry both in the UK and in Eire, which also has a very large horse racing industry. The previous UK government has responded to these concerns; however, mindful that not acting could lead to accusations that it was blind to a hidden epidemic. The administration was also no doubt aware of the potential impact on the civil liberties of citizens and the tax revenue that the country relies on to help fund public services. The former Prime Minister, David Cameron, ordered a review of gambling machines in betting shops, and the view that the stakes should be reduced drastically ultimately held sway. This was in the face of evidence presented that over half of betting shop revenue[35] comes from machines, and restricting them could cause at least 50 per cent of these shops to close. Bearing in mind that racing is paid on a 'per shop' basis for the media rights to relay race broadcasts to these high street premises, this remains a real threat to a significant revenue stream.

The Government also consulted on a ban on advertising betting on daytime television and up to 9.00 pm. The UK racing industry lobbied for an exemption to this, as there were concerns over the viability of racing coverage on Channel Four without bookmaker sponsorship and advertising. Channel Four Racing is a major broadcaster of horse racing in the UK. This ban may yet come into force when the planned new gambling laws are enacted, however. At present, the gambling industry has adopted certain voluntary bans, particularly around televised live soccer matches before 9.00 pm. Other campaigners want the government to go further, for example, veteran England soccer goalkeeper Peter Shilton, who himself has wrestled with a forty-five-year gambling addiction. Shilton is spearheading a push to outlaw gambling advertising on football shirts.[36] This move, if enacted, would mirror the fate of tobacco advertising in sport.

A focus on fixing – 'Spot The Difference'

The introduction of spot betting has created a variety and novel avenues of entertainment for punters, not to mention new revenue streams for gambling providers. It has also created greater opportunities for illegal gains through fixing particular events or incidents within a match, game or race. The relationship between sport and gambling as a whole is almost as old as modern sport itself.[37] Historically, many major sports have had crises of integrity centred on betting as well. For instance, both cricket and baseball have suffered from allegations of match-fixing as long ago as the nineteenth century.[38] What is unprecedented, however, is the current level of concern about the matter. In 2012, the Director General of the World Anti-Doping Agency (WADA) suggested a 'world sports integrity agency'. This would be like WADA but with a much wider remit, namely, combatting 'doping, betting, bribery and corruption'.[39] This call acknowledged that such integrity issues were not always encountered in a silo but often form part of a much wider pattern of international crime. Even local and national police agencies struggle to tackle such criminal activity, which is no respecter of jurisdictional boundaries. The problem is therefore even greater for SGBs and international sporting federations (ISF), and some estimates go as far as to state that the criminal underworld now 'controls' at least 25 per cent of world sport.[40]

Major SGBs have commissioned reports in response to this problem, and since the 2008 Games, the IOC has required all Olympic athletes to explicitly state that they are not involved in betting. In 2010, the UK Government set out a policy requiring sports to protect against fixers. This requirement was not only given to the 'usual suspects' of horse racing and football; all sports are expected to take steps to counter betting-related corruption. Research indicates that sports as diverse as cricket, basketball, tennis, baseball, darts, and snooker have been, or could be, victims of fixing.[41]

Other causes of corruption

There are other causes of betting corruption besides the legalisation of spot betting. Research by prominent economists cites other significant drivers,[42] although one or more of those are still linked to 'single event' betting. Firstly, 'liquidity' is defined as the ease and speed with which a business can convert its assets into cash, and there is a huge growth in this in gambling, caused by far greater amounts wagered compared to the historical position. This expansion is assisted by the greater likelihood of the more 'minor' sports being able to get coverage on television or at least via the web. This is compared to the situation traditionally, before the internet and the modern proliferation of sports channels. The entertainment or 'excitement value' is also multiplied by having a financial stake in the outcome of live action sport.[43] Secondly, the internet has had the effect of driving down bookmakers' profit margins because gamblers can shop around across the globe for the best odds. This in turn has driven down transaction costs, making bribing players and athletes even more profitable. These competition factors also mean betting providers are less likely to be as selective about the kind of bet they will accept. This means there has been an increase in the 'live', 'in-play', 'proposition' or 'spot' betting already discussed. This has in turn been facilitated by new technology and looser regulation of this activity. Inevitably, it is much easier to bribe an individual to bring about the first red card or a throw-in at a specified time than it is to bribe a whole team to lose.[44]

Finally, the traditional bookmaker is not the only provider of gambling anymore. Around the turn of the century, 'betting exchanges' emerged whereby it is now possible to place a 'lay' bet, which means that the bettor is placing money on a participant or team to lose. It is again much more practical, particularly in non-team sports, to offer a financial incentive to a player or athlete to lose, compared to an inducement to win.[45]

Who is particularly vulnerable to corruption?

Betting on sports has a long-established history in countries such as the UK, where regulation is light in relative terms. It is more tightly restricted in countries such as

India and Canada. It is still illegal in some jurisdictions like Pakistan and some US states, but to a certain extent, it continues unlawfully.

The BHA is seen as 'a model for the effective investigation of corruption in sport'[46] in terms of the development of systems and practices that make corruption more difficult. The problem is that the great strides made are largely limited to that one sport. Albeit soccer has come a long way in this regard, of its own volition. These sports have a history of volume betting, whereas equestrianism does not, despite the apparent similarities between some horse-riding disciplines and horse racing. In turn, sports like golf and badminton have no strong association with gambling, but with these more 'minor' sports and others like them, it would be unwise to be complacent about the spectre of betting corruption. This is because research has indicated that many risk factors can be identified in these sports, as well as the giants of soccer and horse racing. Sports like soccer have the greatest liquidity and are at the highest risk because that 'enables large amounts of money to be fed into the market without . . . attracting undue attention'.[47] This discussion is linked to that on levels of wages in sport, however. Where wages are low in relative terms, there is increased vulnerability to this corruption. As in most deviant activities and crimes, a person offered a bribe must make a rational choice, sometimes referred to as the 'pleasure–pain' dynamic.[48] The sportsperson's dilemma revolves around weighing in the balance the potential 'pain' of guilt and/or being caught against the 'pleasure' of the financial uplift the bribe would bring. This monetary reward is more likely to outweigh the negatives if the player is not well remunerated. Sports such as darts or even soccer at the lowest levels are where wages and prize money are relatively low.[49]

Some sports have separate stages in them; tennis and darts 'sets' are instances of this, as are the different disciplines in a triathlon or pentathlon. Research indicates these sports are also more vulnerable to fixing. This is because a bribe can be given to persuade a player to perform poorly or even lose a stage or set. The gambler can bet against the competitor before the match starts, and then, because the odds will have lengthened due to the poor performance early on, the gambler can stake more money with an 'in-play' bet. If the stake is carefully calculated, then it is extremely easy to make a profit.[50] The BHA is alive to this kind of chicanery and employs 'race readers' looking for irregular riding that might be linked to betting corruption. However, few, if any other sports do this to the same degree and with the same expertise. Other sports have unofficial cultures in them, which make them 'fixer-friendly'. For instance, in tennis, there is what is known as 'tanking'. The professional tournament fixtures and the associated travel place somewhat relentless pressure on players. It is therefore tempting for them to make a conscious decision not to give their absolute all in certain, less important matches.[51] A game thrown by a 'player' is harder to spot given this. Furthermore, any guilt and shame felt by the bribed player is bound to be lessened if they allow themselves to lose a game, given that they were planning to play sub-optimally in any event. In fact, any competition in any sport which, win or lose, carries little impact for the competitor is vulnerable to bribery. For example, 'dead rubbers' in cricket are games that must be played, but the outcome is a foregone conclusion. In a five-game test series, all matches will be played, but if a team has already won three of them, then the remaining two will not alter the overall result.[52] There are allegations and proven cases of bribery and corruption in sports that are structured like this, and thus monitoring for unusual patterns of spot betting would be very worthwhile.[53]

The career longevity of a sportsperson varies greatly depending on the sport. Gymnasts may start their journey at nine years old and no longer be at the elite level by their late teens. By contrast, jump jockeys can get a licence at sixteen and still be racing in their forties. A professional soccer player can expect their career to go from age eighteen to late thirties at a push, whereas an equestrian or shooting competitor may compete into their seventies. The oldest competitor at Olympic level in recent years was dressage rider, Hiroshi Hoketsu[54] at the London Games in 2012, aged seventy-one. He was only beaten to the accolade of the oldest Olympian ever by a shooter in the 1930s. These are examples, and there is no suggestion here, of course, that either individual engaged in corruption. Research does indicate that, generally, veteran sports participants are more vulnerable to taking a bribe, however. This is because younger athletes have much more to lose if discovered. Thus, even a seasoned gymnast approaching their twenties must think about what career they will next undertake, perhaps coaching or in the structure of an SGB. This is a strong counterweight to the potential financial incentive of a bribe.[55] The same is true of a soccer player or cricketer in the early years of their playing career. By contrast, a relatively elderly competitor is not usually looking forward to many years of competition, team management or officialdom. There is, therefore, less which pushes back against the desire to take the bribe, other than whatever moral compass they have. Sports where there are athletes and players towards the end of what might be termed their working lives ought, therefore, also to be analysed for signs of betting corruption.

In conclusion, soccer, cricket and horseracing may be the sports that immediately spring to mind when thinking about sporting integrity and betting. A deeper analysis, however, reveals that there are significant risk factors in a range of other sports, including more 'minor' ones. Complacency born of the fact that these sports have no long-term association with volume betting is unsatisfactory. This is why organisations such as WADA and the UK Government are either calling for or mandating a review of policy to address betting-related corruption opportunities across all sports.

Protecting vulnerable gamblers

Problem gambling is defined in various ways in different disciplines; this is because the purpose of the definition changes. For instance, psychiatry and medicine generally have their focus on criteria that aid a clinical diagnosis of addiction. For other disciplines, such as the social sciences, the main factors are those associated with harm. This is often in terms of affecting a wider group than simply the individual gambler, such as family, work colleagues and even society generally.

What is problem gambling? Exploring the definitions

A definition widely used originated in Australia and states that problem gamblers may have 'difficulties in limiting money or time spent gambling with adverse consequences for the gambler, others, or the community'.[56] Consequently, a person might exhibit a tendency for 'excessive' gambling, poor control over gambling behaviour, and a desire to persist in gambling. This is despite significant adverse consequences flowing directly from this inability to self-regulate. The Problem Gambling Severity Index (PGSI)[57] was developed in Canada and uses a series of questions put to participants to assess problem gambling with a Likert Scale response. Data can be gathered on how often in the preceding twelve months the gambler has bet more than they could afford to lose or needed to gamble with larger amounts of money to get the same excitement. Whether they felt their gambling had caused problems for them and their household could also be determined. These answers, amongst others, indicate whether a person has a gambling problem and can be the first step towards treatment. The emphasis here, though, is not on trying to identify addiction *per se*, but rather to establish the wider impact the gambler is having on themselves and others through their behaviour.

Problem gambling statistics

The Gambling Commission conducts a telephone survey of gamblers quarterly. Around 4,000 respondents take a 'lite' version of the PGSI, and the most recent useful figures cover the year from December 2016 through to December 2020. The last year is difficult to draw a pattern from because it contained the most stringent pandemic lockdown measures and thus is unprecedented. The problem gambling figures are split into 'low risk' and 'moderate risk' bands, with a most serious 'problem gambler' category as well. In the years prior to the pandemic, those at low risk represented between 2.7 per cent and 3.7 per cent of respondents; those at moderate risk accounted for between 1.2 per cent and 1.8 per cent, although the trend in both cases was broadly downward. The problem category was fairly stable, however, at 0.5 per cent to 0.7 per cent of those surveyed.[58] These figures are not segregated by gender, but the gambling providers have made strenuous efforts in recent years to increase their appeal to female gamblers.[59] The full extent of female problem gambling is possibly not well enough known yet, as this is a relatively recent development. Even ignoring the low and moderate risk categories and concentrating on the year with the lowest problem gambler figure of 0.5 per cent (2018)[60] this is a significant number of people. Given a UK population of around seventy-one million, that equates to 355,000 people alone. This is still not representative of the true problem, however, as few, if any of these people have no impact on anyone else. Other research[61] indicates that each problem gambler has a negative effect on between six and ten other people. This elevates the harm figure to between 2,130,000 and 3,550,000, to include family members, co-workers and those from the gamblers' wider community. Ironically, public policymakers take very seriously issues which affect much lower numbers of people than this. For instance, in 2019, 1,752 people were killed in road traffic collisions, and 25,945 people received serious injuries.[62] In 2018, 6,507 people committed suicide,[63] a significant increase on the year before. Both societal problems have generated either tighter legislation, high-profile government media campaigns or both.

Finally, even if 0.5 per cent can be considered a small proportion of the UK population as a whole, it is a much higher proportion of total gambling customers, and these gamblers provide a disproportionate amount to the gambling industry's total revenue. It would therefore only be reasonable for the gambling industry itself to also try to do as much as it can about the issue of problem gambling.

Case study on FOB-Ts, problem gamblers and the state's response

Fixed Odds Betting Terminals, 'FOB-Ts', gaming machines or so-called 'One-Armed Bandits', were discussed earlier in this chapter. That was firmly in a horse racing industry context, as the impact of government policy is likely to have the most dramatic effect on that sector. In these paragraphs, the regulation of these machines will be analysed from the point of view of policy aimed at controlling problem gambling.

For background, in 2018–19, the last year unaffected by the pandemic, there were 7,315 licensed betting shops in the UK, and most have FOB-Ts in them, usually the maximum of four. In this year, the GGY for these 'Category B2' machines, as they are also called, fell by 46.4 per cent to £624m. This was largely due to the introduction of the £2 maximum stake in 2019. Category B3 machine GGY has increased by 18.5 per cent to £1.3bn in the same period, and the online sector grew to £2.1bn according to these statistics. In addition, FOB-Ts continued to account for 56 per cent of high street betting office revenue.[64] The reduction in maximum stake was a policy change that was entirely due to concerns about problem gambling. Gambling and religious charities, together with other campaigners, convinced MPs that there were a number of problems specific to these 'B2' machines. These worries included that the then maximum stake of £100 was out of step with the regulatory policy applied to other forms of gambling. Also, staking this sum on a single spin is 'hard gaming', something usually restricted to casinos. The particular issue being that betting shops are so numerous and accessible compared to casinos and less well supervised.[65] High street betting shops are often sited in deprived areas as well, so losing this sum of money has a disproportionate effect on those bettors.[66] It is worth noting as well that before the reduction in maximum stake to £2 was implemented, The Responsible Gambling Trust (now 'Be Gamble Aware')[67] funded more than one study on gamblers' use of B2 machines. There were many findings that supported the reduction in stake, with one respondent even opining that at least one murder and attempted murder of betting shop employees would not have happened without FOB-Ts.[68] Collectively, the surveys also concluded however, that reducing the stake size might reduce B2 machine usage but might not necessarily mitigate overall gambling harm. This is because players may move on to other gambling products and online in pursuit of a similar thrill. On first reading, this does appear to be borne out by the statistics already discussed.

Regulatory moves

Initially, the date for reducing the maximum stake to £2 was set for April 2019, but bowing to pressure from the betting mega-corporations, this was held back until the autumn of that year. This was controversial enough for the sports minister to tender her resignation, citing that delay as the primary cause.[69] There are further harm reduction measures as well, which have been slightly less newsworthy. Gambling with credit cards has been banned, and tighter guidance around the operation of self-exclusion schemes has been forthcoming. In these, a gambler who recognises that they have a problem can exclude themselves from a bookmaker chain. Of course, it was always open to the gambler to simply visit a competitor's venue if they wished to renege on their self-imposed ban. Now, different betting operators have to co-operate in their local area to ensure these schemes are as effective as they can be across different betting operators' outlets. Beyond these measures, all the major gambling providers are experimenting with algorithms designed to look for patterns of play that indicate problem gambling. Unfortunately, this is predicated on the assumption that betting will be account-based, as over-the-counter cash transactions will be much harder to track. A further innovation being trialled, though, is the use of facial recognition systems, which it is hoped would allow all the transactions made by an individual to be aggregated over a given period. This has not been without controversy, as a number of organisations and individuals from 'Big Brother Watch' to the Information Commissioner have raised concerns about the privacy issues involved.

Outside the UK, Norway has made the most extreme regulatory intervention of all. Any form of gambling product, including the state lottery, can only be purchased with a government-issued player card. This allows each individual's gambling behaviour to be tracked over time with a view to developing a programme of detection or intervention to address problem gambling issues. It also imposes an overall upper loss limit on the gambler.[70] Such a move in the UK may well trigger protests from civil liberties groups, given that the comparatively tame regulatory interventions and use of technology so far have already incurred their ire.

Does regulation make gambling fair?

In conclusion, the preceding illustrates that gambling is, at best morally questionable and a potentially harmful product; yet it is legal in many jurisdictions and contributes significantly to annual tax revenues. In this regard, it shares significant similarities with smoking and drinking alcohol. With respect to these potentially addictive activities, so far, no Western government has succeeded in prohibition long term. The United States went the furthest down this road with the alcohol prohibition era, but ultimately moderated its approach. Unless there is a strong underlying culture of aversion to such activities as alcohol and gambling, as in some predominantly Muslim countries, it is unlikely that there would be enough 'buy-in' to a total ban. Consequently, such a move could come with repercussions at the ballot box and also the potential growth of a black market. Modern policies that restrict access to gambling products on the high street may help, but they carry with them the risk that problem gamblers, given that they are addicts, will simply be forced under the influence of even less well-regulated betting operators. These are offshore, online or even in the unregistered illegal gambling sector. A key problem is that gambling is no longer the province of the local high street independent 'turf accountant'. The gambling corporations have enormous influence, and even under the legislation that exists, they can reach a deal with the regulator without facing significant sanctions. The further problem for the state is how to replace the taxation lost if onshore gambling shrinks due to stricter regulation. Paying for the enormous cost of the pandemic aside, the government needs this income to pay for everything from education to highways and defence, and, ironically, anti-addiction policy initiatives. That said, a similar issue arises with regard to climate change. The goal of largely replacing combustion engines with electric vehicles (EVs) by the 2030s brings with it the inescapable fact that petrol and diesel duty will diminish almost to vanishing point. The government will then have to come up with a palatable way to tax road users or face much shrunken coffers. This has not prevented the UK, as well as many other Western countries, from pursuing the policies promoting the EV. This is because they see the end goal of becoming carbon neutral as worth the hurdle of finding tax revenue in other ways. If gambling were viewed in the same way, that is, as socially damaging as climate change is environmentally harmful, it could be more heavily regulated or even marginalised in the way that smoking is. In the final analysis, gambling, even regulated as it currently is, will never be fair because it encourages addiction, cheating, bribery and a myriad other crimes. Also, ultimately, it is the gambling mega-corporations that 'win' with their enormous profit margins. The most egregious in that list, though, is the potential for addiction. No addict is able to rationally apply a 'quitting time' with all that this means for them, their family, sport and society as a whole.

Notes

1 From the Chinese proverb, 'if you must play, decide upon three things at the start: the rules of the game, the stakes, and the quitting time'.

2 Oliver Barnes, Sarah Provan and Akila Quinio, 'William Hill hit with record £19.2mn fine', *Financial Times*, 28 March 2023, https://www.ft.com/content/c80ca492-eac9-434c-9d00-b641059c2cff.

3 'Gambling Commission – Industry Statistic: May 2020', accessed 9 October 2023, https://www.gamblingcommission.gov.uk/statistics-and-research/publication/industry-statistics-april-2020.

4 James Close and Joanne Lloyd, 'Gamble aware – Report: Lifting the lid on loot-boxes chance-based purchases in video games and the convergence of gaming and gambling 2012', accessed 9 October 2023, https://www.begambleaware.org/sites/default/files/2021-03/Gaming_and_Gambling_Report_Final.pdf.

5 See for instance, Virve Pöysti and Maija Majamäki, 'Cultural understandings of the pathways leading to problem gambling: Medical disorder or failure of self-regulation?' *Addiction Research & Theory*, 21, no. 1 (2003): 70–82.

6 Toine Spapens, 'Illegal gambling', in *The Oxford Handbook of Organised Crime*, ed. Letizia Paoli (Oxford: Oxford University Press, 2014), 402–18.
7 See Jeremy Adams and Robert J. Kirkby, 'Excessive exercise as an addiction: A review', *Addiction Research & Theory*, 10, no. 5 (2002): 415–37.
8 Robert Erens et al., *Gambling and Problem Gambling in Britain* (London: Taylor and Francis, 2003), 56.
9 Hansard: Review of the Gambling Act 2005, Volume 699: debated on Thursday 22 July 2021, Column 1242, Scott Benton MP.
10 See David Zendle, Rachel Meyer and Harriet Over, 'Adolescents and loot boxes: Links with problem gambling and motivations for purchase', *Royal Society Open Science*, 6, no. 6 (June 2019), https://royalsocietypublishing.org/doi/full/10.1098/rsos.190049.
11 'World Esports Association (WESA)', Baarerstraße 26300 Zug, Zug, Switzerland.
12 'The Gambling Commission', accessed 9 October 2023, https://www.gamblingcommission.gov.uk/.
13 'The Gambling Commission – Gambling licence information, guidance and advice for businesses and individuals', accessed 9 October 2023, https://www.gamblingcommission.gov.uk/licensees-and-businesses.
14 'The Gambling Commission – Regulatory action against Ladbrookes Betting and Gaming Ltd', accessed 9 October 2023, //www.gamblingcommission.gov.uk/public-register/regulatory-action/detail/108.
15 'Ofwat – Southern water to pay £126m following Ofwat investigation', accessed 9 October 2023, https://www.ofwat.gov.uk/pn-12-19-southern-water-to-pay-126m-following-ofwat-investigation/.
16 Safer Gambling Campaign is overseen by the industry's main trade body, the Betting and Gaming Council (BGC). See 'BGC – "BGC takes over Senet safer gambling remit"', accessed 9 October 2023, https://bettingandgamingcouncil.com/news/senet-group-bgc.
17 Naomi Muggleton and Neil Stuart, 'Our study of gambling and its harms shows it's time to intervene', *New Scientist*, 4 February 2021, https://www.newscientist.com/article/2266799-our-study-of-gambling-and-its-harms-shows-its-time-to-intervene/.
18 Barry Glendinning, 'Gambling affordability checks by control freaks would be threat to civil liberties', *The Guardian*, 8 February 2021, https://www.theguardian.com/sport/2021/feb/08/gambling-affordability-checks-control-freaks-threat-civil-liberties-reform.
19 Evan Osnos, 'Playing fake ball: Why Chinese soccer matters', *The New Yorker*, 20 June 2012, https://www.newyorker.com/news/evan-osnos/playing-fake-ball-why-chinese-soccer-matters.
20 *Ivey v Genting Casinos (UK) Ltd t/a Crockfords* [2017] UKSC 67.
21 'BHA appeal board – Appeals of Maurice Sines, James Crickmore, Peter Gold, Nick Gold and Kirsty Milczarek', 10 April 2012, accessed 9 October 2023, https://www.britishhorseracing.com/press_releases/appeal-board-decisions-regarding-the-appeals-of-maurice-sines-james-crickmore-peter-gold-nick-gold-and-kirsty-milczarek/.
22 'UEFA – Integrity', accessed 9 October 2023, https://www.uefa.com/insideuefa/protecting-the-game/integrity/.
23 *Fallon v HRA* [2006] EWHC 2030 (QB).

24 'British Horseracing Authority – Neville Report 2008', Executive Summary, accessed 9 October 2023, http://www.britishhorseracing.com/wp-content/uploads/2008/05/Neville-Review-Pr-Rel-Exec-Summ-Recomm-City-of-Lon-May-08.pdf.
25 'Cricketer Nasir Jamshed admits bribery conspiracy', *BBC*, 9 December 2019, https://www.bbc.co.uk/news/uk-england-50715653.
26 See David Forrest and Robert Simmons, 'Outcome uncertainty and attendance demand in sport: The case of English soccer', *Journal of the Royal Statistical Society: Series D (The Statistician)*, 51, no. 2 (2002): 229–41.
27 Steven Riess, 'The cyclical history of horse racing: The USA's oldest and (sometimes) most popular spectator sport', *The International Journal of the History of Sport*, 31, nos. 1–2 (2014): 37–8.
28 'HM Government – The UK betting and gaming market: Estimating price elasticities of demand and understanding the use of promotions', 2014, accessed 9 October 2023, https://www.gov.uk/government/publications/the-uk-betting-and-gaming-market-price-elasticities-of-demand-and-use-of-promotions.
29 'The Horserace Betting Levy Board', accessed 9 October 2023, https://www.hblb.org.uk/.
30 'Gambling Commission – Industry Statistics, May 2020'.
31 'Crackdown on fixed-odds betting terminals where ministers are due to announce a new £2 maximum stake on gambling machines is delayed again', *Daily Mail*, 23 April 2018, https://www.dailymail.co.uk/news/article-5645375/Fixed-odd-betting-terminal-crackdown-delayed-local-elections.html.
32 'Gambling Commission – Industry Statistics, May 2020'.
33 Rob Davies, 'Bookmakers prepare for store closures as FOBT stake is cut', *The Guardian*, 30 March 2019, https://www.theguardian.com/uk-news/2019/mar/30/bookmakers-prepare-for-store-closures-as-fobt-stake-cut.
34 Declan Jordan, 'The Economics of Sport – "The external costs of gambling and why Ireland's unhealthy relationship with the horse industries need to end"', March 3, 2016, accessed 9 October 2023, https://www.sportseconomics.org/sports-economics/the-external-costs-of-gambling-and-why-irelands-unhealthy-relationship-with-the-horse-industries-need-to-end.
35 Rob Davies, 'Maximum stake for fixed-odds betting terminals cut to £2', *The Guardian*, 17 May 2018, https://www.theguardian.com/uk-news/2018/may/17/maximum-stake-for-fixed-odds-betting-terminals-cut-to-2.
36 Alistair Magowan, 'Peter Shilton calls for change to gambling sponsorship laws in football', *BBC*, 14 September 2021, https://www.bbc.co.uk/sport/football/58566431.
37 David Forrest, 'Betting and the integrity of sport', in *Sport Betting: Law and Policy* by Paul Anderson et al. (The Hague: T.M.C. ASSER Press, 2011), 14.
38 Ibid., 15.
39 David Howman, 'Supporting the integrity of sport and combatting corruption', *Marquette Sports Law Review*, 23 (2012): 247.
40 Ibid.
41 Forrest, 'Betting and the integrity of sport', 23.
42 Ibid., 18–22.
43 Ibid.
44 Ibid.
45 Ibid.

46 'The British Horseracing Authority – THE BHA and integrity in horseracing, an independent review (The Neville Review)', Executive Summary, para. 1.12, accessed 9 October 2023, http://www.britishhorseracing.com/wp-content/uploads/2008/05/Neville-Review-Pr-Rel-Exec-Summ-Recomm-City-of-Lon-May-08.pdf.
47 Forrest, 'Betting and the integrity of sport', 19.
48 Tim Newburn, *Criminology* (London: Routledge, 2007), 117–19.
49 Forrest, 'Betting and the integrity of sport', 23.
50 Ibid., 20.
51 Ibid.
52 Ibid., 23.
53 Ibid.
54 'Oldest 2012 Olympic athlete – Aged 71', *BBC*, 1 August 2012, http://www.bbc.co.uk/news/world-asia-19073349.
55 Forrest, 'Betting and the integrity of sport', 23.
56 Helen E. Miller, Samantha L. Thomas, Priscilla Robinson and Mike Daube, 'How the causes, consequences and solutions for problem gambling are reported in Australian newspapers: A qualitative content analysis', *Australian and New Zealand Journal of Public Health*, 38, no. 6 (2014): 529.
57 'Gambling Commission – Problem gambling screens', accessed 9 October 2023, https://www.gamblingcommission.gov.uk/statistics-and-research/publication/problem-gambling-screens.
58 'Gambling Commission – Low risk, moderate risk and problem gamblers (according to the PGSI mini-screen) 2016–2020', accessed 9 October 2023, https://www.gamblingcommission.gov.uk/statistics-and-research/publication/year-to-december-2020.
59 See Heather Wardle, 'The "re-feminisation" of gambling', in *Gambling Disorders in Women*, ed. Henrietta Bowden-Jones and Fulvia Prever (London: Routledge, 2017), 173–86.
60 'Gambling Commission – Problem fambling screens'.
61 'The Standard Life Foundation – "Betting in the UK: How to tackle problem gambling"', accessed 9 October 2023, https://www.standardlifefoundation.org.uk/en/our-work/publications/betting-in-the-uk-how-to-tackle-problem-gambling.
62 'Department for Transport – "Reported road casualties in Great Britain": 2019 annual report', accessed 9 October 2023, https://assets.publishing.service.gov.uk/government/uploads/system/uploads/attachment_data/file/922717/reported-road-casualties-annual-report-2019.pdf.
63 'Office for National Statistics – "Suicides in the UK: 2018 registrations"', accessed 9 October 2023, https://www.ons.gov.uk/peoplepopulationandcommunity/birthsdeathsandmarriages/deaths/bulletins/suicidesintheunitedkingdom/2018registrations.
64 'Gambling Commission – Industry Statistic, May 2020'.
65 'Parliament – Fixed odds betting terminals all party parliamentary group, "fixed odds betting terminals – Assessing the impact"', 2017, 34, accessed 9 October 2023, https://www.fobt-appg.com/wp-content/uploads/2017/01/FINAL-FOBT-APPG-REPORT.pdf.
66 'The Standard Life Foundation – "Betting in the UK: How to tackle problem gambling"'.

67 See 'Parliament – Fixed odds betting terminals all party parliamentary group, "fixed odds betting terminals – Assessing the impact"', 2017, for a useful summary of this research.

68 Ibid., 16.

69 Rob Davies, 'Sports minister resigns over delay to gambling curb', *The Guardian*, 1 November 2018, https://www.theguardian.com/uk-news/2018/nov/01/sports-minister-resigns-over-chancellors-delay-to-gambling-curb.

70 See Jonny Engebø et al., '"Regulatory measures" effect on gambling participation: Experiences from norway', *Frontiers in Psychiatry*, 12 (30 June 2021), https://www.ncbi.nlm.nih.gov/pmc/articles/PMC8278013/.

9

Sport and the Modern World Order

Fairness, equity, geo-politics and sport

It is impossible in a work of this size to give a full account of all the ways in which geo-political issues and sport intertwine. Instead, selected topics will be discussed to put sport in the widest political, social and economic context possible. In terms of international relations, the aim is to assess to what extent regimes have sought to use sport to project power and influence at the expense of their 'competitors'. This is with a particular focus on Russia, the Middle East and China as examples. For the section on sport and the climate, the dual problems of environmental activism targeting sport and the challenge of sport itself, reducing its carbon footprint, are addressed.

Geo-politics is generally understood to mean a consideration of international relations and politics in the context of geography. It is often used to differentiate between domestic and global politics. Traditionally, the additional factor influencing political matters would be physical location around the globe, but today it would be hard to exclude the physical climate. This is a topic that geographers study, but also, given the climate change agenda, it would be less than useful to ignore environmental concerns in this chapter, so inextricably are they linked to location. Worldwide shifts in temperature and weather patterns are now noticeably more important to policymakers and politicians, either through genuine concern or, regrettably, as 'political footballs'. For example, in September 2023, the then UK Prime Minister Rishi Sunak made a significant policy change when he pushed back the ban on new petrol and diesel cars from 2030 to 2035. This, as well as a number of other dilutions of targets and rules designed to help the country reach 'Net Zero' carbon emissions, was either lauded as pragmatic or derided. It was criticised on the basis that it was a clear, and ultimately unsuccessful attempt to put distance between his party and his political rivals ahead of a looming general election, whatever the environmental consequences.[1]

International relations

Research indicates that sport-related commerce is particularly impactful in the Global South. Here, 'sport mega-events are increasingly seen as vehicles for increasing a host's power and prestige in global relations and achieving developmental goals across social, economic, and political spheres of life'.[2] That said, the expected social and health benefits need a clear and robust long-term strategy to be implemented to be successful. Both Australia and the UK found this after the 2000 and 2012 Games respectively.[3] Without this planning and ongoing oversight, engagement with grassroots sports quickly drops off, and buildings never fulfil their expected enduring potential for the population. Put another way, the benefits promised to the people by the decision-makers to outweigh the disruption and cost of a large-scale hosting effort never fully materialise. Irrespective of this, developing and developed countries continue to vie for the prestige of hosting premier international events, too often hoping to distract attention from their poor social, economic or human rights record. Key to that is the very often misplaced perception that sport is politically neutral. The picture is usually much more nuanced and convoluted than that.

Sport's efforts to stay out of politics and the difficult choices that this entails have a long and not always fortunate history. The apartheid system of racial segregation in South Africa led to the country being an international pariah prior to the end of white minority rule in 1994. International sanctions were applied by many countries, including the United States, which enacted anti-Apartheid legislation in 1986[4] banning many imports and exports from South Africa. Sportsmen and women were not statutorily banned from competing in that country, however. Many sporting federations did boycott the regime though,[5] including those for cricket, soccer, wrestling and Judo. Having withdrawn the invitation to host the Olympic Games in 1963, the International Olympic Committee (IOC) expelled South Africa in 1970. Individual sportspeople made the decision to compete in the country nevertheless, and a few sports federations disciplined those concerned. In turn, some individual players took a differing view from their SGBs. In *Finnigan v. NZRFU (No. 1) [1985]* 2 NZLR 159, the New Zealand Rugby Football Union accepted an invitation to tour South Africa. Two rugby players challenged this controversial decision. The court decided that there were sufficient political and geo-political issues to allow the claim despite the fact that the SGB was not a public body, a common sport/legal problem discussed at length in Chapter 3. The stand-off between sporting governance and the South African regime only finally came to an end in the early 1990s with the first free elections and a new multiracial government. That thirty-year controversy may be in the past, but there are still regimes that have policies which lead to moral and ethical questions being posed for sport. It is also evident that sport hardly presents a united front when faced with even the most heinous of regimes or egregiousness of human rights abuses. It seems that personal career goals, right up to the commercial concerns of SGBs, can still eclipse calling out the appalling inequity in a society, thus in effect supporting the regime.

'Get On With The Football!'

This adherence to neutrality and impartiality, however extreme the political policy concerned may be, is evident in the mainstream media as well. Broadcasters and journalists who break ranks to highlight unfair treatment by lawmakers can find themselves censured. The BBC's highest-paid sports pundit, ex-England, Tottenham Hotspur FC and Leicester FC soccer player Gary Lineker, courted controversy in 2023.[6] He had previously been outspoken about a number of issues outside sport. These included questions of human rights, LGBTQ+ and women's rights, and the abuse of migrant workers in Qatar. The country had hoped to enhance its global image by hosting the soccer World Cup, but it only emphasised the problems it has in all those areas.[7] Lineker then took to X (formerly Twitter) to decry the government's immigration policies, particularly regarding combatting people-smuggling across the English Channel. Lineker advocated a more liberal approach. This is a contentious issue between the UK and France, with the French regularly being accused of not doing enough to deter the perilous crossing of the Channel by refugees in small boats. Hundreds a day take the appalling risk and all too often die in the attempt. Successive governments appear to be making little progress in tackling the problem in a humane way.[8] Lineker's predecessor at the BBC, veteran sports broadcaster Des Lynam, commented in an interview that Lineker, as a high-profile sports celebrity, should not comment on matters such as this, saying:

> For example, the last World Cup was in Qatar and he went very, very strongly about the limitations of society in Qatar. And he's right, there are, but he's not the person to say it. Get on with the football.[9]

The view that sport, in particular sports personalities, should not get involved in politics or social issues is not new either. Marcus Rashford MBE, a forward for Manchester United FC and England, was disparaged for his work regarding food banks and free school meals in the UK and the criticism of the Conservative Government's unfair policies that accompanied it. Unsurprisingly, the voices critical of his work, complete with the 'stick to football' jibe, came from the right.[10]

This book aims to analyse the extent to which the basic concept of fairness is present in modern sport, away from the playing of the sports themselves. This requires an examination of the legal framework within which sport operates, but also critically analysing the political, social, religious and ideological context from which the law derives. Law does not, after all, grow in a petri dish, unaffected by any contaminants. It follows, then, that the issues affecting sport are rarely unique to that sphere, and the question of how realistic it is to expect sport, politics, and society to occupy distinct spaces is paramount. This is no less so when considering geo-political matters. In fact, there is a convincing argument that sport, particularly sport governance, is a stratum itself in international relations. In modern international legal orders, the term 'normative co-ordinations'[11] has been coined. It used to be that the only international orders that existed came about when treaties were signed by nation states and between distinct geographical jurisdictions. Now, an increasing number of international agreements are in place that do not tie specific nations together but are 'co-ordinations'. This is where groups of citizens with common goals in various countries agree on a mode of operation without the involvement of governments (see Figure 9.1). International sporting bodies, like the World Anti-Doping Agency (WADA)[12] and the International

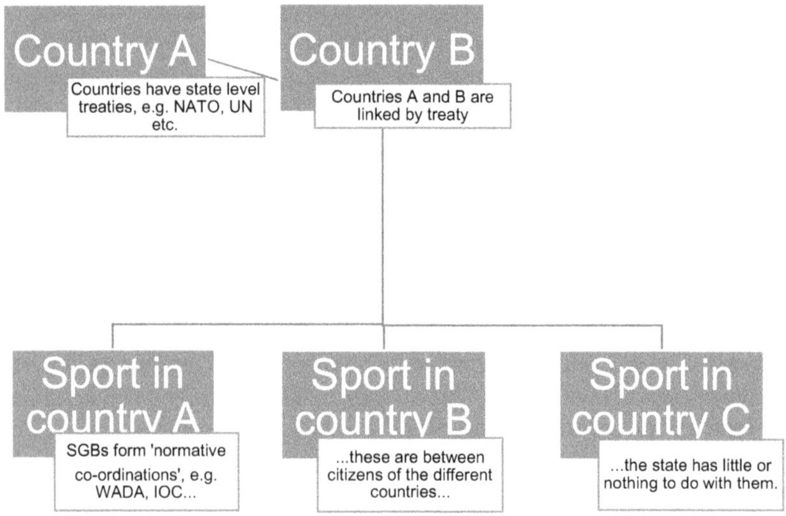

Figure 9.1 Sub-state level normative co-ordinations can have a wider scope and legitimacy than nation state treaties.

Olympic Committee (IOC), are examples, and the trend is increasing.[13] These orders can impose significant rights and duties on people subject to them, not always by their choice. Consider the fact that the IOC can mandate legal restrictions on domestic commerce, based mostly on Intellectual Property (IP) law, as a condition of a country hosting the Games.[14] There is little doubt that the consequences of being the subject of disciplinary proceedings by the sporting international order can be catastrophic for an elite sportsperson. The result can sometimes even be worse than being subject to a sanction under national or international law.[15]

The 'Westphalian' notion of the international order takes its name from the Peace of Westphalia, a series of treaties that ended the Thirty Years War in 1648. This established that all states have a right to their own sovereignty, regardless of size, something taken for granted today. This is no longer considered to be a useful model to understand how the international order works, however.[16] This phrase has been adapted more recently to include a reference to Keynesian economics. This has an emphasis on a market economy with interventions from the government to attempt to mitigate issues such as recessions and inflation. There is evidence that the world is past this stage now and is in a post 'Keynesian-Westphalian' conception of the international legal order.[17] Here, the tidy 'territorially coded, mutual exclusivity of jurisdiction'[18] model, complete with international treaties between these territories, is fading in importance. There are an emerging number of arrangements based on private law that allow for trade, travel, disaster response, humanitarian aid and sport to be better managed across multiple borders.

There have been many intersections between sport and politics. These range from the use of games and sporting events to exert coercion and control over the masses in Roman times to Jesse Owens' famous Olympic gold medals awarded in front of Adolf Hitler in 1936. There are many more in between and beyond. There are too many instances for the scope of this book; instead, some examples are selected for consideration.

Russia

The last hundred years or more have seen Russia and much of the Western world at odds politically, diplomatically and mostly by proxy, militarily for most of that time. It is hard to find any aspect of the societies on either side that was unaffected by this, and sport was no exception. It will be useful to briefly examine where this particularly long-lived animosity has come from.

A brief 'Horrible History' of relations

From the 1917 Revolution, Marxist-Leninist communism in the ultimate form of the Union of Soviet Socialist Republics (USSR) had as a central policy goal the spread of that ideology internationally.[19] This mostly took the form of encouraging and supporting worker revolutionary groups and left-leaning factions in other countries, examples being supporting the leftist Republicans in the Spanish Civil War of 1936–9 and Fidel Castro's communist takeover in Cuba in 1959. These aims were perceived as a threat to liberal capitalist democracies, and chronic suspicion became embedded on both sides of this ideological divide. There was a brief improvement in this situation, necessitated by the need to defeat the Axis powers during the Second World War. However, by 1946, the two blocs were implacably opposed again, and thus began the 'Cold War'. China became a natural ally for Russia after its own communist revolution in 1949, and North Korea followed soon after. The post-war years were marked by proxy wars where each side would support opposing combatants. This was in a bid to increase their geo-political sphere of influence whilst weakening that of the other. The Korean War ended inconclusively, whereas Vietnam was ultimately deeply damaging to the US-led Western nations involved. The Cuban Missile Crisis of 1962 is considered to be the closest both sides came to a nuclear exchange. Ultimately, though, the United States persuaded the USSR not to base nuclear missiles that close to the US mainland by winning a high-stakes game of naval brinkmanship in the Atlantic. The Soviet invasion of Afghanistan in 1979 was a miserable failure over time at the hands of largely US supplied *Mujahidin* rebels. Ironically, included in their number was one Osama Bin Laden. The Communist Party's handling of the Afghan debacle during the 1980s, together with serious failings in dealing with the 1986 disaster at the Chernobyl nuclear power plant, are said to have been key factors in the ultimate break-up of the USSR in 1991. From the mid to late 1990s, there was something of a thawing in relations with the West and a degree of movement towards democratisation in post-communist Russia. Unfortunately, that trend slowed[20] and then reversed under the current premier, Vladimir Putin, who learned his political nous whilst a key operative in the KGB spy agency during authoritarian times. Relations with the West worsened again and reached an all-time low after the invasion of Ukraine in 2022.

Both in the time of the USSR and after the fall of communism in Russia, both sides strove to prove their ideology was the 'best' through a number of non-violent means as well. US chess grandmaster Bobby Fischer's famous match against Boris Spassky of the USSR is one such example. Sport has been a key weapon in these 'hostilities'. Before the fall of the 'Iron Curtain' in 1989, the *Deutsche Demokratische Republik* (DDR), or East Germany, was part of the USSR, and the DDR embarked on a long-term state-sponsored doping programme. It was outrageous, but very successful in terms of medals.[21] The aim was to restore credibility for the state after international condemnation of the building of the Berlin Wall in 1961. The doping campaign started around the same time and lasted for decades. In more recent times, evidence of such systemic doping has arisen again regarding the Russian Federation. This is a country in its own right that emerged from the collapse of the Soviet bloc in 1991. There was evidence that the cover-up of the doping and corruption that surrounded it involved the Russian secret service, the FSB, the successor organisation to the KGB.[22] Russia has struggled to find its place in the world since losing its mantle in the 1990s as one of two dominant superpowers. Much has been made of President Vladimir Putin's efforts to restore the former glory of his country, as he sees it, in order to understand the motivations behind his ordering of the disastrous Ukraine invasion of 2022.[23] Since the 1990s, as Putin consolidated his grip on power, he weakened opposition voices and introduced greater autocracy.[24] This has, in many respects, been an extension of the 'Cold War' that existed from 1946 to 1991. Sport has again been used as a means to further the political needs of Russia. The regime is trying to establish itself as a global superpower again, with international influence enough to rival the reach of the United States, using any means at its disposal. This backfired once the doping scandal erupted. The result was a case before the Court of Arbitration for Sport (CAS), which meant that as far as WADA-compliant sports were concerned, Russian competitors could only compete as neutrals in international competitions. This restriction included the Olympics and was in place from 2019 for initially four years but was reduced to two on appeal.[25]

The ban had barely lapsed when political issues stemming from Russia and its close ally, Belarus, forced many athletes and players from both countries to compete internationally as neutrals again. On 24 February 2022, Russia launched what it called a 'Special Military Operation' to decapitate the regime in Kyiv and install a leader and government loyal to Moscow. Russia had previously annexed the Ukrainian region of Crimea in 2014 and had been supporting Russian-speaking pro-Kremlin militia forces in the east of the country since then. These militias were fighting an ongoing insurgency against the Kyiv government, something very much to the advantage of the Kremlin. The official reason given for the invasion of 2022 was the 'de-Nazification' of Ukraine, despite not providing any credible evidence that a fascist regime existed in the country. The real reason was Ukraine's increasing interest in joining both the European Union (EU) and the North Atlantic Treaty Organisation (NATO). Both moves would have pulled the country further away from Moscow's sphere of influence and weakened Russia's geo-political position.[26] International sanctions on the country and individuals in, and associated with, the regime followed. These have had a profound effect on the Russian economy.[27]

'Oh Those Russians!' – sport's reaction to the war in Ukraine

In a similar way to apartheid, the sporting world has been divided about the extent to which sport should reflect the international opprobrium regarding Moscow's actions, especially with respect to any impact on individual competitors. The IOC has banned the Russian and Belarussian teams from competing at the Olympics at all whilst there is war in Ukraine. However, there have been voices that say allowing these athletes to compete as neutrals would be 'doing more for peace'.[28] Understandably, Ukrainian sports personalities disagree, citing the fact that the war impacts sport, with hundreds of Ukrainian athletes killed or injured in the fighting already, together with many sporting facilities destroyed. They say the ban should mean no Russians or Belarusians competing in any guise.[29] Wimbledon was the only one of the four Grand Slam tennis tournaments to ban individual athletes from these two countries, but it repealed the sanction after trenchant criticism from the tennis tours. Consequently, at Wimbledon 2023, players such as Aryna Sabalenka and Daniil Medvedev were allowed to compete. It is evidently very difficult to find a consensus across the sports regarding how best to respond to geo-political events, even one as grave as this. To do nothing risks sport being seen as out of touch, aloof and insensitive. Conversely, to ban all athletes from an aggressor country for the duration of the war would harm the careers of competitors, and all because of the actions of an autocracy that they can do little to influence.

War is an emotive subject, especially for the citizens of the combatant nations, and athletes have made their views plain on the sports field as well. At the World Fencing Championships in Milan in July 2023, Ukraine's Olga Kharlan beat her Russian opponent, Anna Smirnova, but refused to shake her hand. Tennis players Elina Svitolina and Marta Kostyuk have taken a similar stand, but unlike in fencing, the handshake at the end of a tennis match is not compulsory. Kharlan was disqualified for this rule breach. This incident quickly turned into a war of words between the two countries. The Ukrainian side seized on Smirnova's victory by default as emblematic of how Russia conducts international relations and warfare, in an underhand way.[30] An example, if ever there was one, of how intertwined a 'shooting war' and sport as a 'war minus the shooting' can become.

There is little doubt that sport needs to have a position on the most serious international political matters. Not to do so means a regime, no matter how hellish its crimes, can expect to partake in, or even host, international competitions nonetheless. That offends against all basic notions of humanity. Sanctions may fall on individuals, even if they are privately implacably opposed to the actions of their governments, but this pales into insignificance compared to the fortunes of oppressed and invaded peoples.

Saudi Arabia

The Kingdom of Saudi Arabia's (KSA) economic fortunes improved dramatically with the discovery of vast quantities of oil within its borders in 1938. The KSA's contribution to cultural and religious life has always been profound however, with two of the three holiest sites in Islam being located there, Mecca and Medina. Prior to the abundance of oil export revenues, the Kingdom had been mostly reliant on agriculture and revenues from religious pilgrimages. Today, though, the World Bank categorises the KSA as a high-income economy. This category includes countries with a gross national income of at least $13,845 per capita and places the KSA on a par with most Western developed nations. The country has been an absolute monarchy for all of its modern existence, and the King, with his Council of Ministers rather than a directly elected legislative body, has final authority. The current monarch is 87-year-old King Salman, but given his advanced age, the de facto ruler is his son, Crown Prince Mohammed bin Salman. The prince, who is also the prime minister, is often referred to outside the country by the acronym 'MBS'. MBS has been credited with considerable forward vision, aware that one day the oil reserves will run out or that there will be a significant decline in demand. This latter is a concern because of the efforts many countries are making to reduce reliance on fossil fuels in the face of climate change. In 2016, the Saudi Government launched a policy initiative called 'Saudi Vision 2030', which has the goal of diversifying the country economically, so that it is not so dependent on oil. There is also the aim of doing so in social and cultural terms. One example of social development is a change in the law allowing women to drive cars, which came into force in June 2018. Women can now also attend soccer matches and go to the cinema. However, the KSA's strict guardianship rules mean that women still cannot do things such as open a bank account, have a passport, marry or divorce without the permission of their male guardian.[31]

The economic wealth and political influence that the KSA has, not to mention the oil deposits, have made it a key ally for much of the West. The UK sells arms to the country, for instance. The Kingdom has an antipathy towards the Iranian regime, too. Iran has long been seen as a state sponsor of terrorism by the West and now is an arms supplier to Russia in its Ukrainian campaign.[32] Consequently, diplomatic relations between key powers like the United States and the KSA are relatively good. This is a difficult balancing act to maintain, however. The Kingdom is not a democracy and has often faced criticism internationally, particularly for intervening militarily in the civil war in Yemen, for its demonstrably poor human rights record, and wholesale use of the death penalty. Reprieve, a UK-based human rights charity, alleges that the KSA has carried out 800 executions since 2015.[33] Relations with the West did sour for a time, however, as MBS was alleged to have ordered the murder of a prominent critic, Jamal Khashoggi, by KSA agents in 2018. Diplomatic ties have since recovered somewhat though.[34]

'Sportswashing'

The West's relationship with the KSA is undoubtedly complex, and the Kingdom has a clear desire to modernise and diversify its society and economy. It is unsurprising, therefore, that the MBS government would wish to divert attention from its human rights record and project a positive image of itself abroad. The wealth at the country's disposal and the sums that it is prepared to spend investing in international sport have given rise to claims that it is actively 'sportswashing'. Put another way, the KSA is seeking to cleanse its image as a human rights abuser by seeking legitimacy through funding international sport. This is an example of 'soft power' being exercised where, like with Royal visits and cultural exchanges, a country is seeking to influence other nations using social and economic means. This is preferred over coercion by sanctions or military force. The KSA has an enormous Public Investment Fund (PIF), and some of the expenditure from this has been analysed by the UK's Guardian newspaper. According to the report, the Kingdom has spent over $6.3bn on sport, particularly on soccer and golf, but also boxing and motorsport. This is a close approximation to the entire GDP of either Montenegro or Barbados. Amnesty International, an international human rights organisation, claims this is an attempt to distract from the country's human rights record.[35] Deals include Saudi soccer club *Al Hilal* making a world record bid for the captain of France's national team, Kylian Mbappé. The fees reportedly totalled nearly $325m, with high-profile figures like Cristiano Ronaldo having already been persuaded to play for Saudi teams for large sums. The PIF also bought the soccer team Newcastle United FC in 2021.[36] In terms of golf, the Saudis are now also major stakeholders. In 2021, the PIF created LIV Golf[37] with an estimated $2bn investment. The arrival of this premier, well-funded tournament was seen as an immediate threat by the Professional Golfers' Association (PGA) tour. An antitrust case was filed in the United States, although it was later settled[38] and court documents openly accused the regime of trying to 'sportswash the recent history of Saudi atrocities' with its money.[39] The matter was resolved by LIV taking over the PGA, creating the dominant force in world golf today, with the governor of the Saudi PIF as its chair.

The ethical issues raised here have not gone unnoticed in sporting circles either. England and Liverpool FC player Jordan Henderson has been a staunch supporter of LGBTQ+ causes and has been outspoken in backing the Premier League's Rainbow Laces campaign. Sports federations are 'increasingly promoting and engaging in diversity and social inclusion as an important component of their corporate social responsibility . . . agenda'.[40] This campaign is the contribution of the Premier League with respect to combatting homophobia in soccer. In July 2023, Henderson left Liverpool to join the Saudi team *Al-Ettifaq* for a reported £700,000 per week. This drew criticism from fellow players and supporters, in particular former West Ham, Aston Villa and Everton player Thomas Hitzlsperger. Homosexuality is punishable by execution in the KSA, and Hiltzsberger came out as gay in 2014. He summarised his thoughts with:

> [I'm c]urious to know . . . how the new [Jordan Henderson] brand . . . will look like. The old one is dead! I did believe for a while that his support for the [LGBTQ+] community would be genuine. Silly me.[41]

The Liverpool LGBTQ+ fan organisation ventured thoughts in a similar vein. The Saudis themselves were evidently aware of the clash of cultures here. When *Al-Ettifaq* used video clips of Henderson's career to celebrate his signing, the images had been altered. The player's LGBTQ+ rainbow armband appears in black and white in the footage.[42]

The evidence suggests the Saudis are indeed engaged in sportswashing and, to a degree, it appears to be a successful move for them. They are the dominant global force in golf and are attracting elite soccer players to their teams in increasing numbers. This is not to mention the rising levels of ownership in Premier League clubs in the UK. The efforts may well be part of MBS's 'Saudi Vision 2030' modernisation policies for his country, and there are signs of liberalisation, at least for women. It may be that the Saudi government is implementing change very slowly, wary of any backlash from hard-line clerics and political traditionalists. They must be apprehensive about the possibility of an Islamic uprising, such has been seen in the recent history of a significant number of Middle Eastern and North African countries. In the short term, though, money does appear to be able to overcome significant ethical conundrums for individuals. This was also the case for the Apartheid regime in South Africa for three decades. It may be a similar time frame before the Saudis have Westernised enough for there to be no moral dilemma for sport in this context, however. In the meantime, the regime is able to maintain policies at home that would be deemed deeply inequitable if embedded in the legal systems of Western democracies.

The Chinese Communist Party

This is largely a historical account and for this reason is subtitled as it is, rather than simply 'China'. The relationship between sport and China's dealings with the West is very different today. However, studying how the Chinese Communist Party (CCP) sought to rebuild diplomatic relations between itself and particularly the United States using sport helps to continue the theme of this chapter.

In 1949, the communist troops under their charismatic leader, Mao Zedong, finally prevailed against the Nationalist forces of Chiang Kai-shek after years of civil war. The People's Republic of China (PRC) was formed. The remnant nationalists retreated to the island of Taiwan, which proclaimed itself an independent country. This territory has had the recognition and protection of successive US administrations. The PRC, however, has a policy of viewing the island as a renegade province and openly seeks to reintegrate it into China, with military force if necessary. These events and China's involvement in the Korean War of 1950–3 have led to many years of political distance between the country and the West.[43] This has not been helped by decades of repression and human rights abuses in China. These are exemplified by the 'Cultural Revolution', the Tiananmen Square massacre, and the treatment of China's minority Uyghur population.[44] Other than regular diplomatic stand-offs about Taiwan,[45] the West has had to maintain an uneasy but stable relationship with the PRC, which, as an autocratic state, means a relationship with the CCP. This is because it became such an important trading partner for much of the world once free market reforms were introduced in China in the 1980s. The country may be taking an inward turn now, though, with reductions in investment both flowing out from China and back into it from abroad since the pandemic.[46] In the early days of the People's Republic, however, diplomatic ties with the West were all but non-existent as these were the first years of the 'Cold War'. At the time, China was in some ways more closely allied with the Soviet Union than it is today with Russia. China needed a way to legitimise and reintegrate itself into the global political sphere, and this partly came in the unlikely form of the humble game of table tennis or 'ping-pong'.

Mao, 'Ping-pong', and turning the tables on political isolation

The involvement of the sport of table tennis in the relative thawing of US-China relations is what led to the coining of the term 'ping-pong' diplomacy. Over time, the distance between the PRC and Moscow began to grow, culminating in some border clashes in 1969. Consequently, the United States felt that some form of better diplomatic relations between itself and the PRC would reduce the threat of a Third World War. In addition, anything that further increased the diplomatic rift between the PRC and the USSR was seen as beneficial to the West. During the same period, formal relations with the United States having been severed in 1949, Beijing wanted to be seen as 'a more virtuous communist state than the USSR'. Partly, 'this was driven by Mao Zedong's desire to promote himself globally as the chosen leader of world communism' and further fuel the 'cult of personality' around him.[47] The scene was set for some form of olive branch to be passed between the nations. Whether the actual event that began the process for table tennis to be the medium for a warming of relations was set up or whether it was simply fortuitous may never be known, though. The 1971 World Table Tennis Championships were held in Japan, and for the first time in many years, the PRC sent a team including Zhuang Zedong, the best male player in the world at that time. Glenn Cowan was playing for the United States and found himself on the Chinese team's bus on the way to the venue. The two men had common ground in table tennis, which transcended the political rift between their respective countries. When they got off the bus together, press photographs of the two made headlines around the globe. Mao gave his approval retrospectively to the meeting, and the difficult journey of improving US/PRC diplomatic ties had been started.[48]

As a follow-up, there was much secret diplomacy by the two states. As a result, in 1972, President Richard Nixon was the first Western premier to undertake a state visit to China. This visit allowed a host of new agreements on trade and military co-operation to be made. This distracted the US public from the mounting casualties in Vietnam for Nixon and enhanced Mao as an international political figure both at home and abroad.[49] The Nationalist regime in Taiwan was somewhat sidelined by these moves, and the PRC was admitted to the United Nations (UN) in Taiwan's place. By 1979, the PRC had been given a seat at the IOC as well, although Taiwan remained a member in this instance.[50] Today, the United States and China still 'sabre rattle' over Taiwan, and concerns about Chinese espionage in the West continue. There is no doubt, though, that

China is better integrated into the world, politically and economically, now because of the steps that began with the 'chance' meeting of the two table tennis players. China is now the dominant partner, in terms of economic might, in the BRICS[51] organisation, which hopes to rival the G7 group of leading Western economies in due course.

Sport as 'Soft Power' – concluding remarks

There is a clear theme running through the examples considered in this chapter. In each case, the regimes seeking to extend their influence through sport in one way or another have been autocracies. This does not mean that democracies do not adopt similar policies. It is also true to say, though, that the vast majority of Western states are adopting the self-regulation model of sport discussed in Chapter 2. It is therefore much less likely, if not impossible, for sport to be directly used as a tool by a state in attempting to maximise its power and influence overseas. The relationship between sport and state power is more nuanced than that.

What is also evident is that the autocracies studied here have much to deflect international attention from. The former USSR, with its satellite communist states, and later Russia, obviously believed that sporting prowess in international competitions would improve its image internationally. This is, despite the fact that this was achieved at the expense of its athletes' health and well-being. The aim was to be seen as an alternative political powerhouse to the United States and, in particular, a viable superpower in a 'multi-polar' world. Furthermore, Putin only envisaged that his 2022 'Special Military Operation' against the Kiev regime would last a few days and that there would not be time for much international reaction. In this case, for the most part, sport and its international 'normative co-ordinations' have broadly, but not wholly, aligned with the governments of the Northern hemisphere at least. Russia has, with notable exceptions, been treated as a pariah state by both sets of institutions, with the war in Ukraine dragging on. Having said that, an International Criminal Court (ICC) arrest warrant has been issued for Vladimir Putin, but it does not appear to have deterred him from prosecuting his war. Nor did it preclude President Trump welcoming Putin to the United States with great fanfare in 2025. It is very unlikely, therefore, that the exclusion of Russian athletes from international competition, except as neutrals, will do so either. Sport will want to be seen to be on the right side of history. However, the picture right now is mixed at best.

Both the Saudis and the PRC sought to emerge from periods of political isolation using sport, albeit in very different ways. Both countries have an approach to human rights that diverges from the official position of most Western democracies. In the case of communist China, the interests of the West and the CCP aligned to a limited extent in the late 1960s and 1970s, and sport provided the catalyst for a thaw in relations. In this respect, the West was complicit in allowing the PRC back into the fold without having to address its human rights issues. This was more of a success for China than it was for the rest of the world. On the other hand, the KSA has huge financial resources to utilise when it comes to working its way back into the favour of Western governments and populations. It is too soon to say whether their early successes will translate into a favoured position in the long term, however. In the meantime, sport cannot be said to have done very much against oppression so far.

War only happens when politicians and diplomats have failed. It is easy to see here how sport can be both used and misused in the diplomatic sphere. When not being hijacked by despots, sport can offer a great deal in furthering harmony between nations. The proper use of sport in this way should be encouraged and where peace is the goal, it makes no sense at all to keep politics and sport separate; to do so leaves desperate social inequities unaddressed.

Sport and climate change – playing at social justice?

This is an auspicious time to be discussing climate change. In 2023, it was reported that the warmest twenty-seven days ever recorded on the planet occurred in July. This followed the hottest day ever recorded in the UK the previous year. Also in 2023, many thousands of penguin chicks have drowned in the Antarctic as their icy environment melts and breaks up prematurely.[52] Further, there have been widespread wildfires across the Mediterranean and Canada, with Arizona reporting a significant death toll from an extreme heat event there. Beijing has experienced unprecedented heat and flooding in addition. There are still climate change deniers, and many of these voices have found new vigour, facilitated by Donald Trump's return for a second term in 2025. Even so, there is mounting evidence that what is happening in nature will be as destructive, if not more so, than climate scientists have been predicting for some time.[53] The difference is that extreme weather phenomena are no longer predictions but are in our news feeds almost every week.

Science versus politics

In 2015, 196 countries reached an agreement to attempt to keep global temperature increases to 1.5° Celsius (2.7° Fahrenheit) as a maximum by 2100. This was the Paris Climate Agreement[54] and to achieve this, countries should reach a state of 'Net Zero' by 2050.[55] This phrase means a state of play where human activity is no longer adding to the aggregate amount of carbon dioxide in the atmosphere. Despite this 'legally binding' agreement, attempts to implement Net Zero policies and other environmentally motivated moves are often watered down or reneged on altogether. For instance, the deal was originally signed by 197 countries, but the United States left the pact in 2020 after notice to withdraw was given by the Trump administration in 2017. The United States has been a major force in driving two significant international agreements on climate, the Kyoto Protocol in 1997 and the one in Paris, yet neither is in force in the States. In the case of Kyoto, the US Senate would not ratify the accord.[56] In the UK, politicians on both sides of the political spectrum have signalled their apparent lack of enthusiasm for green initiatives when they are seen as vote losers.[57]

The difficulty with such international agreements is that they are a prime example of 'soft law', previously encountered in Chapter 1. On a breach of the agreement, there is no way to apply legal judgement through a court of law with concrete sanctions. The only outcome is that countries that derogate face little more than a downturn in their international reputation. Soft law differs from 'hard law' on a continuum; they are not absolutes. At one end are legally enforceable statutes under which a court of law can impose outcomes like prison time and fines. These do not exist in the international sphere, only within individual jurisdictions. Some international conventions, such as the European Union's (EU) Lisbon Treaty and its forerunners, come close in that a court can adjudicate between member states and impose redress. The jurisdiction of the European Court of Justice (ECJ) can only be avoided if a nation leaves the bloc, as the UK did in 2020. Most international agreements are really collections of aspirational goals.[58] In research based on the Kyoto Protocol, discussed also earlier in Chapter 1, three criteria were utilised to help analyse whether agreements tend more to the hard or soft end of the spectrum. These are 'binding obligation', 'precise wording', and at least an outline method for 'delegation' to the signatory countries to implement the provisions.[59] If the legal framework is weak in any of these three areas, then the agreement is more soft than hard law. Climate agreements like Kyoto and Paris have to be ratified or accepted by the parliament of the member countries. Furthermore, they consist of a set of aspirations about carbon emissions rather than precise mandated actions that nations are obligated to perform. It is relatively easy, therefore, for politicians facing elections in the near future to acquiesce to the demands of corporations or even fickle voters and for the delegation aspect to fail. Hard law has 'enduring efficacy and normative preferability', but where careful harmonisation between nations is called for and hard law sanctions are not possible, as is the case in the international arena, soft law has merit as the only alternative[60] (see Figure 9.2).

The increase in temperatures and the extreme weather events themselves are a matter of lived experience; they cannot be denied. The debate, outside the overwhelming majority of the scientific community, is whether the changes are human-caused. Climatologists are clear that the speed of the increases in global temperatures and the ferocity of the weather events mean that they would be virtually impossible without human-caused climate change.[61] The fact remains, though, that there is no clear consensus about what the social policy should be in the face of this emergency. Politicians rarely embark on policy initiatives that they believe will be unpopular with their core voters, but more than that, there seems to be a lack of understanding of the science and its complexities. One view is that there are not enough people with a science background in politics today[62] but the result is that movement towards Net Zero seems at times glacially slow.

In light of the overall political and social picture, sport faces two main conundrums. If politics, and indeed society, are not moving as fast as environmental activists want, then sport, with its high media profile, is bound to be one of the targets for environmental activism. Footage of campaigners protesting and being ejected from venues or being arrested is likely to be widely viewed, and disruption of sporting events by environmentalists has come to the fore. Secondly, sport itself has recognised the

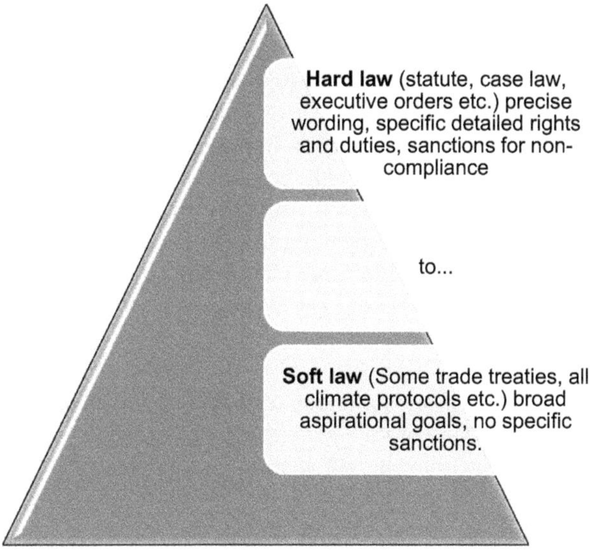

Figure 9.2 The hard law – soft law continuum.

need to address its own carbon footprint. Not all sports are major fossil fuel burners like motorsport, but most sports played at the international level require travel by significant numbers of people, in many cases by air. Reducing sport's imprint on the environment and achieving good public relations by doing so, without affecting viewing and spectator numbers, is a headache for sports governance in most major sports. This section of the chapter will focus on these two problem areas in turn.

Environmental activism and sport

Targeting sporting events to draw attention to a political or social cause has a long history. In 1913, the Suffragette movement was in full swing, campaigning for women's right to vote in the UK. During the Epsom Derby horserace of that year, Emily Wilding Davison of the militant Women's Social and Political Union (WSPU) sought to bring attention to the cause by stepping in front of *Anmer*, King Edward VII's horse. The encounter proved fatal for Davison, and she has achieved a status akin to martyrdom, the centenary of her death being celebrated in 2013. Due in large part to the activities of these suffragettes, some women got the vote in 1918, and full equality with men in this regard was achieved by 1928.[63] It is ironic, therefore, that it was two recent female UK Home Secretaries who have pressed the hardest for changes to the law restricting this kind of protest.[64] Neither would have had the careers they have enjoyed without the disruptive tactics of the suffragettes. The new laws were prompted in particular by protest methods used by environmental activist groups such as 'Extinction Rebellion' and 'Just Stop Oil'. These favour blocking roads and tunnels by protesters gluing and chaining themselves to railings or even tarmac. They also employ slow marches to all but halt traffic and bring attention to what they see as government inaction on the climate crisis. It is fair to say that not all of the public is behind these tactics, and individuals will even take it upon themselves to clear the roads of protestors.[65] However, the actions of the protesters are eerily similar to those employed by the suffragettes. They also famously chained themselves to public buildings to highlight an issue they were passionate about. These are actions which history has since unequivocally validated.[66] They were not universally lauded at the time, though.

Particularly in 2023, activists added large-scale sporting events to their target list. At Wimbledon in June of that year, 'Just Stop Oil' protesters disrupted two matches. The aim of the group is to persuade the government to bar any new projects involving the extraction of oil, gas and coal. The then Conservative administration was unmoved, granting hundreds of new oil and gas exploration licences the following month.[67] On Court 18, two protesters ran onto the grass and scattered pieces of a jigsaw puzzle; oddly, these were bought from the gift shop within the grounds, and they threw 'environmentally friendly orange confetti glitter'. The object was news coverage and disruption arising from the time it took staff to pick up the objects so that play could resume.[68] Both were achieved, although it is fair to say the public reaction, including from those spectating at the event, has been mixed.[69] Another man from the group ran onto the same court a short time later; all three were arrested. Some support for the cause came from a relatively unexpected quarter, though: show business. Activism does not have to be carried out in person to be impactful, and names from the entertainment sector have joined together to highlight environmental concerns. This was prompted by what they see as the poor environmental record of a key sponsor of Wimbledon, Barclays PLC. This bank also received considerable negative press during the 1980s because of its involvement in apartheid-era South Africa, discussed earlier in this chapter. It eventually ceased operations there, citing business efficacy, but the real reason was the opprobrium that the conglomerate received for its relationship with the regime.[70] Several actors, presenters, writers, politicians and others have signed an open letter to the All England Lawn Tennis Club (AELTC) stating their opposition to Barclays being a prominent sponsor of the tournament. Leading this campaign is the organisation 'Make My Money Matter'. This was co-founded by Richard Curtis, who wrote the screenplay for the blockbuster film 'Four Weddings and a Funeral' amongst other notable achievements. This group alleges that Barclays PLC is 'financing and profiting from climate chaos' and the AELTC is endorsing this by entering into partnership with them. The letter goes on to point out that the sponsorship agreement is therefore at odds with the AELTC's climate strategy. This quotes the aim of sustaining the 'Championships in a way that ensures . . . [a] . . . positive impact on our environment'.[71] The problem Barclays faces is that it has provided more than $190bn to the fossil fuel industry since the Paris Climate Agreement was signed. This makes it Europe's largest funder of that sector. The detail of the AELTC's climate policy will be further discussed in the next section.

In Chapter 6, the issue was raised of the difficulties that can be caused for a sponsor or endorser in sport when the sports personality or team does something that might bring the brand concerned into disrepute by association. It was also pointed out that the reverse can be true, as it was regarding the child labour allegations against companies such as Nike. This dispute is potentially an example of the latter. Barclays have, however, responded that they were amongst the first banks to officially aim to achieve Net Zero by 2050. It also maintains that the best outward-facing environmental strategy is to provide the funding and work with clients to achieve their own climate goals. There is still potential for damage to the AELTC and Wimbledon brand through this type of press coverage, however.

Just Stop Oil also targeted the Ashes Cricket series between England and Australia for direct action, and play was interrupted. The official justification for sports events like this one being the focus for protest is a little tangential. The organisers of the protest are quoted as saying, 'Cricket is an important part of our national heritage, but how can we enjoy the Ashes when much of the cricketing world is becoming unfit for humans to live in?'.[72] It seems more likely that this was part of a co-ordinated campaign to gain as much airtime as possible, given the probable viewing figures for such high-level competitions. The 2023 Rugby Union Premiership Final and the World Snooker Championship were almost certainly chosen for protests for the same reason.[73]

It is sport's very success in attracting the viewing public that is going to make it an ongoing target for environmental and other protesters. Situational crime prevention measures such as surveillance, personal searches and more stewards will help to minimise the disruption, as will intelligence gathering and sharing. As discussed in Chapter 5, co-ordination like this has helped to address the general crowd behaviour problems associated particularly with European soccer in the 1990s. They could do much the same here. Complete eradication of such protests is unlikely, however, even with statutory intervention, just as some soccer hooliganism still occurs. It may even be undesirable to completely stop them if governments continue to prevaricate on climate change. The better way forward would be to make the protests unnecessary. Tournaments, teams and SGBs alike would be well advised to look hard at who their commercial sponsors are and what those businesses' responses to the climate emergency have been. Reverse morality clauses in contracts should be worded such that severing ties with a polluter or enabler will not lead to litigation. This is because, despite the complex relationship that politicians and the public have with environmental issues, taking no notice at all of environmental concerns could well bring bad press. Ultimately, it will be morally indefensible as well. Environmental protesters do not have universal support, but then, neither did the suffragettes a little over a century ago; yet now they are seen as heroines in the fight for equality. That would not have been the attitude of many who placed a bet on *Anmer* at the 1913 Epsom Derby, but their views rightly do not feature in our history now.

Sports's carbon footprint

The question arises as to whether sport's leaders are actively and genuinely doing their part in contributing to the Net Zero target or whether they are paying lip service to it. There has been some damning criticism of the IOC, for instance:

> the IOC continues to engage in extreme greenwashing: a public display of concern for the environment and the propensity to claim credit for providing solutions while in actuality doing the bare minimum, if anything, to make material ecological improvements.[74]

This section will consider whether this is a fair point, and/or more generally applicable. Like most organisations, national governing bodies (NGBs) and international sports federations (ISFs) have adopted policies expressing the desire to reach Net Zero. It would not be possible in a work of this size to examine the environmental strategies from very many of the world's sports. Instead, a limited number of examples will be discussed to introduce some key themes.

The AELTC's climate strategy mentioned earlier in this chapter was published in 2021 and is subject to regular updates. It aims to be comprehensive, reports on progress to date and has the aim of 2030. The headline aspects of this policy are '[r]educing emissions from . . . operations to Net Zero by 2030 . . . [b]eing a resource-efficient organisation by 2030 . . . [c]ontributing to a "net gain" in biodiversity by 2030 . . . [and] . . . [u]sing . . . influence to inspire wider action'.[75] This last general aspiration was typical of the types of statements that provoked the open letter regarding Barclays sponsorship discussed earlier. Accepting the sponsorship of a major funder of fossil fuels does seem to run counter to the spirit of those words after all. There is considerable detail in the policy on what the AELTC has done and proposes to do, however. The aim of 2030, which is twenty years earlier than the Government's target, is ambitious. This will require reducing operational emissions through energy efficiency and decarbonisation in heat and transport. It also plans a reduction in the use of resources through recycling and increasing the 'abundance and diversity' of plant and animal species on the AELTC's grounds.[76] There will also have to be 'collaboration with other major events and bodies in the sports industry and beyond' as a means of inspiring wider action. This statement is further alleged to be at odds with having a major fossil fuel funder bank as a sponsor. In its favour, the sport is prima facie not a major polluter, so some of these goals may be achievable but the 'elephant in the room' is travel, however. It is briefly mentioned in the policy, but a major contributor to carbon emissions is air travel at 2.4 per cent globally.[77] Like all international sport, tennis requires competitors, officials, support personnel, their equipment and spectators to travel vast distances by air. It may be that the air travel industry is considered to be outside the remit of the NGB itself, but it is hard to see how Net Zero could be achieved by the AELTC, or any governing body at the elite level, if the airmiles are factored in.

Moving to a sport that has much more of a task ahead of it to become environmentally friendly, motorsport. This sector has nevertheless committed to sustainability. Formula One (F1) has the same ambitious target of achieving Net Zero by 2030.[78] This is particularly audacious, given a report commissioned by F1 itself recorded that the sport generated '256,000 tonnes of [carbon] emissions during the 2019 season' alone.[79] F1 has historically revolved around the use of the internal combustion engine (ICE). In other words, rather than the use of this 'dirty' technology facilitating the sport like many others, it is central to it. That being said, the races themselves are not the only contributors; premises, research, development and production facilities all have to be taken into account as they all consume energy. Nonetheless, F1 has committed to largely the same goals as tennis, with an important addition. The sport has already has developed a hybrid engine that can deliver more than 50 per cent 'thermal efficiency', resulting in less fuel burned on the track without a drop in performance. There is also a future goal to explore greater use of alternative fuels, hydrogen and biofuels for example,[80] the key word being 'goal' in that sentence. Formula E is also leading the way in electric car racing. That in itself is not a panacea, of course, as with respect to the push to increase EV usage on the roads, concerns have been raised about the production of these cars. Inter alia, the extraction of lithium for the batteries and the recycling of them, which causes such significant environmental damage itself.[81] These aspirations might be expected for a sport with the ICE as part of its core activity, but F1 has also acknowledged that the transport of persons and equipment, often by air, is something the sport itself should attempt to address. As a start, F1 reports that the number of staff required to attend tracks for broadcasting and communications purposes has been reduced by introducing 'remote production'. The technical teams required for broadcast coverage, technical data analysis, and transmission now work remotely rather than from the venue wherever possible. Admittedly, this was initially prompted by travel restrictions during the Covid-19 pandemic, but it has apparently achieved a '34% reduction in technical cargo and a 36% reduction in travelling staff'.[82] The weight of equipment needed for these teams when they do travel has also been reduced. Further, there are moves to shipping methods that lend themselves to greater use of rail and sea logistics, or at least to more fuel-efficient types of aircraft.[83]

One area of travel is perhaps the most difficult to address: the need for spectators to get to the venues concerned, and this is a challenge for most sports. The 2023 Dutch F1 Grand Prix does appear to be ahead of the game in this respect. The event took place in the small town of Zandvoort, and its location and facilities there severely restricted the ability of spectators to travel by car. The event organisers wanted to be on record as 'the most sustainable race on the F1 calendar'. To achieve this, spectators have been barred from attending the event by car. The town has 17,000 inhabitants and expected 300,000 visitors for the race, so travelling to the venue via bicycle and public transport was required. Even the police, paramedics and race officials were made to use bicycles to get around the town.[84] The organisers referenced F1's desire to reduce its climate impact, and the initiative was applauded by its CEO, Stefano Domenicali. This was especially true as there was potential to 'to set a precedent for modern era Grand Prix events'.[85] Despite these steps, there are those, including drivers like Sebastian Vettel and Lewis Hamilton, who feel that the sport could still be more environmentally sustainable. It has been said that F1 is too 'reactive' to public pressure, rather than leading the way on its own initiative.[86]

A clear theme that is emerging from the two brief case studies above is that the problem of the travel required for elite competition is a difficult one to surmount. The policy initiatives discussed so far really amount to promises and, at best, tinkering rather than re-engineering. Whether it is the competitors, team support, equipment or spectators, the impact on the environment is considerable. The received truth is that elite sport is only viable if there is a live crowd and that a variety of international locations should be used for competitions. Historically, that made sense, but the Covid-19 pandemic made some inroads into that way of thinking. In particular, there was a significant growth in interest in esports during the lockdowns. Even pre-Covid, the industry was phenomenally successful. In 2017, it was possible to compare a major gaming competition with the pre-eminent traditional sporting event, the US Super Bowl. Over eighty million watched the League of Legends World Championship, which is respectable when compared to the just over 111 million who watched the Super Bowl.[87] Esports managed $1bn in revenue in 2019 and the total prize money paid out was over $110m from 3765 competitions the previous year.[88] Whilst travel to physical venues, so-called 'esports tourism', initially flourished, the pandemic showed the potential for sport to be enjoyed without travelling anywhere. The worldwide travel restrictions meant that not only did esports competitions themselves undergo a boom, but traditional sports started investing in gaming versions of themselves, anticipating that this might insure them against any future barriers to competing in person.[89]

Perhaps esports has the easiest task of all in converting to Net Zero. It is true that games have been held in vast halls filled with monitors that players and spectators travel to watch. However, the entire enterprise can be carried out remotely, thus negating the impact that travel to traditional sports has. The question which few people are asking, however, is to what extent a shift away from being physically present at a 'traditional' venue can be workable without ruining the essence of a competition. For spectating, the answer is easier to discern. Soccer clubs can sometimes be ordered to play games behind closed doors, usually as a result of hooligan trouble[90] and any negative effect of not having live supporters to cheer them on is felt equally by both teams, thus not introducing any unfairness. The vast increase in viewing figures and the money to be made from broadcasting deals, discussed in Chapter 7, shows it is possible for many millions to enjoy sport without actually travelling to it. The thornier problem is that of the competitors and entourage travelling to compete. One answer is, as F1 are seeking to do, to work towards mitigating the carbon footprint attached to that. Another response might be to carefully audit the extent to which competitions have to be held in such a variety of countries or indeed continents. The tennis 'Grand Slam' consists of the Australian Open, the French Open, Wimbledon (UK) and the US Open, for example, necessitating players globetrotting with their backup teams every year. Purists may not like it, but it would be possible to devise a system whereby points from each tournament, based on performance in each final, would establish who could be the winner of all four competitions. That is one example, but there could also be more attention paid to whether initial qualifying rounds of events such as track and field need to be against physical competitors. The question is whether they could be based on monitored time trials or other attainments at the competitor's home stadium with local spectators. This is not entirely without precedent; the sport of dressage has versions at the lower, unaffiliated levels whereby a dressage test can be performed on video locally and sent in to be judged remotely.[91] The carbon footprint is minimal compared to forty to sixty riders, their mounts and equipment being brought in mostly by diesel power, to specific venues. These may seem draconian solutions now, but they may look more realistic if the climate emergency is eventually more generally perceived as a real and present danger in the way that Covid-19 was.

Conclusions on sport and the world

In terms of geo-politics, clearly sport can be usurped as a means to legitimise a regime with a dubious record, attempting to hide the inequity with which it treats its populations. It can also create and maintain international influence for more benign governments. The question of whether sport should be used in this way is rather moot, as it it *is* so used. The notion that sport and politics should not mix must also be confined to theory, as in practice, they do. It is further apparent that politics and society are inextricably linked, and this is never more apparent than when considering international relations. Expecting representatives of two warring nations to behave cordially on the field of competition in all circumstances is to deny the reality of the lived experiences of both. In the same vein, to ignore the egregious human rights abuses of a nation's government by agreeing to compete there is not celebrating the independence of sport; it is enabling and cosseting dictatorship. People play sport; people are subject to oppression. To give succour to autocracies by allowing them influence in the sporting world is to ignore human suffering in an unconscionable way. This is to temporarily suspend humanity. When governments weaponise sport, withholding sporting engagement because of a regime's atrocities is to fight back against unfairness and injustice, almost literally 'war minus the shooting'.

Turning to climate change, the main discussion has been on policies designed to align with the Paris Climate Agreement's aim of net zero carbon emissions by 2050. On paper in many cases, the targets are ambitious and exceed those of nation states. That said, there is little evidence of anything beyond skirting around the issue of the major polluter, which is travel, especially air travel. As the climate emergency worsens, it may be that international travel will be curtailed in some form anyway. In which case, the experience of Covid-19, and perhaps future pandemics, will be useful in reimagining how international sport can function and be truly sustainable. At present, the policies are vulnerable to the charge of being slow to implement, vague and in some cases pure wishful thinking. This is unsurprising as they are not laws in the way that the rules, processes and structures of sports organisations are. These are underpinned by the substantive law of contract and occasionally case law and statute. However, climate-friendly policies are not even at the status of soft law. That said, given that soft law is all that nation states have to bind themselves together in the face of the climate emergency, it is not surprising that the aims and aspirations of SGBs and ISFs are even more nebulous in nature. There is the will to effect change here and there, but like in wider society, there is some lack of appreciation of the urgency of the situation. Social justice is inextricably linked with climate change as different communities and socio-economic groups are impacted to varying degrees. Inevitably, the most marginalised will suffer the greatest as the planet warms, and modern well-funded commercialised sport has enormous power, as can be discerned from the various discussions throughout this book. It is incumbent on the rulers of sport to use that strength to help reduce the harm to the least enfranchised rather than simply talk in terms of aspirations and goals.

Notes

1 Sam Francis, 'Rishi Sunak delays petrol car ban in major shift on green policies', *BBC*, 21 September 2023, https://www.bbc.co.uk/news/uk-politics-66871457.
2 Jay Coakley and Doralice Lange Souza, 'Sport mega-events: Can legacies and development be equitable and sustainable?' *Motriz: Revista de Educação Física*, 19 (2013): 580–9, 581–2.
3 Ibid.
4 Comprehensive Anti-Apartheid Act 1986, United States Congress.
5 See generally, Christopher Merrett, 'Sport and apartheid', *History Compass*, 3, AF 195 (2005): 1–11.
6 Helen William, 'Gary Lineker responds after ex-Match of The Day host Des Lynam tells him to stick to football', *Independent*, 24 July 2023, https://www.independent.co.uk/news/media/gary-lineker-des-lynam-match-of-day-b2380721.html.
7 See generally, Sarath K. Ganji, 'Leveraging the World Cup: Mega sporting events, human rights in Qatar, risk, and worker welfare reform', *Journal on Migration and Human Security*, 4, no. 4 (2016): 221–59.
8 Megan Fisher, Alex Kleiderman and Simon Jones, 'Migrant boat sinks in Channel killing six people', *BBC*, 13 August 2023, https://www.bbc.co.uk/news/uk-66484699.
9 William, 'Gary Lineker responds after ex-Match of The Day host Des Lynam tells him to stick to football'.
10 Tom Ambrose, 'Tory MP who accused Marcus Rashford of "playing politics" has second job', *The Guardian*, 11 November 2021, https://www.theguardian.com/politics/2021/nov/11/tory-mp-who-accused-marcus-rashford-of-playing-politics-has-second-job.
11 Neil Walker, 'Beyond boundary disputes and basic grids: Mapping the global disorder of normative orders', *International Journal of Constitutional Law*, 6, nos. 3–4 (2008): 377.
12 Ibid.
13 Ibid., 373.
14 Mark James and Guy Osborn, 'The Olympics, transnational law and legal transplants: The International Olympic Committee, ambush marketing and ticket touting', *Legal Studies*, 36, no. 1 (March 2016): 93–110.
15 Jonathan Merritt, *Regulating Sport for the Non-Human Athlete* (Lanham: Rowman and Littlefield, 2019), 179–80.
16 Claire Cutler, 'Critical reflections on the Westphalian assumptions of international law and organization: A crisis of legitimacy', *Review of International Studies*, 27, no. 2 (April 2001): 133.
17 Walker, 'Beyond boundary disputes and basic grids: Mapping the global disorder of normative orders'.

18 Ibid.

19 Nicholas Bisley, *The End of the Cold War and the Causes of Soviet Collapse* (Basingstoke: Palgrave Macmillan), 4.

20 Richard Sakwa, 'The cold peace: Russo-Western relations as a mimetic cold war', *Cambridge Review of International Affairs*, 26, no. 1 (2013): 204.

21 Paul Dimeo, Thomas Hunt and Richard Horbury, 'The individual and the state: A social historical analysis of the East German "doping system"', *Sport in History*, 31, no. 2 (2011): 220.

22 Spencer Harris, Mathew Dowling and Barrie Houlihan, 'An analysis of governance failure and power dynamics in international sport: The Russian doping scandal', *International Journal of Sport Policy and Politics*, 13, no. 3 (2021): 360.

23 See, for example, Mark Trevelyan, 'Explainer: Why is Russia's Putin drawing "red lines" over Ukraine?' *Reuters*, 26 January 2022, https://www.reuters.com/world/europe/why-is-russias-putin-so-focused-ukraine-2021-12-15/.

24 'Russia, Navalny: Putin critic given nine-year jail sentence in trial branded "sham"', *BBC*, 22 March 2022, https://www.bbc.co.uk/news/world-europe-60832310.

25 'WADA – Statement on Court of Arbitration decision to declare Russian Anti-Doping Agency as non-compliant', December 17, 2020, accessed 9 October 2023, https://www.wada-ama.org/en/news/wada-statement-court-arbitration-decision-declare-russian-anti-doping-agency-non-compliant.

26 Trevelyan, 'Explainer: Why is Russia's Putin drawing "red lines" over Ukraine?'

27 Pjotr Sauer, 'Russia's central bank to hold extraordinary meeting after rouble falls to 16-month low', *The Guardian*, 14 August 2023, https://www.theguardian.com/business/2023/aug/14/rouble-falls-to-16-month-low-dollar-russian-exports-collapse-war-ukraine-russia-economy.

28 'Paris Olympics: Allowing Russian athletes to compete' "doing more for peace", says IOC boss Thomas Bach', *Sky News*, 12 February 2023, https://news.sky.com/story/paris-olympics-allowing-russian-athletes-to-compete-doing-more-for-peace-says-ioc-boss-thomas-bach-12809354.

29 Rob Harris, 'Ex-Chelsea forward Andriy Shevchenko says Russian and Belarusian athletes should be banned from sports events while war rages', *Sky News*, 2 July 2023, https://news.sky.com/story/ex-chelsea-forward-andriy-shevchenko-says-russian-and-belarusian-athletes-should-be-banned-from-sports-events-while-war-rages-12912942.

30 'Ukraine's Kharlan calls for rule change after disqualification for snubbing Russian opponent', *Reuters*, 27 July 2023, https://www.reuters.com/sports/ukraines-kharlan-disqualified-after-refusal-shake-hands-with-russian-opponent-2023-07-27/.

31 'Saudi Arabia's ban on women driving officially ends', *BBC*, 24 June 2018, https://www.bbc.co.uk/news/world-middle-east-44576795.

32 'Ukraine war: US says Iranian drones breach sanctions', *BBC*, 18 October 2022, https://www.bbc.co.uk/news/world-europe-63294698.

33 Rory Sullivan, 'Saudi Arabia has carried out 800 executions since 2015, says rights group', *The Independent*, 15 April 2020, https://www.independent.co.uk/news/world/middle-east/saudi-arabia-executions-death-toll-human-rights-king-salman-a9466741.html.

34 Frank Gardner, 'Khashoggi murder: US softens towards Saudi leader', *BBC*, 14 July 2021, https://www.bbc.co.uk/news/world-middle-east-57760786.

35 Ruth Michaelson, 'Revealed: Saudi Arabia's $6bn spend on "sportswashing"', *The Guardian*, 26 July 2023, https://www.theguardian.com/world/2023/jul/26/revealed-saudi-arabia-6bn-spend-on-sportswashing?CMP=oth_b-aplnews_d-5.
36 Ibid.
37 LIV is the Roman numeral form of '54', which refers to scoring in a golf match.
38 Ammar Alrefaei, 'LIV Golf and PGA Tour: Reinvigorated issue of antitrust in sport', *European Journal of Law and Political Science*, 2, no. 1 (February 2023): 47.
39 'PGA Tour launches LIV Golf lawsuit counterclaim', *BBC*, 29 September 2022, https://www.bbc.co.uk/sport/golf/63080009.
40 Matilda Hansena et al., 'An analysis of responses on Twitter to the English Premier League's support for the anti-homophobia rainbow laces campaign', *Sport in Society*, 26, no. 2 (2023): 303.
41 Andy Hunter, 'Jordan Henderson no longer an LGBTQ+ ally after Saudi move, says Hitzlsperger', *The Guardian*, 27 July 2023, https://www.theguardian.com/football/2023/jul/27/jordan-henderson-liverpool-lgbtq-saudi-arabia-thomas-hitzlsperger.
42 Ibid.
43 Thomas Carter and John Sugden, 'The USA and sporting diplomacy: Comparing and contrasting the cases of table tennis with China and baseball with Cuba in the 1970s', *International Relations*, 26, no. 1 (March 2012): 101–2.
44 Michael Clarke, 'China and the Uyghurs: The "Palestinization" of Xinjiang?' *Middle East Policy*, 22, no. 3 (Fall 2015): 128–9.
45 'Biden says US will defend Taiwan if China attacks', *BBC*, 22 October 2021, https://www.bbc.co.uk/news/world-asia-59005300.
46 Michael Schuman, 'China and the West are coming apart. Can China's economy continue to rise?' *The Atlantic*, 8 June 2023, https://www.theatlantic.com/international/archive/2023/06/china-economy-xi-jinping-us-relationship-investment-trade/674321/.
47 Carter and Sugden, 'The USA and sporting diplomacy: Comparing and contrasting the cases of table tennis with China and baseball with Cuba in the 1970s'.
48 Ibid., 102.
49 Ibid., 102–3.
50 Fan Hong and Xiong Xiaozheng, 'Communist China: Sport, politics and diplomacy', *The International Journal of the History of Sport*, 19, nos. 2–3 (2002): 336–8.
51 An acronym for a trading and cultural partnership, 'Brazil, Russia, India, China and South Africa'.
52 Jonathan Amos, 'Climate change: Thousands of penguins die in Antarctic ice breakup', *BBC*, 25 August 2023, https://www.bbc.co.uk/news/science-environment-66492767.
53 Damian Carrington, 'Dramatic climate action needed to curtail extreme weather', *Irish Times*, 28 August 2023, https://www.irishtimes.com/environment/climate-crisis/2023/08/28/dramatic-climate-action-needed-to-curtail-extreme-weather/.
54 'United Nations – The Paris agreement 2015', accessed 10 October 2023, https://unfccc.int/process-and-meetings/the-paris-agreement.
55 'What is net zero and how are the UK and other countries doing?' *BBC*, 28 June 2023, https://www.bbc.co.uk/news/science-environment-58874518.
56 Matt McGrath, 'Climate change: US formally withdraws from Paris agreement', *BBC*, 4 November 2020, https://www.bbc.co.uk/news/science-environment-54797743.

57 Michael Savage, Toby Helm and Robin McKie, 'Dropping green pledges would be "political suicide", Sunak and Starmer warned', *The Guardian*, 22 July 2023, https://amp.theguardian.com/environment/2023/jul/22/green-pledges-sunak-starmer-byelections.
58 Sylvia Karlsson-Vinkhuyzen and Antto Vihma, 'Comparing the legitimacy and effectiveness of global hard and soft law: An analytical framework', *Regulation & Governance*, 3 (2009): 400.
59 Ibid., 402.
60 Ibid.
61 See 'World Weather Attribution Report, July 7, 2021 – "Rapid attribution analysis of the extraordinary heatwave on the Pacific Coast of the US and Canada June 2021"', accessed 10 October 2023, https://www.worldweatherattribution.org/wp-content/uploads/NW-US-extreme-heat-2021-scientific-report-WWA.pdf.
62 Sebastian Payne, 'Dominic cummings, remember him? Turns out he was right, after all', *iNews*, 4 August 2023, https://inews.co.uk/opinion/dominic-cummings-remember-him-turns-out-he-was-right-after-all-2524920.
63 Jilly Boyce Kay and Kaitlynn Mendes, 'Gender, media and protest', *Media History*, 26, no. 2 (2020): 137.
64 See 'Priti Patel in fresh bid to push through strict anti-protest measures', *The Guardian*, 21 May 2022, https://www.theguardian.com/politics/2022/may/21/priti-patel-in-fresh-bid-to-push-through-strict-anti-protest-measures and Akiko Hart, 'See you in court, Suella Braverman – Your anti-protest law is an insult to democracy', *The Guardian*, 24 June 2023, https://www.theguardian.com/commentisfree/2023/jun/24/suella-braverman-protest-law-home-secretary-liberty.
65 Lucy Skoulding, 'Angry motorists drag Just Stop Oil protesters out of road as 100 activists arrested', *The Independent*, 9 October 2022, https://www.independent.co.uk/climate-change/news/just-stop-oil-protest-dragged-london-road-b2198970.html.
66 Kerry McInerney, 'Reclaiming space: Enacting citizenship through embodied protest during the British suffragette movement', *Gender, Place & Culture* (2023): 2–3, https://www.tandfonline.com/doi/full/10.1080/0966369X.2023.2249260.
67 'Rishi Sunak defends granting new North Sea oil and gas licences', *BBC*, 31 July 2023, https://www.bbc.co.uk/news/uk-scotland-66354478.
68 Sonia Oxley, 'Wimbledon 2023: Just Stop Oil protesters interrupt play twice, jigsaws taken off sale', *BBC*, 5 July 2023, https://www.bbc.co.uk/sport/tennis/66041547.
69 Ibid.
70 Patrick Bond and Khadija Sharife, 'Apartheid reparations and the contestation of corporate power in Africa', *Review of African Political Economy*, 36 (2009): 116.
71 Jemma Dempsey, 'Wimbledon: Stars call on championships to end Barclays sponsorship', *BBC*, 3 July 2023, https://www.bbc.co.uk/news/business-66084764.
72 Stephan Shemilt, 'Ashes: Just Stop Oil protesters briefly disrupt opening morning of England v Australia Test at Lord's', *BBC*, 28 June 2023, https://www.bbc.co.uk/sport/cricket/6603309.
73 'Premiership final: Protesters force stoppage of Twickenham showpiece between Saracens and Sale', *BBC*, 27 May 2023, https://www.bbc.co.uk/sport/rugby-union/65734664.

74 Jules Boykoff, 'Glitterati and grit: The perils and possibilities of sports mega-event research', *Journal of Sport and Social Issues* (2024) 75: https://doi.org/01937235241247038.

75 'Wimbledon – Sustainability', accessed 10 October 2023, https://www.wimbledon.com/en_GB/atoz/sustainability.html.

76 Ibid.

77 Stefan Gössling and Sara Dolnicar, 'A review of air travel behavior and climate change', *Wiley Interdisciplinary Reviews*, 14, no. 1 (January/February 2023): 2.

78 'Formula one – Sustainability', accessed 10 October 2023, https://corp.formula1.com/sustainability/.

79 Lawrence Barretto, 'Net zero carbon: How formula 1 is going to meet this ambitious target by 2030', accessed 10 October 2023, https://www.formula1.com/en/latest/article.net-zero-carbon-how-formula-1-is-going-to-meet-this-ambitious-target-by-2030.5QsK9NpYbz7pXp7423I3iJ.html.

80 'Formula One – "Countdown to zero – On the track"', accessed 10 October 2023, https://corp.formula1.com/countdown-to-zero/.

81 See, for instance, Anna Stamp, Daniel J. Lang and Patrick A. Wäger, 'Environmental impacts of a transition toward e-mobility: The present and future role of lithium carbonate roduction', *Journal of Cleaner Production*, 23, no. 1 (2012): 104–12.

82 'Formula One – "Countdown to zero – On the move"', accessed 10 October 2023, https://corp.formula1.com/countdown-to-zero/.

83 Ibid.

84 Anna Holligan, 'Dutch Grand Prix 2023: Zandvoort imposes car ban on travelling F1 fans', *BBC*, 26 August 2023, https://www.bbc.co.uk/news/world-europe-66620698.

85 Ibid.

86 Andrew Benson, 'Formula 1 must do more for the environment, says Sebastian Vettel', *BBC*, 3 September 2020, https://www.bbc.co.uk/sport/formula1/54014313.

87 Young Hoon Kim, John Nauright and Chokechai Suveatwatanakul, 'The rise of E-Sports and potential for Post-COVID continued growth', *Sport in Society*, 23, no. 11 (2020): 1861.

88 Ibid.

89 Ibid., 1870.

90 Ros Atkins, 'Why will England v Italy be played behind closed doors?' *BBC*, 10 June 2022, https://www.bbc.co.uk/sport/football/61754571.

91 'E-Riders online dressage', accessed 10 October 2023, https://www.e-riders.co.uk/.

Conclusion

All is fair in love and war . . . also sport management

The main aim of the book is a critical analysis of the true relationship between sport and fairness in the context of the mechanisms to regulate sport. These structures are primarily legal, so a detailed account of the law and its inadequacies, in each of the nine separate but related areas pertaining to sport is provided. The conclusions to be reached in those analyses are in each of the chapters, closest to what they relate to, and it would serve no purpose to restate those here. The supplementary question is therefore the extent to which politics, religion and society contribute to law and therefore affect equity in sport's governance and procedures.

Religion, ideology and sports law

Church attendance in traditional Christian denominations may be declining in the UK, but the influence of the religious right is growing, if anything, particularly, but not exclusively, in the United States. These voices have gained enhanced prominence during Donald Trump's term as forty-seventh president. Before that, the impact of these views on the abortion laws was already plain to see there. In any event, the resurgence of more fundamental interpretations of Islam has had an enormous effect on the law of countries where that is the dominant religion. As discussed primarily in Chapter 5, sport is global, so inevitably this can lead to a clash of cultures. This was exemplified by the trenchant criticism of Qatar being allowed to host the soccer World Cup, given its human rights record and allegations of abuse of migrant labour. The controversy over Jordan Henderson's move to Saudi Arabia is another instance. Both of these countries have much less tolerance for LGBTQ+ issues than most Western governments. In this respect alone, it is evident that considerations of religion and culture must take place in the context of the creation and implementation of the rules of sport. This is not limited to fundamentalist doctrines; it is also true when considering equality legislation in the UK. The design of sportswear must take account of these matters, and the issue of transgender rights is just beginning to be addressed by the major sports governing bodies (SGB), albeit in a desperately haphazard way. Hostility to gender reassignment has its roots in religious doctrine, although nowadays a wider set of interest groups, including women's rights advocates, weigh in. In the United States, there is even more division on the issue, mostly the diverging views are broadly in line with the policies of the two major political parties there, rather than science. Consequently, the treatment of trans competitors by their SGBs can hardly be said to be in accordance with that in respect of other marginalised groups in terms of fairness. Fortunately, traditional views about homosexuality based on fundamentalist Christian morals have not held sway everywhere, and sport, along with society and the law generally, has moved towards much greater inclusivity in this regard. Women continue to be treated unfairly in sport, however. Cricket, cycling and soccer are three examples where sexism and even misogyny continue to be a problem. These are issues that wider society is grappling with too, and sadly, the underlying attitudes are also rooted in conservative interpretations of Judaeo-Christian theology. Until relatively recently, generations of Western society were brought up on the notion that a woman is there to serve man. This is evident from the Genesis story[1] to the writings of St Paul in the New Testament.[2] The traditional view is that passages like these mean that women and men were never intended to be equal, and that there are only two genders. It is of course possible to interpret these writings quite differently or to ignore them. After all, ambivalence towards slavery and support for genocide are evident throughout the Old Testament, but right-thinking believers do not take these literally. It will take many more generations to change minds on gender equality, however, particularly in light of the rather depressing recent United Nations (UN) report on worldwide attitudes to this matter.[3] There are signs that sport is making progress, though. Women's soccer has enjoyed a boost from the Euros and World Cup tournaments, and there is definitely a great improvement in attendance and viewing figures in recent years here. There has also been a key recommendation that cricket moves to equal pay and generally gets its house in order in this context, which is to be welcomed. This was a result of the Independent Commission for Equity in Cricket (ICEC) report commissioned by the England and Wales Cricket Board (ECB).[4]

In Chapter 4, it was highlighted that there is a relationship between social policy regarding illegal recreational drugs and sports governing bodies' (SGB) campaigns against doping. Firstly, both are largely failing. Secondly, each began as a prohibitionist, legalistic approache based on notions of abstinence and moral purity, basic tenets of most religions, especially Christianity. That said, social policy has begun to move towards a public health approach to street drugs, which prioritises treatment over convictions. In some jurisdictions, this is at pace, but there is still considerable resistance to these moves in places such as the UK. Arguments against developments towards decriminalisation or even legalisation mainly revolve around preserving the 'moral fabric of society itself'.[5] It is these underlying notions of morality steeped in religious traditions that go some way to explaining why anti-doping has not moved away from total prohibition as well. There are limited voices about mitigating this position, even challenging the current very notion of 'fair play' in sport, but it is difficult for these to push back against the accepted wisdom. Most strikingly, there is even a planned experiment with 'steroid games' having virtually no limits on performance-enhancing drugs (PEDs). However, the basic approach of a total ban on given substances, based on strict liability, is perceived as the only method possible, however unworkable, unfair and unjust it is proving to be.

In terms of sports gambling, the law in the UK tries to navigate a difficult path between the rights of citizens to enjoy a pastime of their choice and the addiction problems that betting leads to. Some of the most outspoken critics of liberalisation in this area are church leaders, and the UK is somewhat anachronistic in that bishops of the Church of England are automatically members of the upper House of Parliament. Their influence on law, society and therefore law in sport remains significant. Ultimately, the dominance and influence carried by the mega-corporations of the gambling sector mean that inequity prevails here too. This is because commerce, profit and tax take are considered more important than the damage to a significant number of ordinary families.

Ideology presents problems for sport as well; it is not coterminous with politics, but sometimes the two are inextricably linked, hence its inclusion here and not later in this conclusion. As Chapter 2 explores, autocratic regimes tend to want to run sport directly, which then brings them into conflict with international sporting federations (ISFs) such as the *Fédération Internationale de Football Association* (FIFA). FIFA has exercised its power to expel those teams affected from the organisation and would do so again. Secondly, as Chapter 9 examines, money and power are very strong human desires. Sport is a global multi-billion-dollar phenomenon and has the potential to vastly increase both wealth and at least soft power. It is clear that geo-political influence has been sought through sport by regimes, particularly with those that have found themselves isolated due to their own internal excesses towards their populations or minorities therein. In Soviet times, the *Deutsche Demokratische Republik* (DDR) used systematic doping to enhance its chances of winning internationally. Thereby, it hoped to deflect attention from the Berlin Wall and all that it meant for families divided by the Iron Curtain and also dissidents. Russia has gone down the same path more recently to assist in its efforts to carve out a new place in the world, now that it is no longer considered a superpower. Saudi Arabia is using its vast wealth to buy sporting prowess and now owns significant portions of soccer and golf with an eye on further expansion. The stated aims of the regime are to diversify the Saudi economy and liberalise its culture to a degree. However, this is really an exercise in soft power to divert attention away from its poor human rights record and lack of democracy, all the same. China began a process towards some sort of *rapprochement* with the West after its 1949 revolution, with the unlikely aid of table tennis. In this case, though, it may have been that warmer relations suited both the Communist Party and Western powers, but sport was just the means by which this was accelerated. Given China's human rights record since, this relative warming of relations has done little for democracy and freedom of speech for ordinary Chinese citizens, however.

Whether sport should boycott regimes that have offended against basic norms of humanity or not is a long-debated question, and sport has rarely presented a united front in this regard. Even with something as heinous as apartheid, the response was mixed, and in many cases, it was left up to individual conscience. Similarly, Russia's aggression against Ukraine, with the help of its ally Belarus, has not led to a cohesive response from sport either. There is no doubt that enormous swathes of sport, from within Russia itself to international tennis and all the way to the Olympics, have been deeply affected by such bans as there are in place. Nevertheless, to offer a fractured response to authoritarianism in any sphere is *de facto* appeasement, and history has shown what the consequences of that are. Inevitably, those with the least say in the matter suffer most, whether they are conscripted soldiers or oppressed minorities of citizens. Fairness would mean sport always taking a position that benefits these people, not boards of directors or governments.

Capitalism is an ideology, and its proponents have been remarkably successful in presenting it as the only possible economic, political and social system or that it is '"natural" . . . that it could do no other than exist'.[6] This is perhaps the greatest of all ideological impacts on fairness in sport's management. SGBs and ISFs are structured so that there is a 'ruled' class and a cohort of 'rulers' with only a limited form of democracy in place. Inherent ideas about monetisation and commodification absolutely dominate sport, as Chapters 6 and 7 on Intellectual Property (IP) and broadcasting make plain. This creates and exacerbates inequalities, which the law can only ameliorate to a certain degree, as the law itself is limited by the confines of the capitalist paradigm. Here, hierarchies based on wealth and connection are still the norm, and Chapter 2 explains that a lack of diversity and a predominance of men at the management level in a number of national institutions is also reflected in SGBs. However, the reluctance of both Parliament and the courts to intervene in the running of sport means that individuals are often left to seek their own redress against their 'masters'. In addition, clumsy efforts to force systemic reform only come when the crisis point is reached, and public opprobrium is impossible to ignore. The free market also allows some sports clubs to become insolvent, whereas others are able to generate astronomical revenues together with injections of funds from billionaire owners. In soccer and rugby, there are financial fair play rules, but these have limited effect. The UK has also decided it will be financially better off in the global market rather than within the European Union (EU). Evidence that this was based on sound predictions is scant, but Brexit has occurred, albeit in a ragged, piecemeal way. Placing trading opportunities above being involved in possibly the greatest ever human harmonisation project has affected sport, though. Recruitment of foreign players, travel to international competitions, and the downturn in the economy generally produced by Brexit have all created problems for competitors that were not there before. This conclusion will return to that point later.

Perhaps the most egregious matter, though, is the way that sport has been hijacked by the 'rulers' in society to distract the people from their economic or social policy mistakes, corruption and the structural failings of capitalism itself. It is worth restating this here to emphasise the point:

> the collective passion towards sports distracts people from the vagaries and exploitations of everyday life: When the workday is over, I can root for my beloved Rangers/Giants/Titans and not think about my nasty boss.[7]

Taking all the foregoing points together, the conclusion must be that sports law is affected to a great degree by religion and ideology, just as society as a whole is. When both tend to reinforce traditional hierarchies and modes of thinking around the treatment of 'the other', the result is unsurprisingly that fairness is a secondary criterion.

Equality and diversity legislation, athlete welfare and sport

Sport discriminates; that is the nature of competition. There are also good reasons for separating sports into para and able-bodied sections, by gender, age category (in some cases), and so on. This only becomes controversial and potentially unfair, however, when the differentiation is based on traditional notions and not science and experience. The gender split usually means different earning potentials, so this situation can hardly be described as 'separate but equal'. The Equality Act 2010 allows separation in sports where 'physical strength, stamina or physique of average persons of one sex would put them at a disadvantage compared to average persons of the other sex'.[8] This therefore leaves open the question as to what sports are considered to have these attributes as dominant factors. All sports require at least some measure of mental acuity and dexterity, but these are least apparent in weightlifting and more obvious in curling and tennis, for instance. Consequently, there are few, if any, voices challenging the need for different gender categories in boxing, but discontent about the way tennis is segregated is mounting. Mostly, these are about the lower number of sets played and prize money for women players. These are linked to arguments about whether men and women should play against each other; they do, after all, in doubles matches. Horse racing has been in the spotlight for entrenched attitudes not allowing female jockeys a fair run in the sport[9] and much the same is said about Formula One. These long-held biases, reflective of women's experiences in much wider contexts than sport, have been discussed in the previous section. Legislation exists to tackle sexism, but there is only so much that statute can do to encourage positive attitudes to diversity. There has been some progress in attempting to address the patriarchy that exists in the hierarchy of many SGBs, but this is a work in progress. As evidence, the '#MeToo' movement has been in full swing for many years; despite this, a serious scandal about misogyny and sexual harassment in Spanish women's soccer broke from allegations arising from the 2023 World Cup final.

Racism and homophobia are scourges that afflict all of modern life to a greater or lesser degree, and the Equality Act or its predecessors have been successfully utilised from time to time in challenging these in a sporting context. UK soccer has its 'Kick It Out' anti-racism and 'Rainbow Laces' LGBTQ+ campaigns as well, to try to address the attitudes before the law needs to be engaged. The same is not so true of the position of transgender athletes, however. As society has no fully settled moral position on gender reassignment, politicians tend to pick one side or the other to suit their own careers and the perceived fortunes of their parties. The resulting discord has allowed SGBs to issue bans on most male-to-female transitioned athletes, really as a response to public opinion rather than science and experience. The Equality Act has contributed little to intervening here. Much of the resistance to allowing these competitors in anything other than an 'open' category seems to rest on the ridiculous notion that a mediocre male athlete might transition purely to be able to win in the female category and for no other reason. Unsurprisingly, no examples of this behaviour have been produced in support of this fatuous position. It is true that a competitor who undergoes gender reassignment in this way might have a physical advantage, but needing to undergo the trauma of such a process is a genetic factor, not a choice. In the same way, swimmers with genetically abnormally large feet and cyclists with enlarged hearts and lungs are born with those; they did not choose them. The advantages that flow in all of these cases should be treated the same, therefore. The law has not caught up with this because society has not done so either. The ingrained notion that there are only two genders and those are assigned at birth is rooted in conservative interpretations of scripture, particularly in the Abrahamic religions, as discussed in the previous section. In the same vein, disallowing a female athlete who was born with abnormally high testosterone levels defies common sense, given the genetic advantages that are not even questioned when they are in relation to the size of organs or appendages. The result is wholly unfair treatment of transgender athletes based on a predominantly genetic condition, gender dysphoria going largely unchallenged. The further inequity is that this state of affairs only affects men wishing to transition; little, if anything, is said about women athletes transitioning to male.

Turning to where an athlete or player must seek the protection of criminal and civil law, the area where there is particular concern is safeguarding. Some such issues, such as bullying, harassment, or even neglect of mental and physical well-being, do not necessarily engage the law unless they are severe enough. It is encouraging that, in particular, the mental health of competitors is receiving more consideration, especially since the issue was highlighted by the experiences of such as gymnast Simone Biles and tennis player Naomi Osaka. This mirrors a greater awareness of poor mental health in society generally, especially in young people and since the pandemic. Both have unfortunately received pushback from a less empathetic and traditionalist mindset, however. There is, or should be, no difference in harm caused to the bodies of competitors through overtraining or particular playing techniques and avoidable damage caused to their minds. Where either type of injury is caused intentionally or by the negligence of management in clubs, teams or SGBs, it is right that redress should be sought through the courts, of which more later.

Much research in criminology has proved that in society generally, there is a large gap between the amount of sexual offending and versus reporting and/or recording of these offences and ultimately, convictions. There are many reasons for a lack of reporting: fear of the offender, worry about the effect on career prospects in some cases and even failing to recognise the behaviour as criminal. This is especially true when the perpetrator is known to the victim. There are organisational failings too, and the criminal justice system is working to improve those in its structures and processes so that more cases proceed to the courts. Many of the factors from the world outside sport that have hitherto protected offenders also apply to sport. It is now much more likely that historical cases will come to light because of greater awareness of these issues in the general populace. In like vein, cases like UK soccer coach Barry Bennell and US Gymnastics doctor Larry Nassar will help to encourage victims in sport to approach the authorities. Until the poor statistics for convictions in rape and sexual assault cases generally improve, a corresponding improvement in sport is unlikely. One saving grace, however, is that in sport, in many instances the offending takes place when an individual is in a position of authority over the victim, be that as coach, manager, doctor and so on. This may not necessarily be as likely in wider society. What this means is that SGBs could be liable for damages flowing from any convictions. This is because they may well be vicariously liable or negligent themselves for not supervising closely enough or acting on complaints effectively. Improving recruitment and oversight procedures, as well as being the right thing to do, is therefore further encouraged by the threat of civil litigation from the victims or even action by the police. Using negligence or breach of contract claims to obtain compensation when SGBs and clubs fall short is to be welcomed, whether this is for physical, mental or emotional harm. This runs counter to some voices who decry how litigious society has become. That is a narrow view, as greater use of litigation in terms of sports harm has a dual effect. Firstly, it allows the victims to repair their lives to an extent. Secondly, it exerts financial leverage on those who exercise poor governance to put in place fairer and better procedures, which will reduce the risk of being sued. Much of the time, this process does not require litigation anyway, as alternative dispute resolution (ADR) methods result in the vast majority of civil cases being settled without trial. Access to justice issues, mostly financial, are a serious obstacle to achieving fairness through law, but litigation has the potential to improve the welfare of the sporting community collectively.

Politics, geo-politics and the regulation of sport

Politics invades every aspect of our daily lives. The small 'p' politics of our workplace, social pursuits and even family relationships are ever-present, but so too is national and local domestic formal politics. This is why voter apathy is so disappointing. The former type of politics plays a major role in how SGBs and ISFs function, as they must be democratic to attract National Lottery funding in the UK. This means that those who seek membership in the highest echelons of officialdom must gain election and set forth what they hope to achieve to garner votes. In running the organisation, deals will be done and rivalries will arise, sometimes in the pursuit of individual advantage rather than the good of the stakeholders. Corruption may even be a feature. These are all reflective of the sad state of national politics. The policies of political parties affect our healthcare, personal safety, transport networks, job security, education, cost of housing, level of taxation and so much more that impacts on our daily lives. Again, the decisions made by national and local politicians may be about preserving the status and future of the decision-makers, not necessarily to benefit the voters. A good example is Brexit. The leaders of the 'Leave' campaign were almost all very wealthy people. Remaining a member of the EU was favoured by the vast majority of ordinary economists, academics and business organisations, however. There is as yet very little evidence that leaving the bloc has improved the lives of ordinary citizens and plenty that indicates a major contribution to the opposite. The resulting downturn in the economy has made everything, including sport, more expensive and complicated. As discussed earlier in this conclusion, it has made it much harder for competitors to travel to competitions on European soil and more complicated to recruit foreign players, none of which is fair.

International politics tends to highlight a lack of agreement rather than cohesion and expose the fractures in any supposedly united front with respect to all manner of global issues. These range from Russian aggression to how to achieve Net Zero by 2050. The schisms are again reflective of the differing views on these topics within society, and sport has to respond to international issues against that backdrop. As a result, there is no universal accord on how to respond to the invasion of Ukraine. Similarly, it remains unclear whether foreign money in sport means undue influence, to take just two examples. Further, the efforts that sport has made to address the climate crisis must be undermined when the government itself rows back on national climate-related goals. Sport seems to be making an effort where environmental matters are concerned, albeit that may be more apparent than real; therefore, 'greenwashing' occurs in some instances. However, with this area and with the problem of the undesirable, sometimes despicable actions of regimes from Central Asia to the Middle East and beyond, the chief source of inequity is the utter lack of cohesion across sport; a united front is entirely lacking, except sometimes on paper.

Summary

This book was written to examine the concept of fairness in the context of sport, but in terms of its structures, processes and organisation as distinct from when competing on the field of play. It is evident there is cause for optimism, and improvements can be seen, albeit sometimes travelling at a glacial pace. Unfortunately, the overwhelming sense is one of widespread and entrenched inequity. This is a product of the expansion and commercialisation of sport, necessitating complex management structures. Necessarily underpinning these is the law, which would have little part to play in a world of sport played purely under the Corinthian ideals and not monetised at all. With law comes the injustices that subsist from the centuries-old and continuing influence of religion, politics and societal norms on how the law develops. The development of sport from amateur pastime to commercial mega-operation has deepened unfairness in the world, not addressed it.

Notes

1 Genesis c. 2 vs. 19–24 and c. 3 vs. 1–6, NIV.
2 1 Timothy ch. 2, v. 12, NIV.
3 'UN – New UN report reveals chronic bias against women over last decade', 12 June 2023, accessed 10 October 2023, https://news.un.org/en/story/2023/06/1137532.
4 Sean Ingle, 'English cricket is "racist, sexist and elitist," says landmark report', *The Guardian*, 27 June 2023, https://www.theguardian.com/sport/2023/jun/27/english-cricket-is-racist-sexist-and-elitist-says-landmark-report?CMP=oth_b-aplnews_d-5.
5 Stephen Rolles, 'An alternative to the war on drugs', *British Medical Journal*, 341 (2010): 127–8.

6 Antonio Gramsci, *Selections from the Prison Notebooks*, trans. Quintin Hoare and Geoffrey Nowell-Smith (New York: International Publishers, 1971), 157.
7 David Karen and Richard Washington, eds, *Sociological Perspectives on Sport – The Games Outside the Games* (London: Routledge, 2015), 21.
8 Section 195(3) Equality Act 2010.
9 Bridie Jabour, '"Get stuffed": How Michelle Payne and family beat odds to win Melbourne Cup', *The Guardian*, 3 November 2015, https://www.theguardian.com/sport/2015/nov/03/get-stuffed-how-michelle-payne-and-family-beat-odds-to-win-melbourne-cup.

Bibliography

Abbott, Kenneth and Duncan Snidal. 'Hard and soft law in international governance', *International Organisation,* 54, no. 3 (2000): 421–56.

Acohs Pty Ltd v Ucorp Pty Ltd [2012] FCAFC 16.

Act No. 2018-493 of 20 June 2018 (France).

Adams, Jeremy and Robert J. Kirkby. 'Excessive exercise as an addiction: A review', *Addiction Research & Theory,* 10, no. 5 (2002): 415–37.

Adler, Katya. 'Far-right parties on the rise across Europe', *BBC,* 30 June 2023, https://www.bbc.com/news/world-europe-66056375.

Adu, Aletha and Aubrey Allegretti. 'Tory MP under fire for transphobic comments about Eddie Izzard', 26 October 2022, https://www.theguardian.com/culture/2022/oct/26/tory-mp-under-fire-for-transphobic-comments-about-eddie-izzard.

'Advisory, Conciliation and Arbitration Service – ACAS', accessed 6 October 2023, www.acas.org.uk.

Agar v Hyde; *Agar v Worsley* (2000) 201 CLR 552.

'Albanese "proud" of Australian cricketers after British PM weighs in on Lord's stumping', *Sydney Morning Herald,* 3 July 2023, https://www.smh.com.au/world/europe/rishi-sunak-weighs-in-on-jonny-bairstow-dismissal-at-lord-s-20230703-p5dlhe.html.

Alcock v Chief Constable of South Yorkshire Police [1992] 1 AC 310.

Alrefaei, Ammar. 'LIV Golf and PGA Tour: Reinvigorated issue of antitrust in sport', *European Journal of Law and Political Science,* 2, no. 1 (February 2023): 47.

Ambrose, Tom. 'Tory MP who accused Marcus Rashford of "playing politics" has second job', *The Guardian,* 11 November 2021, https://www.theguardian.com/politics/2021/nov/11/tory-mp-who-accused-marcus-rashford-of-playing-politics-has-second-job.

Amos, Anne. 'Inadvertent doping and the WADA code', *Bond Law Review,* 9, no. 1 (2007): 1.

Amos, Jonathan. 'Climate change: Thousands of penguins die in Antarctic ice breakup', *BBC,* 25 August 2023, https://www.bbc.co.uk/news/science-environment-66492767.

Anderson, Jack. 'An accident of history: Why the decisions of sports governing bodies are not amenable to judicial review', *Common Law World Review,* 35, no. 3 (2006): 173–96.

Anderson, Jack. 'Doping sport and the law: Time for a repeal of prohibition?', *International Journal of Law in Context,* 9 (2013): 135–59.

Anderson, Jack. *Modern Sports Law.* Oxford: Hart, 2010.

Anderson, Jack. 'Why drug cheats are still being caught seven years after the 2012 London Olympics', *The Conversation,* 5 August 2019, http://theconversation.com/why-drug-cheats-are-still-being-caught-seven-years-after-the-2012-london-olympics-121123.

Andrews, Lori. 'Is there a right to clone? Constitutional challenges to bans on human cloning', *Harvard Journal of Law and Technology,* 11, no. 3 (1998): 643.

Anheuser-Busch v Budejovicky Budvar Narodni Podnik [1984] FSR 413.

Anwesh Pokkuluri v Union of India W.P.(Crl.) No. 000121 - / 2018.

Armour v Skeen (Procurator Fiscal, Glasgow) (1977) IRLR 310.

Arsenal Football Club PLC v Matthew Reed [2014] EWHC 781 (Ch).

'Ashes: "Wholly unacceptable" – Lord's bosses suspend cricket fans after clashes with Australia players following controversial Bairstow stumping', *Sky News*, 3 July 2023, https://news.sky.com/story/ashes-emotions-were-running-high-lords-bosses-apologise-after-fans-clash-with-australia-players-12913481.

Ashworth, Andrew and Meredith Blake. 'The presumption of innocence in English Criminal Law', *Criminal Law Review*, (1996): pp. 306–17.

Atheraces v British Horseracing Board Ltd, ([2007] EWCA Civ 38.

Atkins, Ros. 'Why will England v Italy be played behind closed doors?', *BBC*, 10 June 2022, https://www.bbc.co.uk/sport/football/61754571.

Aylwin, Michael. 'Rugby union's brutal reality: The physical and mental toll of an elite playing career', *Guardian*, 5 May 2016, https://www.theguardian.com/sport/2016/may/05/rugby-union-brutal-reality-elite-player-welfare.

Baker, Peter. 'Trump's far-right embrace – Why it's important to know more about Nick Fuentes', *New York Times*, 29 November 2022, https://www.nytimes.com/2022/11/29/briefing/nick-fuentes-trump.html.

Bank Mellat v HM Treasury (No 2) [2014] AC 700.

Barnes, Oliver, Sarah Provan and Akila Quinio. 'William Hill hit with record £19.2mn fine', *Financial Times*, 28 March 2023, https://www.ft.com/content/c80ca492-eac9-434c-9d00-b641059c2cff.

Barnett v Chelsea & Kensington Hospital [1969] 1 QB 428.

Barretto, Lawrence. 'Net zero carbon: How formula 1 is going to meet this ambitious target by 2030', accessed 10 October 2023, https://www.formula1.com/en/latest/article.net-zero-carbon-how-formula-1-is-going-to-meet-this-ambitious-target-by-2030.5QsK9NpYbz7pXp7423I3iJ.html.

Bates, Thomas. 'Gramsci and the theory of hegemony', *Journal of the History of Ideas*, 36, no. 2 (April–Junē 1975): 351–66.

BBC v Talksport Ltd [2001] FSR 53.

Beloff, Michael. 'Drugs laws and Versapaks', in *Drugs & Doping in Sports: Socio-legal Perspectives*, by John O'Leary, Abingdon: Cavendish, 2001.

Bennett v Football Association (1998) CA (unreported).

Benson, Andrew. 'Formula 1 must do more for the environment, says Sebastian Vettel', *BBC*, 3 September 2020, https://www.bbc.co.uk/sport/formula1/54014313.

Berberoglu, Berch. *An Introduction to Classical and Contemporary Social Theory: A Critical Perspective*, Lanham: Rowman and Littlefield, 2005.

'"Betting drones" frustrating UK racecourses', *BBC*, 17 January 2019, https://www.bbc.co.uk/news/uk-england-nottinghamshire-46905905.

Betting Levy Act 1961.

Betting, Gaming and Lotteries Act 1963.

'BGC – "BGC takes over Senet safer gambling remit"', accessed 9 October 2023, https://bettingandgamingcouncil.com/news/senet-group-bgc.

'BHA appeal board – Appeals of Maurice sines, James Crickmore, Peter Gold, Nick Gold and Kirsty Milczarek', 10 April 2012, accessed 9 October 2023, https://www.britishhorseracing.com/press_releases/appeal-board-decisions-regarding-the-appeals-of-maurice-sines-james-crickmore-peter-gold-nick-gold-and-kirsty-milczarek/.

'BHA rules of racing, chapter L – BHA investigations and disciplinary action, rules 13 and 53.2', accessed 4 October 2023, https://rules.britishhorseracing.com/#!/book/34/chapter/s3489-bha-investigations-and-disciplinary-action.

'Biden says US will defend Taiwan if China attacks', *BBC*, 22 October 2021, https://www.bbc.co.uk/news/world-asia-59005300.
Birch, Simon. 'How activism forced Nike to change its ethical game', *The Guardian*, 6 July 2012, https://www.theguardian.com/environment/green-living-blog/2012/jul/06/activism-nike.
Bisley, Nicholas. *The End of the Cold War and the Causes of Soviet Collapse*, Basingstoke: Palgrave Macmillan (2004).
Blackford, Russell. 'Human cloning and "posthuman" society', *Monash Bioethics Review*, 24, no. 1 (2005): 10–26.
Bluver, Howard. 'Owner liability for intentional torts committed by professional athletes against spectators', *Buffalo Law Review*, 30, no. 3 (July 1981): 565.
Blythe v Birmingham Waterworks (1856) 11Ex 781.
Board of Education v Rice [1911] AC179.
Bolam v Friern Hospital Management Committee [1957] 1 WLR 582.
Bond, Patrick and Khadija Sharife. 'Apartheid reparations and the contestation of corporate power in Africa', *Review of African Political Economy*, 36 (2009): 115–25.
Bornstein, Avram. 'Institutional racism, numbers management, and zero-tolerance policing in New York City', *North American Dialogue*, 18, no. 2 (Fall 2015): 51–62.
Boykoff, Jules. 'Glitterati and grit: The perils and possibilities of sports mega-event research', *Journal of Sport and Social Issues* (2024), https://doi.org/01937235241247038.
Bradley v Jockey Club [2004] EWHC Civ 2164 (QB).
Brannagan, Paul Michael, Nicolas Scelles et al. 'The 2021 European Super League attempt: Motivation, outcome, and the future of football', *International Journal of Sport Policy and Politics*, 14, no. 1 (2022): 169–76.
Bray, Joe. 'UEFA fine eight clubs for Financial Fair Play breaches and place Man City on watchlist', *Manchester Evening News*, 22 November 2022, https://www.manchestereveningnews.co.uk/sport/football/football-news/uefa-man-city-ffp-fines-24919263.
Bribery Act 2010.
'Britain's Got Talent: Ofcom will not investigate diversity performance', *BBC*, 17 September 2020, https://www.bbc.co.uk/news/entertainment-arts-54188788.
'British Dressage – British Dressage handbook 2023', 118, accessed 4 October 2023, https://www.britishdressage.co.uk/competitions/competition-rules/.
'British Dressage – British Dressage members handbook 2023', 51, accessed 4 October 2023, https://www.britishdressage.co.uk/news/2023-bd-members-handbook-now-live/.
'British gymnastics – Safeguarding policy and procedures', accessed 6 October 2023, https://www.british-gymnastics.org/documents/regions-and-home-countries/london/policies-and-procedures-1/12382-safeguarding-policy-september-2021/file.
'British Horseracing Authority – Neville Report 2008', Executive Summary, accessed 9 October 2023, http://www.britishhorseracing.com/wp-content/uploads/2008/05/Neville-Review-Pr-Rel-Exec-Summ-Recomm-City-of-Lon-May-08.pdf.
'British Horseracing Authority, Rules of racing and guides', accessed 5 October 2023, https://www.britishhorseracing.com/regulation/rules-guides/.
British Horseracing Board v William Hill Organisation [2005] EWCA Civ 863.
Broadcasting Act 1990.
Broadcasting Act 1996.

Brooks, Libby and Severin Carrell. 'Scotland proposes drug decriminalisation in Westminster challenge', *The Guardian*, 7 July 2023, https://www.theguardian.com/uk-news/2023/jul/07/scotland-proposes-drug-decriminalisation-in-westminster-challenge.

Brown, Gregor. 'How did Lizzie Armitstead miss three anti-doping tests? "Whereabouts" system explained', *Cycling Weekly*, 2 August 2026, https://www.cyclingweekly.com/news/racing/olympics/how-did-lizzie-armitstead-miss-three-antidoping-tests-270214.

Brown, James. 'The vicarious liability of sports governing bodies and competition organisers', *Legal Studies*, 43, no. 2 (2023): 221–39.

Bull, Andrew. 'Sports bodies face cuts over lack of women in boardrooms', *The Guardian*, 8 March 2017, 7.

Burrell, Gibson and Gareth Morgan. *Sociological Paradigms and Organisational Analysis*, Aldershot: Ashgate, 2005.

Caldwell v Maguire [2001] EWCA Civ 1054.

California Consumer Privacy Act (CCPA) 2018.

Cantelmo, Rebeca Araujo et al. 'Gene doping: Present and future', *European Journal of Sport Science*, 20, no. 8 (2020): 1093–101.

Caparo Industries PLC v Dickman [1990] 1 All ER 568.

Carrington, Damian. 'Dramatic climate action needed to curtail extreme weather', *Irish Times*, 28 August 2023, https://www.irishtimes.com/environment/climate-crisis/2023/08/28/dramatic-climate-action-needed-to-curtail-extreme-weather/.

Carter, Neil. 'Testing times', in *Medicine Sport and the Body: A Historical Perspective* (Oxford: Bloomsbury Academic, 2012), 105.

Carter, Thomas and John Sugden. 'The USA and sporting diplomacy: Comparing and contrasting the cases of "table tennis with China and baseball with Cuba in the 1970s"', *International Relations*, 26, no. 1 (March 2012): 101–21.

CAS 94/129 *USA Shooting & Quigley v UIT.*

CAS 2002/A/376 *Baxter v IOC.*

CAS 2008/A/1480 *Pistorius v/ IAAF.*

CAS 2008/A/1700 *Deutsche Reiterliche Vereinigung v FEI & Christian Ahlmann.*

CAS 2012/A/2807 *Khaled Abdullaziz Al Eid v. Fédération Equestre Internationale*/CAS 2012/A/2808 *Abdullah Waleed Sharbatly v. Fédération Equestre Internationale.*

Casciani, Dominic. 'The John Terry verdict explained', *BBC*, 13 July 2012, https://www.bbc.co.uk/news/uk-18835915.

Case 36/74 *Walrave and Koch v Union Cycliste Internationale* (1974) ECR 140536/74.

Case 415/93 *Union Royale Belge des Societes de Football Association ASBL v Jean-Marc Bosman* [1995] ECR I-4921.

Case C-51/96 *Christelle Deliège v Ligue francophone de judo et disciplines associées ASBL*, Ligue belge de judo ASBL, Union européenne de judo.

Case C-176/96 *Jyri Lehtonen and Castors Canada Dry Namm-Braine ASBL v Fédération royale belge des sociétés de basket-ball ASBL* (FRBSB).

Case C-201/11 P/C-204/11 P/C-205/11 P, *UEFA and FIFA v Commission* (2013).

Case C-203/02 *The British Horseracing Board Ltd and Others v William Hill Organization Ltd.*

Case C-273/00 [2002] ECR I-11737 *Ralf Sieckmann v Deutsches Patent- und Markenamt.*

Case C-30/14, *Ryanair Ltd v PR Aviation BV.*

Case C-403/08, *Football Association Premier League and Others v QC Leisure and Others.*

Case C-429/08, *Karen Murphy v Media Protection Services Ltd.*

Case C-438/00 *Deutscher Handballbund eV v Maros Kolpak.*

Case C-5/08 *Infopaq International A/S v Danske Dagbaldes Forening.*

Case No. C-90/16 (The English Bridge Union).

Castello, Jay. 'Why do female pro gamers earn millions less than men?', *The Guardian*, 10 October 2021, https://www.theguardian.com/games/2021/dec/02/why-do-female-pro-gamers-earn-less-than-men-esports.

'Centre for European Reform – Hot topics, Brexit', accessed 6 October 2023, https://www.cer.eu/hot-topics/brexit.

'Cheetham Hill raids: Largest haul of fake goods in UK history, say GMP', *BBC*, 4 July 2023, https://www.bbc.co.uk/news/uk-england-manchester-66093295.

'Chief constable: War on drugs has comprehensively failed', *Northern Echo*, 30 September 2013, http://www.thenorthernecho.co.uk/news/10706142.print/.

Children Act 2004.

'CJEU rules bridge card game is not a sport for the purposes of the VAT directive', accessed 5 October 2023, https://eur-lex.europa.eu/content/news/CJ_bridge.html.

Clarke, Michael. 'China and the Uyghurs: The "Palestinization" of Xinjiang?', *Middle East Policy*, 22, no. 3 (Fall 2015): 127–46.

Close, James and Joanne Lloyd. 'Gamble aware – Report: Lifting the lid on loot-boxes chance-based purchases in video games and the convergence of gaming and gambling, 2021', accessed 9 October 2023, https://www.begambleaware.org/sites/default/files/2021-03/Gaming_and_Gambling_Report_Final.pdf.

Coakley, Jay. 'Youth sports: What counts as "positive development?"', *Journal of Sport and Social Issues*, 35, no. 3 (2011): 306–24.

Coakley, Jay and Doralice Lange Souza. 'Sport mega-events: Can legacies and development be equitable and sustainable?', *Motriz: Revista de Educação Física*, 19 (2013): 580–9.

Coe, Sebastien. 'We cannot move from strict liability rule', *Telegraph*, 25 February 2004, http://www.telegraph.co.uk/sport/othersports/drugsinsport/2373729/We-cannot-move-from-strict-liability-rule.html.

Colaguori, Claudio. 'Violence, violent crime, and state violence', in *Crime, Deviance, and Social Control in the 21st Century: A Justice and Rights Perspective* (Toronto: Canadian Scholars, an Imprint of CSP Books Inc, 2023).

'Colin Kaepernick: How the NFL made its U-turn', *BBC*, 6 June 2020, https://www.bbc.co.uk/sport/american-football/52948942.

'College of policing – Investigation of fatal and serious injury road collisions', accessed 6 October 2023, https://www.college.police.uk/app/roads-policing/investigation-fatal-and-serious-injury-road-collisions.

Collins, Nick. 'Famous and infamous sports marketing stunts', *Telegraph*, 16 June 2020, https://www.telegraph.co.uk/news/picturegalleries/7831901/Famous-and-infamous-sports-marketing-stunts.html?image=2.

Collins v Willcock [1984] 1 WLR 1172.

Communications Act 2003.

Companies Act 2006.

Competition Act 1998.

'Competition and markets authority – Ladbrokes and Coral – A report on the anticipated merger between Ladbrokes plc and certain businesses of Gala Coral Group Limited', 26 July 2016, accessed 9 October 2023, https://assets.publishing.service.gov.uk/media/5797818ce5274a27b2000004/ladbrokes-coral-final-report.pdf.

Comprehensive Anti-Apartheid Act 1986 (United States).

Conditional Access (Unauthorised Decoders) Regulations 2000.

Condon v Basi [1985] 1 WLR 866.

Conn, David. 'Hillsborough: David Duckenfield found not guilty of manslaughter', 28 November 2019, https://www.theguardian.com/uk-news/2019/nov/28/hillsborough-david-duckenfield-verdict.

Connor, James and Jason Mazanov. 'Would you dope? A general population Test of the Golden Dilemma', *British Journal of Sports Medicine*, 43 (2009): 871–2.

Connor, Neil. 'China "cloning factory" to produce cattle, racehorses and pets', *Telegraph*, 24 November 2015, http://www.telegraph.co.uk/news/worldnews/asia/china/12013158/China-cloning-factory-to-produce-cattle-racehorses-and-pets.html.

Contract (Rights of Third Parties) Act 1999.

Coombs, Danielle Sarver, Cheryl Ann Lambert, David Cassilo and Zachary Humphries. 'Flag on the play: Colin Kaepernick and the protest paradigm', *Howard Journal of Communications*, 31, no. 4 (2020): 317–36.

Copyright Designs and Patents Act 1988.

Copyright and Rights in Databases Regulations 1997.

Corporate Manslaughter and Corporate Homicide Act 2007.

Coult v Szouba (1982) ICR 380.

Council Directive 2006/112/EC.

Council of Civil Service Unions v Minister for the Civil Service [1985] AC 374.

Council of Europe's European Sports Charter 1993.

Council Regulation (EC) No 40/94 of 20 December 1993.

Coway, Richard. 'FA reform: As MPs debate the issue, is real change a stretch too far?', *BBC Sport*, 8 February 2017, http://www.bbc.co.uk/sport/football/38907978.

'Crackdown on fixed-odds betting terminals where ministers are due to announce a new £2 maximum stake on gambling machines is delayed again', *Daily Mail*, 23 April 2018, https://www.dailymail.co.uk/news/article-5645375/Fixed-odd-betting-terminal-crackdown-delayed-local-elections.html.

Crawford, Netta. 'Brown University "costs of war" project – Blood and treasure: United States budgetary costs and human costs of 20 years of war in Iraq and Syria, 2003–2023', 15 March 2023, accessed 5 October 2023, https://watson.brown.edu/costsofwar/papers/2023/blood-and-treasure-united-states-budgetary-costs-and-human-costs-20-years-war-iraq-and.

'Cricketer Nasir Jamshed admits bribery conspiracy', *BBC*, 9 December 2019, https://www.bbc.co.uk/news/uk-england-50715653.

Crime and Disorder Act 1998.

Criminal Attempts Act 1981.

Criminal Justice Act 1988.

Criminal Justice and Immigration Act 2008.

'Crown Prosecution Service – Hate crime guidance', accessed 6 October 2023, https://www.cps.gov.uk/crime-info/hate-crime.

'Crown Prosecution Service – Offences against the person, incorporating the charging standard', accessed 6 October 2023, https://www.cps.gov.uk/legal-guidance/offences-against-person-incorporating-charging-standard.

'Crown Prosecution Service – Rape and sexual offences – Chapter 7: Key legislation and offences, legal guidance, sexual offences', accessed 7 October 2023, https://www.cps.gov.uk/legal-guidance/rape-and-sexual-offences-chapter-7-key-legislation-and-offences#.

Cuckson, Pippa. 'Clone of "best ever horse" Gem Twist is bought by Olympic show jumping owner', *Telegraph*, 7 July 2012, www.telegraph.co.uk/sport/olympics/equestrianism/9383567/Clone-of-best-ever-horse-Gem-Twist-is-bought-by-Olympic-show-jumping-owner.html.

Cuckson, Pippa. 'Maktoum family endurance horse trainer banned for steroids offence', *Horse Sport Website*, accessed 25 March 2025, https://horsesport.com/horse-news/maktoum-endurance-trainer-banned-steroids-offence/.

Cutler, Claire. 'Critical reflections on the Westphalian assumptions of international law and organization: A crisis of legitimacy', *Review of International Studies*, 27, no. 2 (April 2001): 133–50.

Data Protection Act 2018.

Davies, Gareth. 'Cloning in polo has arrived and set to be talk of the town in Argentine season', *Telegraph*, 21 October 2016, http://www.telegraph.co.uk/polo/2016/10/21/cloning-in-polo-has-arrived-and-set-to-be-talk-of-the-town-in-ar/.

Davies, Karen. *Understanding European Law*, Oxford: Routledge, 2013.

Davies, Rob. 'Bookmakers prepare for store closures as FOBT stake is cut', *The Guardian*, 30 March 2019, https://www.theguardian.com/uk-news/2019/mar/30/bookmakers-prepare-for-store-closures-as-fobt-stake-cut.

Davies, Rob. 'Maximum stake for fixed-odds betting terminals cut to £2', *The Guardian*, 17 May 2018, https://www.theguardian.com/uk-news/2018/may/17/maximum-stake-for-fixed-odds-betting-terminals-cut-to-2.

Davies, Rob. 'Sports minister resigns over delay to gambling curb', *The Guardian*, 1 November 2018, https://www.theguardian.com/uk-news/2018/nov/01/sports-minister-resigns-over-chancellors-delay-to-gambling-curb.

Davis v Carew-Pole [1956] 1 WLR 833.

Davis, Leon. 'From a pub game to a sporting spectacle: The professionalisation of British Darts, 1970–1997', *Sport in History*, 38, no. 4 (2018): 507–33.

Davis, Timothy. 'What is sports law', in *Lex Sportiva: What is Sports Law?* ed. Robert Siekmann and Janwillem Soek, The Hague: T.M.C. Asser Press, 2012.

Dawling, Emily. 'The sports hijab dividing opinions', *BBC*, 10 January 2018, https://www.bbc.com/culture/article/20180110-the-sports-hijab-dividing-opinions.

Dawson, Joanna. 'UK cases at the European Court of Human Rights since 1975, House of Commons briefing paper, Number CBP 8049', 19 December 2019, 3, accessed 5 October 2023, https://researchbriefings.files.parliament.uk/documents/CBP-8049/CBP-8049.pdf.

De Dycker, Stéphanie. 'Good governance in sport: Comparative law aspects', *The International Sports Law Journal*, 19 (2019): 116–28.

Deloitte. 'A balancing act – Annual Review of Football Finance 2023', 6, accessed 9 October 2023, https://www2.deloitte.com/content/dam/Deloitte/uk/Documents/sports-business-group/deloitte-uk-annual-review-of-football-finance-2023.pdf.

Dempsey, Jemma. 'Wimbledon: Stars call on championships to end Barclays sponsorship', *BBC,* 3 July 2023, https://www.bbc.co.uk/news/business-66084764.

'Department for Transport – "Reported road casualties in Great Britain: 2019 annual report"', accessed 9 October 2023, https://assets.publishing.service.gov.uk/government/uploads/system/uploads/attachment_data/file/922717/reported-road-casualties-annual-report-2019.pdf.

Department of Digital, Culture, Media and Sport. *A Sporting Future For All.* London: DCMS, 2000.

'Department of Transport Press release, November 7th, 2014, – 92% of people feel ashamed to drink and drive as 50th anniversary THINK! campaign is launched', accessed 6 October 2023, https://www.gov.uk/government/news/92-of-people-feel-ashamed-to-drink-and-drive-as-50th-anniversary-think-campaign-is-launched.

Devine, John William. 'The Enhanced Games: Letting athletes use drugs could lead to worse problems than cheating', *The Conversation,* 11 July 2023, https://theconversation.com/the-enhanced-games-letting-athletes-use-drugs-could-lead-to-worse-problems-than-cheating-209349.

Devlin, Kate. 'Rishi Sunak to consider law change to protect "biological" women', *The Independent,* 5 April 2023, https://www.independent.co.uk/news/uk/politics/kemi-badenoch-trans-women-biological-b2314144.html.

Dimeo, Paul, Thomas Hunt and Richard Horbury. 'The individual and the state: A social historical analysis of the East German "doping system"', *Sport in History*, 31, no. 2 (2011): 218–37.

Directive 2019/790.

Directive 96/9/EC.

Dobbs v. Jackson Women's Health Organization, No. 19-1392, 597 U.S. (2022).

Donnellan, Laura. 'Dispute resolution in Irish sport: The courts as reluctant interlopers', *Entertainment and Sports Law Journal,* 14, no. 3 (2016): 1.

Donoghue v Poplar Housing & Regeneration Community Association Ltd [2001] 3 WLR 183.

Donoghue v Stevenson [1932] AC 562.

Douglas v Hello! Ltd [2001] QB 967.

DPP v K [1990] 1 WLR 1067.

DPP v Newbury and Jones [1977] AC 500.

DPP v Santana-Bermudez [2003] EWHC 298.

DPP v Smith [1960] 3 W.L.R. 546.

DPP v Smith [2006] EWHC 94 (Admin).

Ducker, James. 'Jose Mourinho to Manchester United Q&A: What is delaying the deal?', *Telegraph,* 25 May 2016, https://www.telegraph.co.uk/football/2016/05/25/jose-mourinho-to-manchester-united-qa-what-is-delaying-the-deal/.

Dunkley, Elaine and Christine McSorley. 'Oxford split over Kathleen Stock's invite to Union debate', *BBC*, 28 May 2023, https://www.bbc.co.uk/news/education-65722845.

Dunlop Pneumatic Tyre Co Ltd v Selfridge and Co Ltd [1915] AC 847.

Dunning, Eric. 'Towards a sociological understanding of football hooliganism as a world phenomenon', *European Journal on Criminal Policy and Research*, 8 (2000): 141–62.

'EC/UEFA joint statement on Financial Fair Play (FFP) rules and state aid control in professional football', 21 March 2012, accessed 4 October 2023, https://ec.europa.eu/competition/sectors/sports/joint_statement_en.pdf.

Edwards v BAF and IAAF [1998] 2 CMLR 363.

Elhauge, Einer. 'Can Health Law become a Coherent Field of Law?', *Wake Forest Law Review*, 41 (2006): 365.

Employment Rights Act 1996.

Enderby Town Football Club Ltd v The Football Association Ltd [1971] Ch 591.

Engebø, Jonny et al. 'Regulatory measures' effect on gambling participation: Experiences from Norway', *Frontiers in Psychiatry*, 12 (30 June 2021): 672471, https://www.ncbi.nlm.nih.gov/pmc/articles/PMC8278013/.

Equal Pay Act 1970.

Equality Act 2010.

'Equality in sport – SCEG project for review and redraft of guidance for transgender inclusion in domestic sport 2020', accessed 6 October 2023, https://equalityinsport.org/docs/300921/Project%20Report%20on%20the%20Review%20of%20the%20Guidance%20for%20Transgender%20Inclusion%20in%20Domestic%20Sport%202021.pdf.

Erens, Robert et al. *Gambling and Problem Gambling in Britain*, London: Taylor and Francis, 2003.

'E-Riders Online Dressage', accessed 10 October 2023, https://www.e-riders.co.uk/.

'European Broadcasting Union', accessed 9 October 2023, https://www.ebu.ch/home.

European Communities Act 1972.

'European Commission Statement IP/03/1105', dated 24 July 2003.

'European Parliament, Briefing Paper – "Audiovisual rights in sports events, an EU perspective"', March 2017, 9–10, accessed 9 October 2023, https://www.europarl.europa.eu/RegData/etudes/BRIE/2017/599320/EPRS_BRI(2017)599320_EN.pdf.

European Union (Withdrawal) Act 2018.

'Ex-football coach Barry Bennell pleads guilty to nine sexual offences', *The Guardian*, 31 July 2020, https://www.theguardian.com/uk-news/2020/jul/31/former-football-barry-bennell-coach-pleads-guilty-to-nine-sexual-offences.

'FA – Know the rules: Betting, match fixing and inside information', accessed 4 October 2023, https://www.thefa.com/football-rules-governance/policies/betting-rules.

FA Premier League Ltd v QC Leisure & Ors. [2008] EWHC 1411 (Ch).

Falkingham, Katie. 'World Athletics bans transgender women from competing in female world ranking events', *BBC*, 23 March 2023, https://www.bbc.co.uk/sport/athletics/65051900.

Fallon v HRA [2006] EWHC 2030 (QB).

'Fédération Internationale de l'Automobile (FIA) 2023 – Formula 1 Technical Regulations, para. 3.7.4, "Coke Panel and Engine Cover Shape"', accessed 4 October 2023, https://www.fia.com/sites/default/files/fia_2023_formula_1_technical_regulations_-_issue_4_-_2022-12-07.pdf.

'Fédération Internationale de Ski et de Snowboard (FIS) – The International Ski Competition rules (ICR) Book III, Ski Jumping 2022/23', 46, accessed 4 October, https://assets.fis-ski.com/image/upload/v1671441414/fis-prod/assets/ICR_Ski_Jumping_2023_clean.pdf.

Fédération Nationale des Syndicats Sportifs (FNASS) and Others v. France (application no. 48151/11 and 77769/13) ECHR.

Feist Publications v Rural Telephone Service Company, Inc. 499 U.S. 340 (1991).

Fiedler, Julie and Paul D. McGreevy. 'Reconciling horse welfare, worker safety, and public expectations: Horse event incident management systems in Australia', *Animals*, 6, no. 3 (2016): 16.

'FIFA – About FIFA', accessed 4 October 2023, https://www.fifa.com/about-fifa.
'FIFA regulations – Article 17', FIFA, accessed 4 October 2023, https://digitalhub.fifa.com/m/41c272bcbc3b19df/original/c83ynehmkp62h5vgwg9g-pdf.pdf.
Finnegan v New Zealand Rugby Football Union [1985] 2 NZLR 190.
Fisher, Megan, Alex Kleiderman and Simon Jones. 'Migrant boat sinks in Channel killing six people', *BBC,* 13 August 2023, https://www.bbc.co.uk/news/uk-66484699.
Flaherty v National Greyhound Racing Club [2005] EWCA Civ 1117.
Flinders, Matthew. 'MP's expenses: The legacy of a scandal', *BBC,* 7 May 2019, https://www.bbc.co.uk/news/uk-politics-48187096.
'Football abuse hotline receives "staggering surge" in calls', *BBC,* 1 December 2016, http://www.bbc.co.uk/news/uk-38161301.
Football Dataco Ltd and Others v Sportradar GmbH and *Others Same v Stan James Plc and Others* [2012] EWHC 1185 (Ch).
Football League Limited v Littlewoods Pools [1959] 1 Ch 637 (ChD).
Football Spectators Act 1989.
For Women Scotland Ltd v The Scottish Ministers [2025] UKSC 16.
Forbes v NSW Trotting Club Ltd (1979) 143 CLR 242.
'Formula one – "Countdown to zero – On the move"', accessed 10 October 2023, https://corp.formula1.com/countdown-to-zero/.
'Formula one – "Countdown to zero – On the track"', accessed 10 October 2023, https://corp.formula1.com/countdown-to-zero/.
'Formula one – Sustainability', accessed 10 October 2023, https://corp.formula1.com/sustainability/.
Forrest, David. 'Betting and the integrity of sport', in *Sport Betting: Law and Policy*, by Paul Anderson et al., The Hague: T.M.C. ASSER Press, 2011.
Forrest, David and Robert Simmons. 'Outcome uncertainty and attendance demand in sport: The case of English soccer', *Journal of the Royal Statistical Society: Series D (The Statistician),* 51, no. 2 (2002): 229–41.
Foschi, Jessica. 'A constant battle: The evolving challenges in the international fight against doping in sport', *Duke Journal of Comparative International Law*, 16, no. 2 (2006): 457.
Foster, Ken. 'Is there a global sports law', in *Lex Sportiva: What is Sports Law?*, ed. Robert Siekmann and Janwillem Soek, The Hague: T.M.C. Asser Press, 2012.
Fox, Aine. 'Man charged with attack on Arsenal goalkeeper Aaron Ramsdale', *Independent,* 17 January 2023, https://www.independent.co.uk/sport/football/aaron-ramsdale-arsenal-tottenham-metropolitan-police-b2263927.html.
Francis, Sam. 'Rishi Sunak delays petrol car ban in major shift on green policies', *BBC*, 21 September 2023, https://www.bbc.co.uk/news/uk-politics-66871457.
Fraud Act 2006.
Froom v Butcher [1976] 1 QB 286.
Futterman, Matthew. 'FINA restricts transgender women from competing at elite level', *New York Times,* 19 June 2022, https://www.nytimes.com/2022/06/19/sports/fina-transgender-women-elite-swimming.html.
Gambling Act 2005.
'Gambling Commission – Industry Statistic: May 2020', accessed 9 October 2023, https://www.gamblingcommission.gov.uk/statistics-and-research/publication/industry-statistics-april-2020.

'Gambling Commission – Low risk, moderate risk and problem gamblers (according to the PGSI mini-screen) 2016–2020', accessed 9 October 2023, https://www.gamblingcommission.gov.uk/statistics-and-research/publication/year-to-december-2020.

'Gambling Commission – Problem gambling screens', accessed 9 October 2023, https://www.gamblingcommission.gov.uk/statistics-and-research/publication/problem-gambling-screens.

Ganji, Sarath. 'Leveraging the World Cup: Mega sporting events, human rrights in Qatar, risk, and worker welfare reform', *Journal on Migration and Human Security*, 4, no. 4 (2016): 221–59.

Gardiner, Simon et al. *Sports Law*. London: Cavendish, 2011.

Gardner, Frank. 'Khashoggi murder: US softens towards Saudi leader', *BBC*, 14 July 2021, https://www.bbc.co.uk/news/world-middle-east-57760786.

Gender Recognition Act 2004.

General Data Protection Regulations 2016.

Gibb, Francis and David Brown. 'Verdict on the judges: Too male, too white, too elitist', *The Times*, July 6 2011, 1.

Gibsen, Owen. 'Paula Radcliffe denies "cheating in any form" after allusions in parliament', *The Guardian*, 8 September 2015, http://www.theguardian.com/sport/2015/sep/08/paula-radcliffe-denies-cheating-parliamentary-committee.

'Glasgow drug consumption room could be approved in weeks', *BBC*, 12 September 2023, https://www.bbc.co.uk/news/uk-scotland-66783640.

Glendinning, Barry. 'Gambling affordability checks by control freaks would be threat to civil liberties', *The Guardian*, 8 February 2021, https://www.theguardian.com/sport/2021/feb/08/gambling-affordability-checks-control-freaks-threat-civil-liberties-reform.

Goldman, Bob and Ronald Klatz. *Death in the Locker Room: Steroids in Sport*. South Bend: Icarus Press, 1984.

Goldman, Bob and Ronald Klatz. *Death in the Locker Room 2*. Chicago: Elite Sports Medicine, 1992.

Gordon, Sarah. 'Women hold just a sixth of senior roles at top UK companies', *The Financial Times*, 15 March 2017, https://www.ft.com/content/0713fe70-18f8-11e6-bb7d-ee563a5a1ccl.

Gössling, Stefan and Sara Dolnicar. 'A review of air travel behavior and climate change', *Wiley Interdisciplinary Reviews*, 14, no. 1 (January/February 2023): e802.

Gramm-Leach Bliley Act (GLBA) 1998.

Gramsci, Antonio. *Selections from the Prison Notebooks*, trans. Quintin Hoare and Geoffrey Nowell-Smith, New York: International Publishers, 1971.

Gramsci, Antonio and David Forgacs. *The Gramsci Reader: Selected Writings, 1916–1935*, New York: Schocken Books, 1988.

'Grand National 2023: Trainer blames delays caused by protesters for horse death', *BBC*, 12 November 2022, https://www.bbc.co.uk/sport/horse-racing/65296693.

Greig v Insole [1978] 1 WLR 302.

Greve, Joan. 'Contraception, gay marriage: Clarence Thomas signals new targets for supreme court', *The Guardian*, 24 June 2022, https://www.theguardian.com/world/2022/jun/24/clarence-thomas-roe-gay-marriage-contraception-lgbtq.

Griffith-Jones, David. *Law and The Business of Sport*, Haywards Heath: Tottel, 2007.

Grinberg, Emanuella and Dani Stewart. '3 myths that shape the transgender bathroom debate', *CNN*, 7 March 2013, https://edition.cnn.com/2017/03/07/health/transgender-bathroom-law-facts-myths/index.html.
Guadamuz, Andres. 'Artificial intelligence and copyright', *WIPO Magazine*, 1 October 2017, https://www.wipo.int/wipo_magazine/en/2017/05/article_0003.html.
Hansard: Review of the Gambling Act 2005, Volume 699: debated on Thursday 22 July 2021, Column 1242, Scott Benton MP.
Hansard HL, 24 November 1997, col 811.
Hansena, Matilda et al. 'An analysis of responses on Twitter to the English Premier League's support for the anti-homophobia rainbow laces campaign', *Sport in Society*, 26, no. 2 (2023): 302–16.
Harris, Rob. 'Ex-Chelsea forward Andriy Shevchenko says Russian and Belarusian athletes should be banned from sports events while war rages', *Sky News,* 2 July 2023, https://news.sky.com/story/ex-chelsea-forward-andriy-shevchenko-says-russian-and-belarusian-athletes-should-be-banned-from-sports-events-while-war-rages-12912942.
Harris, Spencer, Mathew Dowling and Barrie Houlihan. 'An analysis of governance failure and power dynamics in international sport: The Russian doping scandal', *International Journal of Sport Policy and Politics*, 13, no. 3 (2021): 359–78.
Hart, Akiko. 'See you in court, Suella Braverman – Your Anti-protest Law is an Insult to Democracy', *The Guardian*, 24 June 2023, https://www.theguardian.com/commentisfree/2023/jun/24/suella-braverman-protest-law-home-secretary-liberty.
Haystead v Chief Constable of Derbyshire [2000] 3 All E.R. 890.
Health Insurance Portability and Accountability Act (HIPAA) 1996.
Health and Safety at Work Act 1974.
He Kaw Teh v The Queen (1985) 157 CLR 523.
Henley, Jon and Michael Goodier. 'Britons who want to rejoin EU at highest levels since 2016, survey finds', *The Guardian*, 23 June 2023, https://www.theguardian.com/politics/2023/jun/23/britons-who-want-to-rejoin-eu-at-highest-since-2016-survey-finds.
Henson, Mike. 'Enhanced Games: The mind behind the "doped games"', *BBC,* 28 March 2024, https://www.bbc.co.uk/sport/68672104.
Hill v Chief Constable of West Yorkshire [1987] UKHL 12.
'HM Government – The UK betting and gaming market: Estimating price elasticities of demand and understanding the use of promotions, 2014', accessed 9 October 2023, https://www.gov.uk/government/publications/the-uk-betting-and-gaming-market-price-elasticities-of-demand-and-use-of-promotions.
'HM Government – Working together to safeguard children', accessed 6 October 2023, https://www.gov.uk/government/publications/working-together-to-safeguard-children--2.
Holland, Stephen. *Arguing about Bioethics*. Oxford: Routledge, 2012.
Holligan, Ann. 'Dutch Grand Prix 2023: Zandvoort imposes car ban on travelling F1 fans', *BBC,* 26 August 2023, https://www.bbc.co.uk/news/world-europe-66620698.
'Home Office – Football-related arrests and banning orders, England and Wales: 2021 to 2022 season', accessed 7 October 2023, https://www.gov.uk/government/statistics/football-related-arrests-and-banning-orders-england-and-wales-2021-to-2022-season/football-related-arrests-and-banning-orders-england-and-wales-2021-to-2022-season.

'Home Office – Operation *Soteria Bluestone,* Year One Report', https://www.gov.uk/government/publications/operation-soteria-year-one-report/operation-soteria-bluestone-year-one-report-accessible-version.

'Home Office, drugs: International comparators', accessed 6 October 2023, https://www.gov.uk/government/uploads/system/uploads/attachment_data/file/368489/DrugsInternationalComparators.pdf.

Hong, Fan and Xiong Xiaozheng. 'Communist China: Sport, politics and diplomacy', *The International Journal of the History of Sport*, 19, nos. 2–3 (2002): 319–42.

Horton, Jessica and Jonathan Merritt. '"Show me your horse and I will tell you who you are": Brexit, a chance to acknowledge animal sentience in law', *Denning Law Journal*, 31 (2019): 5.

Hotel Cipriani v Cipriani (Grosvenor Street) Ltd. [2010] EWCA Civ 110.

Houben, Jessica. 'Proportionality in the WADC: Is there enough room for flexibility?', *International Sports Law Journal,* 1, no. 2 (2007): 10.

'House of Commons Committee of Privileges matter referred on 21 April 2022 (conduct of Rt Hon Boris Johnson): Final Report, Fifth Report of Session 2022–23', accessed 15 June 2023, https://committees.parliament.uk/publications/40412/documents/197199/default/.

Howman, David. 'Supporting the integrity of sport and combatting corruption', *Marquette Sports Law Review,* 23 (2012): 245.

Human Rights Act 1998.

Hunter, Andy. 'Jordan Henderson no longer an LGBTQ+ ally after Saudi move, says Hitzlsperger', *The Guardian,* 27 July 2023, https://www.theguardian.com/football/2023/jul/27/jordan-henderson-liverpool-lgbtq-saudi-arabia-thomas-hitzlsperger.

Hunting Act 2004.

Hussaney v Chester City Football Club and Ratcliffe EAT 203/98.

'"I hope my son is proud" – Transgender sprinter Valentina Petrillo misses out on Paralympics final', *New York Times*, 16 September 2023, https://www.nytimes.com/athletic/5740197/2024/09/02/transgender-valentina-petrillo-paralympics/.

Imperial Chemical Industries Ltd v Shatwell [1965] AC 656.

Ingle, Sean. 'English cricket is "racist, sexist and elitist", says landmark report', *The Guardian*, 27 June 2023, https://www.theguardian.com/sport/2023/jun/27/english-cricket-is-racist-sexist-and-elitist-says-landmark-report?CMP=oth_b-aplnews_d-5.

Ingle, Sean. 'Lizzie Armitstead becomes latest rider to accuse British Cycling of sexism', *The Guardian,* 31 March 2017, www.theguardian.com/sport/2017/mar/31/lizzie-armitstead-becomes-latest-rider-to-accuse-british-cycling-of-sexism.

Ingle, Sean. 'Semenya loses landmark legal case against IAAF over testosterone levels', *The Guardian,* 1 May 2019, https://www.theguardian.com/sport/2019/may/01/caster-semenya-loses-landmark-legal-case-iaaf-athletics.

Ingle, Sean. 'Simone Biles pulls out of Olympics all-around gymnastics final to focus on mental health', *The Guardian,* 28 July 2021, https://www.theguardian.com/sport/2021/jul/28/simone-biles-withdraws-from-tokyo-olympics-all-around-gymnastics-final.

'Intellectual Property Office – Trademark No. UK00001387589', accessed 7 October 2023, https://trademarks.ipo.gov.uk/ipo-tmowner/page/search?id=1748596&domain=1.

'Intellectual Property Office – Trademark No. UK00002302590', accessed 7 October 2023, https://trademarks.ipo.gov.uk/ipo-tmcase/page/Results/1/UK00002302590.

'IOC Annual Report 2021 – Faster, Higher Stronger – Together', 184, accessed 6 October 2023, https://stillmed.olympics.com/media/Documents/International-Olympic-Committee/Annual-report/IOC-Annual-Report-2021.pdf?_ga=2.4683184.2092531801.1684250454-1859082748.1684250454.

'Ireland's Olympic boss fed up with doping', *Reuters,* 23 August 2008, https://www.reuters.com/article/us-olympics-equestrian-ireland-idUSPEK30997520080823.

Irvine and another v Talksport Ltd [2002] EWHC 367 (Ch).

Israel, M. and Iain Hay. *Research Ethics for Social Scientists*, London: Sage, 2006.

Ivey v Genting Casinos (UK) Ltd t/a Crockfords [2017] UKSC 67.

Jabour, Bridie. '"Get stuffed": How Michelle Payne and family beat odds to win Melbourne Cup,"', *The Guardian,* 3 November 2015, https://www.theguardian.com/sport/2015/nov/03/get-stuffed-how-michelle-payne-and-family-beat-odds-to-win-melbourne-cup.

James, Mark. *Sports Law*. London: Palgrave, 2017.

James, Mark and Guy Osborn. 'The Olympics, transnational law and legal transplants: The International Olympic Committee, ambush marketing and ticket touting', *Legal Studies*, 36, no. 1 (March 2016): 93–110.

James, Meg. 'Murdoch has survived scandal after scandal. Will Dominion-Fox News lawsuit be different?', *LA Times*, March 4, 2023, https://www.latimes.com/entertainment-arts/business/story/2023-03-04/rupert-murdoch-fox-new-accused-spreading-election-lies.

James v Eastleigh Borough Council [1990] IRLR 288.

'Jim Best may seek High Court ruling over rehearing dispute with BHA', *The Guardian*, 28 August 2016, https://www.theguardian.com/sport/2016/aug/28/jim-best-high-court-ruling-rehearing-bha.

JJC v Eisenhower [1984] 3 All ER 23.

'Joe Tidy, "US teenager wins $3m as Fortnite world champion"', *BBC,* 28 July 2019, https://www.bbc.co.uk/news/technology-49146644.

Jones, Chris. 'Premiership rugby: Impossible to draw conclusions from injury crisis', *BBC,* 4 October 2017, http://www.bbc.co.uk/sport/rugby-union/41498498.

Jones v Vernons' Pools Ltd [1938] 2 All ER 626.

Jordan, Declan. 'The Economics of Sport – "The external costs of gambling and why Ireland's unhealthy relationship with the horse industries need to end"', 3 March 2016, accessed 9 October 2023, https://www.sportseconomics.org/sports-economics/the-external-costs-of-gambling-and-why-irelands-unhealthy-relationship-with-the-horse-industries-need-to-end.

Judicial Review and Courts Act 2022.

Karen, David and Richard Washington, eds, *Sociological Perspectives on Sport – The Games Outside the Games*, London: Routledge, 2015.

Karlsson-Vinkhuyzen, Sylvia and Antto Vihma. 'Comparing the legitimacy and effectiveness of global hard and soft law: An analytical framework', *Regulation & Governance*, 3 (2009): 400–20.

Kay, Jilly Boyce and Kaitlynn Mendes. 'Gender, media and protest', *Media History*, 26, no. 2 (2020): 137–52.

Keay, Andrew. 'Comply or explain: In need of greater regulatory oversight?', *Legal Studies,* 34, no. 2 (June 2014): 279–304.

Kelly, Jon. 'How ambush marketing ambushed sport', *BBC,* 17 June 2010, http://news.bbc.co.uk/1/hi/8743881.stm.

Kelso, Paul. 'Bull's-eye! Darts achieves sporting recognition', *The Guardian*, 3 March 2005, https://www.theguardian.com/uk/2005/mar/25/sport.paulkelso.
Keogh, Frank. 'Jockeys to meet horse racing bosses over whip dispute', *BBC*, 16 October 2011, http://www.bbc.co.uk/sport/0/horse-racing/15327053.
Kettle, Martin. 'Suella Braverman is spoiling for a fight on human rights – One that undermines this whole government', *The Guardian,* 8 December 2022, https://www.theguardian.com/commentisfree/2022/dec/08/suella-braverman-human-rights-undermines-rishi-sunak.
Kilbey, Ian. 'The Ironies of *Arsenal v Reed*', *EIPR*, 26 (2004): 479–82.
Kim, Young Hoon, John Nauright and Chokechai Suveatwatanakul. 'The rise of E-Sports and potential for Post-COVID continued growth', *Sport in Society*, 23, no. 11 (2020): 1861–71.
Kitzmiller v Dover Area School District 400 F Supp. 2D 707 (M.D. Pa. 2005).
Kyoung Kima, Joon, Holly Overton, Nandini Bhallac and Jo-Yun Lid. 'Nike, Colin Kaepernick, and the politicization of sports: Examining perceived organizational motives and public responses', *Public Relations Review*, 46, no. 2 (2020): 101856.
Landgericht München, judgment dated 26 February 2014, file no. 37 O 28331/12.
Lando, Ole. 'The lex mercatoria in international commercial arbitration', *International and Comparative Law Quarterly,* 34, no. 4 (October 1985): 747–68.
Law Reform (Contributory Negligence) Act 1945.
Law Reform (Year and a Day Rule) Act 1996.
Law v National Greyhound Racing Club Ltd [1983] 1 WLR 1302.
Lennox v British Show Jumping Association (Scottish Branch) 1996 SLT 353.
Levy, Roy. 'Swiss Federal Tribunal overrules CAS award in a landmark decision: FIFA vs Matuzalem', *International Sports Law Journal,* 12, nos. 3–4 (2012): 35–9.
Liew, Jonathan. 'Saudi golf takeover is blueprint for what they want to do everywhere else', *The Guardian,* 13 June 2023, https://www.theguardian.com/sport/blog/2023/jun/13/saudi-arabia-golf-pga-tour-public-investment-fund.
Lin, Chien-Yu, Ping-Chao Lee and Hui-Fang Nai. 'Theorizing the role of sport in state-politics', *International Journal of Sport and Exercise Science*, 1, no. 1 (2008): 23–32.
London Olympic Games and Paralympic Games Act 2006.
'Lord Hailsham's Dimbleby Lecture', *BBC*, 14 October 1976, audio, 21:25, https://www.bbc.co.uk/programmes/p00fr9gh.
'Luis Rubiales resigns as president of Spanish FA over Jenni Hermoso kiss', *BBC,* 9 September 2023, https://www.bbc.co.uk/sport/football/66637879.
Magowan, Alistair. 'Peter Shilton calls for change to gambling sponsorship laws in football', *BBC*, 14 September 2021, https://www.bbc.co.uk/sport/football/58566431.
Maguire v Western Morning News [1903] 2 KB 100 (CA).
'MCC Laws of Cricket – The Ball Law, para. 4.1', accessed 4 October 2023, https://www.lords.org/mcc/the-laws-of-cricket/the-ball.
McClean, Roan. 'I was so afraid of coming out as transgender that I struggled with OCD and psychosis as a teenager', *Independent,* 13 May 2021, https://www.independent.co.uk/voices/transgender-mental-health-lgbt-b1846149.html.
McCracken v Melbourne Storm Rugby League Football Club [2005] NSWSC 107.
McCutcheon, Paul. 'Sports discipline, natural justice and strict iability', *Anglo-American Law Review,* 28, no. 1 (1999): 37.

McDonald, Henry. 'It's time to end the war on drugs says top UK police chief', *The Guardian,* 28 September 2013, http://www.theguardian.com/society/2013/sep/28/time-end-war-drugs-uk-police-chief.

McGrath, Matt. 'Climate change: US formally withdraws from Paris agreement', *BBC*, 4 November 2020, https://www.bbc.co.uk/news/science-environment-54797743.

McInerney, Kerry. 'Reclaiming space: Enacting citizenship through embodied protest during the British suffragette movement', *Gender, Place & Culture* (2023): 1–22, https://www.tandfonline.com/doi/full/10.1080/0966369X.2023.2249260.

McInnes v Onslow-Fane [1978] 1 WLR 1520.

McLaughlin, Chris. 'Steve Thompson in group of ex-rugby union internationals to sue for brain damage', *BBC,* 8 December 2020, https://www.bbc.co.uk/sport/rugby-union/55201237.

Meca Medina and Majcen v Commission (2006) C-519/04 P.

Merrett, Christopher. 'Sport and apartheid', *History Compass* 3, AF 195 (2005): 1–11.

Merritt, Jonathan. '"Attack of the clones": Problematising equine sports integrity regulation on the ascendancy of the genetically copied athlete', *Contemporary Issues in Law*, 14, no. 3 (2018).

Merritt, Jonathan. '"Don't look a gift horse in the mouth" – Regulating for Integrity, what equestrianism can learn from Thoroughbred racing', *International Sports Law Journal*, 16, no. 3 (2017): pp. 191–216.

Merritt, Jonathan. *Regulating Sport for the Non-Human Athlete*, Lanham: Rowman and Littlefield, 2019.

Merritt, Jonathan and Genevieve Gordon-Thomson. 'European Super League: What can its opponents legally o?', *The Conversation*, 20 April 2021, https://theconversation.com/european-super-league-what-can-its-opponents-legally-do-159393.

Miah, Andrew. *Genetically Modified Athletes: Biomedical Ethics, Gene Doping and Sport*, Oxford: Routledge, 2004.

Michaelson, Ruth. 'Revealed: Saudi Arabia's $6bn spend on "sportswashing"', *The Guardian*, 26 July 2023, https://www.theguardian.com/world/2023/jul/26/revealed-saudi-arabia-6bn-spend-on-sportswashing?CMP=oth_b-aplnews_d-5.

Milieuhandhavingsdecreet (Flemish Environmental Enforcement Decree – 2008).

Miller, Helen E., Samantha L. Thomas, Priscilla Robinson and Mike Daube. 'How the causes, consequences and solutions for problem gambling are reported in Australian newspapers: A qualitative content analysis', *Australian and New Zealand Journal of Public Health*, 38, no. 6 (2014): 529–35.

Milmo, Dan and Alex Hern. 'Wimbledon to introduce AI-powered commentary to coverage this year', *The Guardian,* 21 June 2023, https://www.theguardian.com/sport/2023/jun/21/wimbledon-introduce-ai-powered-commentary-to-coverage-this-year.

Misuse of Drugs Act 1971.

Mitchell, Kevin. 'Maria Sharapova receives two-year ban for failing drug test', *The Guardian*, 8 June 2016, https://www.theguardian.com/sport/2016/jun/08/maria-sharapova-banned-two-years-failing-drugs-test-meldonium.

'Mo Farah and his wife in "Fly Mo" flag kerfuffle', *Telegraph*, 13 August 2012, https://www.telegraph.co.uk/sport/olympics/news/9471720/Mo-Farah-and-his-wife-in-Fly-Mo-flag-kerfuffle.html.

'Mo Farah "wants answers" over Alberto Salazar doping claims', *BBC*, 6 June 2015, http://www.bbc.co.uk/sport/0/athletics/33034350.

Modahl v British Athletic Federation Ltd (1997) CA (Unreported).
Modahl v British Athletics Federation (No 2) [2002] 1 WLR 1192.
'Modern Pentathlon: Vote goes in favour of replacing show jumping with obstacle racing', *BBC,* 12 November 2022, https://www.bbc.co.uk/sport/modern-pentathlon/63611122.
Mohamud v Wm Morrison Supermarkets PLC, [2016] UKSC 11.
Moriarty v Brookes (1834) 172 ER 1419.
Morris v Murray [1991] 2 QB 6.
Muggleton, Naomi and Neil Stuart. 'Our study of gambling and its harms shows it's time to intervene', *New Scientist,* 4 February 2021, https://www.newscientist.com/article/2266799-our-study-of-gambling-and-its-harms-shows-its-time-to-intervene/.
Murphy v Media Protection Services Ltd [2012] EWHC 466 (Admin).
Murray, Rebecca. '"No room for these drugs in sport": Showjumper who lost Olympic place banned for two years', *Horse and Hound,* 3 March 2022, https://www.horseandhound.co.uk/news/australian-showjumper-jamie-kermond-banned-for-two-years-779109.
Murray, Rebecca. 'Sir Mark Todd: Update on disciplinary hearing', *Horse and Hound,* 24 March 2022, https://www.horseandhound.co.uk/news/sir-mark-todd-update-on-disciplinary-hearing-781565.
Mutu and Pechstein v Switzerland (Applications nos. 40575/10 and 67474/10).
Nagle v Fielden [1966] 2 QB 633.
Naidoo, Andre. *Complete Contract Law: Text, Cases, and Materials*. Oxford: Oxford University Press, 2021.
National Lottery Act 1993.
'Nelson Piquet fined £780k for racist and homophobic comments about Lewis Hamilton', *Reuters,* 25 March 2023, https://www.theguardian.com/sport/2023/mar/25/nelson-piquet-fined-lewis-hamilton-comments-f1.
Nethermere (St. Neots) Ltd v Gardiner and Another [1984] ICR 612.
Neville, Elizabeth. 'The British Horseracing Authority and integrity in horseracing, an independent review 2008', accessed 4 October 2023, https://www.britishhorseracing.com/wp-content/uploads/2008/05/Neville-Review-Pr-Rel-Exec-Summ-Recomm-City-of-Lon-May-08.pdf.
Newburn, Tim. *Criminology*. London: Routledge, 2007.
'NHS England – About NHS England safeguarding', accessed 6 October 2023, https://www.england.nhs.uk/safeguarding/about/.
'Nicola Sturgeon: No apology over transgender prisoner row', *BBC,* 30 January 2023, https://www.bbc.co.uk/news/uk-scotland-scotland-politics-64431383.
Norris, Pippa and Jonni Lovenduski. *Political Recruitment: Gender, Race and Class in the British Parliament*, Cambridge: Cambridge University Press, 1995.
'Novak Djokovic questions equal prize money in tennis', *BBC,* 21 March 2016, https://www.bbc.co.uk/news/world-us-canada-35859791.
N.S.K. v. the United Kingdom (application no. 28774/22, formerly *K.N. v. the United Kingdom*).
Nutt, David et al. 'Drug harms in the UK: A multicriteria decision analysis', *The Lancet,* 376, no. 9752 (2010): 1558–65.
O'Leary, John. *Drugs & Doping in Sports: Socio-legal Perspectives*, London: Cavendish, 2001.
O'Reilly v Mackman [1983] 2 AC 237.

Occupiers Liability Act 1957.
Occupiers Liability Act 1984.
'Ofcom – The broadcasting code, section one, protecting the under eighteens', accessed 9 October 2023, https://www.ofcom.org.uk/tv-radio-and-on-demand/broadcast-codes/broadcast-code/section-one-protecting-under-eighteens.
'Ofcom – Press Release: Ofcom revokes RT's broadcast licence', 18 March 2022, https://www.ofcom.org.uk/news-centre/2022/ofcom-revokes-rt-broadcast-licence.
'Ofcom – What is Ofcom', accessed 9 October 2023, https://www.ofcom.org.uk/about-ofcom/what-is-ofcom.
Offences Against the Person Act 1861,
'Office for National Statistics – "Suicides in the UK: 2018 registrations"', accessed 9 October 2023, https://www.ons.gov.uk/peoplepopulationandcommunity/birthsdeathsandmarriages/deaths/bulletins/suicidesintheunitedkingdom/2018registrations.
'Office for Standards in Education (OFSTED) – Safeguarding Policy', accessed 6 October 2023, https://www.gov.uk/government/publications/ofsted-safeguarding-policy/ofsted-safeguarding-policy.
'Ofwat – Southern water to pay £126m following Ofwat investigation', accessed 9 October 2023, https://www.ofwat.gov.uk/pn-12-19-southern-water-to-pay-126m-following-ofwat-investigation/.
'Oldest 2012 Olympic athlete – Aged 71', *BBC*, 1 August 2012, http://www.bbc.co.uk/news/world-asia-19073349.
Oliver, Dawn. *Common Values and the Public – Private Divide*, Oxford: Butterworths, 1999.
'Olympic gold medallist Brianna Rollins handed year ban for missing drug tests', *The Guardian*, 20 April 2017, https://www.theguardian.com/sport/2017/apr/20/brianna-rollins-olympic-100m-champion-one-year-ban.
Orwell, George. *Homage to Catalonia*, London: Penguin Press, 1938.
Orwell, George. *Nineteen Eighty-Four*, Glasgow: Collins, 1949.
Orwell, George. 'The sporting spirit', *Tribune*, 14 December 1945.
Osnos, Evan. 'Playing fake ball: Why Chinese soccer matters', *The New Yorker*, 20 June 2012, https://www.newyorker.com/news/evan-osnos/playing-fake-ball-why-chinese-soccer-matters.
Overseas Tankship (UK) Ltd v *The Miller Steamship Co (The Wagon Mound)* (No. 2) [1967] 1 AC 617.
Oxley, Sonia. 'Wimbledon 2023: Just Stop Oil protesters interrupt play twice, jigsaws taken off sale', *BBC*, 5 July 2023, https://www.bbc.co.uk/sport/tennis/66041547.
'Paris Olympics: Allowing Russian athletes to compete' "doing more for peace", says IOC boss Thomas Bach', *Sky News*, 12 February 2023, https://news.sky.com/story/paris-olympics-allowing-russian-athletes-to-compete-doing-more-for-peace-says-ioc-boss-thomas-bach-12809354.
Paris v Stepney Borough Council [1951] AC 367.
Parker, George. 'UK plan to scrap all EU laws suffers new setback', *Financial Times*, 8 November 2022, https://www.ft.com/content/0c0593a3-19f1-45fe-aad1-2ed25e30b5f8.
'Parliament – Fixed odds betting terminals all pParty parliamentary group, "Fixed odds betting terminals – Assessing the impact"', 2017, 34, accessed 9 October 2023, https://www.fobt-appg.com/wp-content/uploads/2017/01/FINAL-FOBT-APPG-REPORT.pdf.

Parrish, Richard. 'The birth of European Union Sports Law', *The Entertainment and Sports Law Journal*, 2, no. 2 (2003): 20.

Parsons, Ben. 'Hurdler issues apology for unsportsmanlike behaviour as rival placed in neck brace', *Daily Mirror*, 7 March 2023, https://www.mirror.co.uk/sport/other-sports/athletics/jason-joseph-european-athletics-news-29392603.

Parveen, Nazia. 'Jonás Gutiérrez wins case against Newcastle over cancer treatment', *The Guardian*, 14 April 2016, https://www.theguardian.com/football/2016/apr/14/jonas-gutierrez-wins-discrimination-claim-against-newcastle-utd.

Patel, Seema. *Inclusion and Exclusion in Competitive Sport: Socio-legal and Regulatory Perspectives*, Oxford: Routledge, 2015.

Patriot Act.

Paul, Kari. 'Chaotic and crass: A brief timeline of Elon Musk's history with Twitter', *The Guardian*, 25 April 2022, https://www.theguardian.com/technology/2022/apr/25/timeline-elon-musks-history-twitter.

Payne, Sebastien. '"Dominic Cummings, remember him? Turns out he was right, after all', *iNews*, 4 August 2023, https://inews.co.uk/opinion/dominic-cummings-remember-him-turns-out-he-was-right-after-all-2524920.

Peng, Michael et al. 'History and the debate over intellectual property', *Management and Organization Review*, 13, no. 1 (March 2017): 18 and see generally Peter K. Yu. 'The confucian challenge to intellectual property reforms', *WIPO Journal*, 4, no. 1 (2012).

Pepper v Hart [1993] AC 593.

'PGA Tour launches LIV Golf lawsuit counterclaim', *BBC*, 29 September 2022, https://www.bbc.co.uk/sport/golf/63080009.

Pielke, Roger Pielke. 'How can FIFA be held accountable?', *Sport Management Review*, 16, no. 3 (2013): 255–67.

Pitts v Hunt [1991] 3 All ER 344.

Pittsburgh Athletic Co v KQV Broadcasting Co, 24 F Supp 490.

Poland v John Parr & Sons [1927] 1 KB 236.

Popham, Mark. 'Racing: Court paves way for Cook compensation: Judge says jockeys were playing Russian roulette when riding at Doncaster', *The Independent*, 15 July 1993, http://www.independent.co.uk/sport/racing-court-paves-way-for-cook-compensation-judge-says-jockeys-were-playing-russian-roulette-when-1485240.html.

Posner, Richard. *An Affair of State, The Investigation, Impeachment and Trial of President Clinton*. Cambridge, MA and London: Harvard University Press, 2012.

Pöysti, Virve and Maija Majamäki. 'Cultural understandings of the pathways leading to problem gambling: Medical disorder or failure of self-regulation?', *Addiction Research & Theory*, 21, no. 1 (2003): 70–82.

'Premier League captains confirm players to continue taking a knee', *BBC*, 3 August 2023, https://www.bbc.co.uk/sport/football/66443693.

'Premiership final: Protesters force stoppage of Twickenham showpiece between Saracens and Sale', *BBC*, 27 May 2023, https://www.bbc.co.uk/sport/rugby-union/65734664.

Priest v Last [1903] 2 KB 148.

'Priti Patel in fresh bid to push through strict anti-protest measures', *The Guardian*, 21 May 2022, https://www.theguardian.com/politics/2022/may/21/priti-patel-in-fresh-bid-to-push-through-strict-anti-protest-measures.

'Professional Darts Players Association – PDC/BDO, "The Split"', accessed 5 October 2023, https://www.pdpa.co.uk/statistics/unique/.

Protection of Children Act 1978.
Psychoactive Substances Act 2016.
Public Order Act 1984.
Quinlan, Christopher. 'The British Horseracing Authority and integrity in horseracing, an independent review 2016', accessed October 4, https://www.britishhorseracing.com/wp-content/uploads/2017/03/Christopher-Quinlan-QC-Report-29-09-16.pdf.
'Quinlan Review 2016 – Terms of Reference', accessed 5 October 2023, http://www.britishhorseracing.com/wp-content/uploads/2016/06/TERMS-OF-REFERENCE-Review-of-DP-AB-and-LC-01-06-16.pdf.
Quirke v Bord Luthchleas na hÉireann (BLÉ) [1988] IR 83.
R (Miller) v The Prime Minister; Cherry and Ors v Advocate General for Scotland [2019] UKSC 41.
R (Mullins) v Appeal Board of the Jockey Club [2005] EWHC 2197 [2006] ISLR, SLR-30.
R (on the application of Weaver) v London and Quadrant Housing Association [2009] EWCA Civ 587.
R v Adomako [1994] 3 WLR 288.
R v Aitken [1992] 1 WLR 1006.
R v Aldridge, R v Eaton [2012] ECWA Crim 1456.
R v Barnes [2004] EWCA Crim 3246.
R v Billinghurst [1978] Crim LR 553.
R v Bingham Justices ex p Jowitt (1974) QBD.
R v Bow Street Magistrates ex parte Pinochet No (2) [2000] 1 AC 119, (HL).
R v Bradshaw (1878) 14 Cox CC 83.
R v Brown [1993] UKHL 19.
R v Burstow [1997] UKHL 34.
R v Cantona (1995), Times Law Reports, March 25.
R v Chan-Fook [1993] EWCA Crim 1.
R v Church [1966] 1 QB 59.
R v Coney (1882) 8 QBD 534.
R v Cunningham [1957] 2 QB 396.
R v Disciplinary Committee of the Jockey Club, ex parte Massingberd-Mundy [1993] 2 All ER 207.
R v Donovan [1934] 2 KB 498.
R v Football Association Ltd ex parte Football League [1993] 2 All ER 833.
R v Gateway Foodmarkets Ltd [1997] 3 All ER 78.
R v Golding [2014] EWCA Crim 889.
R v Jockey Club ex parte Aga Khan [1993] 1 WLR 909.
R v Jones [1987] Crim LR 123.
R v Kamara (1988), Times Law Reports, April 15.
R v Langford [2017] EWCA Crim 498.
R v Light (1857) D & B 332.
R v Lowe [1973] QB 702.
R v Martin (1881) 8 QBD 54.
R v Matthews and Alleyne [2003] EWCA Crim 192.
R v Miller [1954] 2 QB 282.
R v Misalati [2017] EWCA 2226.
R v Mohan [1976] QB 1.

R v Natera [1995] QSC 1.
R v Panel on Take-overs and Mergers, ex p Datafin plc [1987] QB 815.
R v Saunders [1985] Crim LR 230.
R v Savage; Parmenter [1992] 1 AC 699.
R v Servite Houses ex parte Goldsmith [2000] 5 WLUK 415.
R v Tabassum [2000] 2 Cr App R 328.
R v Thomas (Emyrs) (1985) 81 Cr App R 331.
Race Relations Act 1976.
'Rape crisis – Rape and sexual assault statistics', accessed 6 October 2023, https://rapecrisis.org.uk/get-informed/statistics-sexual-violence/.
Ravikumar, Sachin and M. Muvija. 'Record net arrivals highlight UK's post-Brexit migration dilemma', *Reuters*, 25 May 2023, https://www.reuters.com/world/uk/net-migration-uk-hits-record-606000-2022-2023-05-25.
Rayner, Gordon, 'Queen's gold cup-winning racehorse *Estimate* tests positive for banned drug morphine', *Telegraph*, 22 July 2014, http://www.telegraph.co.uk/news/uknews/queen-elizabeth-II/10984322/Queens-Gold-Cup-winning-racehorse-Estimate-tests-positive-for-banned-drug-morphine.html.
Re Yenidje Tobacco Co Ltd [1916] 2 Ch 426.
Read, Andrew. 'Cloning for gold', *British Journal of Sports Medicine*, 31 (1997): 174.
Ready Mixed Concrete (South East) Ltd v Minister of Pensions and National Insurance [1968] 2 QB 497.
Reckitt & Coleman Products v Borden [1990] 1 All ER 873.
RFU & Nike v Cotton Traders Limited [2002] EWHC 467 (Ch).
Ridge v Baldwin [1964] AC 40.
Riess, Steven. 'The cyclical history of horse racing: The USA's oldest and (sometimes) most popular spectator sport', *The International Journal of the History of Sport*, 31, nos. 1–2 (2014): 29–54.
'Rishi Sunak defends granting new North Sea oil and gas licences', *BBC*, 31 July 2023, https://www.bbc.co.uk/news/uk-scotland-66354478.
Road Traffic Act 1988.
Roan, Dan. 'British cycling to ban transgender women from competing in female category', *BBC*, 26 May 2023, https://www.bbc.co.uk/sport/cycling/65718748.
Roan, Dan. 'FA reform: Former chiefs say, "elderly white men" block change', *BBC*, 12 December 2016, http://www.bbc.co.uk/sport/football/38274152.
Roan, Dan. 'Transgender women banned from female pool category', *BBC*, 24 April 2025, https://www.bbc.co.uk/sport/articles/c1k4gd2vge9o.
Roe v Wade 410 U.S. 113.
Rolles, Stephen. 'An alternative to the war on drugs', *British Medical Journal*, 341 (2010): pp. 127–131.
RSPCA v AG [2001] 3 All ER 530.
Rumsby, Ben. 'Rio Ferdinand's "brutal" eight-month drug ban was the fault of incompetent testers according to Alex Ferguson', *The Telegraph*, 22 October 2013, https://www.telegraph.co.uk/sport/football/teams/manchester-united/Sir_Alex_Ferguson/10397197/Rio-Ferdinands-brutal-eight-month-drug-ban-was-the-fault-of-incompetent-testers-according-to-Alex-Ferguson.html.
Russell v Duke of Norfolk (1949) 1 All ER 109.

'Russia, Navalny: Putin critic given nine-year jail sentence in trial branded 'sham', *BBC,* 22 March 2022, https://www.bbc.co.uk/news/world-europe-60832310.
Saker-Clark, Henry. 'JD sports, rangers and elite sports fined £2m over football kit price fixing', *The Independent,* September, 27, 2022, https://www.independent.co.uk/sport/football/jd-sports-cma-belfast-glasgow-b2176025.html.
Sakwa, Richard. 'The cold peace: Russo-Western relations as a mimetic cold war', *Cambridge Review of International Affairs*, 26, no. 1 (2013): 203–24.
'Saudi Arabia's ban on women driving officially ends', *BBC*, 24 June 2018, https://www.bbc.co.uk/news/world-middle-east-44576795.
Sauer, Pjotr. 'Russia's central bank to hold extraordinary meeting after rouble falls to 16-month low', *The Guardian,* 14 August 2023, https://www.theguardian.com/business/2023/aug/14/rouble-falls-to-16-month-low-dollar-russian-exports-collapse-war-ukraine-russia-economy.
Savage, Michael, Toby Helm and Robin McKie. 'Dropping green pledges would be "political suicide", Sunak and Starmer warned', *The Guardian*, 22 July 2023, https://amp.theguardian.com/environment/2023/jul/22/green-pledges-sunak-starmer-byelections.
Savulescu, Julian et al. 'Should athletes be allowed to use performance enhancing drugs?', *British Medical Journal,* 347 (2013), http://www.bmj.com/content/347/bmj.f6150.
Schmerler, Cindy. 'The mental health of tennis players is no longer in the shadows', *New York Times*, 15 January 2022, https://www.nytimes.com/2022/01/15/sports/tennis/mental-health-players.html.
Schuman, Michael. 'China and the West are coming apart. Can China's economy continue to rise?', *The Atlantic*, 8 June 2023, https://www.theatlantic.com/international/archive/2023/06/china-economy-xi-jinping-us-relationship-investment-trade/674321/.
Scott, Kirsty. 'Straw forced to defend Tyson decision', *The Guardian*, 23 May 2000, https://www.theguardian.com/politics/2000/may/23/uk.boxing.
'Scottish football to ban heading on days before and after matches', *ITV News,* 28 November 2022, https://www.itv.com/news/2022-11-28/scottish-football-to-ban-heading-on-days-before-and-after-matches.
Sean Ingle, 'English cricket is "racist, sexist and elitist," says landmark report', *The Guardian,* 27 June 2023, https://www.theguardian.com/sport/2023/jun/27/english-cricket-is-racist-sexist-and-elitist-says-landmark-report?CMP=oth_b-aplnews_d-5.
Sex Discrimination Act 1975.
Sexual Offences Act 1956.
Sexual Offences Act 2003.
Shakespeare, William. *Much ado about nothing*, ed. Barbara A. Mowat and Paul Werstine, New York: Simon and Schuster, 2015.
'Sharapova's sponsors divided after two-year tennis ban', *BBC,* 9 June 2016, https://www.bbc.co.uk/news/business-36485320.
Shemilt, Stephan. 'Ashes: Just Stop Oil protesters briefly disrupt opening morning of England v Australia Test at Lord's', *BBC*, 28 June 2023, https://www.bbc.co.uk/sport/cricket/6603309.
Simester, Andrew. 'Is strict liability always wrong?', in *Appraising Strict Liability*, ed. Andrew Simester, Oxford: Oxford University Press, 2005.
Skoulding, Lucy. 'Angry motorists drag Just Stop Oil protesters out of road as 100 activists arrested', *The Independent*, 9 October 2022, https://www.independent.co.uk/climate-change/news/just-stop-oil-protest-dragged-london-road-b2198970.html.

Slater, Matt. 'Eni Aluko feels "vindicated" by FA apology but accuses chief executive Martin Glenn of blackmail', *Independent,* 18 October 2017, http://www.independent.co.uk/sport/football/news-and-comment/eni-aluko-football-association-hearing-martin-glenn-conduct-like-blackmail-a8007111.html.

Smith v Baker and Sons [1891] AC 325.

Smith v Chief Superintendent of Woking Police Station [1983] Crim LR 323.

Smoldon v Nolan and Whitworth [1997] ELR 249.

Southern Foundries (1926) Ltd v Shirlaw [1940] AC 701.

Spapens, Toine. 'Illegal gambling', in *The Oxford Handbook of Organised Crime*, ed. Letizia Paoli. Oxford: Oxford University Press, 2014.

Spencer, John and Antje Pedain. 'Approaches to strict and constructive liability in continental criminal law', in *Appraising Strict Liability*, ed. Andrew Simester. Oxford: Oxford University Press, 2005.

Spithoff, Sheryl and Meldon Kahan. 'Cannabis and Canadian youth – Evidence, not ideology', *Canadian Family Physician*, 60, no. 9 (September 2014): 785–7.

'Sport England - About us', accessed 4 October 2023, https://www.sportengland.org/about-us.

'Sport England – A code for sports governance', accessed October 5, 2023, https://www.sportengland.org/campaigns-and-our-work/code-sports-governance.

'Sport England – A code for sports governance – Requirements', accessed 5 October 2023, https://www.sportengland.org/campaigns-and-our-work/code-sports-governance?section=the_requirements.

'Sport England – The recognition process', accessed 4 October 2023, https://www.sportengland.org/our-work/national-governing-bodies/sports-that-we-recognise/.

'Sport England – Safeguarding', accessed 6 October 2023, https://www.sportengland.org/guidance-and-support/safeguarding.

Sporting Events (Control of Alcohol etc.) Act 1985.

'Sporting future: A new strategy for an active nation – Foreword', Department of Digital, Culture, Media and Sport, accessed 4 October, https://assets.publishing.service.gov.uk/government/uploads/system/uploads/attachment_data/file/486622/Sporting_Future_ACCESSIBLE.pdf.

Sports and General Press Agency v 'Our Dogs' Publishing Co. [1917] KB 125 CA.

Stamp, Anna, Daniel J. Lang and Patrick A. Wäger. 'Environmental impacts of a transition toward e-mobility: The present and future role of lithium carbonate production', *Journal of Cleaner Production*, 23, no. 1 (2012): 104–12.

Steinkraus, William et al. *The Horse in Sport*. London: Macdonald Orbis, 1987.

Sterling v Leeds Rugby League Cup [2001] ISLR 201.

Steven Weatherill, '"Fair Play Please!" – Recent developments in the application of EC law to sport', *Common Market Law Review*, 40 (2003): 201–43.

Stretford v The Football Association Ltd & Another [2007] EWCA Civ 238.

Sullivan, Rory. 'Saudi Arabia has carried out 800 executions since 2015, says rights group', *The Independent,* 15 April 2020, https://www.independent.co.uk/news/world/middle-east/saudi-arabia-executions-death-toll-human-rights-king-salman-a9466741.html.

Sweet v Parsley [1970] AC 132.

Sweney, Mark. 'London 2012: Paddy Power wins poster campaign battle', *The Guardian*, 25 July 2012, https://www.theguardian.com/media/2012/jul/25/london-2012-paddy-power.

Taylor, D. J. *On The Corinthian Spirit: The Decline of Amateurism in Sport*, London: Yellow Jersey Press, 2006.
Taylor, Danile. 'Football is heading for trouble over brain injuries caused by the ball', *The Guardian,* 30 September 2017, https://www.theguardian.com/football/blog/2017/sep/30/football-heading-brain-injuries-ball-kevin-doyle.
Taylor, Dianne, Rajeev Syal and Emine Sinmaz. 'Rwanda asylum flight cancelled after 11th-hour ECHR intervention', *The Guardian,* 14 June 2022, https://www.theguardian.com/uk-news/2022/jun/14/european-court-humam-right-makes-11th-hour-intervention-in-rwanda-asylum-seeker-plan.
The Bible 1 Timothy c. 2, v. 12, NIV.
The Bible, Genesis c. 2 vs. 19- 24 and c. 3 vs. 1-6, NIV.
'The British Horseracing Authority – THE BHA and integrity in horseracing, an independent review (The Neville Review)', Executive Summary, para. 1.12, accessed October 9, http://www.britishhorseracing.com/wp-content/uploads/2008/05/Neville-Review-Pr-Rel-Exec-Summ-Recomm-City-of-Lon-May-08.pdf.
The Electronic Communications and Wireless Telegraphy (Amendment) (European Electronic Communications Code and EU Exit) Regulations 2020
'The Equality and Human Rights Commission', accessed 6 October 2023, www.equalityhumanrights.com.
'The Gambling Commission', accessed 9 October 2023, https://www.gamblingcommission.gov.uk/.
'The Gambling Commission – Gambling licence information, guidance and advice for businesses and individuals', accessed 9 October 2023, https://www.gamblingcommission.gov.uk/licensees-and-businesses.
'The Gambling Commission – Regulatory action against Ladbrookes Betting and Gaming Ltd', accessed 9 October 2023, //www.gamblingcommission.gov.uk/public-register/regulatory-action/detail/108.
'The Government Equalities Office', accessed 6 October 2023, www.equalities.gov.uk.
'The Horserace Betting Levy Board', accessed 9 October 2023, https://www.hblb.org.uk/.
'The Legal 500 – discrimination in footall, its most famous cases, the evolution of its regulations and remedies', accessed 6 October 2023, https://www.legal500.com/developments/thought-leadership/discrimination-in-football-its-most-famous-casesthe-evolution-of-its-regulationsand-its-remedies/.
'The Standard Life Foundation – "Betting in the UK: How to tackle problem gambling"', accessed 9 October 2023, https://www.standardlifefoundation.org.uk/en/our-work/publications/betting-in-the-uk-how-to-tackle-problem-gambling.
'Thousands of London protesters call for UK to rejoin EU', *The Guardian*, 22 October 2022, https://www.theguardian.com/politics/2022/oct/22/thousands-of-london-protesters-call-for-uk-to-rejoin-eu.
Trade Marks Act 1994.
Trainor, Niall. 'The 2009 WADA code: A more proportionate deal for athletes?', *ESLJ*, 8, no. 1 (2010): 1, https://www.entsportslawjournal.com › articles › eslj.45 › galley › download.
Tran, Mark. 'Government drug adviser David Nutt sacked', *The Guardian,* 30 October 2009, http://www.theguardian.com/politics/2009/oct/30/drugs-adviser-david-nutt-sacked.
Treaty on the Functioning of the European Union (TFEU).

Trebor Bassett Limited v The Football Association Limited [1997] FSR 211.

Trevelyan, Mark. 'Explainer: Why is Russia's Putin drawing "red lines" over Ukraine?', *Reuters,* 26 January 2022, https://www.reuters.com/world/europe/why-is-russias-putin-so-focused-ukraine-2021-12-15/.

Tuberville v Savage (1669) 1 Mod Rep 3.

Tucker, Ross. 'What makes champions? A review of the relative contribution of genes and training to sporting success', *British Journal of Sports Medicine*, 46 (2012): 555–61.

Uberoi, Elise and Neil Johnston. 'Political disengagement in the UK: Who is disengaged? – Research Briefing, House of Commons Library', 7, accessed 21 November 2022, https://researchbriefings.files.parliament.uk/documents/CBP-7501/CBP-7501.pdf.

Udowitch, Heather. 'The Larry Nassar nightmare: Athletic organizational failures to address sexual assault allegations and a call for corrective action', *DePaul Journal of Sports Law & Contemporary Problems*, 16 (2020): i.

'UEFA – Integrity', accessed 9 October 2023, https://www.uefa.com/insideuefa/protecting-the-game/integrity/.

'UK: Supreme Court outcome "disappointing" but court affirms right of trans people to protection from discrimination and harassment', Amnesty International Press Release, 16 April 2025, https://www.amnesty.org.uk/press-releases/uk-supreme-court-outcome-disappointing-court-affirms-right-trans-people-protection.

'UK Census – Religion, England and Wales, main points', accessed 29 November 2022, https://www.ons.gov.uk/peoplepopulationandcommunity/culturalidentity/religion/bulletins/religionenglandandwales/census2021#main-points.

'UK Sport – A code for sports governance', accessed 4 October 2023, https://www.uksport.gov.uk/resources/a-code-for-sports-governance.

'UK Sport – A code for sports governance: The principles', accessed 4 October 2023, https://www.uksport.gov.uk/resources/a-code-for-sports-governance/the-principles.

'Ukraine war: US says Iranian drones breach sanctions', *BBC*, 18 October 2022, https://www.bbc.co.uk/news/world-europe-63294698.

'Ukraine's Kharlan calls for rule change after disqualification for snubbing Russian opponent', *Reuters*, 27 July 2023, https://www.reuters.com/sports/ukraines-kharlan-disqualified-after-refusal-shake-hands-with-russian-opponent-2023-07-27/.

'United Nations – New UN report reveals chronic bias against women over last decade', 12 June 2023, accessed 6 October 2023, https://news.un.org/en/story/2023/06/1137532.

'United Nations – New UN report reveals chronic bias against women over last decade', 12 June 2023, accessed 10 October 2023, https://news.un.org/en/story/2023/06/1137532.

'United Nations – The Paris Agreement 2015', accessed 10 October 2023, https://unfccc.int/process-and-meetings/the-paris-agreement.

'United Nations – UN General Assembly votes to suspend Russia from the Human Rights Council', 7 April 2022, accessed 6 October 2023, https://news.un.org/en/story/2022/04/1115782.

'United Nations – Universal Declaration of Human Rights', accessed 6 October 2023, https://www.un.org/en/about-us/universal-declaration-of-human-rights.

'United Nations – Universal Declaration of Human Rights 1948', accessed 5 October 2023, https://www.un.org/en/about-us/universal-declaration-of-human-rights.

United Nations General Assembly Resolution 217A.

US Constitution, 15th Amendment, 1870.

Varnish v British Cycling Federation t/a British Cycling UKEAT/0022/20/LA.

Vasey v Surrey Free Inns [1996] PIQR P373.
'Veronica Campbell-Brown tests positive for banned diuretic', *BBC,* 15 June 2013, https://www.bbc.co.uk/sport/athletics/22919193 and 'On this day in 2003: Shane Warne handed 12-month ban after taking diuretic', 22 February 2022, https://www.independent.co.uk/sport/cricket/shane-warne-australia-the-oval-queensland-victoria-b2020183.html.
Verver, John. 'Lessons from the FIFA Corruption Scandal', *Risk Management,* 62, no. 7 (2015): 16–18.
Victoria Park Racing & Recreation Grounds Co Ltd v Taylor (1937) 58 CLR 479.
Vincent,Geraint. 'Zeebrugge: Britain's worst peacetime maritime disaster explained', *ITV News,* 6 March 2017, https://www.itv.com/news/2017-03-06/zeebrugge-britains-worst-peacetime-maritime-disaster-explained.
Voting Rights Act 1865.
Vowles v Evans [2003] EWCA Civ 318.
'WADA – Athlete Biological Passport Operating Guidelines, 8th Version', accessed 6 October 2023, https://www.wada-ama.org/sites/default/files/resources/files/guidelines_abp_v8_final.pdf.
'WADA – Biological Passports', accessed 5 October 2023, https://www.wada-ama.org/en/athlete-biological-passport.
'WADA – Biological Passports', accessed 6 October 2023, https://www.wada-ama.org/en/athlete-biological-passport.
'WADA – Prohibited List 2023', accessed 6 October 2023, https://www.wada-ama.org/en/resources/world-anti-doping-program/prohibited-list.
'WADA – Statement on Court of Arbitration decision to declare Russian Anti-Doping Agency as non-compliant', 17 December 2020, accessed 5 October 2023, https://www.wada-ama.org/en/news/wada-statement-court-arbitration-decision-declare-russian-anti-doping-agency-non-compliant.
'WADA – Statement on Court of Arbitration decision to declare Russian Anti-Doping Agency as non-compliant', 17 December 2020, accessed 9 October 2023, https://www.wada-ama.org/en/news/wada-statement-court-arbitration-decision-declare-russian-anti-doping-agency-non-compliant.
'WADA – Whereabouts rule', accessed 5 October 2023, https://www.wada-ama.org/en/athletes-support-personnel/provide-whereabouts.
'WADA laboratory guidelines – Gene doping detection based on Polymerase Chain Reaction (PCR), Version 1', January 2021, accessed 6 October 2023, https://www.wada-ama.org/sites/default/files/resources/files/wada_guidelines_for_gene_doping_pcr_test_v1_jan_2021_eng.pdf
'WADA Press release January 27, 2022, – WADA publishes testing figures and calls on Anti-Doping Organizations to take full advantage of IOC's long-term sample storage', accessed 6 October 2023, https://www.wada-ama.org/en/news/wada-publishes-testing-figures-and-calls-anti-doping-organizations-take-full-advantage-iocs.
Waddington, Ivan, Ask Vest Christiansen, John Gleaves, John Hoberman and Verner Møller. 'Recreational drug use and sport: Time for a WADA rethink?', *Performance Enhancement & Health,* 2, no. 2 (June, 2013): 41–7.
Walker, Neil. 'Beyond boundary disputes and basic grids: Mapping the global disorder of normative orders', *International Journal of Constitutional Law*, 6, nos. 3–4 (2008): 373–96.

Walker, Peter, Damien Gayle and Jessica Elgot. 'Boris Johnson threatens to use "legislative bomb" to stop European Super League', *Guardian*, 20 April 2021, www.theguardian.com/football/2021/apr/20/uk-government-may-legislate-to-stop-european-super-league-says-minister.
Walker v Crystal Palace [1910] 1 KB 87-.
War Crimes Act 1991.
Wardle, Heather. 'The "re-feminisation' of gambling', in *Gambling Disorders in Women*, by Henrietta Bowden-Jones, ed. Fulvia Prever, London: Routledge, 2017.
'Water sports firm pleads guilty to Mari-Simon Cronje death charge', *BBC*, 22 November 2013, https://www.bbc.co.uk/news/uk-england-london-25056230.
Waterson, Jim. 'BBC licence fee to be abolished in 2027 and funding frozen', *The Guardian*, 16 January 2022, https://www.theguardian.com/media/2022/jan/16/bbc-licence-fee-to-be-abolished-in-2027-and-funding-frozen.
Watson v BBBC and Others [2001] QB 1134.
Watt v Hertfordshire County Council [1954] 1 WLR 835.
'Wayne Couzens sentenced to 19 months in prison for indecent exposure', *The Guardian*, 6 March 2023, https://www.theguardian.com/uk-news/2023/mar/06/wayne-couzens-sentenced-to-19-months-in-prison-for-indecent-exposure.
Welsh, John. 'The European Super League debacle: Why regulation of corporate football is essential', *Soccer & Society*, 24, no. 2 (2022): 172–89.
'Welsh rugby: WRU was in denial on sexism – acting chief exec.', *BBC*, 2 February 2023, https://www.bbc.co.uk/news/uk-wales-politics-64497272.
'What is net zero and how are the UK and other countries doing?', *BBC*, 28 June 2023, https://www.bbc.co.uk/news/science-environment-58874518.
William, Helen. 'Gary Lineker responds after ex-Match of The Day host Des Lynam tells him to stick to football', *Independent*, 24 July 2023, https://www.independent.co.uk/news/media/gary-lineker-des-lynam-match-of-day-b2380721.html.
Wilson, Jonathan. 'A lesson from history: The European Super League battle is not over', *The Guardian*, April 22, 2021, https://www.theguardian.com/football/2021/apr/22/a-colombian-lesson-from-history-the-super-league-battle-is-not-over.
'Wimbledon – Sustainability', accessed 10 October 2023, https://www.wimbledon.com/en_GB/atoz/sustainability.html.
Wolcher, Louis. *Law's Task: The Tragic Circle of Law, Justice and Human Suffering*. Oxford: Routledge, 2008.
Wong, Julie Carrie. 'Zuckerberg says Facebook is pivoting to privacy after year of controversies', *The Guardian*, 6 March 2019, https://www.theguardian.com/technology/2019/mar/06/mark-zuckerberg-facebook-privacy-vision.
Wood, Greg. 'Khadijah Mellah becomes first UK jockey to wear hijab – and wins race', *The Guardian*, 1 August 2019, https://www.theguardian.com/sport/2019/aug/01/khadijah-mellah-first-uk-jockey-to-wear-hijab-wins-race-goodwood-horse-racing.
Woodhouse, John. 'House of Commons Library – Research Briefing: Broadcasting: Listed sporting events', 3 May 2022, https://researchbriefings.files.parliament.uk/documents/SN00802/SN00802.pdf.
Woodley v Metropolitan District Rly (1877) 18 QBD.
Woolridge v Sumner [1963] 2 QB 43.
'World Anti-Doping Agency', accessed 6 October 2023, www.wada-ama.org.

'World anti-doping code international standard for therapeutic use exemptions 2023', 5, accessed 5 October 2023, https://www.wada-ama.org/sites/default/files/2022-09/international_standard_for_therapeutic_use_exemptions_istue_2023.pdf.
'World Cup 2010: FIFA issues ban deadline to Nigeria', *BBC Sport,* 2 July 2010, http://news.bbc.co.uk/sport1/hi/football/world_cup_2010/8780028.stm.
'World Esports Association (WESA)', accessed 9 October 2023, https://www.wesa.gg/.
'World Weather Attribution Report, July 7, 2021 – "Rapid attribution analysis of the extraordinary heatwave on the Pacific Coast of the US and Canada June 2021"', accessed 10 October 2023, https://www.worldweatherattribution.org/wp-content/uploads/NW-US-extreme-heat-2021-scientific-report-WWA.pdf.
'World's first cloned horse is born', *New Scientist,* 6 August 2003, https://www.newscientist.com/article/dn4026-worlds-first-cloned-horse-is-born/.
Zendle, David, Rachel Meyer and Harriet Over, 'Adolescents and loot boxes: Links with problem gambling and motivations for purchase', *Royal Society Open Science,* 6, no. 6 (June 2019), https://royalsocietypublishing.org/doi/full/10.1098/rsos.190049.

Index

Note: Page locators followed by 'n' refer to notes. Page numbers in italics refer to images.

About the Author

Dr **Jonathan G. Merritt** is Senior Lecturer in Law at the School of Law, De Montfort University, Leicester, UK, and gained his PhD whilst teaching there. Jonathan also has an honours degree in law from Nottingham Trent University, a postgraduate certificate in education, and a master's degree in criminology and social policy. Jonathan's teaching career began in 1995, and latterly he has specialised in sports law whilst also being programme leader on the postgraduate law master's pathway. He has written a number of articles for academic journals during this time, as well as four other books on various legal topics. The most recent book, *Regulating Sport for the Non-Human Athlete*, on equine sports law, is available from the same publisher.

Jonathan lives on the Nottinghamshire/Derbyshire border and was active in equestrian sport until a serious accident whilst competing in 2022. He remains passionate about all things related to equine sport and leisure pursuits. Jonathan still owns, breeds and trains horses, and plans to return to competition in due course.

www.ingramcontent.com/pod-product-compliance
Ingram Content Group UK Ltd.
Pitfield, Milton Keynes, MK11 3LW, UK
UKHW020221290926
15470UKWH00001B/305

9 781666 916812